Electoral Integrity in America

Electoral Integrity in America

Securing Democracy

EDITED BY PIPPA NORRIS, SARAH CAMERON,
and
THOMAS WYNTER

Electoral Integrity Project

OXFORD
UNIVERSITY PRESS

OXFORD
UNIVERSITY PRESS

Oxford University Press is a department of the University of Oxford. It furthers the University's objective of excellence in research, scholarship, and education by publishing worldwide. Oxford is a registered trade mark of Oxford University Press in the UK and certain other countries.

Published in the United States of America by Oxford University Press
198 Madison Avenue, New York, NY 10016, United States of America.

Library of Congress Cataloging-in-Publication Data Names: Norris, Pippa, editor. |
Cameron, Sarah, 1983– editor. | Wynter, Thomas, editor.
Title: Electoral integrity in America : securing democracy /
edited by Pippa Norris, Sarah Cameron, and Thomas Wynter.
Description: New York, NY : Oxford University Press, [2019] |
Includes bibliographical references and index.
Identifiers: LCCN 2018026450 (print) | LCCN 2018041081 (ebook) |
ISBN 9780190934187 (Updf) | ISBN 9780190934194 (Epub) |
ISBN 9780190934170 (pbk. : alk. paper) | ISBN 9780190934163 (hardcover)
Subjects: LCSH: Elections—Corrupt practices—United States—Prevention. |
Ballot—Security measures—United States. | Voting—United States.
Classification: LCC JK1994 (ebook) | LCC JK1994 .E435 2018 (print) |
DDC 324.60973—dc23
LC record available at https://lccn.loc.gov/2018026450

CONTENTS

List of Figures   vii
List of Tables   ix
Preface and Acknowledgments   xi
List of Contributors   xiii

PART I   INTRODUCTION

1. Challenges in American Elections   3
   PIPPA NORRIS, SARAH CAMERON, AND THOMAS WYNTER

2. Electoral laws   30
   RICHARD L. HASEN

3. Voting Procedures: Inclusion versus Security   44
   KEVIN PALLISTER

4. Diagnosing Electoral Integrity   60
   MICHAEL LATNER

PART II   CHALLENGES

5. Gerrymandering   83
   DANIEL B. MAGLEBY, MICHAEL D. MCDONALD, JONATHAN KRASNO,
   SHAWN J. DONAHUE, AND ROBIN E. BEST

6. Voter Identification   102
   ELIZABETH BERGMAN, DARI SYLVESTER TRAN, AND PHILIP YATES

7. Fake News   114
LETICIA BODE, EMILY K. VRAGA, AND KJERSTIN THORSON

8. Transparency   134
NANDI VANKA, AVERY DAVIS-ROBERTS, AND DAVID CARROLL

9. Decentralized Administration   151
CRAIG ARCENEAUX

PART III   CONCLUSIONS

10. America in Comparative Perspective   175
CHAD VICKERY AND HEATHER SZILAGYI

11. Lessons for the Reform Agenda   196
PIPPA NORRIS, THOMAS WYNTER, AND SARAH CAMERON

Selected Bibliography   219
Index   247

FIGURES

1.1   Public Confidence in the Honesty of Their Country's Elections in Five
       Anglo-American Democracies, 2006–2016   10
1.2   Expert Assessments of Free and Fair Elections in Anglo-American
       Democracies, 2000–2017   11
1.3   Stages in the Electoral Cycle   15
1.4   The Performance of American Elections throughout the Cycle, 2016   21
1.5   Mapping Perceptions of Electoral Integrity by U.S. State, 2016   22
1.6   Changes in the Performance of U.S. Elections, 2012–2016   23
2.1   "Election Challenge" Cases per Year, 1996–2016   31
2.2   "Election Challenge" Cases by Presidential Election Cycle,
       2000–2016   32
4.1   The Distribution of Global and U.S. Perceptions of Electoral Index
       Scores   67
4.2   Global and U.S. State Comparison of Boundaries and PEI Index
       Scores   70
5.1   U.S. States Categorized by the Presence and Type of Gerrymander   91
5.2   Electoral Bias   92
5.3   Bias in Maryland and Connecticut   94
5.4   Bias in Ohio   96
5.5   Bias in Illinois   98
5.6   Bias in Georgia   99
6.1   Change in Voter Share Due to Voter ID Laws   109
6.2   Plot of Change in Voter Share Due to Voter ID Laws: GOP vs.
       Democrats   110
7.1   Belief in Misinformation Statements   121
8.1   Citizen Observation Access in U.S. States   141
8.2   International Observation Access in U.S. States   142
10.1   Approval of Winning the Presidency without the Popular Vote   183

10.2   State Photo Identification Laws   187
10.3   Partisan Administration of Elections   190
11.1   Voting Participation by Perceptions of Electoral Integrity, U.S.,
        2016   209
11.2   Confidence in Fair Elections and Voter Turnout, U.S., 2012   210
11.3   Partisans Differ in Their Assessments of the Performance of U.S.
        Elections   212
11.4   Recommended Sequence of Reforms   212

TABLES

1.1   Electoral Integrity in Postindustrial Democracies, 2017   18
3.1   Inclusion and Security: Trade-offs and Complementarities   48
4.1   Stages of the Election Cycle, Using Perceptions of Electoral Integrity (PEI) Indicators   63
4.2   The Dimensions of the PEI Index   68
4.3   Global and U.S. PEI Index Invariance Model Comparisons   69
4.4   Stages of the Election Cycle, with Alternative U.S. Integrity Indicators   73
4.5   PEI and Alternative Measures of Electoral Integrity   76
6.1   The Number of U.S. Counties with a Voter ID Law, 2016   106
6.2   Voter ID Law Coding by U.S. State with the Number of Counties, 2016   107
6.3   Impact of Voter ID Laws on Expected Vote Share   109
6.4   Probabilities That Voter ID Impacted the Election Results   111
7.1   Predicting Belief in Congruent and Incongruent Misinformation   123
7.2   Predicting Belief in Congruent Misinformation for Trump and Clinton Voters   127
7.3   Predicting Belief in Incongruent Misinformation for Trump and Clinton Voters   128
7.4   Predicting Belief in Individual Statements   129
7.5   Appendix Sources, Scales, and Question Wordings   130
9.1   Federal Institutions in the United States, Canada, Mexico, and Brazil   167
10.1   Proportionality in North Carolina and Maryland   180
11.1   Electoral Integrity in U.S. States, 2016   198
11.2   Predicting Democratic Satisfaction and Voting Participation, World Values Survey, 2017   208

PREFACE AND ACKNOWLEDGMENTS

This book focuses on the challenges of electoral integrity in America, understood in a comparative context. Many issues were highlighted by the 2016 U.S. presidential elections, but their roots go far deeper and their consequences are far more profound than any single contest or country. The study is part of the Electoral Integrity Project (EIP), an academic research project established in 2012. Research for the project has been generously supported by the award of the Kathleen Fitzpatrick Australian Laureate from the Australian Research Council, as well as grants from International IDEA, Global Integrity, the Association of World Electoral Bodies (A-WEB), the University of Sydney, and at Harvard University by the Weatherhead Center for International Affairs, the Roy and Lila Ash Center for Democratic Governance and Innovation, and the Australian Studies Committee.

The Electoral Integrity Project is based at Harvard University's John F. Kennedy School of Government and the Department of Government and International Relations at the University of Sydney. We are indebted to many colleagues at Sydney, notably Michael Spence, Duncan Ivison, Gaby Ramia, and Colin Wight for facilitating the arrangement, as well as the department. The book would not have been possible without the research team at Sydney who have played an essential role in stimulating ideas, providing critical feedback and advice, developing the Perception of Electoral Integrity (PEI) data set, and generating related publications. The team organized the workshop in San Francisco prior to the 2017 American Political Science Association annual meeting, where the draft book chapters were initially presented and invaluable feedback was gathered from participants and discussants. We thank all the presenters and workshop attendees. EIP owes an immense debt to all the team who have contributed to the research and now moved on in their careers: Ferran Martinez i Coma (Griffith University), Richard W. Frank (Australian National University), Alessandro Nai (University of Amsterdam), Holly Ann Garnett (Royal Military College of Canada), Max Grömping (Heidelberg University), Jeffrey

Karp (Brunel University London)—as well as invaluable support from Megan Capriccio, Alexandra Kennett, and Andrea Abel van Es and all the fellows visiting the project. The project would not have been possible without the help of several interns who worked with the EIP over the years, notably Laura Welty, Elena Escalante-Block, Miguel Angel Lara Otaola, Thomas Powell, and Elias Christofi.

EIP has collaborated closely with many international development agencies, including the United Nations Development Program, the United Nations Electoral Assistance Division, the Australian Election Commission, the Carter Center, the International Foundation for Electoral Systems (IFES), International IDEA, the Organization for Security and Cooperation in Europe, the Organization of American States, the Kofi Annan Commission, the Sunlight Foundation, the National Democratic Institute, USAID, the U.K. Electoral Commission, the Australian Electoral Commission, the Association of World Electoral Bodies, the Varieties of Democracy project, and many others.

Finally, as always, the support of Oxford University Press has proved invaluable, particularly the patience, efficient assistance, and enthusiasm of our editor, Angela Chnapko, as well as the helpful comments of the reviewers.

Pippa Norris, Harvard University and the University of Sydney
Sarah Cameron, University of Sydney
Thomas Wynter, University of Sydney

CONTRIBUTORS

Craig Arceneaux is a Professor of Political Science at California Polytechnic State University, San Luis Obispo. His interests focus on Latin American politics, democratization, and political institutions. He is the author of *Bounded Missions* (Penn State University Press, 2001), *Transforming Latin America* (with David Pion-Berlin, University of Pittsburgh Press, 2005), and *Democratic Latin America* (Routledge, 2016). Arceneaux contributed to *Election Watchdogs* (Pippa Norris and Alessandro Nai, eds., Oxford University Press, 2017).

Elizabeth Bergman is the Chair of and an Associate Professor in the Department of Political Science at California State University, East Bay. Her work is focused primarily on access to the instruments of democracy, and she has published on a range of topics, including voter access, vote-by-mail, and electoral reform. Her work has been funded by the U.S. Election Assistance Commission and the Pew Center for the States and has appeared in *Legislative Studies Quarterly*, the *Election Law Journal*, the *California Journal of Politics and Policy*, and two edited volumes: *Latino America* and *Why Don't Americans Vote*.

Robin E. Best joined the Political Science Faculty at Binghamton University (SUNY) in 2013 after holding positions at the University of Missouri, Leiden University, and Syracuse University. Her research and teaching interests include political parties, elections, electoral rules, voting behavior, and representation in democratic systems of government. Her work has been published in *Comparative Political Studies*, *Electoral Studies*, the *European Journal of Political Research*, *Political Analysis*, and elsewhere.

Leticia Bode is an Associate Professor in the Communication, Culture, and Technology Program at Georgetown University. Her work lies at the intersection of communication, technology, and political behavior, emphasizing the role communication and information technologies play in the acquisition and use of political information. She holds a PhD from the University of Wisconsin.

Sarah Cameron is the Electoral Integrity Project Manager and Senior Research Associate at the University of Sydney. Her research interests include elections and political behavior in cross-national comparison. She has contributed to the Australian Election Study and the Comparative Cross-National Electoral Research project. Cameron holds a PhD and Master of Studies from the Australian National University and a Master's from Ashridge Business School. She has held a Visiting Fellowship at Harvard University.

David Carroll is the Director of the Carter Center's Democracy Program, leading efforts on election observation and consensus-building on international standards. He has worked on Carter Center projects on democracy and elections in Africa, Latin America, the Middle East, and Asia. Carroll received his PhD in International Relations from the University of South Carolina, taught at Georgia State University and Sewanee–the University of the South, and has published research on issues of democracy, elections, and human rights.

Avery Davis-Roberts is Associate Director of the Democracy Program at the Carter Center, where she leads the Center's Human Rights and Election Standards initiatives. She has managed Carter Center election observation missions in Asia, Africa, South America, and the Middle East. Davis-Roberts gained her undergraduate and Master of Laws degrees from the School of Oriental and African Studies at the University of London.

Shawn J. Donahue is a doctoral candidate at Binghamton University (SUNY). His research and teaching interests include voting rights, redistricting, gerrymandering, and constitutional law. His dissertation focuses on electoral manipulation by state and local governments on voting rights in the United States, including gerrymandering. Donahue has an undergraduate degree in Political Science and History from Indiana University, Bloomington, and a Juris Doctor from the Indiana University School of Law.

Richard L. Hasen is Chancellor's Professor of Law and Political Science at the University of California, Irvine. He is a nationally recognized expert in election law and coauthor of a leading casebook on election law. He was named one of the 100 most influential lawyers in America by the *National Law Journal* in 2013. His op-eds have appeared in many publications, including the *New York Times, Politico*, and *Slate*. Hasen also writes the often-quoted *Election Law Blog*.

Jonathan Krasno is an Associate Professor of Political Science at Binghamton University (SUNY). His research focuses on public opinion, congressional elections, campaigns, and campaign financing. He is the author of *Challengers, Competition, and Reelection* (Yale University Press, 1994), *Buying Time* (Brennan Center, 2000), and articles in *American Journal of Political Science, Journal of Politics*, and elsewhere.

In addition, Krasno has been an active participant in ongoing debate over campaign finance reform, serving as an expert witness in federal trials.

Michael Latner is an Associate Professor of Political Science at California Polytechnic State University, San Luis Obispo, faculty scholar at the Institute for Advanced Technology and Public Policy, and Kendall Voting Rights Fellow at the Union of Concerned Scientists. Most recently, he coauthored *Gerrymandering in America* (Cambridge University Press, 2016), and his research has appeared in *Comparative Political Studies, Electoral Studies,* and *Election Law Journal.*

Daniel B. Magleby is an Assistant Professor of Political Science and a Fellow in the Center on Democratic Performance at Binghamton University (SUNY). His research interests focus on American political institutions, elections, and political geography. He received his PhD and MA in Political Science from the University of Michigan, and he holds an MSc in Mathematical Methods in the social sciences from Northwestern University. His work is published in the *American Economic Review, Political Analysis,* and *the Election Law Journal.*

Michael D. McDonald is a Professor of Political Science and the Director of the Center on Democratic Performance at Binghamton University (SUNY). He serves on the steering committee of Berlin's Wissenshaftszentrum project on Manifesto Research on Political Representation. His research focuses on democratic representation processes in U.S. and European contexts. He has also served as a consultant and expert witness on questions of legislative districting and voting rights.

Pippa Norris is ARC Laureate Professor of Government and International Relations at the University of Sydney, Paul McGuire Lecturer in Comparative Politics at Harvard University, and Director of the Electoral Integrity Project. Major honors include the Johan Skytte Prize, the Karl Deutsch Award, the Kathleen Fitzpatrick Australian Laureate Fellowship, the Sir Isaiah Berlin Prize for Lifetime Contribution towards Political Studies, the Brown Medal for Democracy, and Fellowship of the American Academy of Arts and Sciences. She has published around 50 books, including *Advancing Electoral Integrity* (Oxford University Press, 2014), *Checkbook Elections* (with Andrea Abel van Es, Oxford University Press, 2016), and *Election Watchdogs* (with Alessandro Nai, Oxford University Press, 2017). @PippaN15.

Kevin Pallister is an Assistant Professor of Political Science at Bridgewater College. His research focuses on election administration and democracy, with a regional focus on Latin America. His published work includes *Election Administration and the Politics of Voter Access* (Routledge, 2017) and articles in *Latin American Politics and Society, Revista de Ciencia Política,* and the *Routledge Handbook of Comparative Political Institutions.*

Heather Szilagyi is a Research Officer at the International Foundation for Electoral Systems (IFES), focusing on issues of electoral integrity. She contributes to research and the development of assessment methodologies for IFES's technical leadership initiatives, including projects on the abuse of state resources and electoral leadership. She has been involved in researching, writing, and editing IFES electoral integrity assessments in Burma/Myanmar, Sri Lanka, The Gambia, and Tanzania and has contributed to revisions of the assessment methodology based on lessons learned. She graduated from Dartmouth College with a BA in Government and minor in Geography.

Kjerstin Thorson is an Associate Professor in the College of Communication Arts & Sciences at Michigan State University. Her research explores the effects of digital and social media on political engagement, activism, and persuasion, especially among youth. Recent research projects have investigated political uses of Facebook, the spread of climate change communication on social media, and the contributions of media use in shifting conceptions of politics among young adults.

Dari Sylvester Tran is an Associate Professor of Political Science at University of the Pacific. She earned her PhD from SUNY Stony Brook University in 2006. She specializes in election law and election administration. Tran's research has been funded by the Pew Charitable Trusts and the Help America Vote Act. Her work has appeared in *Election Law Journal* and edited volumes including *Why Don't Americans Vote?* (ABC-Clio, 2016) and *More Votes That Count: A Case Study in Voter Mobilization* (IGS Press, 2012).

Nandi Vanka joined the Carter Center in 2015. She works on the Democratic Republic of the Congo Human Rights House team and has conducted research for the Center's U.S. Elections project. Previously, Nandi assisted with the Carter Center's international election observation mission in Guyana and interned at the White House Office of Public Engagement. She holds degrees in International Studies and French studies from Emory University and Sciences Po Paris.

Chad Vickery is the Senior Director of applied research, learning and strategy at the International Foundation for Electoral Systems. Vickery's programmatic experience includes leading electoral integrity assessments and projects designed to ensure the development of impartial legal frameworks for elections, increasing professionalism of election management bodies, and establishing effective election dispute programs. He holds a Master's degree in International Relations from Georgetown University, a Juris Doctorate from the Catholic University of America, and a Bachelor's degree in Political Science from the University of Washington.

Emily K. Vraga is an Associate Professor in the Department of Communication at George Mason University. Her research examines how individuals respond to news and information about contentious political, scientific, and health issues, particularly when they encounter disagreement on digital media. She is especially interested in detecting and correcting misinformation on social media, using news media literacy messages to limit biased processing and improve news consumption habits, and encouraging attention to more diverse political content online.

Thomas Wynter is a Senior Research Associate at the Electoral Integrity Project and Program Manager of the Perceptions of Electoral Integrity survey. His research is concerned primarily with political psychology and public opinion, employing survey-experiments to examine policy preferences. His work has been published in the *Journal of Global Security Studies, Conservation Letters,* and *Marine Policy.* Wynter completed his PhD and Master's degrees in Political Science at the University of Sydney.

Philip Yates is an Assistant Professor in the Department of Mathematical Sciences at DePaul University. He was previously an Associate Professor in the Department of Mathematics at Saint Michael's College and an Assistant Professor in the Department of Mathematics and Statistics at Cal Poly Pomona. He earned his PhD in statistics at the University of South Carolina and his MS in Biostatistics at the University of Vermont.

Electoral Integrity in America

PART I

INTRODUCTION

Challenges in American Elections

PIPPA NORRIS, SARAH CAMERON, AND THOMAS WYNTER

The contemporary era has raised a series of red flags about the integrity of American elections. Problems include plummeting public trust, exacerbated by Republican claims of widespread electoral fraud. Confidence in the impartiality and reliability of the news media has eroded. And Russian meddling has astutely exploited both these vulnerabilities, through breaches of cybersecurity in state election records and misinformation campaigns online. It is by no means evident that the political response to these serious threats has been effective or sufficient to reverse the damage. The challenges to electoral integrity in America are far from novel; the seismic fault lines were established many years earlier, in the litigious wars over Floridian ballots in *Bush v. Gore* in 2000 (Wand et al. 2001; Hasen 2012). Earlier decades witnessed historic battles over cleaning up elections and expanding civil rights (Campbell 2006; Keyssar 2009; Foley 2016). But the 2016 campaign highlighted several long-standing weaknesses and revealed new risks.

Partisan polarization over contentious elections heightens the risks of outcomes resolved through the courts, not the ballot box (see Hasen, chapter 2). It becomes more difficult to pass effective reforms (Kropf and Kimball 2011). Where elections are seen as rigged and fraudulent, public confidence in representative institutions can drain away (Birch 2008; Norris 2014), eroding satisfaction with democracy (Fortin-Rittberger, Harfst, and Dingler 2017), depressing voter turnout (Birch 2010; Martinez i Coma and Trinh 2017), and triggering massive protests (Beaulieu 2014). Authoritarian-populist rhetoric typically exploits conspiratorial suspicions that elections don't work, all politicians are corrupt, and the system is rigged, thereby weakening the legitimacy of institutional checks and balances curbing the potential abuse of executive power (Norris and Inglehart 2018). Evaluations of the quality of American elections and democracy have been downgraded recently by leading watchdog agencies, including Freedom House (2018) and the Economist Intelligence Unit (2018).

To understand these issues, this chapter starts by identifying the major concerns arising during and after the 2016 U.S. presidential elections, including issues about fraud, fakery, and meddling. To place these issues in a broader perspective and establish whether systematic evidence justifies these sorts of anxieties, the second part clarifies the core concept of electoral integrity as the key yardstick used to evaluate elections around the world and outlines the sequential steps in the electoral cycle, as well as how this concept can best be measured. The third part demonstrates that many countries face multiple challenges in meeting international standards of electoral integrity. Compared with similar affluent democracies, American contests perform particularly poorly. The analysis also uses expert and public evaluations to diagnose the electoral performance of all fifty U.S. states. Finally, to understand the reasons for these ratings in more depth, the fourth part outlines the chapters contained in the rest of the book. Contributors analyze evidence for a series of contemporary challenges facing American elections, including the weaknesses of electoral laws, photo ID requirements for electoral registers, gerrymandering district boundaries, fake news, the lack of transparency, and the hodgepodge of inconsistent state regulations. The conclusion sets these challenges in comparative context and draws out the broader policy lessons for improving electoral integrity and thereby strengthening American democracy.

The challenges facing American elections

The 2016 U.S. presidential elections highlighted a mélange of concerns involving claims of massive voter fraud and lack of public confidence in the media, combined with Russian meddling designed to exacerbate both these weaknesses. In an era of heightened partisan and ideological polarization and low media trust, Americans often interpret new information through a partisan lens. Theories of motivated reasoning suggest that new information reinforces opinions, allowing us to make reasoned arguments supporting our preexisting beliefs rather than changing minds (Kunda 1990; Edelson et al. 2017). When new risks of any sort come to light— terrorism, climate change, electoral malpractices—anxiety is thought to intensify most among people already the most concerned. Others become less worried or indifferent when presented with the same claims. Thus Trump supporters, already prone to concern about illegal immigration, are likely to dig in following the president's renewed allegations of massive voter fraud by noncitizens. Meanwhile intelligence and news reports about Russian meddling in the 2016 election on behalf of the Trump campaign provide additional ammunition, which makes Democrats become more intense in their belief that the contest and media coverage were unfairly skewed against Hillary Clinton. The combination of problems understood primarily through diametrically opposed partisan lenses, with little common ground between Republicans and Democrats and little faith in the news media as an impartial information gatekeeper, has the potential to trigger a perfect storm to further damage public confidence in the legitimacy of American elections and democracy.

Where trust and legitimacy are lacking, even accidental mistakes or minor procedural flaws in future elections are likely to reinforce contentious outcomes, especially in wafer-thin contests. In Virginia's Newport News, for example, during the
2017 state elections, officials mistakenly assigned around two dozen electors to
the wrong district, which may have cost the Democrat candidate the race and thus
upended the balance of power in the Virginia House of Delegates (Vozzella and
Melinik 2018). Details matter in elections—and without a reservoir of trust, cases
of maladministration, happenstance, and human errors can erode confidence in the
process and provoke bitter partisan battles.

Fraud

One major issue concerns claims that electoral fraud is a widespread occurrence
in American elections. This long-standing allegation among Republicans has been
reinforced on steroids by the barrage of populist rhetoric in recent years, when
President Trump has repeatedly declared that the system is rigged, with "substantial evidence of voter fraud" (White House 2018). President Trump asserted that
he won the popular vote "if you deduct the millions of people who voted illegally."[1]
During the campaign, on October 18, 2016, Trump's urged his supporters, "Get out
and vote. But they even want to try and rig the election at the polling booths where
so many cities are corrupt. And you see that. And voter fraud is all too common."[2]
Sore losers in contentious elections have an incentive to disrupt the process
and undermine the legitimacy of close outcomes, such as by crying wolf, falsely
alleging fraud, and/or engaging in electoral boycotts or protests (Norris, Frank, and
Martinez i Coma 2015b). But victors rarely question the results. Yet even after winning the Electoral College and entering the White House, President Trump continued to assert that more than three million fraudulent votes were cast in the 2016
elections: "In many places, like California, the same person votes many times. You
probably heard about that. They always like to say, 'Oh, that's a conspiracy theory.'
Not a conspiracy theory, folks. Millions and millions of people" (Kesslar 2016). The
assertion was not about the general risks of random acts of fraud across America;
instead it was about ballots allegedly cast by illegal aliens and non–U.S. citizens on
temporary visas in states such as California, Virginia, and New Hampshire.[3]

Trump's speeches could be dismissed as partisan hot air and rhetorical hyper-
bole, an attempt to bolster his popular authority among his base and to link the claim
with anti-immigrant sentiments, without factual foundation or policy consequence
(Cottrell, Herron, and Westwood 2018; Udani and Kimball 2018). Republicans
have repeated similar arguments for years, long before Trump descended the golden
escalator to declare his candidacy, to justify more restrictive state laws tightening
voter identification requirements to register and cast a ballot (Bentele and O'Brien
2013; Biggers and Hanmer 2017; Hicks et al. 2015). Specific irregularities can arise
from out-of-date or inaccurate official registers (Pew Research Center 2012). A few

sporadic cases of double-voting are reported to occur, often accidentally, when an individual casts multiple ballots, each under a different registration record, in the same election (Goel et al. 2017). But there is no credible evidence of *massive* fraud in American elections, refuting Trump's allegation of three to five million illegal ballots cast in the 2016 contest (Levitt 2007; Minnite 2010); indeed the Pence-Kobach Presidential Advisory Committee on Electoral Integrity was dissolved in disarray after a year, without publishing any findings (Jacobson 2018). Leaders in the Republican Party, including secretaries of state, commissioners of elections, the chair of the U.S. Electoral Commission, and the congressional leadership, have all spoken out in rejecting unsubstantiated claims of voter fraud and election rigging (Brennan Center for Justice 2017b). Democrats argue that these claims are spurious justifications for cleaning electoral rolls and tightening voter registration requirements, thereby suppressing eligible citizens' voting rights (Wang 2012). Nevertheless, influenced by motivated partisan reasoning and presidential cues, many Trump supporters find these discredited assertions plausible (Edelson et al. 2017). In April 2018, for example, a Pew Research Center poll found that the majority of Republicans (58%) believed that "some ineligible voters are permitted to vote" (Doherty 2018). This matters: when people lack confidence in the legitimacy of their elections, they can lose faith in core institutions and democracy as well (Norris 2014; Levitsky and Ziblatt 2018).

Fakery

The second problem concerns President Trump's constant attacks on "fake media," which tap into the widespread erosion of trust in the information Americans receive from the media, generating growing partisan divides when assessing their performance (Pew Research Center 2018b). Since the inauguration, estimates suggest that, on average, Trump has used the word "fake" in his public utterances more than once a day (over 500 times), assailing "fake news," "fake polls," "fake media," and "fake stories."[4] He tweeted on May 9, 2018, "The Fake News is working overtime. Just reported that, despite the tremendous success we are having with the economy & all things else, 91% of the Network News about me is negative (Fake). Why do we work so hard in working with the media when it is corrupt? Take away credentials?" He accuses journalists of being "enemies of the American people" and threatens to reduce legal protections for the press and revoke broadcast licenses. The legacy news media like CNN, the *New York Times*, and the *Washington Post* provide a convenient target for mobilizing the base, with attacks generating noise and confusion serving to discredit fact-based information. Again, American conservatives have complained about "liberal media bias" since the mid-1950s, so this battle cry is far from novel, leading to the development of explicitly ideological right-wing alternative media such as magazines, talk radio, and Fox News (Hemmer 2017).

But American conservatives have rarely threatened to use the law to undermine or restrict the free press (Boczkowski 2018).

The "fake news" mantra fuels a "post-truth" world, with populist ideologues denying the Enlightenment idea that there can be such a thing as objective knowledge, scientific evidence, or impartial journalism (McIntyre 2018). Declining use of legacy news media and the rise of social bubbles and echo chambers in online media reinforce dogmatism fueled by ideology, not fact (Allcott and Gentzkow 2017; Dutton et al. 2017; Fletcher et al. 2018). Where news or social media provide repeated distortions impacting citizens' perceptions of events, these can give rise to deep-seated misinformed beliefs and cause significant harm. Attacks on journalistic elites as "enemies of the people" are part and parcel of authoritarian populist rhetoric, with a crackdown on mainstream media by leaders such as the Philippines' Rodrigo Duterte, Hungary's Viktor Mihály Orbán, and Turkey's Recep Tayyip Erdoğan. At a joint press conference in Manila, when Duterte called the media "spies," Trump laughed (Cillizza 2017).

This climate of mistrust in legacy journalism, exacerbated but not triggered by Trump, provides fertile soil for disinformation campaigns. These are designed to spread intentional falsehoods disguised as news stories or documentaries in order to advance political goals (Bennett and Livingstone 2018). Disinformation includes all forms of false, inaccurate, and misleading information designed, presented, and promoted to intentionally cause public harm or for profit. Russian activity during the 2016 U.S. campaign exacerbated the proliferation of domestic disinformation, where the erosion of trust in legacy media and access to the internet has opened the door to social media and political websites mimicking journalism as alternative information sources. In the EU as well, Russian disinformation campaigns, cyberattacks, fake news, and propaganda aiming to destabilize the West have been reported by the European Council president—including in elections in Germany, Britain, and Spain (Rankin 2017). The European Commission's (2018) High Level Expert Group study on fake news suggested several strategies that could help overcome disinformation, including enhancing transparency in political advertising, promoting media literacy education, and developing tools to empower users. The impact of disinformation campaigns (coupled with presidential mendacity) may be that certain falsehoods and myths become widely accepted as true but also that the very notion of objective fact is questioned (Richey 2018). The Knight Foundation (2018) reported that today public trust in the media is at an all-time low; three-quarters of Americans believe that the spread of inaccurate information online (fake news) is a major problem, while two-thirds of Republicans and almost half of the Democrats view the media unfavorably. The majority of Americans believe it is harder to be informed today due to the plethora of news sources available.

Meddling and information warfare

Public concern about electoral fraud and info fakery were heightened following warnings by the joint U.S. intelligence services about the risks of Russian cyberhacking and propaganda in American elections (Office of Director of National Intelligence 2017). The latter involves the use of social media like the 3,517 Facebook ads bought by the Russian Internet Research Agency to spread disinformation and sow discord in the electorate. The ads emphasized polarizing negative messages, stoking fears about race and the police, Muslims, and immigration, which were subsequently spread in America by online networks and amplified by mainstream reporters (Richey 2018; Power 2018; Penzenstadler, Heath, and Guynn 2018). This meddling has not stopped; the Alliance for Securing Democracy, a transatlantic initiative funded by the German Marshall Fund, continues to track Russia's ongoing efforts to undermine democracy and elections in the United States and Europe through cyberattacks, disinformation, and illicit funding.[5]

During the campaign, the Russians successfully hacked into emails belonging to the Clinton campaign and the Democratic National Committee, with the results distributed through WikiLeaks, sparking damaging internal rows dividing Clinton and Sanders supporters (Brazile 2017; McFadden 2018; Isikoff and Corn 2018). An even more serious danger to public trust in electoral integrity was revealed when the Senate Intelligence Committee (2018) reported that Russians attempted to break into the official election records in twenty-one states, scanning them for vulnerabilities. Russians had penetrated the official voter registration rolls of several U.S. states, including Illinois, and they stayed inside the system for several weeks prior to the 2016 presidential election. They had opportunities to alter voter registration data and vote tallies, although the Senate Intelligence Committee (2018) concluded that they did not actually do so. Following his investigations, the special counsel, Robert Mueller, has indicted several Russians and charged them with "information warfare against the United States."[6]

Ordinary citizens have paid attention to the stream of news about hacking of social media, campaign websites, voting machines, and voter registration files. In November 2016, the Survey of the Performance of American Elections by YouGov reported that 17% of respondents thought that computer hacking in the 2016 U.S. elections was a major problem nationwide.[7] By March 2018, this proportion had doubled, to 38%. Moreover, although public concern grew across the board, the partisan divide widened, as the biggest shift during 2016 and 2017 was among Democrats, with the proportion of those expressing concern about election hacking rising from 23% in 2016 to 56% in 2018 (Stewart 2018a).

In response to these threats, the Department of Homeland Security has worked with around thirty states to tighten cybersecurity in their election infrastructure (Halper 2017a; Fidler 2017; U.S. Election Assistance Commission 2017). Behind the scenes, several states have also been improving the nuts-and-bolts of their election administration, such as by implementing automatic voter registration (Brennan Center for Justice 2017a). In March 2018, Congress allocated $380 million to bolster electoral security. But advances have been piecemeal and, despite the threats, it seems highly unlikely that a comprehensive bipartisan federal program of legislative reforms will address major flaws in the security of the American electoral process, such as by adopting voting machines with paper ballot backups, instituting routine vote audits, and updating software systems. Prospects for passage of the bipartisan Secure Elections Act, designed to mitigate the risks of cyberthreats, seem bleak.[8] Even acknowledging the serious nature of the threat in a timely fashion is doubtful, given the general partisan stalemate in Congress, the lackluster and laggard response of the White House to the intelligence reports of Russian meddling, partisan disputes about the nature and causes of any problems of electoral malpractice, and an atmosphere of intolerance poisoned by bitter arguments about alleged collusion between the Russians and the Trump campaign. Some challenges facing the integrity of U.S. elections, like partisan gerrymandering and onerous voter registration requirements, are being addressed through the courts (see Hasen, chapter 2). But the capacity of the legislative and executive branches to secure future American elections against threats seems broken.

The flaws that came to light during the 2016 contest may therefore potentially signify a critical tipping point capable of doing lasting harm that will undermine faith in the legitimacy of the electoral process and damage confidence in American democracy. Partisan differences on policy issues such as healthcare, tax cuts, and immigration are all part of any healthy pluralistic debate. But lack of a bipartisan consensus about the basic rules of the electoral game is likely to prove far more dangerous for the stability of any democracy (Klass 2017; Levitsky and Ziblatt 2018). The 2016 U.S. presidential election saw an exceptionally brutal campaign, characterized by harsh personal attacks and intolerant rhetoric, leaving an enduring legacy of bitterness and division in American society.

Claims of fraud, fakery, and meddling have reinforced public doubts about the legitimacy and fairness of the electoral process. Not surprisingly, as a result, public trust in American elections has fallen sharply during recent years; for example, the Gallup World Poll reports that in 2016 one-third of Americans (30%) expressed confidence in the honesty of their elections, down from a majority (52%) a decade earlier.[9] Moreover this is not just a reflection of a more general phenomenon of declining trust found in Western societies. If we compare public confidence in the honesty of their own country's elections during the past decade, Figure 1.1 demonstrates that American trust has been consistently lower than several comparable Anglo-American democracies.

Public concern about elections seems well-founded, not a conspiracy. As illustrated in Figure 1.2, evidence from the Varieties of Democracy (V-Dem)

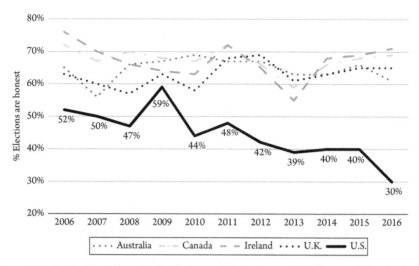

Figure 1.1 Public Confidence in the Honesty of Their Country's Elections in Five Anglo-American Democracies, 2006–2016.

Note: Q: "In this country, do you have confidence in each of the following, or not? How about honesty of elections?" Response options: Yes, No, Don't know. (% Yes). Source: Gallup World Poll, http://www.gallup.com/analytics/213704/world-poll.aspx.

project suggests that, during the decade after Florida, U.S. elections were consistently rated as less free and fair than contests in comparable Anglo-American democracies, such as Canada, Australia, and the U.K., as well as far lower than in Scandinavian and Western European societies. V-Dem assessments of the quality of American contests rose temporarily in the 2012–2014 elections, then plummeted sharply in the 2016 presidential election, where the official results were regarded by experts as having little, if anything, to do with the "will of the people."[10] Similar concerns about the state of American elections and democracy have been highlighted by many scholars (Klass 2017; Sunstein 2018; Levitsky and Ziblatt 2018; Mounk 2018). Leading watchdog agencies concur, thus Freedom House's 2018 report notes that "in recent years (U.S.) democratic institutions have suffered erosion, as reflected in partisan manipulation of the electoral process," downgrading the country's political rating from 1 to 2 "due to growing evidence of Russian interference in the 2016 elections" (Freedom House 2018). Similarly the Economist Intelligence Unit's (2018) annual report downgraded its rating of the U.S. in 2016 from a "full democracy" to a "flawed democracy," noting the problems of growing party polarization, partisan gerrymandering, and the erosion of public trust in government, ranking America 21st in the 2017 global comparison. Reports by the Electoral Integrity Project, Reporters without Borders, Transparency International, and Human Rights Watch largely concurred with these assessments of the risks facing U.S. elections and democracy (Roth 2016; Reporters without Borders 2017).

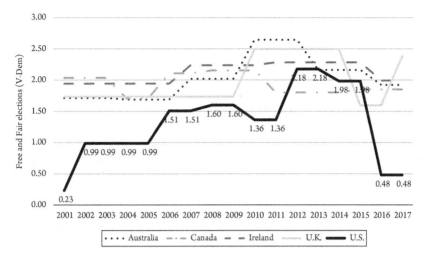

Figure 1.2 Expert Assessments of Free and Fair Elections in Anglo-American Democracies, 2000–2017.

Note: V-Dem 8.0 Q: "Taking all aspects of the pre-election period, election day, and the post-election process into account, would you consider this national election to be free and fair? Clarification: The only thing that should not be considered in coding this is the extent of suffrage (by law). Thus, a free and fair election may occur even if the law excludes significant groups (an issue measured separately)." Responses: "0: No, not at all. The elections were fundamentally flawed and the official results had little if anything to do with the 'will of the people' (i.e., who became president; or who won the legislative majority); 1: Not really. While the elections allowed for some competition, the irregularities in the end affected the outcome of the election (i.e., who became president; or who won the legislative majority); 2: Ambiguous. There was substantial competition and freedom of participation but there were also significant irregularities. It is hard to determine whether the irregularities affected the outcome or not (as defined above); 3: Yes, somewhat. There were deficiencies and some degree of fraud and irregularities but these did not in the end affect the outcome (as defined above); 4: Yes. There was some amount of human error and logistical restrictions but these were largely unintentional and without significant consequences." Scale: Ordinal, converted to interval by the measurement model. Source: Varieties of Democracy project (V-Dem) 8.0, https://www.v-dem.net/en/.

The concept and measure of electoral integrity

These sorts of problems need to be understood from a broader comparative perspective since America is far from alone in encountering problems at the ballot box. Numerous types of flaws and failures regularly undermine elections around the globe (Norris 2015; Flores and Nooruddin 2016; Norris and Nai 2017): Opponents are disqualified. District boundaries are gerrymandered. Campaigns provide a skewed playing field for parties. Independent media are muzzled. Citizens are ill-informed about choices. Balloting is disrupted by bloodshed. Social media spreads fake news and hate speech. Ballot boxes are stuffed. Vote counts are fiddled. Opposition parties withdraw. Contenders refuse to accept the people's choice. Protests disrupt polling. Officials abuse state resources. Electoral registers are out of date. Candidates distribute largesse. Votes are bought. Airwaves favor incumbents. Campaigns are awash with hidden cash. Political finance rules are lax. Incompetent local officials run out of ballot papers. Incumbents are immune from effective challengers. Rallies trigger riots. Women candidates face discrimination. Ethnic minorities are persecuted. Voting machines jam. Lines lengthen. Ballot box seals break. Citizens cast more than one ballot. Laws restrict voting rights. Polling stations are inaccessible. Software crashes. "Secure" ink washes off fingers. Courts fail to resolve complaints impartially. Foreigners meddle. For all the challenges facing American elections, American democracy remains resilient, and these malpractices are obviously far less severe than those in contests around the globe ending in bloodshed, boycotts, or even military coups.

What binds these diverse sorts of problems together?

Several alternative positive terms have commonly been deployed in diplomatic language, election observer reports, and scholarly studies, where contests are described as "competitive," "credible," "acceptable," "genuine," "clean," "democratic," reflecting the "will of the people," and the older rhetoric of "free and fair" (Elklit and Svensson 1997). More recently the metaphor of a "level playing field" has become popular as a way to describe party competition, although it is conceptually ambiguous (Levitsky and Way 2010; Helle 2016). Related notions include negative phrases such as "electoral malpractice," "flawed elections," "misconduct," "manipulated contests," "rigged" or "stolen" elections, as well as the popular notion of "electoral fraud."

Each of these terms often has narrower technical meanings (discussed further in chapter 10). For example electoral *fraud* can be defined as illicit acts intentionally interfering with the election process and outcome, exemplified by vote buying, identity theft, rigging the count, or stuffing the ballot box (see chapter 10; Lehoucq, Edouard, and Jiménez 2002; Lehoucq 2003). These are certainly serious problems when they occur in countries such as Mexico, Ukraine, and Zimbabwe, as they are capable of undermining public confidence, generating legal prosecutions and court appeals, and triggering protests (Alvarez, Hall, and Hyde 2008; Collier and Vincente 2011). International observers devote considerable efforts to deterring cheating in polling places and in the count (Daxecker 2012). American elections in the past have certainly suffered from these problems (Campbell 2006). Yet, at the same time, the available evidence suggests that in *modern* American elections, fraudulent acts such as cases of identity-theft impersonation, double voting, or vote buying are extremely rare (Minnite 2010). And many other types of major malpractice are not necessarily illegal—or even intentional. Contests can be sunk by accidental errors, incompetence, and maladministration—all failures of governance—as much as by malice aforethought. The infamous "butterfly ballot" in Florida, designed by a local Democratic official, exemplifies such flaws (Hasen 2012).

An alternative way to conceptualize these problems is to refer to practices involving the systematic and intentional *manipulation* of elections (Schedler 2002).

Again the intentional abuse of electoral laws is problematic, for example, where voting regulations systematically discriminate against minority populations or where incumbents seek to discourage challengers through the allocation of public campaign funds. But all electoral systems "manipulate" contests to some degree, such as by the rules used when translating votes into seats. Moreover procedures undermining free and fair contests can also be perfectly legal, such as the 2012 Hungarian electoral reforms, which favored Orbán's Fidetz government (OSCE 2014); Malaysia's and Singapore's ethnic gerrymandering, which maintains the power of the ruling parties (Fetzer 2008); U.S. state laws disenfranchising felons and prison inmates (McGinnis 2018); and Turkey's high vote threshold, designed to exclude Kurdish nationalists.

Another approach common among scholars is to use notions of electoral or liberal democracy as the primary benchmark, seeking to examine whether elections meet the criteria that Joseph Schumpeter used to define minimalist notions of party competition or that Robert Dahl described as components of "polyarchy." The V-Dem project adopts this method when seeking to measure the former: "The electoral principle of democracy seeks to embody the core value of making rulers responsive to citizens, achieved through electoral competition for the electorate's approval under circumstances when suffrage is extensive; political and civil society organizations can operate freely; elections are clean and not marred by fraud or systematic irregularities; and elections affect the composition of the chief executive of the country" (Coppedge et al. 2018). This approach is not unreasonable if the goal is to compare types of democratic regimes, but it fails to specify exactly what counts as "systematic irregularities" or "clean elections," which remain open to interpretation. The primary focus is upon classifying regimes rather than monitoring the severity of the myriad types of problems capable of undermining voting procedures and electoral processes. Moreover, while democratic theorists provide conceptual clarity for scholars, they are not acknowledged as a legitimate source of authority for practitioners in the international community.

The concept of electoral integrity

Accordingly, instead of these approaches, the notion of *electoral integrity* has proved a useful way to conceptualize many of the desirable practices in the conduct of elections, and use of the term has grown in recent years (Global Commission on Elections, Democracy and Security 2012; Alvarez, Atkeson, and Hall 2012a; Norris 2014).

⌈ The overarching concept of electoral integrity used in this book refers broadly to whether contests meet international commitments and global norms, endorsed in a series of authoritative instruments (conventions, treaties, protocols, and guidelines) through the UN General Assembly, regional intergovernmental organizations, and related multilateral bodies, exemplified by the 1948 Universal Declaration of Human

Rights (Carter Center 2014; International IDEA 2014). There are two main types of instruments: declarations and conventions. Declarations are not legally binding, but they do have political and moral impact. Conventions are legally binding under international law. Member states that endorse conventions agree to observe and enforce these standards and to implement them in domestic laws. The Carter Center (2014) published the comprehensive *Election Obligations and Standards* (*EOS*) database of international legal obligations and standards governing the conduct of elections compiled from over 200 sources; the database identifies which countries have ratified or endorsed international and regional treaties. These universal standards are understood to apply to all countries worldwide throughout the electoral cycle, including during the pre-electoral period, the campaign, on polling day, and its aftermath. Governments in nation-states committed to these agreements are bound to uphold these obligations. Core principles include the right to vote (requiring a universal franchise) and respect for freedoms of the press, association, and assembly. The standards employed in electoral integrity thereby derive their authority from human rights frameworks, authorized by member states within the international community. Many of these principles reflect core aspects and values of liberal democratic theory, but this is not the primary source of their legitimacy in international jurisprudence and national legal frameworks. Some of the administrative criteria used in regional guidelines developed by electoral monitoring organizations also reflect pragmatic issues of good governance rather than the values of liberal democracy, such as whether elections meet professional standards of electoral management, whether campaign finance is transparent, and whether contests are well planned, budgeted and implemented. Conversely, the term "malpractice" is used throughout the book to refer to violations of standards of electoral integrity.

The international community has also learned that standards of electoral integrity do not apply just to the final stages of voting on polling day and counting the results; instead elections are understood to operate throughout the extended cyclical process, well before the campaign starts, during the campaign, on election day, and during its immediate aftermath. These stages can be understood as a sequence broken down into eleven components, ranging from the election laws, electoral procedures, and boundary delimitation to the voting process, vote count, and declaration of results. Figure 1.3 sets out the key steps—and how the chapters in the book address these in the American context. Some stages occur well before the glare of the spotlight on the election campaign gets under way, such as implementing effective, accurate, secure, and inclusive electoral registers, determining fair and impartial district boundaries, and using open and fair party rules and procedures for nominating candidates. Others involve steps happening later in the process, such as the implementation of convenient balloting facilities, transparent and accurate vote tabulations, and effective dispute resolution mechanisms.

The steps in the electoral process are now usually treated as cyclical rather than a single event. In the time sequence, the cycle restarts in a continuous loop, and

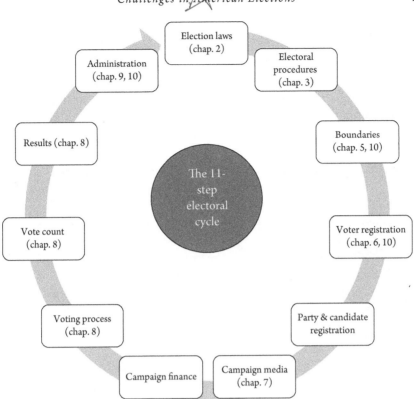

Figure 1.3 Stages in the Electoral Cycle
Source: *Why Electoral Integrity Matters* (Norris 2014).

there is a learning process from one election to the next. Conducting an election is one of the most complex, delicate, and challenging activities undertaken by governments—especially since many contests are now being held in inauspicious circumstances, such as in societies emerging from conflict as part of the peace-building process, in countries with little or no prior experience of democracy, and in poorer states with weak capacity, inadequate resources, and poorly trained staff for the task (Flores and Nooruddin 2016). Given the importance of establishing legitimate results in contentious and close elections, there is often no room for even minor errors or any time for recovery from mistakes at the polls. For effective management and implementation, certain features—such as reforms to electoral laws and administrative procedures—need to occur temporarily well prior to others, such as the commencement of the primary and general election campaigns and the declaration of the final results and allocation of offices.

In addition, like broken links in a chain or a tumbling row of dominoes, violating standards in any one of the sequential steps has the capacity to undermine confidence that the principles of electoral integrity are being genuinely observed, generating public protests, legal challenges, or worse, for example, if a local polling station fails to open on time, a candidate violates campaign finance spending rules, or computerized voting records crash. (For a related notion, see Schedler 2002.) Thus many contests around the world are flawed by illegal acts of electoral fraud on polling day and its immediate aftermath, such as vote buying or ballot stuffing, attracting media headlines. But these make up only one type of problem and not necessarily the most common one today (Frank and Martinez i Coma 2017). Instead it is more efficient in electoral autocracies for leaders to use more subtle means to control the outcome, for example, by appointing judges and electoral commissioners willing to disqualify political opponents from ballot access based on trumped-up charges, or by adopting an electoral system which stacks the deck against opposition parties. Thus election day can be relatively free and fair, with observers reporting peaceful and well-run polling stations, efficient and impartial electoral officials, and accurate and transparent ballot counts. But the contest can still fail to meet international standards of electoral integrity due to the earlier stages of the process, where ballot access laws restrict the eligibility of candidates and parties to run for office, where political money and campaign media coverage fail to provide a level playing field for all parties, and where district boundaries grossly favor incumbents (Frank and Martinez i Coma 2017).

The measurement of electoral integrity

Given this conceptualization, how can electoral integrity be measured and compared? Multiple sources of evidence and techniques are now available to evaluate the quality of elections in each country, such as surveys of the electorate and of front-line poll workers, reports from election observers, forensic techniques of votes cast, and common performance indices, including counting voter turnout, the number of legal appeals, or the proportion of women in elected office. Each has pros and cons (Alvarez, Atkeson, and Hall 2012b; Burden and Stewart 2014). Until recently, less systematic evidence has been available for cross-national comparisons, and studies were forced to rely upon proxy indicators that provide imprecise and noisy measures of the quality of elections per se, such as standard measures of liberal democracy by Freedom House or Polity IV or surveys monitoring public attitudes toward elections like the Gallup World Poll or World Values Survey. Recent years have seen considerable advances in the availability of cross-national and time-series data, however, either by compiling data from election observer and news media reports (Hyde and Marinov 2012) or by applying the techniques of expert surveys. Thus the V-Dem project asks experts to assess nationwide parliamentary and presidential elections, such as the extent of the suffrage, the availability of public funding, the presence of election boycotts or violence, and the autonomy of the election management body.

In this chapter, we examine how far American contests meet international standards by the Perceptions of Electoral Integrity (PEI) expert rolling survey. This standardized instrument has been used since 2012 to compare the performance of national presidential and parliamentary elections around the world, as well as to compare the performance of states and provinces within and across large federal countries, including Russia, Mexico, India, and the United States. The global PEI (v. 6.0) covers 285 elections from July 2012 to December 2017 in 164 countries, drawn from 3,253 expert assessments (Norris, Wynter, and Cameron 2018a). Experts are consulted around one month after polling day for each contest. Around 50 questions monitor all the stages of the electoral cycle in more detail than the V-Dem measures, and these standard items generate the overall PEI 100-point Index summary score for each election, as well as standardized scores for each of the 11 stages of the electoral cycle. Additional thematic batteries rotated each year expand the topics under analysis. The global PEI Index is strongly correlated with independent measures, such as the V-Dem assessments of the same elections, lending confidence to the external validity of the PEI estimates. (For a discussion, see also Latner, chapter 4.)[11] One considerable advantage of using this source is that identical methods have been used by PEI to assess the performance of U.S. states in successive American elections since 2012. Thus PEI-US-2016 evaluated elections in each of the 50 U.S. states, drawing upon a survey of 726 election experts, as well as an index of U.S. state election laws coded from the regulations used in each state (Norris, Garnett, and Grömping 2017). In its publications, the Electoral Integrity Project has not made direct comparison of the global and state-level results (for example, by comparing countries against states), but the availability of both measures using identical methods facilitates across-country and also within-country comparisons on a consistent basis.

Challenges in contemporary American elections

This systematic body of evidence allows us to examine several interrelated questions: How does the quality of American elections compare with those in comparable democracies and postindustrial societies? What are the major challenges arising during recent American contests, including the weakest and strongest stages of the electoral cycle? Has the performance of American elections actually declined over successive congressional and presidential contests, as some fear? And finally, how do U.S. states vary in their levels of electoral integrity?

Comparisons across similar countries

We have already seen that V-Dem rates the quality of free and fair elections lower in America compared with those in several similar Anglo-American countries. To look more broadly, Table 1.1 illustrates the performance of a wider range of over 40 comparable democracies, classified as "free" by Freedom House (in the

Table 1.1 **Electoral Integrity in Postindustrial Democracies, 2017**

Rank	Country	PEI index	Electoral laws	Electoral procedures	District boundaries	Voter registration	Party and candidate registration	Media coverage	Campaign finance	Voting process	Vote count	Results	Electoral authorities
1	Denmark	✓	✓	✓	✓	✓	✓	✓	✓	✓	✓	✓	✓
2	Finland	✓	✓	✓	✓	✓	✓	✓	✓	✓	✓	✓	✓
3	Norway	✓	✓	✓	✓	✓	✓	✓	✓	✓	✓	✓	✓
4	Iceland	✓	✓	✓	✓	✓	✓	–	✓	✓	✓	✓	✓
5	Germany	✓	✓	✓	✓	✓	✓	✓	✓	✓	✓	✓	✓
6	Sweden	✓	✓	✓	✓	✓	✓	–	✓	✓	✓	✓	✓
7	Netherlands	✓	✓	✓	✓	✓	✓	✓	✓	✓	✓	✓	✓
8	Estonia	✓	✓	✓	✓	✓	✓	✓	–	✓	✓	✓	✓
9	Switzerland	✓	✓	✓	✓	✓	✓	–	✗	✓	✓	✓	✓
10	Slovenia	✓	✓	✓	✓	✓	✓	–	–	✓	✓	✓	✓
11	Lithuania	✓	✓	✓	✓	✓	✓	✓	–	✓	✓	✓	✓
12	Austria	✓	✓	✓	✓	✓	✓	–	✓	✓	✓	✓	✓
13	Czech Republic	✓	✓	✓	✓	✓	✓	✗	–	✓	✓	✓	✓
14	New Zealand	✓	✓	✓	✓	–	✓	✗	–	✓	✓	✓	✓
15	Uruguay	✓	✓	✓	✓	✓	✓	✓	–	✗	✓	✓	✓
16	Canada	✓	✗	✓	✓	✓	✓	✓	✓	✓	✓	✓	✓
17	France	✓	✓	✓	–	✓	✓	–	✓	✓	✓	✓	✓
18	Slovak Republic	✓	✓	✓	–	✓	✓	–	✗	✓	✓	✓	✓
19	Portugal	✓	✓	✓	✓	✗	✓	–	–	✓	✓	✓	✓
20	Poland	✓	✓	✓	✓	✓	✓	✗	–	✓	✓	✓	✓
21	Israel	✓	✓	✓	–	✓	✓	–	–	–	✓	✓	✓
22	Korea, Rep.	✓	✗	✓	–	✓	✓	✗	–	✓	✓	✓	✓

Rank	Country	PEI index	Electoral laws	Electoral procedures	District boundaries	Voter registration	Party and candidate registration	Media coverage	Campaign finance	Voting process	Vote count	Results	Electoral authorities
23	Latvia	✓	✓	✓	✓	!	✓	!	×	✓	✓	✓	✓
24	Belgium	✓	✓	✓	!	✓	✓	!	!	✓	✓	✓	✓
25	Ireland	✓	✓	✓	✓	×	✓	!	×	!	✓	✓	✓
26	Chile	✓	✓	✓	!	!	✓	×	!	!	✓	✓	✓
27	Australia	✓	✓	✓	✓	!	✓	×	×	✓	✓	✓	✓
28	Cyprus	✓	✓	✓	!	✓	✓	×	×	✓	✓	✓	✓
29	Spain	✓	×	✓	!	✓	✓	×	×	!	✓	✓	✓
30	Japan	✓	×	✓	×	✓	✓	×	!	!	✓	✓	✓
31	Italy	✓	×	✓	✓	✓	✓	×	×	!	✓	✓	✓
32	Greece	✓	×	✓	×	✓	✓	×	×	!	✓	✓	✓
33	United Kingdom	✓	×	✓	×	×	✓	×	×	✓	✓	✓	✓
34	Argentina	!	✓	✓	!	✓	✓	×	×	!	✓	✓	✓
35	Croatia	!	!	✓	×	×	!	×	×	!	✓	✓	✓
36	Malta	!	×	✓	×	✓	✓	×	×	!	✓	✓	✓
37	United States	!	×	✓	×	×	✓	!	×	✓	✓	✓	✓
38	Panama	!	×	✓	×	!	!	×	×	!	✓	!	✓
39	Hungary	×	×	✓	×	✓	!	×	×	!	✓	✓	!
40	Romania	×	×	!	×	×	!	!	×	×	✓	✓	!
41	Bahamas	×	×	!	×	×	×	!	×	×	✓	✓	!
	Total	✓	✓	✓	!	✓	✓	×	!	✓	✓	✓	✓

Note: Selected countries are those classified as "free" by Freedom House in the year of the election(s) with per capita GDP in purchasing power parity over $20,000. Categories ✓ = High (60+) ! = Moderate (50–59) × = Low (less than 50).

Source: PEI-2017 (v. 6.0), www.electoralintegrityproject.com.

year of the election) with per capita GDP of $20,000 or more. The performances for each country are averaged for presidential and parliamentary elections held during the period 2012–2017. This procedure allows us to compare both the overall 100-point PEI Index for each nation, as well as the scores for each of the 11 stages of the electoral cycle. Ratings for electoral integrity are categorized by the 100-point PEI scales into three groups: high/very high (scoring 60+), moderate (50–59), and low/very low (less than 50). The use of categories is more reliable and robust than comparing relatively modest differences in the continuous scales.

The results in Figure 1.4 show that when the PEI Index is compared across 41 high-income democracies, elections in the United States rank 4th from the bottom. Worldwide, the U.S. PEI Index ranks 55th out of 164 countries. By contrast, many of the Nordic and Northern European democracies cluster at the top of the evaluations, such as Denmark, Norway, and Germany; this is not surprising, since these countries also rank high on most of the standard indices of liberal democracy and human rights. What is perhaps more unexpected about the comparison is that experts regard the quality of U.S. elections as close to those in several third-wave democracies, such as Croatia, Argentina, and Panama, and a long way behind countries such as Estonia, Lithuania, and Uruguay. But this is no accident or anomaly; elections in several other long-established liberal democracies rank close to the U.S. score, including those in the U.K., Greece, Australia, Italy, and Spain. Moreover, strikingly similar results are generated, lending confidence to these conclusions, if we rely upon the V-Dem independent estimates of "free and fair elections" (see Figure 1.2) during the same years (2012–2017), where again the United States is ranked 55th out of 167 countries worldwide, far below many similar affluent societies and long-standing democracies.

Weaknesses and strengths in the American electoral cycle

To break down these results in more detail we need to examine scores for each of the subdimensions, as several stages are often particularly poorly rated in American elections ("low or very low"), notably district boundaries, electoral laws and voter registration, media coverage, and campaign finance. Subsequent chapters discuss the underlying reasons behind these sorts of concerns in more depth, including the process of electoral registration and the consequences of the stricter requirements for voter identification that have been adopted most often by many Republican-held states (see chapter 6 for details), the problem of gerrymandering (chapters 5 and 10), the role of campaign media, including issues of the fair and balanced journalistic coverage of the candidates and the spread of "fake" news and misinformation online (see chapter 7), and whether there is equitable access for parties and candidates to campaign finance (see chapter 11). The book's conclusions also draw together the broader lessons and what can be done to tackle some of these issues through policy reforms.

By contrast to these types of problems, experts rate U.S. elections relatively well in electoral procedures, party and candidate registration, and the final stages of the voting process, vote count, results, and electoral authorities (Figure 1.4). Thus an imbalance can be observed between the media and the expert agendas. The event-driven news media agenda typically focuses attention on issues raised by politicians on polling day, such as alleged cases of fraud or voter suppression at the ballot box or the mechanical breakdowns in election machines and logistical flaws in local polling places. For example, news media reports in the 2016 election highlighted some specific challenges about the voter registration and balloting process at precinct and state levels, ranging from long lines and malfunctioning and outdated voting machines in some precincts to incorrect registers, confusion over registration requirements, and reports of intimidation in others (Brennan Center for Justice 2016b). Media reporting of the Russian disinformation campaign has also been extensive. Yet the assessments of the election expert reflect greater concern about more long-term structural issues, the legal framework, and more technical

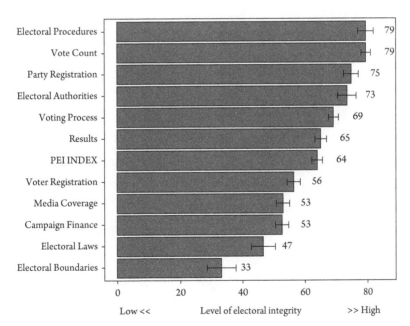

Figure 1.4 The Performance of American Elections throughout the Cycle, 2016.
Note: The mean score at each stage of the electoral cycle in the 2016 U.S. elections calculated from state-level data (N = 51), with 95% confidence intervals.
Source: The Electoral Integrity Project PEI-US 2016 (1.0), www.electoralintegrityproject.com.

aspects of American elections, which typically occur behind the scenes and much earlier during the electoral cycle.

Comparisons across U.S. states

As chapter 9 emphasizes, American elections are a vast mosaic administered in states and thousands of localities. Most countries have a national election management body that determines uniform standards across the country, but the process of electoral administration is highly decentralized in the United States. Figure 1.5 maps how experts evaluated the performance of the 2016 presidential election across all 50 U.S. states and the District of Columbia. The states that experts rated most high in electoral integrity were Vermont, Idaho, New Hampshire, and Iowa. By contrast, states scoring worst on the electoral integrity index in this election were Arizona (ranked last), followed by Wisconsin, Tennessee, Oklahoma, and Mississippi. Several of these states had also been rated low previously in related studies, such as the 2014 Pew Election Performance Index and the Franchise Project Voting Access Scorecard (Pew Research Center 2016a; see chapter 4). It is important to be cautious when interpreting absolute rankings, however, since differences in state performance were often relatively modest.

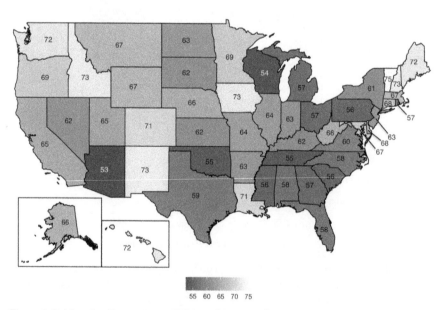

Figure 1.5 Mapping Perceptions of Electoral Integrity by U.S. State, 2016.
Source: Electoral Integrity Project, PEI- US 2016 (1.0), www.electoralintegrityproject.com.

Changes over time

Is there systematic evidence to show that the quality of American elections deteriorated in recent contests, as declared by widespread claims of electoral fraud and media fakery? Figure 1.6 shows the results of the expert survey assessments taken one month after the 2012, 2014, and 2016 elections. The evaluations suggest that several long-standing issues, such as gerrymandering and electoral laws, were regarded as equally problematic across these contests.

Compared with previous elections, the expert ratings fell furthest from 2012 to 2016 for two stages of the electoral cycle. This included evaluations of media coverage of the campaign (discussed in chapter 7), which may reflect the relentlessly negative tone, false equivalence (of the candidate's fitness for office), the disproportionate coverage of Trump, the divisive personal attacks, and focus on the horse race (42% of the total news coverage) rather than policy debate (10%) (Patterson 2016). Yet expert assessments were unable to take into account the issues of misinformation and disinformation on social media that became apparent only later. Despite the use of these techniques by the Russian Internet Research Agency in June 2016, and release of the hacked DNC emails during the same month, President Obama waited until after the election to ask the security services to investigate Russian involvement; their report was published

	PEI Index	Electoral laws	Procedures	Boundaries	Voter registration	Party registration	Media coverage	Campaign finance	Voting process	Vote count	Results	Electoral authorities
2014 Congressional election	62	31	75	11	35	80	69	46	67	76	77	72
2012 Presidential election	63	38	70	16	40	74	63	44	68	85	84	75
2016 Presidential election	59	38	72	16	43	80	46	54	69	76	46	71
Change 2012–2016	**–4**	**0**	**+2**	**0**	**+3**	**+6**	**–17**	**+10**	**1**	**–9**	**–38**	**–4**

Figure 1.6 Changes in the Performance of U.S. Elections, 2012–2016.

Source: Electoral Integrity Project, PEI 2017 (v. 6.0), www.electoralintegrityproject.com.

on January 6, 2017. Beyond rumors, therefore, further information on Russian meddling came to light only after the period of the expert survey.

In addition, experts also rated as poor the announcement of the results stage, which may reflect mass protests due to deep Democratic resentment with the way President Trump won the Electoral College despite losing the popular vote to Clinton by three million votes. This discontent was exemplified by the Women's March, when protesters turned out in massive numbers the day after the presidential inauguration, and by the subsequent waves of mobilization in anti-Trump protest rallies over the Muslim ban, Black Lives Matter, the MeToo movement, and the March for Our Lives antigun rallies. It is estimated that these protests engaged up to eight million Americans during 2017 (Chenoweth and Pressman 2017).

The plan of the book

Alleged electoral fraud, tighter voter registration processes, and eroding public confidence, fake news, and Russian disinformation and hacking are only some of the issues highlighted during the 2016 campaign about the integrity of American elections. Many other long-standing concerns include the partisan gerrymandering of U.S. House districts, lack of transparency and access for monitoring organizations, the role of the Electoral College when translating popular votes into presidential office, major flaws in campaign finance regulation, the lack of uniform laws and professional standards in electoral administration, the paucity of women and minority candidates standing for office, low levels of U.S. voter turnout, and many others (Fife 2010; Alvarez and Grofman 2014; Burden and Stewart 2014; Norris 2017b). Given the importance of understanding the problems of American elections in more depth, this volume brings together a range of legal scholars, political scientists, and electoral assistance practitioners to provide new evidence-based insights and policy-relevant recommendations on key challenges throughout the electoral cycle. For benchmarking, comparisons are often drawn with equivalent democracies. More accurate diagnosis helps to identify effective reforms that could potentially restore confidence in the American electoral process; the comparison of policies adopted by U.S. states also provides an invaluable laboratory for experimentation in election reforms (Cain, Donovan, and Tolbert 2008).

Introduction

To expand upon this introduction, in chapter 2 Richard Hasen provides an overview of the legal and political integrity issues raised in the 2016 elections. He begins by describing the now "normal" voting wars between the hyperpolarized parties, a series of lawsuits aimed at shaping the rules for the registration of voters, the conduct of voting, and the counting of ballots. Restrictive voting laws have increased in number and severity in many states with Republican legislatures, and the judiciary itself often divides along partisan lines in determining the controversial laws' legality. So far, the pace of litigation has remained at more than double the pre-2000 rate, and litigation in the 2016 election period is up 23% compared to the 2012 election period. Hasen then turns to the troubling escalation in the wars, from candidate Trump's unsubstantiated claims of fraud and election rigging, to Russian (and other) meddling in American elections and the rise of the "fake news" issue, and to problems with vote-counting machinery and election administration revealed by Green Party candidate Jill Stein's recount efforts and further hyped by conspiracy theories. Hasen concludes by considering the role that governmental and nongovernmental institutions can play in attempting to protect American elections from internal and external threats and to restore confidence in the electoral process.

In chapter 3, Kevin Pallister discusses the "access versus integrity" framing of debates about registration and balloting procedures, particularly as it has developed in the United States. He clarifies the concepts of voter inclusion (so that all eligible citizens can cast a ballot) and election security (so that no ineligible votes are cast). Pallister identifies several areas where the choice of voting procedures does present a trade-off between these values, including the use of the secret ballot, the rules for changing voters' place of residence on the electoral rolls, mail and absentee voting, mobile polling places, voter identification requirements, and internet voting. But he also identifies several areas where both inclusion and security may be simultaneously enhanced, including the use of automatic voter registration, Election Day registration, online and automated voter registration, posting provisional voter rolls prior to Election Day, early (in-person) voting, and decentralized polling places. Evidence illustrating these issues is drawn from the United States and abroad. Thus the "access versus integrity" framing, suggesting two mutually exclusive values, is only partially correct, and there are certain ways that these values could be combined through policies designed to strengthen electoral integrity and bipartisan agreement.

In chapter 4 Michael Latner considers the sources of systematic evidence that are available to diagnose problems in American elections. Many claims and counterclaims about alleged malpractices are often heard in partisan debates and journalistic commentaries. During an era of low trust in the legacy news and isolating bubbles in social media, what might help to sort out fact from fiction? What are the pros and cons of alternative sources of evidence? Latner compares electoral performance data on issues of voter registration permissiveness, ballot access, system security, and gerrymandering from several expert indices, institutional measures, and mass surveys.

Challenges

The next section of the book turns to more detailed studies of particular issues and problems. Chapter 5 by Daniel B. Magleby and colleagues turns to the contentious issue of partisan gerrymandering, a process of designing the boundaries of electoral districts to favor either the Republican or Democratic candidate. They argue, and then show, that determining what constitutes a partisan gerrymander revolves around how, when, and where a districting plan dilutes some people's votes. Manipulated district boundaries, often with bizarre shapes and associated with seemingly excessive wins by one party, receive more attention than they are due. More states than not choose to manipulate district boundaries in ways that are out of line with what may be expected from any sort of partisan-blind process. The authors present a valid and reliable indicator that can be used to distinguish between manipulations that violate electoral integrity and those that do not.

Chapter 6 by Elizabeth Bergman, Dari Sylvester Tran, and Philip Yates examines another major controversy: the role of voter identification requirements to register and cast a ballot. Many states have sought to implement tighter regulations, and studies have examined the effects of these measures on turnout. By contrast, these authors seek to determine the impact on the popular share of the vote won by Trump and Clinton—and thus whether registration requirements could have made a difference to the outcome of the 2016 presidential election. Evidence is drawn from a county-level data set based on public records of votes cast for the two major party candidates. The research design examines the effects of lax and strict voter registration requirements in 50 U.S. states plus D.C. on the number of votes won by Clinton and Trump at the county level, controlling for the demographic characteristics of counties, such as educational and poverty levels. The authors conclude that, even with these controls, the type of voter ID laws did significantly impact the outcome; in the 2016 election, the estimates suggest that voter ID laws increased Republican support by 1.8% and lowered support for Democrats by 0.7%. In close contests this made a difference. The GOP margin of victory in Arizona, Georgia, and Wisconsin was comparatively small, in the single digits, indicating close contests; in those states voter ID significantly influenced the vote in favor of the GOP.

In chapter 7 Leticia Bode, Kjerstin Thorson, and Emily Vraga tackle the challenges posed by misinformation campaigns and fake news, an issue of growing concern in America and numerous other countries. Following the 2016 U.S. presidential elections, academics and pundits alike struggled to make sense of what had happened. Many pointed to the role of "fake news," and misinformation more broadly, in leading voters astray in their assessments of the two major candidates for president. In particular, social media was widely blamed for disseminating false and misleading information to large groups of people, which could have been enough to swing a very close election. At the same time, increasingly partisan media has also been found to value ratings over accuracy and has been fingered as a major amplifier of fake news. What has been the impact? This chapter seeks to determine how media use in general, and use of social media and partisan media specifically, affected belief in seven fake news stories directly following the 2016 election. The research employs survey data to determine whether use of different types of media affected how fully people believed in misinformation, including messages congruent and incongruent with their own candidate preferences. These results provide insight into what was to blame for belief in fake news in the 2016 elections, and the authors suggest potential remedies or points of concern for future electoral contests.

Chapter 8 by Nandi Vanka, Avery Davis-Roberts, and David Carroll from the Carter Center focuses on issues of transparency, particularly how far U.S. states allow nonpartisan observers to scrutinize the electoral process and results. This is a common practice abroad, where United Nations standards have strengthened the role and rights of international election observers, but it remains a relatively obscure activity at home, with a patchwork of regulations for access across America. The authors conclude that rules across the 50 U.S. states regulating processes of electoral observation are relatively limited and ambiguous, that GOP states are often more restrictive than Democratic, and that a gap exists between legal provisions and state practices. Amid deteriorating trust in U.S elections, these authors discuss the general disregard for nonpartisan observers, while noting the important potential benefits of greater transparency for restoring confidence in American elections.

Craig Arceneaux in chapter 9 starts by laying out guidelines for assessing how federalism affects electoral integrity, both in cross-national perspective and in the U.S. case. The argument itself is rather simple: the impact of federalism varies because federalism itself can be designed in many different ways and because the impact of these arrangements is affected by the broader institutional setting. Though the argument itself is simple, the consequences are more complex: federalism does indeed weigh upon electoral integrity, but its significance must be appreciated in the context of the country under consideration. Arceneaux offers a general survey on the relationship between federalism and electoral integrity and draws evidence from selected cases of federalism in the Americas—Canada, Mexico, and Brazil—for comparison with the United States.

Conclusions

The conclusions to the book set these studies in a broader context and consider their theoretical and policy implications. In chapter 10 Chad Vickery and Heather Szilagyi from the International Federation on Electoral Systems draw on a wealth of experience and knowledge of international electoral assistance to consider the lessons for evaluating the quality of the structural features of U.S. contests. Taking a comparative perspective, they highlight a confluence of factors in the United States that produce a high percentage of wasted votes (those cast for either a losing candidate or in excess of those required by a winning candidate) and a system of governance that largely fails to reflect the will of the majority of voters, widely considered a cornerstone of democracy. Vickery and Szilagyi judge the fundamental integrity of key elements of the electoral process in the United States by applying the same standards used to evaluate developing democracies around the world. They focus on several key areas that observers and academics have regularly noted pose acute challenges to the U.S. electoral process: boundary delimitation for the House of Representatives, the role of the Electoral College in presidential contests, processes of voter registration, and the decentralized administrative framework. They conclude that despite obvious vulnerabilities, the United States is extremely resistant to acknowledging these problems, to reform its electoral process in line with international standards, or to learn from the experiences of other countries that have effectively strengthened their elections over time. This is unfortunate since the practical lessons learned from experience elsewhere could be invaluable if the United States had the political will to address reforms at home.

Finally, chapter 11 draws together the major conclusions from each of the chapters and considers their implications for the policy reform agenda. The consequences of electoral malpractice can be grave. Failures generate contentious elections characterized by lengthy court challenges, opposition boycotts, and public demonstrations (Norris, Frank, and Martinez i Coma 2015). As Pippa Norris, Thomas Wynter, and Sarah Cameron illustrate, major flaws weaken the legitimacy and credibility of elections, and thus corrode the foundation of liberal democracy (Norris 2014). Their study advocates four practical steps designed to improve the quality of American contests: improving the independence and professionalism of electoral administrators, implementing impartial dispute resolution mechanisms to deal with challenges, introducing registration and balloting facilities that maximize both security *and* convenience, and strengthening accountability and transparency. These steps could potentially reduce party polarization and expand a broad consensus about a bipartisan package of reforms. The authors summarize the core argument and the recommended policies helping to strengthen the quality of elections both at home and abroad.

Notes

1. Donald Trump, Twitter, November 27, 2017: "In addition to winning the Electoral College in a landslide, I won the popular vote if you deduct the millions of people who voted illegally."
2. Available at https://www.cnn.com/2016/10/18/politics/donald-trump-rigged-election/index.html.
3. Donald Trump, Twitter, November 27, 2016: "Serious voter fraud in Virginia, New Hampshire and California—so why isn't the media reporting on this? Serious bias—big problem!" See also National Public Radio 2018.

4. See "Fake" at *Factbase*, https://factba.se/search#fake.

5. See GMF, Alliance for Securing Democracy, http://dashboard.securingdemocracy.org/.

6. The filing is available from the U.S. Department of Justice, https://www.justice.gov/file/1035477/download.

7. CalTech/MIT Voting Technology Project, "Survey of the Performance of American Elections," Harvard Dataverse, https://dataverse.harvard.edu/dataverse/SPAE.

8. The text of the bill is at https://www.congress.gov/bill/115th-congress/senate-bill/2261/text.

9. Gallup World Poll, http://www.gallup.com/analytics/213704/world-poll.aspx. Q: "In this country, do you have confidence in each of the following, or not? How about honesty of elections?" Response options: Yes, No, Don't know.

10. Varieties of Democracy Country, Year dataset 8.0, https://www.v-dem.net/en/.

11. The PEI Index (v. 6.0) at country level is strongly correlated (R = .78*** N.153) with the Varieties of Democracy (v. 7.1) Electoral Component index, as well as with standard indicators such as Freedom House's measure of political rights and civil liberties (R = .75** N.159). For all details, see www.electoralintegrityproject.com.

2

Electoral laws

RICHARD L. HASEN

If the "voting wars" that have broken out across the post-2000 election land-scape in the United States could be characterized as a kind of trench warfare, the 2016 election saw a major escalation in weaponry—from the irresponsible rhetoric of a candidate who became commander-in-chief, to foreign interference and a flood of social media-driven propaganda, troubling machine breakdowns, and human error in election administration. The escalation threatens to under-mine the public's confidence in the fairness of the U.S. election process and, ul-timately, American democracy itself. We live in dangerous times, which could get worse, and it is not easy to conceive of simple solutions for de-escalation and bolstering of legitimacy, especially given rapid technological change that has interfered with mediating and stabilizing democratic institutions (Gronke, Sances, and Stewart 2016; Enten 2017).

This chapter provides an overview of the legal and political integrity issues in the 2016 elections. It begins by describing the now "normal" voting wars between the hyperpolarized parties, a series of lawsuits aimed at shaping the rules for the registration of voters, the conduct of voting, and the counting of ballots. Restrictive voting laws have increased in number and severity in many states with Republican legislatures, and the judiciary itself often divides along partisan lines in determining the controversial laws' legality. As the data show, the pace of litigation has remained at more than double the pre-2000 rate, and litigation in the 2016 election period is up 23 percent compared to the 2012 election period.

The chapter then turns to the troubling escalation in the wars, from candidate Donald Trump's unsubstantiated claims of fraud and election rigging to Russian (and other) meddling in American elections, the rise of the "fake news" issue, and problems with vote-counting machinery and election administration revealed by Green Party candidate Jill Stein's self-serving recount efforts and further hyped by conspiracy theories. It concludes by considering the role that governmental and nongovernmental institutions can play in attempting to protect American election administration from internal and external threats and to restore confidence in American elections.

The "normal" voting wars of 2016

American fights over the rules for conducting voting and recounts date back to the beginning of the Republic, but the modern period of escalation dates to the disputed 2000 presidential election between George W. Bush and Al Gore, which the U.S. Supreme Court ultimately resolved in its controversial *Bush v. Gore* decision. The very close election taught political operatives that the rules of the game matter, and in the post-2000 period we have seen a rise in new election legislation as well as litigation (Foley 2016; Hasen 2012; *Bush v. Gore* 2000, 531).

Since 2000 the amount of election-related litigation has more than doubled compared to the period before 2000, from an average of 94 cases per year in the period just before 2000 to an average of 258 cases per year in the post-2000 period.[1] See Figure 2.1.

Even compared to the 2012 presidential election cycle, litigation is up significantly; it was 23 percent higher in the 2015–2016 presidential election season than in the 2011–2012 presidential election season, and is at the highest level since at least 2000 (and likely ever). See Figure 2.2.

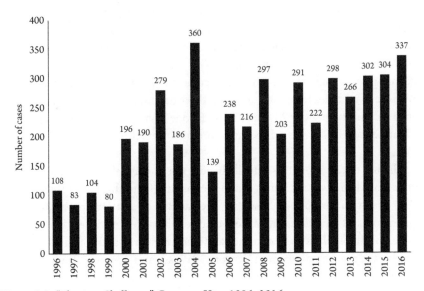

Figure 2.1 "Election Challenge" Cases per Year, 1996–2016.
Source: Author's calculation of data from Lexis/Nexis court databases.

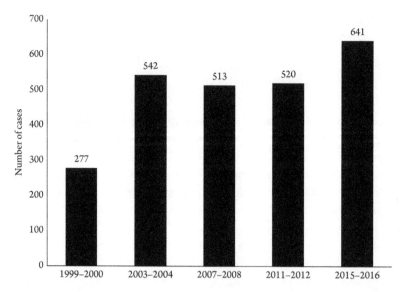

Figure 2.2 "Election Challenge" Cases by Presidential Election Cycle, 2000–2016.
Source: Author's calculation of data from Lexis/Nexis court databases.

Part of the reason for the increase in litigation over election rules is that in the United States's hyperpolarized election environment, controversial election laws—such as voter identification laws and automatic voter registration laws—pass along party lines, and any restrictions invite litigation. This emergence of "red state election law" and "blue state election law" has meant that many states with Republican majorities have passed laws making it harder to register and vote, and those states with Democratic majorities have passed laws making it easier to register and vote. According to a count by the Brennan Center, since 2010, 23 states have passed laws making it harder to register and vote, three of which have been blocked by the courts. All but two of the 23, Illinois and Rhode Island, had majority Republican legislatures when they passed the laws (Brennan Center for Justice 2017c; NCSL 2017a).

Whether or not legislators actually believe the rhetoric about fraud prevention, public confidence, voter suppression, or enfranchisement that they sometimes espouse to support or oppose these laws, the partisan calculation appears to be that registration and identification barriers tend to fall hardest on voters likely to vote for Democrats (such as poor, minority, and student voters), and that at the margins, these laws can make a difference (Newkirk 2017; see also Bergman, Tran, and Yates, this volume).

The 2015–2016 election cycle litigation in some ways resembles battles in the past, and many of the cases involve issues not directly related to registration or the casting and counting of votes. Among the more notable cases during the period are those over ever more restrictive voting and registration restrictions in Kansas, North Carolina, and Texas; redistricting battles in Alabama, Wisconsin, and Texas, and a fight over the constitutionality of redistricting commissions for congressional elections used in Arizona; a campaign finance dispute over the constitutionality of limits on party "soft money" fundraising; and Supreme Court rulings on the constitutionality of limiting judicial candidates' personal solicitation of campaign funds, the meaning of "official action" for bribery laws, and the scope of the "one person, one vote" rule.

In litigation most closely tied to the voting wars, there is no escaping the fact that judges appointed by presidents of different parties often tend to view differently the legality of, and the costs and benefits of, laws making it harder to register and vote. I do not believe judges consciously vote the interests of their party; it is that these judges are chosen because of their background and ideological views that make them predisposed to favor one side or another.

Consider, for example, *North Carolina State Conference of the NAACP v. McCrory*, high-profile litigation over North Carolina's strict 2013 voting law, commonly known as HB 589. Among other things, the law imposed a strict voter identification requirement, cut back on the days of early voting before elections, eliminated same-day voter registration, banned the counting of votes cast by a voter in the wrong precinct even for those races in which the voter was eligible to vote, and ended the practice of preregistering 16- and 17-year-olds as voters. Voting rights groups and the U.S. government filed cases in federal court raising both constitutional and Voting Rights Act claims. The Republican-appointed district judge upheld the law; three Democratic-appointed appeals court judges reversed; and the U.S. Supreme Court split along party lines in deciding whether or not to put the case on hold pending full Court review. (Eventually the Court did not hear the case on the merits for technical reasons.)[2]

The continued hyperpartisanship surrounding rules for conducting elections and the increased litigation has enmeshed the courts in ever more difficult decisions about the scope of voting protections under U.S. constitutional and statutory law. This turn of events would be bad enough for the legitimacy of both the election system and respect for courts and the rule of law, especially as judicial decisions in the hardest cases seem to break down across party lines, and as all the justices currently on the Supreme Court who are conservative were appointed by Republican presidents and all the justices who are liberal were appointed by Democratic presidents.

But these normal, if accelerating voting wars seemed of secondary importance in the 2016 elections, where conflict over voting rules and campaigns reached new, unprecedented heights, including efforts at delegitimization by a major party presidential candidate, Donald Trump, the rise in foreign interference and social-media-driven propaganda, and new concerns over the accuracy of voting technology and election administration.

Donald Trump and delegitimization of the electoral process

Among the most surprising and unusual developments in the 2016 election season was Republican presidential candidate (and now president) Donald J. Trump's repeatedly making outrageous and completely unsupported statements about the extent of the voter fraud problem in the United States. The remarks continued even after Trump won the election, stunning for an election winner, perhaps reflecting the unusual candidate's unhappiness with losing the U.S. popular vote (while winning the Electoral College vote) (Gorman 2016).

Anthony J. Gaughan (2017, 71) summarized some of the statements Trump made on the issue of election integrity:

> Throughout the campaign, and even after his victory, Donald Trump impugned the integrity of the electoral process. For example, when he lagged in the polls in mid-October, Trump claimed without evidence that the election was "rigged" against him "at many polling places" by "large scale voter fraud happening on and before [E]lection [D]ay." Even more remarkable were allegations that Trump made after the election. When the states' certified election results revealed that Hillary Clinton had won the popular vote by nearly 3 million votes, Trump baselessly claimed that "millions" of people had voted illegally for Clinton. On Twitter he declared, "In addition to winning the Electoral College in a landslide, I won the popular vote if you deduct the millions of people who voted illegally." In a subsequent Tweet he wrote, "Serious voter fraud in Virginia, New Hampshire and California—so why isn't the media reporting on this? Serious bias— big problem!" Without offering evidence, Trump later told congressional Republicans that three to five million illegal votes were cast against him in the election, a figure that conveniently exceeded Clinton's popular vote margin of victory.[3]

It was not just that Trump claimed, without evidence, that voter fraud was a problem in the United States; he insinuated that the fraud was more prevalent in minority communities. At a campaign rally in Pennsylvania a few weeks before the November 2016 presidential election,

> Mr. Trump began the day urging the almost entirely white crowd outside Pittsburgh to show up to vote, warning about "other communities" that could hijack his victory. "So important that you watch other communities, because we don't want this election stolen from us. . . . We do not want this election stolen." Later, at the evening rally in Wilkes-Barre, Mr. Trump

raised more concerns about voting fraud. "I just hear such reports about Philadelphia. . . . I hear these horror shows, and we have to make sure that this election is not stolen from us and is not taken away from us." He added for emphasis: "Everybody knows what I'm talking about." (Parker 2016)

Trump later claimed, offering no evidence whatsoever, that all the illegal voting in the United States benefited Clinton. He told *ABC News* anchor David Muir soon after inauguration, "Of those [supposed three to five million fraudulent] votes cast, none of 'em come to me. None of 'em come to me. They would all be for the other side. None of 'em come to me" (Blake 2017).

Over the past two decades, the public heard this type of rhetoric from some other Republicans hyping a false scourge of voter fraud, but Trump's comments went far beyond those. The parade of Republican election officials and others coming forward during and right after the 2016 election to debunk Trump's unsupported rhetoric of massive voter fraud was a welcome respite, but Trump's remarks were deeply troubling.

In addition to hyping the supposed dangers of voter fraud from urban areas such as Philadelphia, Trump set up a sign-up sheet on his campaign website for supporters to organize against fraud at the polls. Trump allies such as Roger Stone Jr. also purported to set up "poll watching activities" via the website StoptheSteal. org. It was not clear whether these efforts were serious or just means to raise funds, rile up supporters, and collect names. Nonetheless the activities attracted the attention of Democrats and inspired new legal maneuvering.[4]

After the election, President Trump issued an order creating the Election Integrity Commission to study the voter fraud issue.[5] He named Vice President Mike Pence as chair and Kansas Secretary of State Kris Kobach as vice chair. Kobach has been a controversial figure, known for exaggerating the amount of voter fraud and for seeking to tighten voter registration rules to prevent (the small amount of detected) noncitizen voting. Kobach was the only prominent election official to support Trump's claims of massive voter fraud in the 2016 elections, telling a reporter in late November 2016 that Trump "is absolutely correct when he says the number of illegal votes cast exceeds the popular vote margin between him and Hillary Clinton at this point." He offered no evidence for his claim (Davis 2017; Berman 2017; Woodall 2016).

The commission did not follow the format of earlier postelection commissions, each of which had been coheaded by leading Democratic and Republican figures. Although the executive order called for a commission of up to 15 members, it did not reach that number, and it contained more Republicans than Democrats. Trump eventually named three more controversial Republican members: Hans von Spakovsky, who was well known for making incendiary and unsupported claims about the extent of the voter fraud problem; Ken Blackwell, who was involved in a notorious incident when he served as Ohio's secretary of state and issued an order rejecting voter registration forms that were not printed on heavy enough paper (a decision he later reversed); and J. Christian Adams, a former Justice Department lawyer who later led efforts to increase purges of voters from the voting rolls. The commission's work got tied up in litigation, and eventually it was disbanded after failing to produce a written report (Levine 2017; Stewart 2018a).

Foreign meddling and "fake news"

At the same time that Trump was telling people on the campaign trail that the election was "rigged"—a vague term that could mean anything from complaining about a legal but unfair aspect of the electoral process (such as the Electoral College or campaign finance rules) to someone illegally manipulating vote totals—foreign actors from Russia and perhaps elsewhere were engaged in unprecedented interference in the 2016 U.S. elections. Russian agents unleashed cyberattacks on election registration databases and other election systems across the United States. And, thanks to Russian hacking, websites posted stolen emails and other electronic files from the Democratic National Committee (DNC) and spread misinformation as a means of trying to influence the outcome of the presidential vote (McFaul 2016).

Russian agents ran social media campaigns, apparently to try to tilt the election to Trump, buying at least $100,000 in Facebook ads for the purpose (Shane 2017; Shane and Goel 2017). At the time of writing, an investigation continues into whether any members of the Trump campaign colluded with Russian agents on any of this activity (Cohen 2017). While all available evidence indicates that vote totals and reporting were not affected by cyberattacks, it is impossible to say whether the stolen DNC emails and misinformation affected election results. It seems likely, however, that the chicanery will contribute to decreased legitimacy of the American electoral system.[6]

A joint report issued in January 2017 by the U.S. Central Intelligence Agency, the Federal Bureau of Investigation, and the National Security Agency confirmed Russian attempts to influence the outcome of the 2016 U.S. elections, to create instability, and to favor Trump over Democratic candidate Clinton: "We assess Russian President Vladimir Putin ordered an influence campaign in 2016 aimed at the US presidential election. Russia's goals were to undermine public faith in the US democratic process, denigrate Secretary Clinton, and harm her electability and potential presidency. We further assess Putin and the Russian Government developed a clear preference for President-elect Trump. We have high confidence in these judgments" (Office of Director of National Intelligence 2017).

As to the specific means employed by the Russian government during the 2016 elections, the report concluded, "Moscow's influence campaign followed a Russian messaging strategy that blends covert intelligence operations—such as cyber activity—with overt efforts by Russian Government agencies, state-funded media, third-party intermediaries, and paid social media users or 'trolls'" (Office of Director of National Intelligence 2017). The two most prominent Russian activities that achieved broad public attention during the 2016 elections were the release of stolen emails of the DNC and the infiltration of many state election databases.

The DNC emails revealed embarrassing facts about the party and the Clinton campaign strategy (Sainato 2016; Frizell 2016). Specific emails about the party's poor treatment of Senator Bernie Sanders during the Democratic primary season when Sanders faced Clinton led Representative Debbie Wasserman-Schultz to resign as the DNC chair (Martin and Rappeport 2016). The revelations dripped out when released over a period of months by Wikileaks, D.C. Leaks, and a hacker associated with the Russian government under the of name Guccifer 2.0 (Bennett 2016). Trump adviser Stone admitted contact with the person tweeting as Guccifer 2.0 as well as (through an intermediary) Julian Assange of Wikileaks. Rosenberg and Haberman (2017) reported in the *New York Times*, "In August [2016], Mr. Stone wrote on Twitter that John D. Podesta, Hillary Clinton's campaign chairman, would soon go through his 'time in the barrel.' Weeks later, WikiLeaks began publishing a trove of Mr. Podesta's hacked emails, the daily release of which was seen as damaging to the campaign."

As to the infiltration of state voter registration databases, the best information available indicates that the attempted cyberattacks were widespread, with one report claiming that the hacking hit systems in 39 states and the government confirming attacks in 21 states. "In Illinois, investigators found evidence that cyber intruders tried to delete or alter voter data. The hackers accessed software designed to be used by poll workers on Election Day, and in at least one state accessed a campaign finance database" (Periroth, Wines, and Rosenberg 2017). The level of attacks was so high that Obama administration officials used the "red phone" to warn Moscow against further attacks. Following the involvement of and assistance from the U.S. Department of Homeland Security (DHS), "thirty-seven states reported finding traces of the hackers in various systems. . . . In two others—Florida and California—those traces were found in systems run by a private contractor managing critical election systems" (Riley and Robertson 2017). According to one report, in one (unnamed) state, hackers successfully changed voter data in a county database, but the database was corrected before the election (Calabresi 2017a).

Jeh Johnson, who served as secretary of DHS during the election period, explained in his June 2017 testimony the nature and extent of the Russian cyberattacks, as well as the efforts he took to help state and local election officials. He also detailed the pushback he received over trying to designate the U.S. election system as "critical infrastructure" for DHS purposes, over the objections of election officials who feared loss of their power over running elections. DHS nonetheless later gave infrastructure the "critical" designation, which the Trump administration then reaffirmed.

Secretary Johnson concluded, "To my current knowledge, the Russian government did not through any cyber intrusion alter ballots, ballot counts or reporting of election results. I am not in a position to know whether the successful Russian government-directed hacks of the DNC and elsewhere did in fact alter public opinion and thereby alter the outcome of the presidential election."[7]

Russia also undertook an extensive propaganda effort, which involved more than publishing negative stories about Clinton and U.S. interests. It also spread "fake news": false stories aimed at influencing the outcome of the election for Trump (Calabresi 2017b). "For example, [the Russian news website] Sputnik published an article that said the Podesta email dump included certain incriminating comments about the Benghazi scandal, an allegation that turned out to be incorrect. Trump himself repeated this false story" at a campaign rally (Carroll 2016). Russia used Facebook to spread false reports to specific populations, including aiming certain false reports at journalists who might be expected to further spread the propaganda and misinformation. Russia also used automated "bots" to spread false news across social media platforms such as Facebook and Twitter (O'Connor and Schneider 2017; Office of Director of National Intelligence 2017).

The so-called fake news problem extended beyond Russia and beyond anti-Clinton propaganda. A group of young Macedonians spread a huge amount of pro-Trump fake news as a way of making money on social media advertising (Silverman and Alexander 2016). A false story from one of the Macedonians saying that Clinton would be indicted in 2017 got 140,000 shares and comments on Facebook, generating good revenue. An American from Clearwater, Florida, started a fake news site as a joke, gaining one million views in two weeks (Gillin 2017).

One fake news story led to actual violence. The so-called Pizzagate scandal started when a false story claimed that a D.C. restaurant, Comet Ping Pong, was being used by Clinton associates to run a child sex ring. The reports led a 28-year-old man to go to the restaurant to check things out. He ended up firing an AR-15 rifle, though fortunately no one was hurt (Kang and Goldman 2016).

After Trump gained the presidency, Democrats and others on the left increasingly began falling for fake news. Senator Ed Markey of Massachusetts made false claims on CNN about grand juries being empaneled to look into the Trump campaign's ties to Russia. Harvard Law professor Laurence Tribe also spread false claims on Twitter, including a false claim that a White House adviser, Steve Bannon, was physically assaulting White House staffers. Both Markey and Tribe fell for false reports coming from a group of sources allied with Louise Mensch (Beauchamp 2017). It does not appear that "fake news" has yet spread on the left as widely as it has on the right, but that may change over time (Heer 2017; Nyhan 2017).

Meanwhile, the term "fake news" risks becoming devoid of meaning, as many people, including President Trump, have attached the label to any news or reporting with which they disagree (Gendreau 2017). Trump used the term constantly on Twitter, such as in a June 2017 tweet proclaiming, "The Fake News Media has never been so wrong or so dirty. Purposely incorrect stories and phony sources to meet their agenda of hate. Sad!"[8]

A new round of voting machine concerns, election administration snafus, and conspiracy theories

In the final report of the Obama-appointed Presidential Commission on Election Administration, headed by Bob Bauer and Ben Ginsberg, which the Trump administration removed from government servers after Trump took office, the commission warned about an "impending crisis" with voting technology reaching the end of its useful life (Hasen 2017b).[9] Many jurisdictions in the United States replaced their voting machines after Congress provided funding in the 2002 Help America Vote Act, following the 2000 Florida voting debacle, but now the replacement machines need replacing. Poor voting machine technology, in the era of hyperpolarization, hacking, and "fake news," would be a disaster in another razor-thin presidential election. After 2016 problems and threats to cybersecurity, more jurisdictions are finally contemplating voting technology upgrades.

A postelection recount that began (but was not completed) in Michigan right after the 2016 presidential election nicely illustrates the voting technology problem. Trump was able to put together a surprising Electoral College victory by narrowly winning three midwestern states that had previously trended Democratic in presidential races: Michigan, Pennsylvania, and Wisconsin. The vote difference was roughly 80,000 votes among the three states (Bump 2016). The Clinton campaign calculated that there would be no reason to request a recount, as the relatively close margin was not close enough that a recount would likely change the results (Cillizza 2016). But Green Party candidate Jill Stein, whom many Democrats blamed for siphoning votes away from Clinton and helping Trump, raised millions of dollars for recounts in these states (Rocheleau 2016). The call for recounts came after some on the left raised concerns that Russia could have hacked voting systems to change election results, even though there was no evidence such hacking actually took place. Some Trump and Clinton supporters believed Stein was engaging in the recount for her own purposes (such as to build up her mailing list for future solicitation), but the Clinton campaign participated in the recounts as observers of the process (Bauer 2016).

The recounts proceeded to various points in the three states, and, unsurprisingly, the results did not change (Ax 2016). But the Michigan recount, where the final tally showed Trump beating Clinton by 10,704 votes out of approximately 4.8 million cast, hit a snag in the City of Detroit before courts called it off as unauthorized by state law (Michigan Department of State 2017). The recount revealed very disconcerting facts about the state of U.S. voting technology and inadequate training of election workers, and the problems led to a quick spread of conspiracy theories (Rosenblatt 2016).

Under Michigan law, votes from a particular precinct may be included in a recount only if the number of voters recorded as having voted in the electronic poll book listing voters' names matches the number of votes tabulated by its corresponding optical-scan voting machine. In Detroit, however, approximately 392 precincts had mismatched numbers. (In election administration parlance, they were not "in balance.") Under Michigan law these precincts could not be included in a recount. In one of the worst examples, Precinct 152, 306 voters were recorded as having voted, but there were only 50 ballots in the sealed ballot box.

The anomalies were very concerning and sparked claims by the right of widespread fraud. *World Net Daily*'s (2016) headline blared, "Stealing the Vote: Recount Uncovers Serious Fraud in Detroit." The story reported a ballot potentially being cast six times. *Fox News Insider* (2016) declared, "Oops! Stein's Recount Turns Up More Votes than Voters in Detroit." The report included the link to a *Fox & Friends* video as well as a *Fox & Friends* tweet: "Jill Stein's crusade to expose voter fraud blows the lid off ballot box fraud in Detroit where Hillary Clinton won big."[10] Even the sober *Detroit Free Press* headline read, "Detroit's Election Woes: 782 More Votes than Voters" (Wisely and Reindl 2016).

At first it was unclear exactly what went wrong in Detroit, but even at the beginning of the recount it appeared likely that a combination of machine failure, such as numerous instances of optical-scan ballots jamming in the tabulation machines, and human error were major culprits. A subsequent investigation by the Michigan secretary of state's Board of Elections (BOE) placed the blame more squarely on human error:

"BOE found no evidence of pervasive voter fraud or that widespread voting equipment failure led to the imbalances, yet the audit uncovered a multitude of human errors that prevented (or would have prevented) the presidential recount from proceeding in a significant number of precincts" (Michigan Department of State 2017, 2). Many of the problems stemmed from election workers not knowing how to properly record information in the electronic poll books, such as recording a spoiled ballot, as well as mishandling of provisional ballots. Furthermore, many ballots were not properly put in the tabulation machines. During the later audit, BOE was able to balance almost half of the 392 unbalanced precincts by figuring out the election workers' errors on election night.

The report continued:

> In other instances, BOE determined that election workers left counted ballots in the tabulator bin at the end of the night instead of placing all ballots in a sealed container. The example of Precinct 152, widely cited in news media reports, is illustrative. When the sealed ballot container for this precinct was opened at the recount, it was found to contain only 50 ballots despite the fact that the poll book included the names of 306 voters. During the audit, BOE was able to confirm that all but one of the voted ballots had been left behind in the tabulator on Election Night. The

audit refutes suspicions that the relatively small number of ballots placed in the ballot container could have been illegally tabulated again and again. (Michigan Department of State 2017, 2)

The Detroit situation recalls the election administrator's prayer: "Lord, let this election not be close." It is hard to imagine how much worse the 2016 election would have been had the results come down to a Michigan recount and social-media-driven stories of ballot snafus, poorly trained poll workers, aging technology, all in a heavily African American city that voted overwhelmingly for Clinton over Trump.

The tough road to de-escalation and improvement to American election administration and democracy

As terrible as the 2016 voting wars were compared to the past, it is important to have no illusions about the future (Perlroth 2017). Things could get much, much worse. Next time cyberattacks could try to alter or erase voter registration databases, bring down our power grids or transportation infrastructure, or do something else to interfere with actual voting on Election Day (Hasen 2016b). The next hacks could include malicious, false information interspersed with accurate stolen files, which could influence election outcomes; public confidence in the fairness of our electoral process could decrease further, as incendiary and unsupported claims about voter fraud, cheating, and altered vote totals spread via social media. Already public confidence in the fairness of the election process is largely driven by who wins and who loses elections (Stewart 2017b). If increased mischief accompanies a razor-thin election, social-media-driven anger threatens the peace of our democracy.

What is to be done? There are no easy answers to these unique challenges now facing U.S. democracy, and longer-term solutions to deal with some of the problems, such as moving to national, nonpartisan election administration, seem further away than ever.

In the short to medium term, we need cooperation among federal, state, and local officials, assisted by technology companies and nongovernmental organizations (NGOs), to deal with internal and external threats to the integrity of voting systems and the threat that such hacks bring to public confidence in election legitimacy. Officials should ensure that voter databases and vote-casting machinery is secure and free from hacking. Votes should be cast only on systems producing a paper ballot that can be recounted. Adequate resources and professionalization and training of local election officials is essential. Transparency in every stage of the vote-counting process, followed by random postelection audits to assure accuracy and fairness, guards best against both malfeasance and incompetence.[11]

Irresponsible rhetoric (from the president on down) about massive voter fraud needs to be repeatedly condemned across the political spectrum, with attention to provable facts and not innuendo. Media and NGOs need to provide timely and accurate information to counter both deliberate and unintentional misinformation.

Given the rhetoric of the president, NGOs need to take the lead on fostering cooperation across levels of government and parties. Efforts of the Bauer-Ginsberg commission, the Pew Charitable Trusts, the Bipartisan Policy Center, and others show that this kind of work can be effective. NGOs should begin by fostering bipartisan cooperation on areas of agreement to improve voting processes, as we saw with the Presidential Commission on Election Administration. Online voter registration, for example, ensures voters are more likely to be correctly listed in voter registration systems, empowers voters, and saves money. As of September 2017, 35 states had adopted online voter registration programs (NCSL 2017e). It is a win-win prospect, and the same coalition that has had success with online voter registration needs to move next to issues of cybersecurity. This is an area where Democrats and Republicans should have reason to cooperate.

But even here there are issues. Pew Charitable Trusts (2017), which has been a leader in this area, has announced it is leaving this policy area. The U.S. Election Assistance Commission, which should provide a clearinghouse and coordination role for state and local governments, has been continually attacked by the National Association of Secretaries of State for intruding on their turf and has been targeted for defunding by House Republicans (Katz 2017). Pushback from the demand for voter data by Trump's Election Integrity Commission may have made states more suspicious of federal intervention.

The judiciary also needs to struggle with conflicting worldviews coloring voting wars cases in the federal courts, looking for means of assuring that states have the capacity to run fair elections without unnecessarily burdening voters. When possible, judges should strive for decisions that cross party lines. Perhaps the most difficult question is how to combat the rise of social-media-driven propaganda and false information in the face of declining mediating institutions like political parties and the mainstream media (Persily 2017, 63). I address that issue elsewhere (Hasen 2018).

Things are not likely to get easier as we approach the 20th anniversary of *Bush v. Gore*. We cannot wait until 2020 to make improvements. Those who would manipulate voting and our elections are not taking a few years off to rest on their laurels.

Acknowledgments

Thanks to Bob Bauer, Bruce Cain, Doug Chapin, Ned Foley, and conference participants for useful comments and suggestions, and to Julia Jones for excellent research assistance. An earlier version of this paper appears in the *William and Mary Bill of Rights Journal* (2018) and is republished here with permission.

Notes

1. The data and the list of cases are posted at *Election Law Blog*, http://electionlawblog.org/wp-content/uploads/Election-Litigation-1996-2016.xlsx.
2. H.B. 589, 2013 N.C. Sess. Laws 381. North Carolina State Conference of the NAACP v. McCrory, 182 F. Supp. 3d 320, 331–332 (M.D.N.C. 2016), *rev'd*, 831 F.3d 204 (4th Cir. 2016), *stay denied*, 137 S. Ct. 27 (2016), *cert. denied*, 137 S. Ct. 1399 (2017).
3. Gaughan (2017, 71–73), also collected evidence demonstrating that Trump's claims were "completely baseless."
4. Democratic Nat'l Comm. v. Republican Nat'l Comm., No. 81-03876, 2016 WL 6584915 (D.N.J. Nov. 5, 2016); Mich. Democratic Party v. Mich. Republican Party, No. 2:16-CV-13924 (E.D. Mich. Nov. 17, 2016); Pa. Democratic Party v. Republican Party of Pa., No. 16-5664, 2016 WL 6584832 (E.D. Pa. Nov. 7, 2016); Ariz. Democratic Party v. Ariz. Republican Party, No. CV-16-03752-PHX-JJT, 2016 WL 8669978 (D. Ariz. Nov. 4, 2016); Ohio Democratic Party v. Ohio Republican Party, No. 16-CV-02645, 2016 WL 6542486 (N.D. Ohio Nov. 4, 2016), *stayed* No. 16-4268, 2016 WL 6608962 (6th Cir. Nov. 6, 2016); *appl. to vacate stay denied* 137 S. Ct. 15 (2016); N.C. Democratic Party v. N.C. Republican Party, No. 1:16-CV-01288 (M.D.N.C. Nov. 3, 2016); Nev. State Democratic Party v. Nev. Republican Party, No. 2:16-CV-02514 (D. Nev. Oct. 30, 2016).
5. Exec. Order No. 13799, 82 Fed. Reg. 22, 389 (May 11, 2017).
6. "At least 12 Trump associates had contacts with Russians during the campaign or transition" (Cohen 2017).
7. Hearing before the H. Permanent Select Comm. on Intelligence, 2017, 115th Cong. 2–6.
8. Donald Trump, Twitter, June 13, 2017, https://twitter.com/realDonaldTrump/status/874576057579565056.
9. The material has now been posted on a mirror site, hosted by MIT: http://web.mit.edu/supportthevoter/www/ (see Stewart 2017c).
10. *Fox & Friends*, Twitter, December 14, 2016, https://twitter.com/foxandfriends/status/809003930516496384.
11. For thoughts on how to improve the security of the U.S. election system, see Norden and Vandewalker 2017.

3

Voting Procedures

Inclusion versus Security

KEVIN PALLISTER

Over the past 15 years it has been common for voting rules in the United States to be discussed in terms of the trade-off values of "access" versus "security" (Carter and Baker 2005; Century Foundation 2005; Minnite and Callahan 2003; Hasen 2012, 163; Gerken 2013b; Bauer et al. 2014). That is, rules that make registering to vote and casting a ballot easy for eligible citizens also risk security by allowing ineligible persons to vote. By contrast, measures to ensure that only eligible voters cast ballots also risk excluding some eligible citizens (see Hasen, this volume).

Despite the common "access versus security" framing of many partisan debates, there is little comparative analysis of how these trade-offs manifest themselves and how they are resolved in different contexts. Do all measures that make voting easier for eligible voters also increase the potential for election fraud? Are there election administration policies that can increase both voter access and election security simultaneously?

This chapter addresses these questions by drawing on evidence from the United States and other countries. I begin by discussing the "access versus security" framing of voting procedures, particularly as it has developed in the United States. I then clarify the core concepts. The following section identifies areas where the choice of voting procedures presents a trade-off between access and security: the use of the secret ballot, voter registration requirements, rules for changing voters' residence on the voter rolls, purging deadwood from the electoral registry, mail and absentee voting, the use of mobile polling places, voter identification requirements, and internet voting. I also discuss areas where both access and security may be simultaneously enhanced: automatic voter registration, Election Day registration, online and automated voter registration, posting provisional voter rolls prior to Election Day, early (in-person) voting, and decentralized polling places. At the same time, the trade-offs between goals will vary across different social and political contexts.

The inclusion-versus-security framing
of voting rules

The potential trade-off between voter inclusion and election security has been a long-standing issue in election administration in the United States. The introduction of voter registration requirements in the early 19th century and the secret ballot around 1890, for instance, helped prevent voter coercion, multiple voting, and voting by ineligible persons, but they also posed obstacles to participation (Campbell 2006). Likewise, historical impediments to immigrant voting—such as requirements to present naturalization papers to election officials—were justified as measures to prevent fraud (Keyssar 2009, 111–112).

These issues have frequently been infused with partisan conflict. Thus the introduction of voter registration in the United States was not only a measure to prevent fraud but a way for Republicans to reduce participation in heavily Democratic urban areas (Keyssar 2009, 123–127; Wang 2012, 23). In recent years, debates over access versus security have again been colored by partisan politics, with Democrats and Republicans taking sharply polarized positions on electoral procedures. In the United States since at least the 1980s, Democrats have favored measures reducing barriers to voting, while Republicans have favored measures ostensibly designed to ensure ballot security. A similar pattern has been evident in Britain, where Labour has sought "to lower the cost of voting and thereby increase participation (particularly among key Labour constituencies)," while Conservatives "have invoked the specter of fraud in pushing for greater controls on access to voting" (Elmendorf 2006, 432).

The partisan acrimony over voting rules has tended to reinforce the notion that election administration poses inherent trade-offs between inclusion and security. As one set of authors puts it, "In legislative debates, the two policy goals are often set in opposition and against one another in a zero-sum framework" (Kimball et al. 2013, 554). This sentiment is reflected in the words of a Democratic congressman who in 2002 noted, "You can do things that make it easier to vote, but also make it easier to cheat. Or you can do things that make it harder to cheat but can also impede voting" (quoted in Keyssar 2009, 264). The notion that inclusion and security stand in tension with one another has become widely ingrained, as evident in a federal court ruling in a 2004 case concerning the counting of provisional ballots in Michigan:

> Any sensible laws regulating the time, place and manner of voting in a democracy ought to focus on two goals: maximizing the participation of eligible voters and eliminating fraud. However, these goals often are in tension, since regulations that guard against fraud may also raise barriers so high that some eligible voters may not be able to pass. Similarly, relaxing

the rules that protect against voting more than once in a single election and verify eligibility may increase the possibility of fraud.[1]

Yet despite how entrenched this idea has become, we know surprisingly little about exactly what types of registration and voting procedures pose trade-offs between maximizing access and preventing electoral fraud, and what areas of election administration provide opportunities to pursue both goals simultaneously. Some scholars are circumspect about the trade-offs between these goals, arguing that there is no tension between inclusion and security, at least concerning certain policies like voter identification (Ansolabehere 2008), Election Day registration (Minnite and Callahan 2003), and early voting (Gerken 2013b). Some argue more broadly that "efforts to make it easier to register and vote are compatible with the prevention of election fraud" (Minnite and Callahan 2003, 10). Yet comparative research shows that some efforts to clean up elections have the potential to disenfranchise some voters (Schaffer 2002, 2008), and in the U.S. popular concerns about voter fraud and partisan acrimony over voting procedures persist. Concerns about voter fraud continue to be used to justify not only voter identification policies but also regulations on voter registration drives and cutbacks in early voting. In Florida, for example, Republican legislators and the secretary of state claimed that a controversial bill cutting back on early voting and imposing restrictions on third-party registration activities was designed in part to "combat voter fraud" (Herron and Smith 2014, 648).

Because partisanship surrounds contemporary debates over election administration procedures, it can be difficult to distinguish between strategic efforts to shape voting rules for partisan advantage and genuine ideological or pragmatic differences over competing goals of electoral integrity. It is thus important to have evidence-based analysis of how different election administration practices affect voter access and election fraud.

Electoral malpractice and voter fraud

As Norris, Cameron, and Wynter discuss in their chapter in this volume, electoral malpractices come in many forms, including voter impersonation, multiple voting, voter intimidation, ballot box stuffing, altering vote counts, illegal use of state resources for campaign purposes, and many other tactics (Calingaert 2006; Schedler 2002). While the rules and institutions of election administration play a role in facilitating or preventing most of these forms of malpractice, only some types implicate voter access to the ballot. It is predominantly safeguards against the illegal casting of ballots—that is, voter fraud—that can pose barriers to the participation of eligible voters. Preventing wholesale fraud, such as the alteration of vote totals or other forms of misconduct in which election officials are complicit, often does not involve regulations pertaining to voter access. Therefore, many precautions against electoral fraud have no implications for voter access, for example, enforcement of regulations against the use of state resources for campaigning; regulations that provide transparency during the vote tally, such as allowing observers to monitor the process and posting disaggregated vote totals for each precinct (as discussed by Vanka, Davis-Roberts, and Carroll, this volume); standard operating procedures used by election officials to maintain secure chains of custody over voting materials (Alvarez and Hall 2008); and cybersecurity measures to prevent hacking of voter registries and voting machines. All of these help deter fraud. Even some measures specifically designed to prevent voter fraud pose few obstacles to participation, such as the use of indelible ink on voters' fingers to prevent multiple ballots.[2]

This chapter focuses on measures to prevent fraud that do bear on voter access, either by making balloting by eligible electors more difficult or easier. In doing so, I largely accept the common "access versus security" framing of election procedures, which distinguishes between the two concepts and values of voter access and election security. Voter access or inclusion refers to how far the administration of the electoral process—particularly voter registration and voting procedures—facilitates the ability of eligible citizens to vote with minimal inconvenience. Election security refers to contests in which only eligible electors cast ballots, where each elector casts no more than the legally allowed number of votes, and where electors cast their ballots free of coercion or illegal influence.

Trade-offs: Where voter access and election security conflict

Some regulations pose a trade-off between voter access and election security. The secret ballot, and the requirement that eligible electors register to vote, have become widely accepted practices whose cost in voter access has been outweighed by their value in preventing electoral malpractices. On other measures, however, there is less consensus about how the goals of inclusion and security should be balanced. Table 3.1 summarizes which procedures pose trade-offs and which allow for the simultaneous pursuit of inclusion and security.

The secret ballot

Perhaps the earliest election measure that posed a trade-off between electoral security and voter access was the adoption of the secret ballot around 1890. Before the adoption of the secret (or Australian) ballot, voting was conducted publicly or by using paper ballots printed and distributed by political parties and candidates,

Table 3.1 **Inclusion and Security: Trade-offs and Complementarities**

Trade-offs	Complementarities
Secret ballot	Automatic voter registration
Voter registration requirement	Election Day registration
Rules for changing voter residence	Online and paperless voter registration
Purging deadwood from voter registry	Posting provisional voter rolls
Mail and absentee voting	Early (in-person) voting
Mobile polling places	Decentralized polling places
Voter identification	
Internet voting	

such that it was clear which party or candidate a voter was supporting when casting his vote.

The secret ballot disenfranchised some voters in the United States, especially illiterate voters who could not fill out complicated ballots lacking party symbols (Kousser 1974, 51–52). For instance, Schaffer (2008, 22–23) documents the effect of the secret ballot in Arkansas, where illiterate voters, especially African Americans, did not trust election officials to assist them in completing their ballot and did not want to reveal that they could not fill out their ballot unassisted. Yet despite the secret ballot's disenfranchising effects, the measure was (and is) widely seen as a necessary protection against vote buying and voter coercion (Wang 2012, 14). The right to vote in elections "held by secret vote or by equivalent free voting procedures" is even enshrined in Article 21 of the Universal Declaration of Human Rights and is endorsed in the International Covenant on Civil and Political Rights (Article 25). Of course, with the expansion of literacy, the secret ballot's disenfranchising effects have become less important today, and many countries include political party symbols and candidate pictures on the ballot to assist voters (Reynolds and Steenbergen 2006).

Voter registration requirement

Another early election measure that posed a trade-off between access and security was the introduction of a voter registration requirement (see Vickery and Szilagyi, this volume). Registration helps protect against voting by ineligible people and helps ensure that each voter votes only once. But voter registration can pose an additional burden for electors, who must complete a registration process in advance of Election Day. Indeed registration laws in the United States were originally justified to prevent election fraud, while opponents saw complicated registration procedures as intended to disenfranchise the poor (Keyssar 2009, 123–127).

While the requirement of registering to vote can pose an obstacle to voters—an obstacle mitigated by measures such as automatic registration (see below)—the impact on inclusion and security depends on the exact voter registration rules and processes. Given that registration is required in order to vote, some registration procedures pose inclusion-security trade-offs, while some others present complementarities.

Rules for changing voter residence

One aspect of voter registration that poses a trade-off is the procedure for changing one's residence for voting purposes. Specifically, rules that make it easy to change one's residence on the electoral registry increase access for mobile voters, but they can also facilitate registration fraud. In many countries, fraudulent residency on voter registration applications is a common means of manipulation, mainly in local elections. Residency fraud typically involves a local candidate arranging for voters from outside jurisdictions to register to vote in the candidate's jurisdiction by falsely claiming to live in the area. The phenomenon has variously been called colonizing, pipe-laying, and pre-electoral residential registration (Campbell 2006, 19, 23; Fukumoto and Horiuchi 2011) and has been documented in many countries, including the United States, Japan, Bulgaria, and across Latin America. Fukumoto and Horiuchi (2011, 588) note that "the simplicity of the registration process" in Japan makes residential registration fraud a feasible method of electoral malpractice, as Japanese voters can easily change their registered address without providing evidence of residence (such as a utility bill).

While the ease of claiming residence can facilitate fraud, stringent requirements for establishing one's residence in an electoral district can result in de facto disenfranchisement. This happened in the 1997 municipal elections in Bosnia-Herzegovina, for example, where restrictive residency documentation requirements designed "to counter widespread manipulation of voter residency claims during the 1996 elections" effectively disenfranchised many voters (Prather and Herron 2007, 362). Similarly, El Salvador and Guatemala have prohibited changes of residence on the voter registry within one year (or longer) prior to Election Day as a way of combatting residency fraud, but at the cost of reducing voter access (Pallister 2017).

Steps put in place to prevent residential registration fraud thus may pose obstacles to the participation of eligible voters, but requirements to prove residence can be made more or less inclusive. For example, registrars may allow many forms of documentation, such as a receipt for a utility service, school enrollment, or pay stub. In contrast, registrars may require residence to be demonstrated with a limited selection of documents, which may provide stronger protections against fraud but also be more onerous for legitimate voters. If the requirements for changing one's registered residence are too onerous—such as requiring a new identity card that lists one's current address—they may be counterproductive, as many eligible voters will fail to update their residence and the registry will accumulate inaccuracies. These voters may then abstain from voting or vote in a jurisdiction in which they no longer reside.

Purging voter rolls of deadwood

Another dimension of voter registration poses a trade-off between access and security: the mechanisms used for purging the voter rolls of "deadwood," or voters thought to be deceased or no longer living in a jurisdiction. Removing from the voter rolls names of people confirmed as being deceased or not living in a jurisdiction is a normal part of keeping the register up to date, of course, and election authorities vary in their procedures for doing so (see NCSL 2012).

One method of aggressively purging the rolls is to remove voters for not voting in a specified number of consecutive elections (as is done in Bolivia and Panama, for example). This approach has the benefit of removing from the voter rolls deceased or emigrated voters who were not detected by other mechanisms of voter list maintenance, thus preventing the use of those voters' information for voter impersonation. But such purges also risk removing eligible citizens who vote irregularly.

Voter registry purges in the United States are restricted by the National Voter Registration Act, but variations in voter list maintenance across states are still the source of much controversy and litigation. Those concerned about voter fraud push for aggressive purges of ineligible individuals from the rolls, while voting rights advocates fear that eligible voters will be swept up in such purges (as has happened in some cases, such as Florida and Ohio) (Wines 2017). While this area of election administration poses a trade-off between access and security, certain measures can be employed to mitigate that trade-off. Rules limiting voter roll purges can be complemented by other provisions—such as using "inactive" voter lists, giving advance notice to affected voters before removal from the registry, and data-sharing arrangements between various state agencies—to keep voter lists up to date and to prevent the use of deadwood for election fraud (see, e.g., Minnite and Callahan 2003, 24–25; Project Vote 2010).

Absentee and mail voting

While some access-security trade-offs pertain to voter registration, others are related to voting procedures, including various forms of absentee and mail balloting. Absentee voting and voting by mail facilitate the participation of voters who are away from their normal residence or who are confined to a hospital or other institution at election time, and more generally can increase the convenience of voting.

Absentee voting can take place in person, with many possibilities as to how it is administered: a voter may be able to cast a ballot in a different precinct within his or her electoral district, or in any polling place within or outside of the electoral district, or at special polling stations set up for absentee voters. In general, the more options available to voters, the more administrative controls must be in place to prevent voter fraud. Making in-person absentee voting available at all voting sites increases accessibility but poses challenges for election management, especially in distributing ballots to polling stations (which may need to issue different ballots from various districts to voters) and maintaining integrity controls over all voting materials. These requirements are reduced by offering absentee voting at more limited locations, but with a resulting reduction in accessibility.

These challenges were seen in Ukraine's elections in 2002 and 2004. The electoral commission did not exercise effective control over the issuance of absentee voting certificates that allowed an elector to vote at any polling place in the country. Observers noted cases of forged certificates and buses of voters arriving at polling places and all voting with the use of absentee certificates (OSCE 2005b, 11, 28).

Regardless of the number of absentee voting sites available to voters, steps need to be taken to ensure that a voter does not cast a ballot at a normal polling station and at an absentee voting site, or at multiple absentee sites. Methods such as requiring prior registration as an absentee voter can help protect against fraud (ACE Electoral Knowledge Network n.d.).

Absentee voting can also take place through the mail. Twenty-seven U.S. states offer no-excuse absentee balloting, allowing voters to request an absentee ballot without offering a reason why the voter cannot make it to a polling place on Election Day. Three U.S. states use voting by mail rather than traditional polling places (NCSL 2017b). Several countries, including Australia, Great Britain, and New Zealand, use mail voting in at least some local elections (Qvortrup 2005; Gronke 2013, 139).

While voting by mail and no-excuse absentee voting increase voter access by eliminating the time and inconvenience of traveling to a polling place, they may also be open to abuses such as vote buying, voter coercion, and multiple voting. Because absentee and mail voting take place outside of the traditional polling place, the voter may be subject to intimidation or vote buying when completing his or her ballot. As Burden and Gaines (2013, 8) explain, "someone in possession of an absentee ballot can . . . easily complete it in the presence of another interested party in exchange for payment, or can sign the ballot and turn it over to another person for completion." The possibility of outside influence on voters may be especially acute in institutions for the elderly or military bases, but may also occur in the home, where spouses or children may be subject to coercion in completing an absentee ballot. The secrecy of the vote may also be compromised by election officials, who typically utilize a multiple-envelope system to protect the secrecy of the ballot; such systems can be complex and subject to error (Burden and Gaines 2013, 7, 9; Century Foundation 2005, 53). Where a third party can handle a voter's absentee ballot, as is allowed in some U.S. states, even greater potential exists for violating the secrecy of the vote or other forms of misconduct (Burden and Gaines 2013, 12).

At the same time, election officials, party observers, and nonpartisan monitors cannot directly observe the voting process in the case of mail voting, unlike voting in traditional polling places. Mail voting also requires stringent safeguards to provide for the security of voting materials traveling through the postal system, and a particular problem is lost votes—either blank ballots that are not received by voters or completed ballots that do not reach election officials (ACE Electoral Knowledge Network n.d.; Burden and Gaines 2013, 12; Stewart 2011). Steps must also be taken to ensure that voters do not vote multiple times (e.g., once by mail and once in person) (ACE Electoral Knowledge Network n.d.; Minnite and Callahan 2003, 26). Mail voting also poses challenges in verifying voter identity, and jurisdictions vary in their procedures, although all three vote-by-mail states in the United States rely on matching a signature accompanying the mailed ballot to the voter's signature on file with election officials (Pérez 2017, 16). While these procedures may minimize voter fraud, they nevertheless may be less secure than the safeguards available in polling places.[3] The potential for fraud resulting from extensive absentee and mail voting has led even strong advocates of voter access to conclude that extensive use of absentee balloting may not be worth the risks (e.g., Wang 2012, 14).

Mobile polling stations

For some populations that are unable to travel to a polling place, an alternative to absentee voting through the mail is the use of mobile polling stations. This can involve a special voting unit or staff from a regular polling place traveling to locations such as hospitals, institutions for the elderly, or remote population centers, either on Election Day or during an early voting period (ACE Electoral Knowledge Network n.d.). Although mobile polling places are less common than absentee voting through the mail in the United States, at least 18 countries use mobile polling stations (Massicotte, Blais, and Yoshinaka 2004, 139).

Mobile stations may provide more control over election security than mail voting, as election officials remain in control of voting materials throughout the balloting process (ACE Electoral Knowledge Network n.d.). Nevertheless, mobile polling stations may provide greater opportunity for voter intimidation, as the voters casting ballots under such circumstances "are often those who rely on the state for their well-being and are subordinate to agents of the state" (Prather and Herron 2007, 355). In Argentina, Costa Rica, and Ecuador, for example, mobile polling places are used in prisons. Mobile polling stations may provide opportunities for partisan election officials to pressure voters or tamper with ballots away from the watchful eyes of opposition party observers—a problem documented in Ukraine (Calingaert 2006, 145; OSCE 2005b, 28–29).

Voter identification

The area of election administration that has gained the most attention in the United States for posing a trade-off between access and security is voter identification (see Bergman, Tran, and Yates, this volume). On the one hand, strict requirements to show photo identification at the polls can help prevent voter impersonation. While all the available evidence strongly suggests that this form of voter fraud is exceedingly rare in the United States (Ahlquist, Mayer, and Jackman 2014; Levitt 2014), requiring voters to show identification might provide a marginal increase in electoral security. On the other hand, voter ID requirements can impede the participation of eligible voters who lack the requisite identification documents, thus lowering inclusion.[4]

Although voter identification poses a trade-off, the potential for disenfranchisement depends on the exact rules concerning what types of ID are accepted, the simplicity and cost of obtaining the necessary ID, and what procedures are in place for voters who lack documentation at the polls (such as casting a provisional ballot and whether poll workers or witnesses can vouch for the identity of voters). U.S. states vary widely on these criteria, as do other countries (Schaffer and Wang 2009). In the United States, sizable numbers of eligible electors lack photo identification, and in at least some cases, obtaining the required ID can be costly in terms of time and money (see, e.g., Horwitz 2016b).

The effects of strict ID laws in promoting electoral security also depend in part on the rules for absentee voting. ID laws may prevent voter impersonation at the polling place, but where strict ID rules apply to in-person voting but not to absentee voting—as is the case in some U.S. states—ID laws may actually increase the potential for fraud by driving voters who lack ID to cast absentee ballots (Levitt 2012, 116–117).

Online voting

A final election administration measure posing a clear trade-off between access and security is online voting. Online voting can be conducted either through an online portal or by emailing voted ballots, and its use to date has been limited. Estonia has used online voting since 2005, when it was first employed for local elections, and 32 U.S. states allow overseas and military voters to return their ballots electronically (Arthur 2014; Verified Voting 2017). In recent years Alaska has begun allowing all voters to return absentee ballots online.

While online voting would increase convenience and access for many voters, computer security experts warn that online voting is highly vulnerable to hacking and "denial of service" attacks that could undermine the legitimacy of an election. It is very difficult to verify voter identity, to maintain the secrecy of the vote, and to audit election outcomes when voting is conducted online, and hackers could potentially alter votes without being detected (Ambinder 2014; Verified Voting 2017). These risks were demonstrated in 2010 when the Washington, D.C., elections board invited specialists to test the security of a new online voting system. University of Michigan computer scientists hacked into the mock election trial, allowing them to gain control of the system and alter votes and violate ballot secrecy. And while Estonia's online voting system appears to have worked well so far, vulnerabilities have been found by computer security analysts (Arthur 2014).

Complementarities: Enhancing both voter access and election security

While trade-offs between access and security are posed by the use of the secret ballot, various voter registration procedures, absentee and mail voting, mobile polling stations, voter ID requirements, and online voting, there are numerous election administration procedures that, if implemented carefully, can pursue both access and security.

Automatic voter registration

Automatic voter registration, whereby the state registers all eligible citizens rather than citizens taking the initiative to register to vote, can be an inclusive safeguard against electoral malpractice. Automatic registration increases voter access by eliminating a time-consuming step for voters and results in a much more inclusive voter registry than systems of voter-initiated registration. It also presents less risk of registration fraud because the state conducts voter registration. Third-party groups or other nonstate actors play little role in collecting registrations; as Heather Gerken (2013a) has put it, "countries with universal registration don't have ACORNs" (Friess 2009). Countries with automatic registration utilize data-sharing processes between different state agencies—such as civil registries or postal services—to incorporate newly eligible citizens, remove deceased voters from the rolls, and in some cases update voters' residence when they move. As a result, voter rolls are more accurate than in voter-initiated registration systems, and thus less vulnerable to fraudsters exploiting outdated registry entries for voter impersonation or multiple voting.

The experiences of other countries demonstrate these advantages. In a survey of democratic countries, Massicotte, Blais, and Yoshinaka (2004, 67–73) found slightly more than half had state-initiated voter registration systems, and since 2015 10 U.S. states have approved some form of automatic voter registration. While critics express concerns that automatic registration will lead to noncitizens and other ineligible individuals being placed on the voter registry (Voting Integrity Institute 2017), these concerns are unfounded. It is fairly easy to confirm the citizenship of applicants before adding their names to the voter registry (as Oregon does, for example). There is no evidence that automatic registration is more vulnerable to noncitizens registering than is voter-initiated registration, nor is there evidence that automatic registration is a source of fraud in other countries. In the case of Canada, for example, automatic registration "works efficiently and with no allegations of fraud" (Rosenberg and Chen 2009, 1). Many countries in Latin America also use automatic registration, including those with quite clean elections, like Chile, Costa Rica, and Panama.

Online and paperless voter registration

Other voter registration practices short of automatic registration can also pursue access and security simultaneously. Paperless voter registration—either online or through motor vehicle and other public agencies—improves both the accuracy of the voter registry and voter access. Where voter registration is paper-based, completed registration forms may be illegible, and errors may occur when data from paper forms are entered into the registry database. Combined with a crush of last-minute registrations, paper-based registration diverts the focus of election administrators from other issues, such as preparing election logistics (Pew Center on the States 2010). Paper-based registration systems are thus prone to accumulating errors in the registry data,[5] a source of potential malpractice, and prone to disenfranchisement, as some voters show up at the polls to find that their name does not appear on the rolls or their identifying information does not precisely match the information on the rolls.

Online voter registration provides easier access to many voters, who no longer have to visit a registry site or mail a paper form. By making it easier for voters to update their information and reducing the likelihood of data entry errors, online registration can improve the accuracy of the voter registry (Underhill 2013). This can increase access, as voters are less likely to encounter delays at polling places caused by voter roll inaccuracies (Bauer et al. 2014, 24–25).

Online registration also provides safeguards against fraudulent registrations. Duplicate registrations can be automatically flagged, and the IP addresses of online registration applications can be tracked to help monitor for suspicious activity (Pérez 2017, 6). The Bipartisan Policy Center (Daschle et al. 2014, 42) concludes that online registration offers both access and security, noting that it provides "checks against inadvertently providing incorrect information that could result in a voter not being successfully registered" and that election officials "have the capacity to check the source of online submissions, an important means of reducing opportunities for voter-registration fraud."

Nevertheless, concerns remain that online registration may permit fraudsters to use the personal information of voters (obtained legally or illegally) to change voters' residence, delete registrations, or request absentee ballots online (what researchers call "voter identity theft") (Sweeney, Yoo, and Zang 2017). For online registration to enhance both inclusion and security, it is necessary for elections agencies to utilize a range of safeguards, such as logging all site visitors and reviewing all address changes (see NCSL 2017e; Pew Charitable Trusts 2014, 4).

Election Day registration

Election Day registration (EDR), which allows citizens to register to vote and cast a ballot on Election Day, is another measure that can achieve both inclusion and security. EDR increases access by eliminating the additional step of registering weeks or months in advance of Election Day, and research on U.S. states finds that EDR boosts voter turnout (see, e.g., Knack 2001). And it seems to achieve this effect without compromising security, possibly even enhancing the accuracy of the voter rolls. Nevertheless, opponents of EDR often suggest that it increases the opportunity for voter fraud by permitting individuals to vote multiple times at different polling places and limiting the ability of election officials to verify the identity and eligibility of Election Day registrants (Von Spakovsky 2013). Election administrators also sometimes express concerns about EDR's administrative requirements (Carbó and Wright 2008, 71; NCSL 2013, 2).

Yet the evidence from American states that use EDR does not support such fears. There is no evidence that states with EDR have higher levels of voter fraud than do states with earlier registration closing dates (Hall 2013, 595; Minnite 2007). When voters register on Election Day with EDR, they do so in person with election officials rather than through other state agencies or third-party groups. Safeguards typically include requiring the registrant to provide proof of identity and residence, and mailing a nonforwardable notice to the registrant's address and investigating if the mailing is returned as undeliverable (Carbó and Wright 2008, 74; Minnite and Callahan 2003, 26, 28; NCSL 2013, 2). Registry databases that can be accessed by election officials in real time can also help prevent people from exploiting EDR to register and vote at multiple locations under the same name (Callahan 2002, 14). Less high-tech methods, such as the use of indelible ink on voters' fingers, can also help prevent multiple voting that might arise with EDR, while "ballots of Election Day registrants can be segregated and their eligibility validated before they are counted" (NCSL 2013, 2). Publicizing the penalties for voter registration fraud and requiring Election Day registrants to sign an affidavit are additional safeguards to minimize the risk of voter fraud resulting from EDR (Callahan 2002, 15; Minnite and Callahan 2003, 27). EDR can also help keep information on the voter rolls up to date—and thus contribute to electoral security—as voters can update their residence information on Election Day.

The experiences of other countries seem consistent with those of U.S. states. There is no evidence that countries with EDR are more susceptible to voter fraud. Canada, for example, allows for same-day registration (Rosenberg and Chen 2009, 7, 41) and seems to suffer no significant voter fraud as a result. However, registration closing dates vary widely across countries, and the number of countries allowing EDR is limited. In a 2004 survey of 63 countries, Massicotte, Blais, and Yoshinaka (2004, 74) found only seven that use EDR. Voter registration deadlines of three to six months before Election Day in many countries suggest that EDR may not be appropriate in all conditions. Much may depend on a country's technological infrastructure, the legal and administrative framework, and the general climate of trust surrounding voter registration and voting. Identifying the most appropriate conditions for EDR requires more research by the elections community.

Posting provisional voter rolls

While some measures that make registering to vote and updating one's registration easy can improve the accuracy of the voter rolls, widespread inaccuracies in voter registry data generate concerns about both fraud and disenfranchisement. Many voters do not cancel their old registration when they move, and thus citizens who no longer live in a jurisdiction remain on its voter registry. Efforts to purge those voters from the rolls can mistakenly purge eligible voters.

Some steps to verify and maintain the accuracy of the voter rolls may increase both voter access and electoral security. Allowing voters to consult their registration status in the weeks or months leading up to Election Day is one way to accomplish this. Many countries publicize the provisional voter rolls before Election Day. This can be done by posting the voter rolls in local public spaces, mailing personalized registration information to voters, offering online lookup tools, and distributing the voter registry to political parties. Voters are then allowed the opportunity to correct any errors (Rosenberg and Chen 2009, 20). Distributing provisional registry information thus increases inclusion by allowing voters to correct errors that would prevent them from being allowed to vote at the correct polling place. It also increases security by allowing for the detection of deadwood or fraudulent registrations. Where provisional voter rolls are posted publicly, only nonsensitive personal information (such as name and address) should be included.

Where the voter registry contains serious inaccuracies, posting the provisional rolls can be an important safeguard to help prevent disenfranchisement, multiple voting, and residency fraud. Even where the voter rolls are fairly accurate, posting the provisional rolls—or, at a minimum, offering online lookup tools to registered voters—increases transparency and may increase the confidence of political parties and citizens.

Early (in-person) voting

Early (in-person) voting is another election administration measure that achieves convenience for voters while potentially reducing the risk of fraud. Early voting increases voter access by providing more times that voters can cast a ballot and by reducing lines at polling stations by extending the voting process beyond one day. At the same time, early in-person voting procedures are the same as those on Election Day, and thus pose no additional complexities for election officials (Gronke 2013, 139). In fact, "the comparatively calmer period of early voting also allows poll workers to gain experience fulfilling their responsibilities before the crush of Election Day voting" (Daschle et al. 2014, 42). By spacing out the voting process, poll workers may be better able to accurately verify voter identity and follow proper voting procedures. In contrast, overcrowded voting centers can overwhelm poll workers, who may become less diligent in following protocols such as checking voter identification (or, in other countries, checking indelible ink on voters' fingers). As a result, as Gerken (2014) has noted, "early voting is at the 'sweet spot' of election reform . . . where the so-called 'access/integrity tradeoff' isn't a tradeoff" (see also Gerken 2013b). This conclusion depends on local conditions, however. The security benefits of early voting are likely to be maximized where political parties and nonpartisan election observer groups have the resources to monitor early voting sites.

Decentralized polling places

The location of polling places can also have implications for both inclusion and security. Inclusion is enhanced when polling places are highly decentralized, such that voters do not have to travel a long distance to reach their polling station and do not have to navigate an overcrowded polling place. Indeed some research finds that longer distance between voters' residences and polling places is associated with lower turnout (Brady and McNulty 2011; Haspel and Knotts 2005). At the same time, highly decentralized polling places can help protect election security by allowing for easier detection of voter impersonation and fraudulent registrations. When polling places are dispersed in local communities, poll workers, party poll watchers, and voters will be likely to know many of the residents assigned to vote at that polling place. Any organized attempt to bus in fraudulently registered voters from out of town or to impersonate local residents at the polls would quickly be detected. It should be noted that this safeguard is likely to apply more to small rural and suburban communities than to urban areas, where residents may not know many of their neighbors.

Conclusion

The widespread notion that registration and voting procedures pose inherent challenges in balancing voter access and election security has some merit. A number of election administration measures—such as absentee balloting, voter ID rules, and procedures for updating the voter registry—can pose such trade-offs. Yet election administration does not always pose a problem of access versus security; in fact some policies can provide for both. Measures such as automatic voter registration, early in-person voting, and publicizing provisional voter rolls can help facilitate voter access while also making some types of election fraud more difficult to carry out.

This chapter has drawn on the experiences of the United States and several other countries to identify some of the areas of election administration that pose difficult trade-offs between access and security, as well as areas in which these two goals are complementary. Yet there is much we do not know about how electoral procedures might be designed to pursue both goals, and further study should focus on identifying the variables that determine the severity of trade-offs (and the degree of complementarity) between access and security for particular electoral practices.

Nevertheless, we have sufficient knowledge of the effects of different voting procedures to move past the simple access-versus-security framing of all voting rules. Election reform in the United States can build on areas of common interest across the two major political parties by pursuing policies that enhance inclusion and security simultaneously. In other areas, parties and other stakeholders will need to grapple with the trade-offs between access and security, as well as other considerations such as cost.

Notes

1. Bay County Democratic Party et al. v. Land, 2004, 04-10257-BC (E.D. Michigan). Quote on p. 3.
2. However, the use of indelible ink may facilitate "negative vote buying," whereby voters are paid to abstain from voting and dip their fingers in ink as a means of enforcing the agreement (see, e.g., Schaffer 2002, 78).
3. For instance, there were cases of vote-by-mail local election results being thrown out by the courts in England in 2005 because of fraud (Calingaert 2006, 145).
4. Studies come to different conclusions about whether voter ID requirements lower turnout, at least enough to be discernible by statistical tests. Among other studies, see Hajnal, Lajevardi, and Nielson (2017) and Grimmer et al. (2017).
5. For instance, in Maricopa County, Arizona, in 2009, paper registration forms accounted for 15.5% of voter registrations, but "they made up more than half of those registrations containing incomplete, inaccurate, or illegible information" (Brennan Center for Justice 2016a, 10).

4

Diagnosing Electoral Integrity

MICHAEL LATNER

Controversy over the integrity of electoral systems in the United States has increased with recent close presidential elections, influential Supreme Court decisions affecting election laws, and renewed attention to the administration and management of elections. A growing body of literature has demonstrated persistent flaws in the conduct of U.S. elections (see Hasen 2012, this volume; McGann et al. 2016; Wayne 2018). But consensus has not emerged on which metrics are superior for evaluating electoral integrity among U.S. states. Several previous attempts to construct a truly comparative index of electoral integrity, that could be applied across all types of electoral systems, leave much to be desired. It is in this context that the work of the Electoral Integrity Project (2017, EIP) is so relevant.

The availability and quality of these tools is relevant for assessing outcomes, but also for initiating policy. Billions of dollars are invested every year by governments and nongovernmental organizations, within and outside the United States, based on indices used to target electoral malpractice, improve democratic governance, and build responsive institutions (Drew 2016; Norris 2017a; UNDP 2017; USAID 2016). Every index carries the theoretical and normative judgments and the methodological choices of its designers, and these decisions have significant political implications (Cooley and Snyder 2015; Merry, Davis, and Kingsbury 2015).

The EIP's Perception of Electoral Integrity (PEI) expert survey seeks to provide a global and multidimensional index of electoral integrity. This chapter provides a multilevel assessment of how well the PEI meets the challenges of accurately estimating electoral integrity across U.S. states, from a globally comparative perspective.

In the first section, the concept of electoral integrity is treated as a component of liberal democracy, as this conceptualization largely determines how integrity is empirically specified and measured, although differing from the human rights approach discussed in the book's introductory chapter. The second section describes the specification of PEI survey components and reviews previous research on the challenges of configuration, aggregation, and measurement of such indices.

Empirical tests assess equivalence between the global and U.S. PEI data sets (Norris, Wynter, and Grömping 2017; Norris, Nai, and Grömping 2016). Both statistical and case analysis help to determine whether expert respondents are measuring the same thing, in the same way, given use of the same indicators. The third section compares the PEI index with alternative U.S. electoral integrity measures, assessing the degree to which indicators are measuring the same components of electoral integrity. Deviations between these indices are analyzed and potential sources of bias are explored. The final section reconsiders the potential of a general measure of electoral integrity in light of the analysis and provides suggestions for avoiding bias in future electoral integrity research.

Integrity and democracy

The integrity of elections can be linked to the quality of liberal democracy, as the electoral process embodies both the mechanisms that convert individual values into social choices as well as the cultural rituals that signify a delegation of authority as being democratic. International standards that define the integrity in elections often reflect broad democratic principles, which, in their simplest form, reduce to institutional manifestations of or procedures that sustain political equality and majority rule (Dahl 1989; Madison 1792). These two principles are complementary, in that majority rule signifies political equality in a social decision rule. Indeed it is the only decision rule that treats each voter equally (May 1952; McGann 2006). Thus, by this standard, elections have integrity when they embody political equality. But what does that look like in action, and how can we measure it?

According to the United Nations International Covenant on Civil and Political Rights (ICCPR 1966), integrity in elections is characterized by periodic elections (so as to regularly measure public preferences); universal (nobody is excluded) and equal (one person, one vote) suffrage (see Pallister, this volume); an equal right to vote or stand for public office; equal freedom of expression through a secret ballot (so as not to reduce the value of one's vote through coercion), in a "genuine" election, meaning an election where all the votes are actually counted; and electoral majorities determine the public will. Similarly, the Global Commission on Elections, Democracy, and Security describes an election as having integrity when it is "based on the democratic principles of universal suffrage and political equality . . . and is professional, impartial and transparent in its preparation and administration throughout the electoral cycle" (Stedman 2015).

At numerous points in the electoral cycle, integrity can reinforce confidence in election outcomes, hold representatives accountable, and facilitate effective management of social problems (Gerring and Thacker 2008; Norris 2012). Conversely, malpractices, whether by design, coercion, or accident, at any stage of the electoral cycle can infringe on civil and political rights, erode support for the process, inflame social divisions, and destabilize regimes. The question analysts face is how to accurately model deviations from integrity wherever they might occur throughout the electoral cycle.

What counts as integrity, and how much should it count for?

Minimally, three analytically distinct phases compose an electoral cycle (Gerken 2009; Huefner et al. 2011; USAID 2013). Pre-election, an exploration phase, is a necessary condition to achieve electoral integrity, in the sense that potential voters should be equally free to learn about their electoral ecosystem, consider alternative choices, and convert their preferences into votes (Berger-Tal et al. 2014; Page 2008, 134). If the conditions for freely exchanging and evaluating information about social choices are not met, or there is not a legible set of management practices and administrative procedures in place to process that information, the range of possible outcomes will be stunted before the election takes place (Norris 2015). Next, the exploitation of that knowledge requires that preferences be converted into votes in accordance with the equality principle, which requires free and equal access to the ballot. Finally, votes must be processed in a postelection phase that adheres to the equality principle, avoiding any distortion or biasing of collective choices that advantages the preferences of some voters over others.

The PEI survey designers, following conventions found in the ACE Electoral Network's (2017) research on electoral systems, further distinguish 11 steps within these phases which they seek to empirically specify with multiple indicators, illustrated in Table 4.1: the choice of *electoral laws* that specify rights of expression and association; the fairness, transparency, and management of *electoral procedures*; the fairness of *electoral boundaries*; inclusiveness and accuracy of *voter registration*; inclusivity and equal opportunity regarding *party registration*; press freedom and speech rights in *campaign media*; equity and fairness with regard to *campaign finance*; freedom, equality, and choice in the *voting process*; fairness, security, and transparency in the *vote count*; impartial and professional behavior on the part of *electoral authorities*; and *postelection* resolution of disputes in a legal, peaceful manner. I have categorized "boundaries" as a postelection component because that is where they affect vote counts, though their influence feeds back into pre-election conditions (Shugart and Taagepera 2017).

The PEI indicators are quantified using 49 ordinal (5-point scale) instruments to collect information from political scientists and state-specific experts regarding the degree to which each condition was met in the previous election cycle. The final index is an additive function of the 49 variables with imputations for missing data, standardized to 100 points. The survey was deployed in each

Table 4.1 **Stages of the Election Cycle, Using Perceptions of Electoral Integrity (PEI) Indicators**

Pre-election (exploration)	Election (selection)	Postelection (processing)
Electoral laws	**Voting process**	**Vote count**
favor small parties?*	threat of violence?	secure ballots?*
favor incumbent groups?	voter fraud?*	timely results?
restrict citizens' rights?*	easy voting?*	fair counting?*
	genuine choice?	restrict international
Electoral procedures	postal ballots?*	monitors?
well managed?*	disabled facilities?*	restrict local monitors?*
voter information?*	voting abroad?*	
fair officials?	internet voting?	**Electoral authorities**
rule of law?		impartial?
		provided information?*
Voter registration		allowed scrutiny?*
voter roll complete?*		performed well?
voter roll accurate?*		
ineligible voters?*		**Electoral boundaries**
		discriminatory?*
Party registration		diluted some party votes?*
favored incumbents?		impartial?*
banned candidates?		
women's opportunity?		**Postelection results**
minority opportunity?		results challenged?
closed candidate selection?*		peaceful protests?*
rallies prohibited?		violent protests?*
		legal resolution?
Campaign media		
balanced news?		
favor incumbents?		
fair access?		
fair coverage?		
social media?		
Campaign finance		
equitable access to subsidies?*		
equitable access to donations?*		
transparent finances?*		
rich buy elections?		
improper use of state funds?		

Note: Indicators marked with * have complementary alternative U.S. indicators.

Sources: Norris, Wynter, and Grömping (2017), country-level; Norris, Nai, and Grömping (2016), state-level. See www.electoralintegrityproject.com.

of the 50 states and Washington, D.C., in order to collect the same data after the 2016 U.S. elections, providing a rare opportunity to compare the global index with electoral integrity among a large number of state units under the same election cycle.

The PEI index offers some real advantages over other conventional indices of electoral integrity and democracy, though external validity tests confirm that they tend to be strongly correlated (Teorell et al. 2014). The specific focus on electoral integrity (as opposed to democracy) also provides hope that researchers can over- come two frequent deficiencies of other indices, namely, the tendency of those who focus on development to truncate the upper bound of their measures by assuming that all "democracies" get high scores since elections are frequently pulled off with little violence, and the tendency of those intent on studying electoral performance in stable regimes to not consider the lower bounds of democratic performance, instead selecting only cases where, or assuming that, pre-election conditions of equality are essentially met. The challenge of a general electoral integrity index, and the motivating question behind this analysis, is to what extent electoral attributes can be accurately measured across the full array of electoral systems, from Alaska to Zimbabwe.

The 11 PEI Index subdimensions can be broken out for separate analyses across contexts. This provides a workable compromise between the more comprehen- sive but less theoretically coherent information provided by data sets like V-Dem (Lindberg et al. 2014) and specific but narrow measures like the Vanhanen Index (Vanhanen 2000). Moreover, the PEI Index allows researchers to test how the use of different components or aggregation rules might impact the structure of the data, something often missing in older measures (Munck and Verkuilen 2002). The ability to open up components gives more flexibility in the use of data for specifying research questions, though it also opens the door to selective use of only statistically significant results, which can contribute to type I errors (Head et al. 2015).

Ideally, a theory of political institutions should guide researchers in modeling how various attributes of an electoral system *should* be linked, then data should be transformed using aggregation rules that fit the theory (Taagepera 2008). The ad- ditive aggregation rule (indicator values are added together for the overall index) of the PEI Index suggests that any break in the chain undermines the integrity of the cycle, but it also assumes that the magnitude of breaks is linear across meas- urement units and equal across links. Such a configuration raises the question of whether a deficit in one component of electoral integrity can be compensated by another, achieving the same average level of integrity across contexts (Møller and Skaaning 2010). Engaging that question requires an analysis of three interlinked conditions, all of which are necessary to establish cross-system equivalence in index measurement (Van Deth 2013; Vijver and Tanzer 2004). Indices may fail tests of equivalence (1) in the manner in which they are constructed, (2) in their method of measurement, and (3) in the act of measuring.

First, the underlying traits that index components are designed to measure may be configured differently in different contexts (Stark, Chernyshenko, and Drasgow 2006). For example, the relevant attributes of integrity regarding electoral boundaries could be different in Ohio compared to a system like Bahrain's. Both use single-seat districts (SSD) for their (elected) chambers, so they could both be susceptible to the known pathologies of SSD, namely disproportionality in vote-to-seat ratios, malapportionment and gerrymandering (Shugart and Taagepera 2017). However, it is also possible that boundary "integrity" includes broader, multidimensional traits across U.S. states, given the level of administrative attention and litigation surrounding the impact of district boundaries in states like Ohio. If so, this could result in the same indicators showing different strengths of association with the latent trait that they are intended to reflect.

Assuming that the constructs are equivalent, indicators that accurately reflect an integrity component in one context might do so less accurately in a different context. For example, measuring the integrity of campaign finance with an instrument that records equity in access to contributions may be more relevant in some systems compared to others (Vijver and Tanzer 2004). In U.S. states, where campaign finance laws are widely perceived as having a strong impact on the electoral process (Lessig 2015), equity could be a more accurate measure of integrity, compared to a system like Belgium's, where many activities linked to campaign finance (corporate lobbying, campaign advertising) are more heavily regulated or subsidized.

At the most granular level of measurement, there may be further variance in how instruments are being used to measure attributes. In this instance, the assumption that "strong agreement" in a survey item reflects the same condition in different contexts may not be valid (Stark, Chernyshenko, and Drasgow 2006). To continue with the above example, what should be considered equitable in terms of access to campaign contributions may vary between systems where there are large differences in the distribution of wealth, or cultural conditions that affect how measurements translate across contexts, or issues of literal translation in the case of survey items (Johnson et al. 2005). Patterns of "hot" scoring or "extreme response" bias, where respondents use instrument scales in systematically different ways, can also produce nonequivalence (Cheung and Rensvold 2000). Similarly, if U.S. experts are using only other U.S. states as their reference point, rather than the global universe of electoral systems, it could be reflected in variance between U.S. and global results (King et al. 2004).

In anticipation of these last sorts of problems, the PEI survey incorporates a set of anchoring vignettes (King et al. 2004) into their survey questionnaire. The goal of anchoring is to measure (and then statistically account for) nonequivalence in personal item response in the evaluation of several conditions that are identical across respondents, such that the variance in answers provides an estimate of respondent nonequivalence. PEI relies on three vignettes for the U.S. Respondents are asked to use a 10-point scale ranging from "not seriously undermined" to "seriously undermined" to answer the question "How seriously do you think that electoral integrity is undermined if in [STATE]": (1) "some voters had to wait in long lines to vote?"; (2) "the opposition decides to boycott an election, so that the government wins most seats by default?"; and (3) "election results lead to widespread violence throughout the country?"

Responses are then used to "anchor" or locate respondents to a standardized point as a means of controlling for interpersonal response nonequivalence. However, even if global and U.S. experts can be anchored to a common reference point with regard to these conditions, the degree to which such recalibration can adjust for variance caused by other perceptual differences is empirically unclear. Fortunately, there are a variety of techniques that can be used to estimate nonequivalence at various levels where it occurs, including multigroup confirmatory factor analysis (Cheung and Rensvold 2002; Hirschfeld and von Brachel 2014), which is employed in the next section.

Diagnosing equivalence in the Global and U.S. PEI indices

Figure 4.1 displays the distribution of PEI scores for both the global (light) and U.S. (dark) data sets. For the global index, the mean PEI score is 55.4, with a standard deviation of 14.4 points. This compares to a mean U.S. state score of 63.9 and standard deviation of 6.1 points. The highest scoring U.S. state is Vermont, at 75.2, comparatively high but significantly lower than the highest scoring nation-state, Denmark, at 86.5. At the other end of the index, Arizona (53.0) scores the lowest among U.S. states. In the 5.5 round of the PEI survey, Ethiopia (24.2) barely edged out Syria for the lowest electoral integrity score, though confidence intervals (roughly 10 points in this case) confirm that such differences are not significant.

To test whether these scores are comparable in a straightforward manner, we test for equivalence between the global and U.S. data sets. Equivalence testing involves a hierarchical series of assessments that probe for increasingly finer degrees of invariance in measures. Rather than probing all the way down to the level of individual questions, our primary interest is in the equivalence of the PEI Index and its components across units, as that is where the most policy-relevant questions about deviations from political equality in the electoral cycle occur. Components are thus treated as the item-level indicators of electoral integrity rather than the 49 individual indicators.

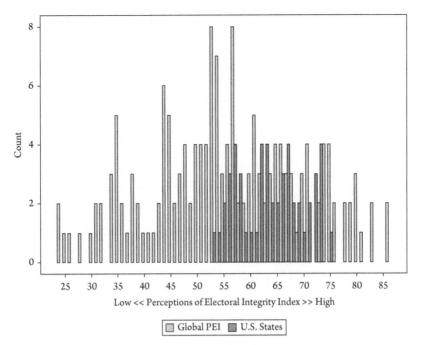

Figure 4.1 The Distribution of Global and U.S. Perceptions of Electoral Index Scores.
Note: Global PEI covers 161 countries; U.S. States covers the 50 U.S. states plus the District of Columbia.
Source: Norris, Wynter, and Grömping (2017), country-level; Norris, Nai, and Grömping (2016), state-level.

First, a baseline model is estimated so that structural equivalence can be established if the model applies equally well across the U.S. and global contexts. If the model has a good fit, and components have similarly significant loadings across groups, then stronger tests of lower-level sources of nonequivalence can be estimated. Measurement equivalence of components across contexts is tested by constraining variance in factor loadings, and then intercepts, to evaluate whether the constrained model is a significantly worse fit (based on chi-squared statistics and other indicators of fit) than the baseline model. The lowest level of invariance is established when a model that constrains factor loadings, intercepts, and residual variances is not significantly worse than the baseline model.

A single-factor model of electoral integrity is fit to the pooled data using the 11 election cycle components as parameters. Table 4.2 displays the measurement model with parameter estimates.[1] Overall each of the components is at least moderately associated with the latent variable. In other words, there is evidence of a latent "integrity" trait being measured.[2]

Next, sources of potential nonequivalence are explored. Comparison of the global and U.S. groups is implemented by imposing equality constraints between

Table 4.2 **The Dimensions of the PEI Index**

Dimension	Estimate (std.)
Electoral laws	0.631
Electoral procedures	0.958
Voter registration	0.776
Party registration	0.848
Campaign media	0.721
Campaign finance	0.834
Voting process	0.859
Vote count	0.953
Postelection results	0.760
Electoral authorities	0.963
Electoral boundaries	0.342

Note: Confirmatory factor analysis model with pooled global-U.S. components.

Sources: Norris, Wynter, and Grömping (2017), country-level; Norris, Nai, and Grömping (2016), state-level. See www.electoralintegrityproject.com.

the two groups. For example, in the first test, the baseline model allows loadings between the two groups to vary. Loadings are then constrained to be equal, and the models are compared to estimate change in goodness of fit, using the comparative fit index (Cheung and Rensvold 2002). Increasingly strict tests similarly constrain the intercepts, then the residuals (Table 4.3).

The series of model comparisons suggest that the loadings are near equivalent, as the Δ CFI is close to the proposed cutoff point of .01. We can be fairly confident that the latent construct of "electoral integrity" is reflected across both the U.S. and nation-state samples. However, when the intercepts are constrained, the measurement equivalence assumption cannot be met (Δ CFI = 0.12, Δ RMSEA = 0.048). This indicates that the average value of one or more components when the latent variable (electoral integrity) is zero varies significantly between the data sets. By inspecting the modification indices that pertain to individual parameters, it is possible to test for partial invariance by relaxing the constraints on individual parameters and looking for improvement in the goodness of fit.

Sorting through the modification indices (available in online materials) indicates that the boundaries component shows the largest measurement variance between groups, followed by the laws component. When I allow these two components to vary between groups, nearly half of the baseline-constrained difference in the

Table 4.3 **Global and U.S. PEI Index Invariance Model Comparisons**

	Configural *(baseline)*	*Loadings* *(weak)*	*Intercepts* *(strong)*	*Means* *(strict)*
Degrees of freedom	88	501.14	108	109
Chi-squared	501.14	567.95	887.75	938.91
Chi-squared difference		66.81	319.8	51.16
Confirmatory fit index	0.84	0.818	0.698	0.678
Confirmatory fit index difference		0.022	0.12	0.019
Root mean square error of approximation	0.21	0.213	0.261	0.268
Root mean square error of approximation difference		0.002	0.048	0.007

Note: Suggested cutoff point for the change in confirmatory fit index is 0.01 (Cheung and Rensvold 2002).

Sources: Norris, Wynter, and Grömping (2017), country-level; Norris, Nai, and Grömping (2016), state-level. See www.electoralintegrityproject.com.

comparative fit index is accounted for. The change in CFI is reduced from 0.12 to 0.091 when Boundaries is allowed to vary, and further reduced to 0.067 when the laws component is allowed to vary between the two groups.

An exploration of the lower end of the boundaries component illustrates the point. In the United States the 10 states with the lowest scores on this component are North Carolina, Wisconsin, Ohio, Pennsylvania, Michigan, Texas, South Carolina, Florida, Virginia, and Utah. To anyone familiar with controversies surrounding racial and partisan gerrymandering, many of these states are among the usual suspects. The 10 nation-states with the nearest, most comparable scores are Malaysia, Singapore, Bahrain, Togo, Swaziland, Uganda, Hungary, Zimbabwe, Cambodia, and Syria.

Figure 4.2 displays the clustering by data set, with a plot fitted with the electoral boundaries index scores on the x-axis and the full PEI index on the y-axis. With the exceptions of Malaysia, Singapore, and possibly Bahrain, U.S. states are the worst of the worst on the boundary component, with a distinct cluster scoring significantly lower than the lowest scoring nation-states.

U.S. readers may initially discount these statistics as incomparable, given that many of the nation-states in question are widely considered to be authoritarian regimes, and at least one (Syria) was embroiled in a civil war during its most recent election. It is crucial to keep in mind, however, that this component is designed to measure the integrity of electoral boundaries and how they operate, distinct from the performance of the rest of the political system. The question to be answered, for authoritarian regimes as well as U.S. states, is to what degree electoral boundaries are used to bias representation in favor of those in authority.

North Carolina and Wisconsin, for example, are recognized for their use of partisan gerrymandering and ballot access laws that entrench incumbent parties, and several states, including Wisconsin and Virginia, have manipulated boundaries to entrench minority government rule (Archer et al. 2014; McGann et al. 2016). Such states are accurately described as having electoral boundaries that (1) discriminate against some parties, (2) favor incumbents, and (3) are not impartial, the three items used to measure boundary integrity.

Nevertheless, when compared to several nation-states that achieve higher boundary integrity scores, U.S. experts, myself included (as a respondent for the California sample), appear overly pessimistic. First, comparative scholars might be surprised that so many different systems have similar ratings in the PEI survey, because they are known to have very different effects on party competition and representation. While some of these nation-states (Bahrain, Malaysia, Uganda,

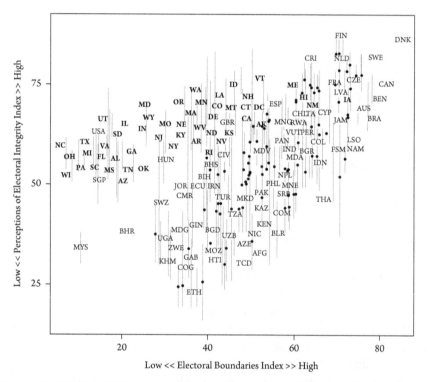

Figure 4.2 Global and U.S. State Comparison of Boundaries and PEI Index Scores.
Note: U.S. states have two-letter abbreviations; nation-states have three-letter abbreviations; dots indicate unlabeled countries; vertical point ranges are 95% confidence intervals for the PEI Index scores.
Source: Norris, Wynter, and Grömping (2017), country-level; Norris, Nai, and Grömping (2016), state-level.

Zimbabwe) share with U.S. states a reliance on single-seat districts and could suffer similar pathologies, others, like Singapore and Cambodia, use some form of multimember districts. Hungary is an especially odd case, a parallel system (two sets of electoral rules for the legislature) with an extremely majoritarian plurality, multimember component. One trait that ties these varied regimes together is that nearly all of them have implemented severely malapportioned (unequal population) districts to underrepresent targeted populations, but this is a discriminatory boundary practice that has been constitutionally prohibited in the United States for over a generation. Malapportionment cannot explain why U.S. states fair so poorly. Even if gerrymandering (the manipulation of district boundaries to gain electoral advantage; see Magleby et al., this volume) has replaced malapportionment as a discriminatory tool in the United States, there are worse practices occurring in these other regimes.

Singapore's use of multimember plurality districts has long allowed the founder Lee Kwan Yew's People's Action Party to sweep entire constituencies with minority vote shares (Amnesty International 2002). Similarly, a combination of malapportionment and single-seat plurality rules basically assures that the governing Fidesz Party retains its coalition in Hungary (Fumarola 2016). Unlike U.S. states, however, Fidesz changed the law to require a supermajority to change the biased boundaries that they designed! In Cambodia, Zimbabwe, and Uganda, the link between electoral boundaries and the dominance of governing parties is not clear, though malapportionment contributes to their dominance. In Bahrain and Swaziland, the legal status of opposition parties and electoral competition is not even clear. Such realities on the ground beg the question of relevance for electoral boundaries in these contexts, and how much weight should be given to their role in assessing electoral integrity.

Whether some U.S. boundary cases are unduly depressed as a result of their salience, or experts in nation-states with little actual competition are overly optimistic about how boundaries function, these findings highlight a construct validity problem raised at the beginning of this chapter: Can the performance of electoral boundaries meaningfully be assessed in the absence of knowledge about prerequisite conditions?

These equivalence tests show modest coherence of electoral integrity as a scalable trait across both U.S. states and more than 100 nation-states. This marks an improvement in comparative social science and a building block upon which more precise models of electoral integrity can be refined. At the same time, there are clear limits to the comparability of individual components as they are currently configured. Specifically, the integrity of electoral boundaries and electoral laws appears to operate with such variance across these two contexts that relevant differences between states are being muddled. I should note that reducing the boundary scores to an ordinal scale (low, medium, high) also reduces measurement error (not shown), a tactic that can exclude noise by minimizing irrelevant distinctions (Burden and

Stewart 2014). Nevertheless researchers should be cautious about assuming the external validity of those component measures.

The fact that many U.S. states previously known to have boundary defects also received lower boundary scores suggests that U.S. interstate comparability may nevertheless be unaffected by nonequivalence with global data. In the next section, I turn the analysis inward to assess comparability between the PEI Index and alternative measures of electoral integrity in U.S. states.

Diagnosing alternative measures of electoral integrity in the United States

In an effort to match comparable items to those used in the PEI Index, I accessed multiple sources of data on U.S. electoral integrity. Two data sets are particularly useful for their comprehensive coverage of electoral cycle stages. The first is the Pew Charitable Trusts' Electoral Performance Index (2016; EPI), which has compiled data through the 2014 U.S. election cycle (Burden and Stewart 2014). The EPI takes a distinctly records-intensive approach. It is the first comprehensive assessment of election administration across U.S. states and the District of Columbia and is designed to facilitate comparative evaluation across states and across election cycles. Seventeen key indicators, focusing on how recorded ballots are processed and converted into votes, are themselves compiled from numerous sources, including the Voting and Registration Supplement of the American Community Survey estimates of disability- and illness-related voting problems, registration or absentee ballot problems, and voter registration rate; the Survey of the Performance of American Elections' estimates of voter wait times; the U.S. Election Assistance Commission's Election Administration and Voting Survey estimates of various types of ballots cast and rejected; the United States Election Project estimates of turnout for voter-eligible populations; and several Pew reports assessing the provision of online voter tools. Table 4.4 marks indicators from the EPI, along with all the indicators used in the analysis below, within their comparable PEI components.

A second comprehensive source of integrity indicators, based on a purely legal-institutional approach to integrity, is made available through the Franchise Project's (2017; TFP) Voting Access Scorecard. The Franchise Project is an electoral reform advocacy organization, largely organized by staff from Hillary Clinton's presidential campaign, who have compiled a battery of mostly dichotomous indicators of electoral permissiveness and security standards, based on 30 metrics that include barriers to registration, early and in-person voting procedures, voter list maintenance, voting machine standards, vote-by-mail provisions, website tools, voter ID requirements, and degree of felon enfranchisement.

Table 4.4 **Stages of the Election Cycle, with Alternative U.S. Integrity Indicators**

Pre-election (exploration)	Election (selection)	Postelection (processing)
Electoral laws	**Voting process**	**Vote count**
registration barriers (TFP)*	voting problems (EPI)*	mail ballots rejected (EPI)*
voter ID? (TFP)*	residual vote rate (EPI)*	mail unreturned (EPI)
felons vote? (TFP)*	turnout (EPI)*	overseas ballots rejected
assembly size	wait time (EPI)*	(EPI)*
district magnitude *	early voting (TFP)	overseas ballots unreturned
	early and mail voting (TFP)*	(EPI)
Electoral procedures	election day return mail	provisional cast (EPI)
data completeness (EPI)*	(TFP)*	provisional rejected (EPI)*
easy registration validation		paper trail (TFP)*
(TFP)		type of observers (NCSL)*
poll worker training (TFP)*		
voting tech info (EPI)(TFP)*		**Electoral authorities**
check status online (TFP)*		audit (EPI)*
all-mail election (TFP)		federal standards (TFP)*
Voter registration		**Electoral boundaries**
registration rate (EPI)		partisan bias *
registration problems (EPI)*		responsiveness *
registration rejected (EPI)*		
voter list managed (TFP)*		**Postelection results**
online registration (EPI)(TFP)		litigation
late registration deadline (TFP)		protest (CNN)*
election day registration (TFP)		violence (SPLC)*
opt-out registration (TFP)*		
fines or penalties (TFP)		
ease of mail vote (TFP)		
Party registration		
primary type (NCSL)*		
Campaign finance		
public financing (NCSL)*		
disclosure requirements		
(NCSL)*		

Note: Indicators marked with * have complementary PEI indicators.

Sources: EPI: 2014 Pew Elections Performance Index; TFP: The Franchise Project's (2017) Voting Access Scorecard; NCSL: National Council of State Legislatures; SPLC: Southern Poverty Law Center (2017); CNN: Cable News Network.

Other sources that aided in filling in remaining gaps for comparable PEI components included the National Council of State Legislatures' (NCSL 2017d) data on state party registration requirements, which provided information on how permissive primary voting is for voters and minor parties in each state. NCSL data also provided ratings on the extent of public financing and disclosure requirements to measure the integrity of campaign finance, and election observer access to help assess the integrity of the vote count. The Southern Poverty Law Center's (SPLC 2017) "Hatewatch" report provided occurrences of postelection violence for the postelection component, and CNN (2016) news coverage documented cities where postelection protests erupted in the days following the 2016 election. The indicators that were determined to most closely match PEI indicators, shown in Table 4.4, were combined with equal weight and converted to component scores ranging from 0 to 1, for the state receiving the highest integrity score.

The most difficult component to identify reliable state-by-state indicators was the campaign media component. In principle, it would be possible to disaggregate exposure to biased news coverage across U.S. states if one could get reliable data from sources like Allsides.com or Pew studies of polarization and news coverage. However, every measure that I could readily access measured consumption rather than content, reflecting media preferences as much as anything else. Substituting Fox News consumption by state as a proxy for campaign media integrity tells us more about the voters than it does about the press. As a result, this component is left out of the more detailed component analysis that follows.

First, I compare the three complete indices, PEI, EPI, and TFP, as they are. The only change made to the data is a conversion of the values for each index into z-scores to facilitate cross-index state comparisons. The PEI Index is not correlated with the EPI (R = 0.13, t-value = 0.94). To some extent, we already know that the two indices are measuring variant aspects of electoral integrity. Because the EPI is more narrow in focus, the PEI Index reflects more components of electoral integrity, including electoral laws, party registration, campaign media and finance, in addition to the impacts of boundaries and postelection protest and violence.

While the EPI designers have verified "fairly consistent" scaling among the multiple items that make up the index, investigators have also noted the absence of underlying "quality" parameters captured by averaging values for specific components of electoral performance, including voter registration (Burden and Stewart 2014, 29; Ansolabehere and Hersh 2014, 83). That is, states typically perform poorly on one set of indicators but better on others. The conditions that weaken or strengthen integrity by these estimates (the type of voting machines used, maintenance of registration lists, etc.) are themselves not correlated, partially a result of the decentralized nature of election administration in the United States (see Arceneaux, this volume).

For this reason, most of the analyses conducted with the EPI have focused on just one or two indicators rather than the index as a whole. By contrast, TFP's Voting Access Scorecard is intended to be used in much the same way as the PEI

Index, as an overall "grade" for states, although there have not been other peer-reviewed publications using it to date. Perhaps not surprisingly, the broader reach of TFP index, which covers election laws, including voter eligibility restrictions, yields a better, but still modest, correlation with PEI ($R = 0.41$, t-value = 3.13). New Hampshire, Idaho, and Louisiana stand out for their high ranking by PEI relative to TFP, while Wisconsin and Arizona receive much higher ratings with TFP but are among the lowest scoring states on the PEI Index. Because TFP index is loosely correlated with both PEI and EPI ($R = 0.32$, t-value = 2.38), it stands out as the only parameter in an unconfirmatory factor analysis. Principal components analysis also shows no statistical indication of an underlying parameter reflected in the full indices (not shown). The indices might reflect complementary but not equivalent aspects of electoral integrity.

In the absence of a single dimension of electoral integrity, assessing the fit of components can tell us a good deal about what *is* being jointly measured and how measures might be used to diagnose specific pathologies within the electoral cycle. For this section, I have selected only those alternative indicators that have close face validity with indicators used in the PEI Index. For example, the electoral laws component indicators from TFP that measure barriers to registration and voting map closely with the PEI indicators that ask about civil rights restrictions. Further, at least in principle, small district magnitudes tend to punish smaller parties, which PEI asks about in the laws component. In practice, magnitude will be a near constant in U.S. states, as only a few use two-seat districts for their state legislatures.

Similarly, I use indicators of postelection violence and protest to match the PEI indicators on that component, but not the legal resolution of disputes. While it is possible to track postelection litigation (Hasen 2012), at the time the questionnaire was implemented, very little postelection litigation would have been resolved, so it is not clear that measuring litigation by state would pick up anything relevant. In selecting indicators to measure components, I also tried not to pick indicators that replicate other items. Each indicator was scaled to range from 0 to 1, and the components are derived from an additive aggregation rule, as is the PEI Index.

Table 4.5 displays the correlation coefficients between the PEI and alternative U.S. components, with the exception of campaign media. The pre-election components appear to be the least congruent between the two data sets. None of components is significantly correlated across the two data sets. This is counterintuitive, as we expect the extent to which state laws and procedures reflect the design principle of equality to be readily observable. I return to this puzzle in the concluding section.

The voting process component is significantly correlated. Most of the closest indicator matches, access and use of postal ballots, voting for the disabled, and occurrence of voting problems, are in this component. Nevertheless, with only about one quarter of observed variance between component measures accounted for, there remains a great deal of noise in evaluations of the voting experience.

Table 4.5 **PEI and Alternative Measures of Electoral Integrity**

Pre-election (exploration)	Election (selection)	Postelection (processing)
Election laws	**Voting process**	**Vote count**
(0.14)	(0.49)*	(0.05)
Electoral procedures		**Electoral authorities**
(-0.17)		(0.12)
Voter registration		**Electoral boundaries**
(0.20)		(0.54)*
Party registration		**Postelection results**
(0.20)		(0.49)*
Campaign media		
N/A		
Campaign finance		
(0.07)		

Note: * indicates statistically significant correlations. Ordinal correlation tests were also conducted on components with two or fewer indicators, with no difference in effect size.

Sources: Norris, Nai, and Grömping (2016) and author's compilation. See www.electoralintegrityproject. com.

Two of the four postelection sets of components also show significant positive correlations. Not surprisingly, the boundaries component measures are correlated, a promising sign for PEI, as the alternative measures are direct measures of electoral inequality (partisan asymmetry and responsiveness). The fact that the alternative measures are from 2012 and not 2016, increasing the probability of decay in the accuracy of the values, lends further credit to the notion that the PEI is picking up relevant aspects of boundary integrity. At the same time, the level of precision available and the demanding evidentiary standards used in U.S. voting rights research may be beyond what the PEI Index is capable of producing (McGann et al. 2015; Grofman 2003).

Postelection protest and violence also tracked modestly well across the PEI and alternative measures. As protests erupted in cities across the country after the presidential election of Donald Trump, and acts of violence spiked, directed primarily against religious minorities and people of color, it was well documented in the national media, providing a common reference point. Additionally, two of the three anchoring vignettes used in the PEI survey addressed two (voting process and postelection) of the three components that are significantly correlated with alternative measures. This is not proof of the efficacy of vignettes, but it does suggest that common signals, as well as the more observable, "moving" parts of the electoral cycle (as opposed to laws and procedures), may be easier to track and evaluate impartially.

Conclusion and Discussion

At least since the days of Tocqueville (2003, 418–419), scholars of comparative politics have been searching for the "imperfect but necessary expedient" of a single metric that does not "lose as much in accuracy as it gains in comprehensiveness." Summary assessments allow us to reduce a bewildering amount of information into something that facilitates learning, not only about the relative standing of a large variety of electoral systems, but also about how differences in various phases of the election cycle affect overall outcomes. At this stage, the loss of accuracy in measurements across U.S. systems is substantial. This warrants not only caution among researchers going forward but further consideration of why the noise-to-signal ratio is low, and what can be done to improve it. It is especially important to get it right early, because the long-term value of an index like the PEI is not so much the focus of this analysis, that is, the cross-sectional validity of the diagnostics. The long-term value is what we learn over multiple electoral cycles, measuring changes in performance over time, changes that will allow us to better understand and forecast the impact of institutional changes on electoral performance.

This analysis has highlighted both strengths and weaknesses of the PEI Index as applied to the United States. The strength of its design is an explicit focus on consequences, with indicators that assess *how well* rights are protected, which groups are *favored*, how *easy* is the act of voting, how *fair* the counting of votes. This emphasis on function over form surely accounts for some of the variance between measures that was discovered, as it aims to overcome the major weakness of legal-institutional approaches to assessment. The downside of a purely institutional approach is that it largely measures the potential for malpractice, as opposed to how much malpractice is actually practiced.

Consider the case of voter eligibility requirements in general, and voter identification laws in particular. A measure of institutional integrity like the analysis from TFP might score a state with no registration requirements or same-day registration without any ID requirement, quite high on integrity, say a 10, and a state with a strict, early registration deadline and strict photo requirement with selective identification credentials very low, say 1. This may be an accurate measure of how permissive, or open, the voting process is, but it is not a direct measure of discrimination. That depends on whether or not those laws actually produce a differential impact on the participation of voters of one type or another. In the specific case of voter ID laws, while it is fairly clear that the intent, as currently applied, is discriminatory (Douglas 2017), there is no consensus on their discriminatory impact (Hajnal, Lajevardi, and Nielson 2017; Hasen 2017a). A key area of future research is the determination of which configurations of laws and procedures have the greatest impact on outcomes.

Of course, as has already been pointed out, the PEI advantage is also potentially its greatest weakness. It is, after all, *perceptions* that are being measured, not actual impact, and perceptions come with their own baggage. In addition to recall error and similar noise introduced by random perceptive mistakes, making normative judgments necessarily draws on the values of respondents in a way that can introduce systematic bias, such as we likely saw in the boundaries measures, relative to the global index.

In light of these two weaknesses, the importance of recorded counts of registration, voting problems, and ballots that the EPI focuses on becomes apparent. Even though these estimates are also largely dependent on survey data and have their own accuracy problems, the administrative records leave less room for value judgments. Moreover, it is in this field where some of the greatest advances have been made in election science. Increased sensitivity in statistical tests are able to identify ever smaller deviations in election returns that signal fraud and selective suppression, and the field of election forensics is developing powerful sets of tools to detect electoral manipulation (Alvarez, Atkeson, and Hall 2012b; Mebane 2017).

Alas, such granular data requirements are the weakness of this approach, limiting its application for global comparative analysis. This feature of electoral systems reflects a more general challenge for global electoral studies. The data intensity of technologically advanced electoral systems likely increases the significance of distinctions that might not be as relevant elsewhere. That, in turn, changes the nature of the problems that become the focus of electoral integrity. Half a century ago, electoral integrity challenges in the United States concerned districts with vastly unequal populations and rather crude methods of preventing citizens from voting. Today challenges to voting rights and electoral integrity involve subtler attempts to discriminate (see Bergman, Tran, and Yates, this volume), requiring ever more demanding techniques to reveal discriminatory effect. The arms race between strategies of political equality and political discrimination grows more complex.

In a relevant sense, then, U.S. election scholars frequently drill down on first world electoral problems. Not unlike the attention now devoted to food allergies in schools throughout the United States, most other countries devote proportionally fewer resources to limiting the dangers of peanuts, as they are still primarily focused on meeting children's basic nutritional needs (Davis 2013). I am not suggesting that such pathologies are not real or that they don't exist in other parts of the world (Boye 2012), but that our food systems have reached a stage where finer distinctions in the nutritional landscape receive more scientific attention.

Nor do I intend to suggest that U.S. elections operate at a higher normative level. The 2017 Senate elections in Alabama saw media reports of long lines, failing voting machines, subtle voter suppression tactics, and negligent underestimation of turnout, leaving many voting precincts ill-prepared for what hit them. Claims of voter suppression may be exaggerated (Lopez 2017), but it is evident that gerrymandering in the state proved so severe that the winning candidate for the U.S. Senate, a Democrat, carried just one of seven congressional districts. Alabama scores low on electoral integrity on many indices for good reasons, but they are different reasons from what was observed 50 years ago. This example demonstrates just how much work remains to be done, both in our scientific study and in the application of evidence-based election policy, which should go hand in hand. As we develop better metrics and better theory about the operation of political institutions, our knowledge will expand, and we will continue to build on the important advances that the Electoral Integrity Project is making.

Notes

1. Principal component analysis confirms that a single integrity factor accounts for 68% of observed component variance in the combined data sets, with a scree plot that shows a single, dominant dimension. Confirmatory factor analysis was conducted using the R package Lavaan, with the addition of semPlot and semTools packages used to inspect model diagnostics.

2. The boundaries component has the lowest loading on electoral integrity (.34) and the highest standardized variance (.88). Overall fit statistics (detailed in online materials) suggest that analysts can be moderately confident in assuming overall equivalence. For the Comparative Fit (CFI) and Tucker-Lewis (TLI) scores, values closer to 1 reflect better fit, while for the root mean squared error (RMSEA), values close to zero indicate better fit.

PART II

CHALLENGES

5

Gerrymandering

DANIEL B. MAGLEBY, MICHAEL D. MCDONALD, JONATHAN KRASNO,
SHAWN J. DONAHUE, AND ROBIN E. BEST

Partisan gerrymandering threatens electoral integrity under two circumstances: either by silencing minority voices or by entrenching one party in majority legislative status regardless of its vote support. In barely competitive states, district lines can be manipulated so that the partisan minority receives no or, at most, de minimis representation. In highly competitive states, district lines can be manipulated so that a party entrenches itself in legislative majority status even when it receives a minority of the vote. Gerrymandering also threatens democratic integrity indirectly, by undermining an electorate's sense of political efficacy and accountability. In the face of partisan gerrymanders, representation and the policy choices that flow from it depend not so much on voters' choices as on mapmakers who organize the outcomes.

At the very least, what we are saying about gerrymandering captures what expert observers of U.S. politics have sensed in recent years. Former U.S. Supreme Court justice John Paul Stevens (2014, 33–56) has called for an antigerrymander constitutional amendment to protect democratic principles. Former president Barack Obama dedicated the early years of his postpresidency to correcting gerrymandering abuses.[1]

The first question is whether alarm sirens about gerrymandering in the American process are justified. The short answer is yes. Our analysis shows that over 60% of the states that could have chosen to manipulate their congressional district lines did so in the 2010–2012 round of redistricting. Given the extent of the problem, what can be done to protect electoral integrity against gerrymandering's corrupting manipulations? One possibility is to let the political process run its course and, where necessary, ask the courts to intervene. To date, but for a few tentative turns in that direction (*Davis v. Bandemer* 1986; *Whitford v. Gill* 2016), courts asked to take that step have seen it as a bridge too far. Why? The U.S. Supreme Court has yet to be convinced there is a manageable standard by which to distinguish a harmful partisan gerrymander from normal politics. Another possibility is to empower people of goodwill to enact fair and effective districts. Such empowerment would surely be an improvement, but it is also likely to prove to be a half-measure. Why? Even people of goodwill need an intelligible standard as a guide for what constitutes fair and effective districting. In either case, therefore, whether anything can be done rests on the ability to apply a standard that validly and reliably identifies a gerrymander.

A valid and reliable standard is possible. We argue, and then show, that coming to such a standard necessarily pivots around the concept of how, when, and where a districting plan dilutes some people's votes. The trappings of gerrymandering, manipulated district boundaries, often with bizarre shapes and associated with seemingly excessive wins by one party, are possibly noteworthy but receive more attention than they are due. More states than not, we find, choose to manipulate district boundaries in ways that are out of line with what could be expected from any sort of partisan blind process. Showing this is not enough. A valid and reliable indicator is needed to distinguish between manipulations that violate electoral integrity and those that do not. The evidence we present seeks to do just that.

Vote dilution: Gerrymander's pivotal characteristic

Partisan gerrymandering is the "practice of dividing a geographical area into electoral districts, often of highly irregular shape, to give a political party an unfair advantage by diluting the opposition's voting strength" (*Vieth v. Jubelirer* 2004, 271n1, quoting *Black's Law Dictionary* 1999, 696). While each of the definition's four elements—irregular shapes, intention, one-party favoritism, and vote dilution—has some role to play when trying to identify and police gerrymandering, the first three are symptoms of gerrymandering that, alone, do not tell us as much as we need to know. For any of those first three elements to play its useful role, it has to be conjoined with the last, vote dilution.

Bizarre district shapes draw attention both because the origin of the word "gerrymander" comes from a lampooning of a salamander-like district shape advanced by Massachusetts governor Elbridge Gerry and because bizarre shapes are a possible sign that mapmakers went out of their way to do something unnatural. However, unless the unnatural something can be shown to impose a decided disadvantage on one group of partisans, reading a gerrymander from shape alone confuses district form with district function.

A focus on intention is also a partial measure. In some situations, handing over mapmaking powers to a body that ignores partisan information can and has worked well in avoiding gerrymanders, for example, under Iowa's Legislative Service Agency (*Economist* 2002; Martin 2016). Elsewhere, as with Arizona's citizen-empowered Redistricting Commission, the case is less clear (*Harris v. Arizona Redistricting Commission* 2016). And in the case of Florida's citizen-adopted state constitutional directive to forbid drawing districts with the intention to favor a political party or incumbent, it is clear that the provision did not prevent a partisan gerrymander (*Romo v. Detzner* 2014). Moreover, as the Supreme Court remarked long ago, in response to an allegation of partisan gerrymandering in Connecticut, a "politically mindless approach may produce, whether intended or not, the most grossly gerrymandered results" (*Gaffney v. Cummings* 1973, 753). Perhaps even more troubling is this: the gerrymandering allegation in that Connecticut case was an objection to the admitted fact that district lines were "drawn with the conscious intent to create a districting plan that would achieve a rough approximation of the state-wide political strengths of the Democratic and Republican Parties" (*Gaffney v. Cummings* 1973, 752). In other words, it was directed at producing an outcome closer to proportional representation than a partisan blind process could be expected to produce. If the challenge had been successful, therefore, reliance on intention alone to outlaw the challenged districts would have resulted in overturning an intention to create fairness, not undermine it, by overcoming the perceived unfairness that partisan residential patterns would have imposed (*Gaffney v. Cummings* 1973, 753–54).

The point of a partisan gerrymander is to favor one party, but claims of favoritism must be considered relative to the votes a party receives, and it is far from clear what a fair translation of votes into seats would look like. The one-time popular cube law (Kendall and Stuart 1950) suggests a party should receive 50% of the seats for 50% of the votes, and for each percentage point above 50 it should win an additional 3% of the seats. More recently, a gerrymandering detection proposal by Nick Stephanopoulos and Eric McGhee (2015) proposes that for each percentage point above 50 a party should win an additional 2% of the seats. Even more widespread, though outside the American political tradition, is a view that fairness requires a one-to-one seat-vote percentage match—that is, direct proportional representation (e.g., Lakeman 1982; Richie and Hill 1999).

The lack of consensus regarding the fair translation of votes into seats makes seat-based claims of gerrymandering problematic; however, the way that biased maps dilute the influence of some votes constitutes a gerrymander's more fundamental attack on electoral integrity. Moreover, the Court's definition of gerrymandering requires that those making the allegation of gerrymandering show that an electoral map dilutes votes. Recall, an enacted plan is a gerrymander when it intends to dilute and does in fact dilute the votes of one set of partisans so much that the districts give the other party an unfair advantage. One way to dilute votes is by undervaluing a vote's weight in determining representation. That sort of dilution is most easily recognized when multimember or at-large election systems are used in conjunction with plurality decision rules. For instance, in an at-large system with patterns of strongly polarized voting one party can win all the seats in a jurisdiction—state, county, city—with just over 50% of the votes. A slate of, say, seven city council members could be elected through an at-large system where seven Democrats versus seven Republicans contest the seats, and the 51% Democratic voters outvote the 49% Republicans with regard to each and every seat and elect seven Democrats.

The same can happen through clever cracking gerrymanders. In a strongly polarized voting jurisdiction, in which party support is more or less stable from election to election, all districts can be drawn so that one party holds a reliably predictable majority in all districts.

Where voting patterns are more fluid, a second form of gerrymandering can be used. In packing gerrymanders votes can be diluted by collecting a large segment of the voters likely to support one party and packing them in one or some small number of districts. The outcome produces a guarantee that the packed partisans win a small number of districts with surplus vote majorities but come up short of vote majorities in all the remaining districts, even if the disadvantaged partisans cast a majority of votes statewide. With that, the party's votes have to have been diluted, underweighted, since such a violation of majority rule can occur only if all votes do not count equally. This form of dilution is an offense to the fairness element in the democratic promise of *fair* and effective representation, inasmuch as the votes of individuals in the two partisan groups are weighted differently.

In short summary, it is vital to recognize that gerrymandering's offense is a violation of core democratic principles, not a mere partisan complaint that "my party deserves more representation." The voices of all people count in their official sovereign capacity as voters, with no exclusion based on political preferences, and all votes are to carry equal weight, with no persistent violation of majority rule. Justice Byron White put it this way: in line with fair and effective representation, combating gerrymandering shows a "preference for a level of parity between votes and representation sufficient to ensure that significant minority voices are heard and that majorities are not consigned to minority status" (*Davis v. Bandemer* 1986, 125n9).

Recognizing gerrymanders and their effects

The leading indicators of the vote dilution associated with both cracking and packing gerrymanders can be read from characteristics of the vote percentage distribution among districts. Spreading votes as uniformly as practical in a cracking gerrymander compresses the vote distribution's standard deviation. For instance, extreme cracking would have all districts with identical vote splits—say, 58:42—so that the standard deviation is zero. Differential packing's leading indicator is observable in the skew of the vote percentage distribution. Skew is readily observable by comparing the median district vote percentage to the mean district vote percentage (McDonald and Best 2015; Best et al. 2018). In a five-district state with a typical 52:48 partisan split, a packing gerrymander could be enacted by arranging voters so that the expected vote percentage distribution is 30, 30, 35, 82, and 83. The median district percentage is 35 (i.e., the vote percentage in the middle district after arranging all percentages from low to high), and the mean district percentage is 52. Absent an unlikely large vote shift in its favor, the 52% vote-majority party can expect to continue to win only a minority of seats, just two of five districts. If we presume that partisan votes accrue uniformly across all districts, the median versus mean difference in our simple example (35–52 = –17) indicates that the vote-majority party wins its two packed districts, and only its two packed districts, when it receives anything less than two-thirds of the statewide vote.

Setting a baseline

A standard deviation that is too small and a vote percentage distribution that is too skewed are relative matters. The relativity of interest is properly set by a state's partisan residential patterns. This is so for two reasons. First, if residential patterns have Republicans and Democrats residentially integrated (e.g., as are, say, men and women for an extreme example) or if they are strongly residentially segregated (e.g., as are people of different races in several states and communities), then a small standard deviation or a large skew associated with a set of districts reflect residential patterns, without, necessarily, an intention to gerrymander. Second, by using a state's residential patterns as the benchmark, an inquiry into intentions becomes self-executing, as opposed to having to deal with the potential discomfiture associated with trying to discern what was in the minds of a collective decision-making body.[2] Given both a rule that commands that the standard deviation and skew remain within specified bounds and a proposed plan that fails to abide by the rule, it becomes self-evident that the enactment knowingly, with intention, ignored the rule's directive.

To arrive at benchmark readings for states where congressional district lines could have been gerrymandered (states with three or more districts), the power of computers developed in recent years can be employed to organize a counterfactual by drawing thousands of maps of each state's districts (e.g., Chen and Rodden 2013; Cho and Liu 2016; Magleby and Mosesson 2018). Our partisan-blind map drawing relies on a graph-partitioning algorithm method proposed and implemented by Daniel Magleby and Daniel Mosesson (2018). Graph-partitioning algorithms assign related computational tasks to cores in a computer's processor (or nodes in a cluster or supercomputer) in a way that balances computational load across processors. In its application to drawing district maps, the algorithm assigns adjacent (contiguous) voter tabulation districts (VTDs) to legislative districts in a way that balances population counts across districts.[3] A graph-partitioning approach proves highly efficient and so far as can be determined shows no indication of bias (see Magleby and Mosesson 2018). The only constraints we impose in the analysis that follows are that each district's territory is contiguous and all districts have roughly equal populations (+/– 1%).

In sequence, we first use the VTDs shape files provided by the U.S. Census Bureau to draw 10,000 computer-generated partisan-blind plans for 36 of 38 states, not including Oregon due to its reliance on vote-by-mail, nor Kentucky due to its choice not to participate in the Census Bureau's geographical information system for reporting of precinct boundaries. We limit our analysis to the 38 states with three or more congressional districts, making a gerrymander possible; the remaining 12 states have only one or two congressional districts, making packing and cracking gerrymanders impossible. For each of the 10,000 partisan-blind plans, we next aggregate the VTDs-level *Daily Kos* political data to the computer-generated districts and calculate the standard deviation and median-mean difference for the distribution of each map of the districts drawn by the computer (see Wolf 2014). The pattern we observe in standard deviations and median-mean skewness that arise in a state's set of partisan-blind maps characterizes the patterns of cracking and packing that would arise as a consequence of that state's residential patterns.

Since data provided by the *Daily Kos* and computer-generated maps are an important element of our analysis, it is worth pausing for a moment to discuss both. First, the *Daily Kos* provides election returns for statewide elections in all 50 states. Stephen Wolf (2014) of the *Daily Kos* provides versions of these data disaggregated to VTDs. Using county-level returns, Wolf assigns votes to VTDs according to votes cast in the VTD in the 2008 presidential election and the proportion of the county's population living in a VTD. The disaggregation of Democratic votes to VTDs can be characterized by the following equation:

$$d_i^t = \delta_i D^t,$$

where d_i^t is the estimated number of votes cast for a Democratic candidate in VTD i in election t, δ_i is the proportion of a county's votes cast in VTD i for Barack Obama in 2008, and D^t is the county-level count of Democratic votes for election t. To understand how this equation works, suppose in 2008 a VTD cast 10% of a county's votes for Obama and 15% of a county's votes for McCain. Now suppose 100 votes were cast for the Democratic candidate for governor and 200 votes were cast for the Republican in an election. The equation estimates the VTD-level Democratic vote total will be 10% of the county Democratic vote, or 10 votes for the Democrat. Wolf estimates Republican votes by substituting the proportion of a county's 2008 McCain vote cast in VTD i for δ_i and the county-level count of Republican votes in election t for D^t. Applying the equation to the Republican returns, Wolf would estimate that the hypothetical VTD-level Republican vote is 15% of the county-level Republican vote, or 30 votes for a Republican candidate.[4]

Analytical sequence

Technological developments make it possible to ask, first, whether an enacted district plan shows signs of manipulation out of line with expectations consistent with partisan residential patterns in a state. Being "out of line" requires a statement about the qualities of interest and their magnitude. Because compressing the standard deviation of a vote distribution is a necessary consequence of cracking, it is the quality to look for as the leading indication of a cracking gerrymander. A large skew in a vote distribution is a necessary consequence of a packing gerrymander, making it the quality to look for as the leading indication of a packing gerrymander. The magnitude for how far out of line with expectations is a judgment call. The decision rule we use is to say that a standard deviation is too low or a skew is too large when it is more likely than not out of line with expectations. We implement that rule, a sort of preponderance of the evidence rule, by looking for whether an enacted plan's standard deviation or skew is within the interquartile range (i.e., the middle 50%) from the 10,000 partisan-blind plans generated through our computer algorithm. It is not just any single election outside the range that we take to indicate manipulation. We are looking for structural manipulations that could be expected to persist under a variety of vote distributions from various elections. Thus we are looking for states where all elections available for analysis are persistently outside the interquartile range (barring special circumstances, such as hugely lopsided percentages where one party receives 60% or more of the vote).

From that first step we have good information about cracking and packing that, with respect to analytical trappings, appear to be intended rather than the consequence of partisan residential patterns. To take account of whether the manipulations dilute votes, further checks are needed. This requires checking whether one partisan group suffers a harm of the sort produced by cracking or packing. Where a standard deviation is lower than expected, the check on vote dilution involves looking at whether disadvantaged partisans are able to gain nothing more than de minimis representation. Where a skew is larger than expected, the question is whether the disadvantaged partisans are able to win a majority of the congressional delegation seats when they win a majority of the votes in a state.

In all, the election data we use cover 365 statewide elections among the 36 states analyzed. The average number of elections per state is 13 (median number is 11), with Nevada (3 elections), Arkansas (5), Maryland (5), and Tennessee (5) on the low end, and Texas (22), North Carolina (23), and Alabama (24) on the high end. All elections are for statewide office, which is both necessary and proper. It is necessary because to establish benchmarks for partisan residential patterns there is no sensible way to rearrange votes from legislative elections in our 10,000 alternative district plans. It is proper because U.S. House election results reflect more than the placement of district boundaries. In other words, the results of congressional elections are influenced by the first-order effect of district boundaries on district partisan dispositions but also by the endogenous second-order effects on the nature of the within-district two-party competition. That is, candidate quality, campaign contributions, campaign organization, and the like depend on where district lines are placed, to say nothing about districts that go uncontested.

Findings, determinations, and cautions

We begin as a mapmaking authority could, by looking at the lay of the land in a state, at the expected standard deviations and skew likely to arise as a result of the partisan residential patterns. After surveying the manipulations and detailing their types, we turn to a series of case-specific applications. The first makes clear how it is possible to use the standard deviation and skew as leading indicators to show that a gerrymander has been enacted. The second follows on with two other case-specific applications to demonstrate how a cautious application of the proposed analysis holds safe districting plans that at first sight might appear to be a gerrymander but really are not.

Findings

Of the 36 states we can check for whether they could have drawn maps outside the bounds of expectations associated with cracking (suppressed variation) or packing (skew in the distribution), 22 did so. That is a remarkable number. More than 60% of the states that could have manipulated their maps did manipulate them. We hasten to add, ours is a conservative count. We infer a gerrymander only in those states for which *every* election for which we have data exhibits patterns consistent with manipulation through district delineation. We refrain from making conclusions in states where even one election fails to show a significant difference from what we might expect based on the set of neutral, partisan-blind maps. Three states miss inclusion because just a small number of elections had an outcome within the middle 50% of computer-drawn hypothetical maps: Indiana (1 of 11 elections), Missouri (1 of 15), and Texas (2 of 22).

A map of the 48 U.S. continental states shown in Figure 5.1 identifies the mapmaking manipulation by type and party favoritism. Five states enacted maps with standard deviations persistently lower than could reasonably be expected from their residential patterns: Connecticut, Iowa, Maryland, Nebraska, and Utah. Two of those, Connecticut and Maryland, favor Democrats. Not surprisingly, in all three elections from 2012 to 2016 Democrats were elected to all five of Connecticut's House seats and seven of eight of Maryland's House seats. Nebraska and Utah tilt strongly Republican, but despite the apparent cracking in both states, a Democrat was able to win a 2014 election in Nebraska's Omaha-based district, and a Utah Democratic incumbent was able to win reelection in 2012 (and then retired). Iowa does not lean strongly in one partisan direction or the other, and in 2012 Iowans elected two Democrats and two Republicans to the U.S. House.

The choice to enact maps that persistently pack one group of partisan voters more than residential patterns indicate is more widespread and decidedly more favorable to Republicans. Of the 18 states that packed one set of partisans beyond

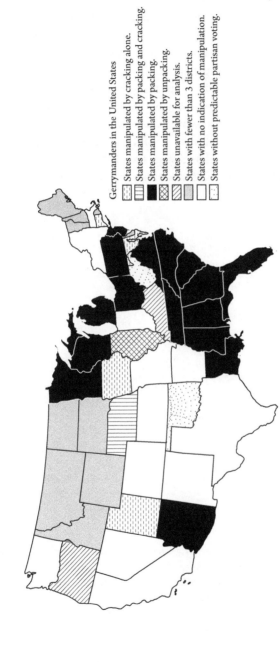

Gerrymanders in the United States

░ States manipulated by cracking alone.
▦ States manipulated by packing and cracking.
■ States manipulated by packing.
▨ States manipulated by unpacking.
▧ States unavailable for analysis.
▒ States with fewer than 3 districts.
░ States with no indication of manipulation.
⣿ States without predictable partisan voting.

Figure 5.1 U.S. States Categorized by the Presence and Type of Gerrymander.
Note: States are categorized as exhibiting no indication of a gerrymander, exhibiting patterns of packing gerrymanders, exhibiting patterns of cracking gerrymanders, having fewer than three districts, not sharing their VTD boundaries with the Census Bureau, or exhibiting unpredictable patterns of partisan voting.

expectations, only two states did so in favor of Democrats: Arizona and Illinois. The other 16 states created maps that could hamstring Democrats with a form of electoral bias that makes it difficult for them to win a majority of a delegation's seats even when Democrats cast a majority of votes.

Figure 5.2 offers a graphic view of the magnitude of the differences in bias the map-making authorities chose in the 18 states that packed, in two cases, unpacked relative to expectations. The 45-degree line indicates a precise match between observed and expected bias from residential patterns. States above that line chose a degree of bias more favorable to Democrats than expected, and states below it chose a degree of bias favorable to Republicans. Arizona stands out for its favoritism to Democrats, resulting in about 1.4 points of bias favorable to Democrats, whereas Arizona's residential patterns run about 1.4 points in favor of Republicans. Illinois and Nebraska also stand out. Illinois manipulated its district lines in a manner strongly favorable to Democrats relative to a partisan-blind process, and Nebraska's manipulation did

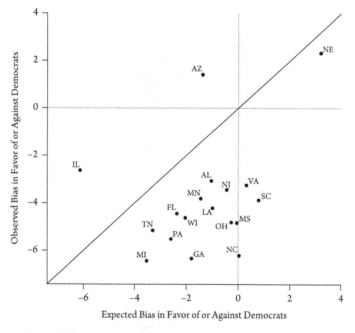

Figure 5.2 Electoral Bias.
Notes: The match between observed and expected electoral bias, symmetry, among U.S. states is persistently biased in favor of one party beyond expectations. States above that line chose a degree of bias more favorable to Democrats than expected (e.g., Arizona), and states below it chose a degree of bias favorable to Republicans (e.g., Michigan). *Persistent* bias means that every election available for analysis in a state has observed bias running against one party. *The expected bias* is based on 10,000 computer-generated districts requiring contiguity and near-equal populations (+1%) and using only population counts as input. *Beyond expectations* means a value of observed bias in each and every election is outside the interquartile range (the middle 50%) of the null set of 10,000 computer-generated partisan-blind districting plans.

something similar in favor of Republicans. As we discuss below, however, neither of the Illinois nor Nebraska manipulations can be read as troubling, let alone invidious. The remaining 15 states chose districting plans biased against Democrats. Several of the most strongly anti-Democratic biases are in southern states: North Carolina, Mississippi, South Carolina, Georgia, Virginia, and Louisiana. They added biases of 3.25 and 6.25 points disadvantaging Democrats. Ohio's anti-Democratic bias is also in that range, while Wisconsin, Michigan, Pennsylvania, and New Jersey are not far behind.

It certainly can be considered alarming that more that 60% of the states that could possibly manipulate their district lines to favor a party did so in the 2012 round of congressional redistricting. That set of findings alone, however, is not all that needs to be known for the manipulations' potential effects on electoral integrity to be combated. In particular, we need to know whether the standard deviation and skew indicators we have been focusing on are up to the task of revealing vote dilution. And we need to know whether their use can be applied in ways cautious enough that they do not overreach and indict as a gerrymander a districting plan that needs to be held safe because it does not actually produce vote dilution harm.

Determinations

On the question of whether the standard deviation and skew are valid and reliable leading indicators of manipulations that result in harmful gerrymandering, we work through the details of Maryland's possible cracking gerrymander and Ohio's possible packing gerrymander. Is the harm self-evident as we look for whether the voices of one set of partisans are largely excluded from representation as a result of an artificially reduced standard deviation? And, we ask, is the harm self-evident as we look for whether the votes of one set of partisans are undervalued because mapmakers have chosen to enact a set of districts that skew the vote percentage distribution?

Maryland. We have the results of five statewide Maryland elections from 2008 to 2012: 2008 President; 2010 Governor, U.S. Senate, and Comptroller; 2012 President. As we know, Maryland leans strongly in favor of Democrats, and in these five elections the Democratic candidate won between 57 and 64% of the two-party vote statewide. This is the kind of weakly competitive circumstance when a cracking gerrymander can be quite effective.

The left portion of Figure 5.3 traces the actual and expected district win percentages across the five elections.[5] In each case, regardless of the vote received, the Democrat carried seven of eight districts (87.5% of the seats). A generous majority bonus of about a 4-to-1 responsiveness, for example $(87.5 - 50) / (59.4 - 50) = (37.5 / 9.4)$, is remarkable on its face but arguably plausible depending on partisan residential patterns. This indicates that an increase in statewide vote of 1% yields a 4% increase in seats carried. The plausibility is belied by the comparison

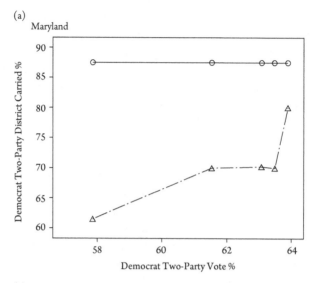

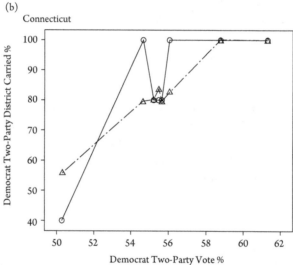

Figure 5.3 Bias in Maryland and Connecticut.

Note: ○ = observed. △= expected. Traces of observed and expected seat-vote correspondence illustrating evidence of districting plans that crack a minority party's votes and lead to vote dilution, in Maryland but not Connecticut, through near-exclusion of minority party members. Expectations are based on 10,000 computer-generated districting plans, requiring contiguity and near-equal populations (+1%) and using only population counts as input.

to expected districts carried at each and every level of the vote. In all five elections Republicans are expected to carry two or three of the eight districts.

The inference is even more convincing when set in contrast to another state with a suppressed standard deviation, Connecticut. The right side of Figure 5.3 traces the same actual and expected district win percentages across Connecticut's eight elections for which we have data. Here we see that Republicans do better than expected in one election, as well as expected in five of eight elections, and worse than expected in two of the eight elections. These results, unlike Maryland's, are unremarkable. The difference is that Connecticut's residential patterns by themselves produce small standard deviations in the vote percentage distributions and that while the district lines as drawn produce persistently lower standard deviations than expected, the persistence of the observed versus expected standard deviation differences are not especially large.

The inference is clear and, we think, indisputable. Combining the fact of Maryland's cracking of Republican votes, as indicated by an unexpectedly small standard deviation, with the unfavorable results for Republican candidates, supplies essential evidence that Maryland enacted a cracking gerrymander.

Ohio. Ohio's mapmaking enterprise, prior to both the 2002 and 2012 elections, found agreement across party lines. This was despite the fact that in both instances the Democrats were fully aware that what was about to be enacted was essentially acknowledged as a pro-Republican gerrymander (see Barone and McCutcheon 2013, 1291–92; McDonald and Best 2015, 325–26). Despite their foreknowledge, Ohio Democrats were apparently willing to trade away dilution of their voters' votes to secure favorable treatment of their incumbents. One revealing consequence of their 2012 trade was that President Obama won the state in 2012 with upward of 51% of the two-party vote but won a majority in just 4 of 16 congressional districts. In 2012, 2014, and 2016 Democratic House candidates won those same four districts, and only those four. The average skew, median district percentage minus mean district percentage, among the 10 Ohio elections is 4.8 points adverse to Democrats, in comparison to a residential pattern Democratic disadvantage of 0.3. That Democrats would have to overcome the 4.8 percentage point bias working against them when they receive a vote majority implies that Democrats would need something on the order of 55% of the statewide vote to win a majority of the state's districts.

Figure 5.4 traces the actual and expected seat percentage returns across the wide range of votes in 10 statewide elections, running from about 41 to 60%. As expected, based on the median-mean comparison, in the three elections when Democrats won 51.7, 52.4, and 53.3% of the vote, they won seat minorities of four, five, and six seats (of 16). Clearly the districts are arranged in ways that dilute Democrats' votes—a Democratic vote majority of even 53% does not have them carrying a majority of the delegation's seats. One other matter requires mention. The graph reveals that the shortfall in seats is a poor indicator of vote dilution, for it shows that Democrats actually carry more seats than expected in 4 of the 10 races examined. Those above-expected wins come, however, when Democrats are winning less than 45% of the vote or more than 58%. This tells us not to try to read packing gerrymanders from seat rewards above and below expectations in some sort of general sense. Rather the focal point has to be on violations of majority rule. In other words, the critically

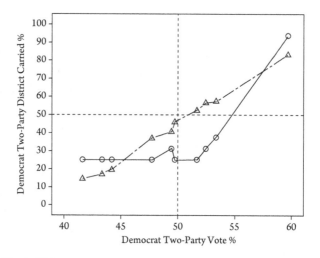

Figure 5.4 Bias in Ohio.

Note: ○ = observed. △ = expected. Observed and expected seat-vote correspondence in Ohio, illustrating the shortfall in winning a seat majority with a vote majority. Expectations are based on 10,000 computer-generated districting plans, requiring contiguity and near-equal populations (+1%) and using only population counts as input.

important matter as it relates to vote dilution via a packing gerrymander is not per se winning too few districts. Rather, the democratic offense from a packing gerrymander is entrenching one party in legislative majority status even when it is the vote-minority party. Packing gerrymanders are willing to guarantee the disadvantaged party a few seats, even a few seats above fair expectations, but they do so at the cost of keeping the disadvantaged party in minority status even when they win a vote majority.

Cautions

While Ohio is a clear example of a packing gerrymander, what about states where majority rule is never violated? We consider two states where there are reasonable suspicions of manipulation outside the bounds of expectations associated with residential patterns, Illinois and Georgia, but their congressional maps might not be confidently labeled as gerrymanders. Both, of course, have huge population centers that are very heavily Democratic (Chicago and Atlanta). Democrats often hold sway in Illinois politics, but Republicans have still managed to win several statewide elections. In contrast, Republican dominance of Georgia politics is so complete that Democrats have not been winning statewide vote majorities and are not likely to do so anytime soon (although the gap in presidential elections has been narrowing). In fewer words, these two states serve as useful examples of how caution should be applied in interpreting vote dilution from packing.

Illinois. A few weeks before the legislature passed and the governor signed the Illinois congressional redistricting plan, a writer for the *Christian Science Monitor* labeled it "a radical Illinois gerrymander" (Greenbaum 2011). After enactment, and in response to a challenge in federal court by Republicans, one court called the plan "a blatant political move to increase the number of Democratic congressional seats," and another said it was "enacted in large part to give Democrats a partisan advantage" (quoted in Pearson 2011). The allegations beg important questions: Radical by what standard? An increase in Democratic seats or a grant of a Democratic advantage relative to what, exactly?

Our analysis, starting with the display in Figure 5.2, makes the suspicions understandable and also indicates why they are misplaced. Relative to how biased against Democrats a partisan-blind plan in Illinois could have been, the enacted plan reduced the bias. Importantly, however, it did not do away with the bias. Even with the manipulation relative to a partisan-blind effort, the Illinois congressional district plan operated with a bias against Democrats. That such a manipulation ought to be overturned because the bias against Democrats should be worse is an affront to sound reasoning. Who is to say it is or should be impermissible to reduce the unfairness that residential patterns would have otherwise created?

Figure 5.5 traces the observed and expected districts carried by Illinois Democrats contesting statewide office in relation to their vote percentages. Two important facts stand out. Most important, even with the manipulations that helped Democrats, reducing the would-be anti-Democratic bias of between 4 and 7.5 points from residential patterns to an anti-Democratic bias of 1.5 to 4.5 points, Democratic candidates carried 6 of 16 districts with 49% of the vote and 7 of 16 districts with 50.5% of the vote. Manipulated? Yes. Harm to Republicans? No. Second, overall, whatever relative advantage the Democrats' corrective provided, it did nothing more than structure a pattern of district wins by Democratic candidates much in line with expectations.

Georgia. The Georgia congressional districting plan is 4 to 5 points more biased against Democrats than expectations from our 10,000 partisan-blind maps, which by themselves show Democrats would be disadvantaged by bias running 1.3 to 2.2 points against them. Taken together, residential bias plus additional chosen bias, the overall bias would appear to severely hamstring Democrats by a need to win something on the order of 56 to 57% of the statewide vote in order to carry a majority of the state's 14 districts. There might be truth to that in theory, but the facts of Georgia politics undercut the theory in practice.

Democratic candidates in Georgia, among the 15 elections on which we have data, typically receive about 43% of the vote. None of the 15 elections shows a Democrat winning more than 47%. In short, it is not all that plausible to think Democrats can win a majority of the vote. If they did, a skew of 4.5 to 7.5 points adverse to Democrats would be a large handicap to overcome just to abide by democracy's majoritarian ethic. Without the reasonable prospects of winning a majority, however,

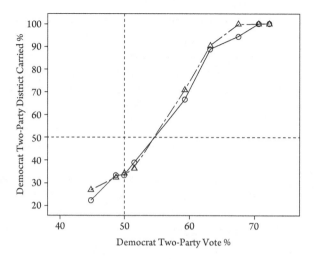

Figure 5.5 Bias in Illinois.
Note: ○ = observed. Δ = expected. Expectations are based on 10,000 computer-generated districting plans, requiring contiguity and near-equal populations (+1%) and using only population counts as input. In this case, allegations of gerrymandering are not reflected in a partisan advantage.

labeling Georgia's packing a districting plan that dilutes Democratic votes is not factual. Indeed a look at the trace of districts carried relative to votes in Figure 5.6 shows that among the 15 available elections Democratic candidates carried more districts than expected 14 times. That, as was true in the Ohio analysis, is the nature of packing gerrymanders. When the disadvantaged party receives relatively low voter support, the districts carried can actually run above expectations. Because the packing causes no knowable harm in this sort of circumstance, it is wrong to label such a districting plan a gerrymander.

Conclusion

Democracy as a philosophy and as a procedure holds that the majority and minority are entitled to some voice in government, and in forming a majority every voter counts the same. Gerrymandering has the power to undermine both precepts. In the United States, as many observers have sensed, gerrymandering is undermining the democratic integrity of U.S. House elections, and likely very many state legislative elections. Our evidence reveals that a sizable majority of states, over 60%, that could have gone out of their way to manipulate district boundaries in ways unexplainable by the kinds of districts that partisan-blind processes produce did engage in some form of manipulation. That, by itself, is an important fact: given the opportunity to manipulate, districting processes currently in use often take the opportunity. In the run-up to the 2012 House elections it can be added that this was

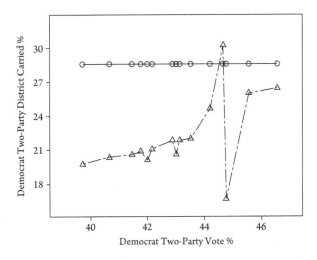

Figure 5.6 Bias in Georgia.

Note: ○ = observed. △ = expected. Expectations are based on 10,000 computer-generated districting plans, requiring contiguity and near-equal populations (+1%) and using only population counts as input. This case illustrates how packing of Democrats does not disadvantaged the party where its vote totals are neither observed nor expected to reach a majority.

true in four states that have rules imposing a supposed form of neutral or bipartisan process: Iowa (cracked more than a partisan-blind process), along with Arizona, Florida, and New Jersey (packed more than a partisan-blind process).

Sometimes offenses to what is thought to be the right and proper course of action are problems we just have to live with because we do not have knowledge about how to confront them. For at least some observers, including the U.S. courts to date, this is their reaction to trying to combat gerrymandering. In sequence we have shown, first, that recent advances in technology make it possible to know whether a districting plan is inside or outside the bounds of what a partisan-blind process would produce. Second, by knowing what qualities of the vote distribution to look to for leading indications of gerrymandering—that is, standard deviation and skew in the vote distribution—it is possible to know when manipulations are suspect. Third, for a districting plan with suspicious manipulation, it is straightforward to check for whether a suspicious manipulation is likely to produce gerrymandering harm in the form of vote dilution:

1. Does a districting plan show signs of cracking (low standard deviation) or packing (large skew) outside the bounds that is more likely than not to be the result of residential patterns?
2. Does a districting plan with an unreasonably low standard deviation thwart the ability of a minority to win anything more than a de minimis number of districts?

3. Does a districting plan with an unreasonably large skew thwart the ability of a party to win a majority of the districts when it wins a majority of the vote?

Each of these questions is answerable as a factual matter. A willingness to ask them, or a rule that requires asking them, would carry us a long way toward combating gerrymandering.

Notes

1. See National Democratic Redistricting Committee 2017, at https://democraticredistricting. com/.
2. We accept, without endorsing, that as a definitional and legal matter, gerrymandering requires a showing of intent. Our reluctance to endorse rests on a recognition of the practical and constitutional arguments that warn against making intention a necessary condition. In *Reynolds v. Sims* (1964, 566) the Supreme Court emphasized its role in protecting a constitutional right: "We are admonished not to restrict the power of the States to impose differing views as to political philosophy on their citizens. We are cautioned about the dangers of entering into political thickets and mathematical quagmires. Our answer is this: a denial of constitutionally protected rights demands judicial protection; our oath and our office require no less of us." Reading those words in conjunction with Justice Marshall's quoting of John Hart Ely's words on the role of intention gives one pause. When the element of intention took an elevated position in racial vote dilution jurisprudence, Justice Marshall objected: "It . . . cannot be emphasized too strongly that analysis of motivation is appropriate only to claims of improper discrimination in the distribution of goods that are constitutionally gratuitous. . . . However, where what is being denied is something to which the complainant has a substantive constitutional right—either because it is granted by terms of the Constitution, or because it is essential to the effective functioning of a democratic government—the reasons for its denial are irrelevant" (Justice Marshall dissenting, *City of Mobile v. Bolden* 1980, 121n21; Ely 1978, 1160–1161, emphasis and footnotes omitted).
3. Voter tabulation districts roughly correspond to state-designated voting precincts; however, the correspondence to actual voting precincts is not precise. In practice, states reprecinct more frequently than they redistrict. States share their precinct boundaries with the Census Bureau once every 10 years, so the VTDs we use to develop our neutral maps were almost certainly out of date by the 2012 and 2014 elections, requiring us to rely on estimated vote totals by VTD, described below. On the other hand, the Census Bureau does ensure that the population reported for VTDs is accurate.
4. To arrive at these estimates, Wolf (2014) clearly assumes that VTDs will perform roughly as they did in the 2008 presidential election. Of course, estimating VTD performance relies on the additional assumption that VTD-level vote tallies for the 2008 election are accurate. Even if the assumptions hold true, the process of disaggregation introduces measurement error. To check the amount of error, we compared the *Daily Kos* data to official VTD returns in Wisconsin, where the state provides official tallies of VTD-level votes. For every election covered by the data, we found the estimated returns provided by the *Daily Kos* were closely correlated with the official returns. Correlations of the *Daily Kos* numbers and official vote totals range from 0.87 to 0.97.
5. These figures combine the observed seats carried by a party in various elections and the average seat carried by that party in the set of 10,000 hypothetical maps. For each of the elections included in our analysis we aggregate votes cast for a candidate for statewide office to the district boundaries of the official congressional districts; we make the same

aggregation to each of the districts in the hypothetical, computer-drawn maps of congressional districts. We denote the percentage of seats carried in the actual map with a circle, and the average percentage of seats carried in the hypothetical maps with a triangle. For example, suppose a candidate for statewide office received 45% of the vote, but received more than 50% of the vote in only 1 out of 5 districts. Likewise, suppose that, aggregating the same votes to the districts in the hypothetical maps, the candidate received more than 50% of the vote in 2 out of 5 districts on average. For 45% of the votes, we would record the observed seat percentage (from the actual map) as 20% and the expected seat percentage (from the hypothetical map) as 40%. We do these calculations for each statewide contest for which we have data.

6

Voter Identification

ELIZABETH BERGMAN, DARI SYLVESTER TRAN, AND PHILIP YATES

> For all the fervor of the current debate over voter ID laws, there's a star-
> tling lack of good data on their effects.
>
> Newkirk (2017)

Free and fair elections are of paramount importance, considered by many to be the lifeblood of a thriving democracy. The act of voting is thought to be one of the most fundamental means of holding elected officers accountable and providing a check on power. For these reasons, the integrity of democratic elections needs to be secure. However, electoral integrity involves several rival values that can be in tension with one another, including access to voting rights and holding secure elections free from fraud (see Pallister, this volume). Specifically, election laws that aim to reduce purported fraud may do so at a cost of disenfranchising qualified citizens.

One reform that has garnered much attention in the past several years is voter identification laws. In states where voter ID laws are in place, they vary considerably. The laws can be strict, where identification is required before a voter is eligible to cast a ballot, or not strict, where ID is requested, though not required.[1] In recent years, more U.S. states have been adopting increasingly strict measures, with proponents arguing that voter fraud is pervasive and must be stopped with definitive legal measures such as voter ID laws. Republicans, including Kansas secretary of state Kris Kobach and President Donald Trump, have claimed that anywhere from thousands to millions of ineligible voters were allowed to vote in the 2016 presidential election, leading many to question the integrity of the election. Data from Gallup World Poll (2018), for instance, shows that in America, those believing that their country's elections are honest declined from 42% in 2012 to 30% in 2016.

On the other hand, opponents of ID laws argue that they are an exaggerated, often politically motivated response to an extremely rare phenomenon (Minnite 2010). Moreover, several critics have claimed that ID laws are tantamount to a new poll tax; laws requiring state-issued identification to ensure voter eligibility may ultimately overburden individuals without the resources to obtain ID, thus acting as an effective means of suppressing targeted groups (see de Alth 2009; Hasen 2016a). They further reason that it is no coincidence that Republicans are the strongest advocates for ID laws because the true motivation behind such laws is to keep voters more likely to vote Democratic from the polls (Horwitz 2016a; Wines 2016). To date, we are not aware of any empirical investigation of this claim, even if there seems to be evidence that party elites espouse this view (Graham 2016). This chapter provides initial empirical analysis to shed light on the question: Do voter ID laws have partisan effects on election outcomes?

Prior to the 2016 presidential election, a number of events began to shift the landscape of voter identification laws in the United States (see Hasen, this volume), particularly as states increasingly found themselves mired in legal battles over the legislation. Among the most prominent were the U.S. Supreme Court's allowing an appeal court's decision to stand to invalidate North Carolina's voter identification law and the loosening of Texas's voter identification law. Nevertheless, by November 2016, poll worker and public misunderstanding of the status of these changes caused voters to face inconsistent application or misapplication of voter identification laws. Election Protection, a nonpartisan organization led by Lawyers' Committee for Civil Rights under Law (2016), reported widespread problems with voter identification law application in Texas, Wisconsin, and even in areas where no such laws exist, such as California and New Jersey. For example, while Texas has one of the strictest ID laws on the books, ongoing legal battles led to a court-ordered temporary fix that would allow individuals without required ID to sign an affidavit and cast a vote. Despite the temporary fix, voters without ID were not informed of this option and were turned away from polling booths. Michigan also has a nonstrict voter ID law on the books, such that poll workers may request a voter to show ID, but it is not a requirement to vote. Nevertheless poll workers incorrectly denied voters without ID the right to vote (Lawyers' Committee for Civil Rights under Law 2016).

The cumulative deleterious impact of the misapplication of voter identification laws ranges from inconveniencing voters who are asked to produce identification when none is required to the outright suppression of voting rights of individuals who are legally entitled to vote. Moreover, the existence of such laws may discourage voters from ever appearing at the polls in the first place, to avoid the possibility of being turned away due to a lack of appropriate identification. This effect would be more difficult to verify, though the 2016 Survey of the Performance of American Elections found that 52% of voter respondents in states with nonstrict voter ID laws believed that they would not have been allowed to vote had they not provided photo identification (Stewart 2017a).

What, then, are we to make of voter identification requirements? In this chapter we first provide an overview of what scholars have found to date in terms of causes and consequences of voter identification requirements in the American states. After describing some of the limitations in the current body of work, we offer new research to illuminate the debate about the impact of voter ID on elections. More specifically, in the wake of the 2016 presidential election, when 32 states had a voter identification law in place (and 14 of those states had new restrictions), did voter ID laws impact party vote share?

Causes and consequences of voter ID laws

Scholarly work on the political causes and consequences of voter ID laws is emerging, although findings are mixed. A small body of work has focused on the variables that increase a state's likelihood of adopting ID laws. For example, McKee (2015) and Hicks et al. (2015) found that state legislator support for stricter voter ID laws was significantly predicted by the racial and electoral composition of districts, even more so than partisan affiliation. Biggers and Hanmer (2017) find that change of control from Democratic state leadership to Republican in both the executive and legislative branches predicts the adoption of voter ID laws.

Other studies have explored the consequences of adopting voter ID laws, though much of the notable work on the impact of the laws was published prior to 2010, before many states had adopted strict versions of voter ID. One could surmise that studies conducted in the time period before many states adopted strict ID laws would be less likely to find significant effects of ID requirements on voter behavior. Nevertheless, several studies found the presence of ID laws decreased turnout levels in general and particularly among historically marginalized groups (de Alth 2009, 185–202; Barreto, Nuno, and Sanchez 2009). Specifically, Barreto, Nuno, and Sanchez found that particular demographic groups—the elderly, racial minorities, and low-income individuals—are significantly less likely to possess the necessary identification required to vote compared to their Caucasian, nonelderly, and higher income counterparts. Still, other studies found that there could be factors that mitigate the negative effects of voter ID on turnout. This includes time for voters to become aware of and adjust to new voting requirements, and active campaigns to increase awareness of changes in voting requirements (Vercellotti and Andersen 2009; Citrin, Green, and Levy 2014; de Alth 2009, 185; Lynch and Bright 2017).

The most recent work has tried to zero in on the differential effects that voter identification laws have on subgroups. Analysis of voter identification laws by Hajnal, Lajevardi, and Nielson (2017) found turnout depressing effects on racial and ethnic minority groups across elections utilizing Cooperative Congressional Election Studies survey data that was cross-checked against official voting records. However, this finding has not been met with unanimous agreement. In a research note, Grimmer et al. (2017) concluded that Hajnal et al.'s research was unable to produce a conclusive relationship between ID laws and minority turnout due to data inaccuracies, unreliability of findings, and misinterpretation of results. Recent work by Burden et al. (2017) analyzed the partisan impact of election reforms such as early voting and Election Day registration and found evidence that voter ID laws decreased the Democratic vote in two out of three elections. While voter ID laws were not the main focus of their analysis, this finding has prompted a need for further inquiry.

This chapter extends the literature discerning the differential partisan effects of one reform among a set of increasingly restrictive election laws: voter identification laws. By utilizing actual party voter share derived from official vote records from 3,109 counties in the 48 contiguous states and the District of Columbia, including data on more than 129 million voters, we avoid the common pitfalls associated with using survey data.[2] Previous studies have addressed partisan motivations for the adoption of voter ID laws and consequences on voter turnout; however, no work has specifically examined the impact of voter ID laws on party vote share.

Data and findings

To examine the impact of voter identification laws on vote share, we created a unique county-level data set from various data sources. Combining sources was necessary to capture the various county-level characteristics of interest. These county-level data included 2016 presidential election results by party obtained by McGovern (2016), who scraped the data from Townhall.com; demographic data on race from the Pew Research Center (2016b) and Olson (2014); educational attainment for adults age 25 and older in 2011–2015 by county (U.S. Department of Agriculture 2016); urban-rural county classifications (U.S. Department of Agriculture 2016); poverty and median household income by county (U.S. Census Bureau 2015); and the National Conference of State Legislatures (NCSL 2018b) and the Brennan Center for Justice (2015) on state voter ID laws. Because these data are not self-reported and are the absolute values and totals for each variable in every county in the contiguous states, our data set contains the most detailed and reliable data available for this type of analysis, to the best of our knowledge. Furthermore, we are not relying on sampling in this study, but rather analyzing the universe of more than 60 million Republicans and 62 million Democrats who voted in 3,109 counties in November 2016.

We coded the presence of voter identification laws in the states as a dichotomous variable. States were coded "1" where a limited set of photo IDs (usually issued by a government) is required to cast a vote; all other states were coded "0," indicating that either no ID requirements or optional ID requirements are in place. Using this coding approach, Table 6.1 shows the number of countries with voter ID laws in place in 2016, while Table 6.2 shows the coding of voter ID laws by state, along with the number of counties in each state.

The goal in this study is to explain party vote share in the 2016 general election. The unit of analysis is the county. Using counties as the level of analysis is appropriate

Table 6.1 **The Number of U.S. Counties with a Voter ID Law, 2016**

	Frequency	*Percentage*
ID required	1,182	38
ID not required	1,926	62
Total	3,108	100

Note: The presence or absence of voter ID laws is coded dichotomously. "ID required" refers to counties where a limited set of photo IDs (usually issued by a government) is required to cast a vote. "ID not required" refers to counties where either no ID requirements or optional ID requirements are in place.

Source: Data on state voter ID laws sourced from the National Conference of State Legislatures (NCSL 2018b) and the Brennan Center for Justice (2015).

for this study for two reasons. First, counties provide more granularity than would be possible with state-level data. Second, counties are governing units of states and, especially as it relates to election administration, have substate responsibilities for the implementation and execution of voter ID laws. Even though the counties implement and execute the voter ID laws, whether a county has those laws depends on the state. Since counties are contained within a specific state, our model controls for the impact of Republican majority legislatures, drawing on the theory that the presence of voter ID laws is related to how strongly the state leans Republican. This is measured using Mitt Romney's vote share in the 2012 presidential election. Our Bayesian multilevel modeling approach uses the framework presented by Katz and King (1999).[3] An online appendix provides further details on the methods and modeling approach.[4]

In this chapter, we ask whether identification laws impact partisan vote share. To do this we examine whether the presence of voter identification laws serve to increase or decrease party vote share. We developed a model to transform each party's respective vote shares for each county in the study. Using the methods of Katz and King (1999) and Tomz, Tucker, and Wittenberg (2002), our model was used to assess the causal impact of voter ID laws on each party's vote share. The predictor variables were set to their respective means, except for the voter ID variable which was set to "1" when voter ID was present and "0" when voter ID was not present. The difference between these two values is the impact of the voter ID law on each party's vote share.

Figure 6.1 shows the density curves for the distribution of change in voter share due to voter ID laws for the GOP and Democrats, respectively. Table 6.3 outlines the probabilities that voter ID impacted the election result for the GOP and the

Table 6.2 **Voter ID Law Coding by U.S. State with the Number of Counties, 2016**

State	ID Required	ID Not Required
Alabama	0	67
Arizona	15	0
Arkansas	75	0
California	0	58
Colorado	0	64
Connecticut	0	8
Delaware	0	3
District of Columbia	0	1
Florida	0	67
Georgia	159	0
Idaho	0	44
Illinois	0	102
Indiana	92	0
Iowa	0	99
Kansas	105	0
Kentucky	0	120
Louisiana	0	64
Maine	0	16
Maryland	0	24
Massachusetts	0	14
Michigan	0	83
Minnesota	0	87
Mississippi	82	0
Missouri	0	115
Montana	0	56
Nebraska	0	93
Nevada	0	17
New Hampshire	0	10
New Jersey	0	21
New Mexico	0	33
New York	0	62

(continued)

Table 6.2   **Continued**

State	ID Required	ID Not Required
North Carolina	0	100
North Dakota	53	0
Ohio	0	88
Oklahoma	0	77
Oregon	0	36
Pennsylvania	0	67
Rhode Island	0	5
South Carolina	46	0
South Dakota	0	65
Tennessee	95	0
Texas	254	0
Utah	0	29
Vermont	0	14
Virginia	134	0
Washington	0	39
West Virginia	0	55
Wisconsin	72	0
Wyoming	0	23
Total	1182	1926

Note: The presence or absence of voter ID laws is coded dichotomously. "ID required" refers to states where a limited set of photo IDs (usually issued by a government) is required to cast a vote. "ID not required" refers to states where either no ID requirements or optional ID requirements are in place. The figures provide the number of counties for each state.

Source: Data on state voter ID laws sourced from the National Conference of State Legislatures (NCSL 2018b) and the Brennan Center for Justice (2015).

Democratic Party, respectively. The distribution of change in voter share due to voter ID laws for the GOP had a mean of 0.018 (1.8%) and a standard deviation of 0.045 (4.5%). The 2.5th percentile and 97.5th percentile for the distribution was −0.067 (−6.7%) and 0.101 (10.1%). The distribution of change in voter share due to voter ID laws for Democrats had a mean of −0.007 (−0.7%) and a standard deviation of 0.042 (4.2%). The 2.5th percentile and 97.5th percentile for the distribution was −0.087 (−8.7%) and 0.075 (7.5%). The probability that there is a larger increase in voter share for the GOP than the Democratic candidate when voter ID laws are present is 61%. These values are all calculated from 1,000 draws from the

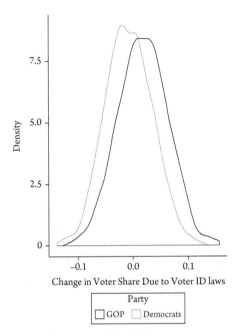

Figure 6.1 Change in Voter Share Due to Voter ID Laws.
Note: Based on 1,000 draws from the posterior distributions.
Source: Authors combined county-level data from a range of sources, as discussed in the text.

Table 6.3 **Impact of Voter ID Laws on Expected Vote Share**

	Mean	St. Dev.	2.5th Percentile	97.5th Percentile
GOP	0.018	0.045	−0.067	0.101
Democrat	−0.007	0.042	−0.087	0.075

Note: Table outlines the probabilities that voter ID impacted the election result for the GOP and the Democratic Party, respectively.

Source: Authors combined county-level data from a range of sources, as discussed in the text.

posterior distributions based on modeling the transformed vote shares as a multi-variate student's t distribution. In particular, the 61% was calculated by the number of 1,000 points in Figure 6.2 that are black, indicating the change in voter share is greater for the GOP than for the Democrats.[5] This means that the probability that there is a larger increase in voter share for the GOP than the Democratic candidate when voter ID laws are present is 61%.[5]

These results are not definitive with respect to whether voter ID laws systemat-ically favor one party over the other, but there is a greater than 50-50 chance that voter ID laws are producing partisan results—increasing the GOP voter share and decreasing the Democrats' voter share. Another way of looking at the results is to

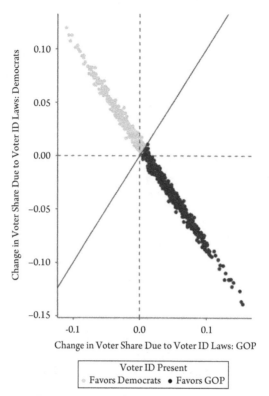

Figure 6.2 Plot of Change in Voter Share Due to Voter ID Laws: GOP vs. Democrats.
Note: Based on 1,000 draws from the posterior distributions. The probability that there is a larger
increase in voter share for the GOP than the Democratic candidate when voter ID laws are present is
61% (the proportion of black points in this figure).
Source: Authors combined county-level data from a range of sources, as discussed in the text.

look at the odds of this particular event occurring. The odds are the probability
that an event occurs divided by the probability that the event does not occur. The
odds that voter ID laws produce partisan results for the GOP are $\frac{0.61}{0.39} = 1.564$ times
greater than the voter ID laws producing partisan results for the Democrats. While
not quite the 2-to-1 magnitude found by Burden et al. (2017), these results serve to
further back up their claim.

Wisconsin and other states with voter ID laws

We use the Wisconsin experience with voter ID regulation as instructive regarding
political consequences in terms of specific election outcomes. In Wisconsin in
November 2016 candidate Clinton lost to candidate Trump by 22,871 votes. This

was a difference in vote share for the two parties of 0.008 (0.8%). When looking at the mean of each of these changes in vote share distributions for each party, in the absence of voter ID laws Trump's vote share would decline from 47.2 to 45.4%, while Clinton's vote share would increase from 46.5 to 47.2%. Still, there is no way of knowing what the actual vote totals would be for both candidates (the actual difference between Trump and Clinton in Wisconsin being 0.77%). Nevertheless, by using the results from the posterior distribution produced from modeling the transformed voter shares as a multivariate student's t-distribution (Figure 6.1), we can say there is a 57.9% chance that this difference was due to Wisconsin's voter ID laws. Thus candidate Trump's benefit from the voter ID law in Wisconsin was 7.9% better than a coin toss, and not inconsequential in such a close election.

We apply the same approach to 10 other states that have passed voter ID laws. Table 6.4 illustrates for these states the GOP margin of victory and the probability that the voter identification laws affected the outcome in favor of the GOP.[6] Furthermore, the results from Table 6.3 show the difference (or impact) of vote share for each party when voter ID laws are present versus when voter ID laws are not present after controlling for all other factors of interest. We found that, on average,

Table 6.4 **Probabilities That Voter ID Impacted the Election Results**

State	GOP Margin of Victory (%)	Probability Win Due to Voter ID
Arkansas	26.9	0.003
Arizona	3.5	0.465
Georgia	5.1	0.393
Indiana	19.0	0.023
Kansas	20.4	0.015
Mississippi	17.8	0.035
North Dakota	35.7	0.000
South Carolina	14.3	0.087
Tennessee	26.0	0.004
Texas	9.0	0.231
Wisconsin	0.8	0.579

Note: Table highlights states with voter ID laws, illustrating the GOP margin of victory, and the probability that the voter identification laws affected the outcome in favor of the GOP.

Source: Authors combined county-level data from a range of sources, as discussed in the text.

voter ID laws increase GOP support by 1.8% and lower support for Democrats by 0.7%. In Bayesian analysis, credibility intervals are reported instead of confidence intervals; the intervals are the 2.5th and 97.5th percentiles. Thus such an analysis indicates that 95% of all possible values will fall between these two points. This means that one could expect that voter ID laws could increase support for the GOP by as much as 10.1% but also could lower support for the GOP by as much as 6.7%. Likewise voter ID laws could lower support for the Democrats by as much as 8.7% but also could increase support for Democrats by as much as 7.5%. Hence it is not definitive that voter ID laws would always benefit the GOP candidate.

In sum, these state examples, shown in Table 6.4, tell us the odds of voter ID laws impacting partisan vote share in an election; whether that's consequential to electoral outcomes depends on the closeness of an election. The GOP margin of victory in Arizona, Georgia, Texas, and Wisconsin was comparatively small, in the single digits, indicating close elections; in those states voter ID significantly influenced partisan vote share in favor of the GOP.

Conclusions and discussion

The implementation and strengthening of voter identification laws across some American states has brought with it a wave of controversy. We need to understand the political ramifications of the existence and enforcement of such laws. While previous work has focused almost exclusively on the impact voter identification has had on turnout, in general and among subgroups, no work has specifically addressed whether requiring voter identification can impact partisan vote share directly. Our findings show that when strict voter ID laws are present, these laws are 61% more likely to benefit the GOP share of the vote than the Democratic candidate. Though voter ID laws do not systematically favor one party over the other, we have shown that more often than not, these laws do impact partisan vote share in the states and counties where they are present. In any elections where the winner is determined by a few votes, reforms like voter ID laws can have a significant impact in the margins, and in close elections the margins count.

For the United States to be a legitimate democracy elections must be free and fair and certainly avoid even the perception of partisan manipulation for electoral advantage. It is likely that the trade-off between security and voter access will continue to be a contentious topic upon which determinations about the appropriate public policy may be arguable and litigious, especially among partisans. We believe this research will be useful for policymakers, courts, and others who seek to ascertain the specific consequences of voter ID laws.

Notes

1. In addition to the distinction between the strict and not strict categories, laws may require that the identification bears a photograph or does not require a photograph. Thus strict photograph ID laws are considered to be the strictest among the state voter ID laws.

2. The limitations of survey data are well documented and include reliability and validity problems that stem from social desirability bias, faulty memory, and lack of comprehension of the question (see Rosenthal and Rosnow 1991).

3. The main reasons that the Bayesian modeling approach is being used in this analysis are due to the type of response variable of interest and the nesting of counties in states. If GOP support was the only support of interest, a logistic regression model with counties nested in states would have been appropriate to use. Unfortunately, GOP, Democratic, and other support in each county are of interest, with emphasis put on the first two groups. These types of data are compositional data, making the model's response variable multivariate in nature. Combine this multivariate response with the nesting of counties in states, and the Bayesian framework appears to be an innovative approach to address these issues.

4. For the online methods appendix see Electoral Integrity Project, "Books," www. electoralintegrityproject.com/books-1/.

5. These values are all calculated from 1,000 draws from the posterior distributions based on modeling the transformed vote shares as a multivariate student's t distribution. See the online appendix for description of student's t.

6. Virginia was omitted from this table because it is a state where the Democrat won; Clinton had a margin of victory of 5.32%.

7

Fake News

LETICIA BODE, EMILY K. VRAGA, AND KJERSTIN THORSON

In the months following the 2016 presidential elections in the United States, academics and pundits alike struggled to make sense of what had happened (see Hasen, this volume). As the introduction to this volume discusses, a growing number of voices pointed to the role of "fake news" and misinformation more broadly in leading voters astray in their assessments of the two major candidates for president, Hillary Clinton and Donald Trump. Social media was widely blamed for disseminating misleading information that might have affected the election results (Solon 2016). Partisan media, too, received widespread blame: for propagating misleading beliefs, for promoting partisan polarization, and for suppressing the possibility of trusting the "other side" (Garrett, Weeks, and Neo 2016; Hindman 2009; Levendusky 2013). Mainstream news media outlets like CNN and the *New York Times* also came under fire for failing to cover substantive issues while devoting large volumes of coverage to scandals related to the Clinton campaign (Faris et al. 2017; Patterson 2016).

The purpose of this chapter is to examine the relationship between media use and beliefs in seven false or misleading election narratives. We use a survey data set collected in the days immediately following the 2016 election to investigate whether different types of media use are related to the extent to which people believed in congruent misperceptions (misperceptions that align with existing candidate support) versus incongruent misperceptions (those that would not match up with candidate support) broadly, as well as their belief in each of the seven misperceptions specifically. Within this framework, we test the role of partisan media, social media, mainstream media, and entertainment media to determine whether particular news habits were more likely to enhance or depress belief in these prominent misleading claims that emerged during the presidential campaign. We also address the nature of misinformation and related difficulties with measuring associated beliefs. Our findings confirm that news media consumption is related to beliefs in election narratives that were not backed up by expert evidence. The results also show that news media had a varied role to play—partisan television media and online news media use are more closely related to misperceptions than other forms of news media consumption, including use of social media for news—but also that overall the predictors of belief in any specific misleading narrative were quite varied.

Literature review

Misinformation and motivated reasoning

Extensive research shows that strongly held social identities spur people to use media in ways that reinforce their beliefs and preferences, and that people are more likely to be persuaded by information that confirms their preexisting beliefs and more likely to reject information that challenges their worldview (Jerit and Barabas 2012; Kunda 1990; Taber and Lodge 2006). The majority of empirical research on this topic has been conducted under the rubric of motivated reasoning, a widely used framework for understanding how motivations to process information are related to persuasive outcomes. Motivated reasoning arises from cognitive dissonance theory (Festinger 1957) and is driven by a desire to protect existing cognitions and avoid the uncomfortable arousal that results from holding two incompatible beliefs. As a result, people require more evidence to accept information incongruent with their worldview, attempting instead to counter or rebut this incongruent information rather than being driven by accuracy motivations (Edwards and Smith 1996; Erisen, Redlawsk, and Erisen 2017; Kunda 1990; Taber and Lodge 2006). This process tends to be stronger among the highly sophisticated, who have greater resources to counter incongruent information (Erisen, Redlawsk, and Erisen 2017; Meirick 2013; Taber and Lodge 2006; Zaller 1992).

As a result of these tendencies, motivated reasoning also tends to explain misperceptions about the world. Motivated reasoning processes not only lead people to hold misperceptions about the world around them but also make people more resistant to efforts to correct misinformation (Lewandowsky et al. 2012; Lewandowksy and Oberauer 2016; Meirick 2013; Nisbet, Cooper, and Garrett 2015). In the case of political information exposure, it is typically partisan identity that leads to biased reasoning. Strong partisans or those with a strong candidate preference in an electoral context are more likely to have both the incentive and the sophistication required to engage in motivated reasoning to protect their beliefs, and thus should be more likely to hold misperceptions (Erisen, Redlawsk, and Erisen 2017; Weeks and Garrett 2014; Weeks 2015).

Partisan-motivated reasoning is of increasing importance given the rise in partisan polarization over time (Hare and Poole 2014), and especially the rise in affective polarization (Iyengar and Westwood 2015); among partisans, partisan social identity has become more central to self-concept and more closely tied to emotional response (Huddy, Mason, and Aaroe 2015). This emotional component of partisanship is particularly important, as scholars have suggested that motivated reasoning works by a process of "hot cognition," driven by affective tags linked to our beliefs (Kraft, Lodge, and Taber 2015).

Likewise the rise in partisanship has also strengthened the alignment between party affiliation and candidate selection; in the 2016 election, for example, exit polls suggested that Clinton won 89% of Democratic votes while Trump won 90% of Republican votes (*New York Times* 2016). By comparison, exit polls found Bill Clinton won 85% of Democrats in 1996, while 81% of Republicans voted for Bob Dole (Roper 2015). This is part of a long-standing trend. Smidt (2017, 379) argues in analyzing data from 2012 and earlier, that compared to the past 30 years, "Americans now exhibit the highest observed rates of party allegiance when voting across successive presidential elections."

While misperceptions are often easily defined when considering health and scientific topics, where scientific consensus can serve as an important cue about "expert opinion" (Bode and Vraga 2015; Nisbet, Cooper, and Garrett 2015; Lewandowsky et al. 2012; Lewandowsky and Oberauer 2016), such a definition becomes more problematic in political spheres. In many cases, elite consensus does not exist about the truth behind a specific claim or the effects of a particular policy (Meirick 2013; Shin and Thorson 2016; Thorson 2016). In the absence of elite consensus, partisans are more likely to fracture in their beliefs about correct information, and motivated reasoning suggests they are more likely to believe information (whether true or false) that aligns with their existing beliefs (Taber and Lodge 2006; Zaller 1992).

Therefore it becomes important to distinguish between congruent and incongruent political misperceptions. Much existing research has focused on *congruent* misperceptions, which we define as holding incorrect beliefs that align with preexisting worldviews (Craft, Ashley, and Maksl 2017; Meirick 2013; Nisbet, Cooper, and Garrett 2015; Thorson 2016). Thus voters who supported Hillary Clinton would be more likely to find information (whether true or false) that favors her—either by highlighting Trump's flaws or excusing Clinton's faults—to be congruent with their beliefs and thus be inclined to believe it. Less is known about *incongruent* misperceptions—or holding incorrect beliefs that run counter to an existing worldview—and the ways in which media habits contribute to these misperceptions. In this case, that would mean a Clinton supporter who believes information that excuses Trump's mistakes or highlights Clinton's flaws, and vice versa for Trump supporters.

We think it important to distinguish between these types of misinformation as they may arise from different sources. While beliefs in congruent misperceptions are likely driven by motivated reasoning to protect existing worldviews (Bode and Vraga 2015; Hart and Nisbet 2012; Jerit and Barabas 2012; Kunda 1990; Meirick 2013; Taber and Lodge 2006), belief in incongruent misinformation could be driven by other forces, such as a simple lack of knowledge, uncertainty about expert opinion, or the plausibility of a given claim (Hinze et al. 2014; Pasek, Sood, and Krosnick 2015; Starbird et al. 2015). However, these same explanations could also contribute to beliefs in congruent misinformation, with an added layer of motivated reasoning. In line with existing research (Weeks and Garrett 2014; Weeks 2015), we propose that belief in congruent misinformation will be higher than belief in incongruent information (Hypothesis 1 [H1]).

Our next set of expectations examines the relationship between media use and misperceptions. Existing research suggests that formation of beliefs in political misperceptions is closely related to biased processing of political information (Bode and Vraga 2015; Erisen, Redlawsk, and Erisen 2017; Nisbet, Cooper, and Garrett 2015; Weeks and Garrett 2014). In general, research on the ways in which a range of diverse media habits contribute to beliefs in congruent versus incongruent misinformation is relatively limited, with few studies focused on comparing partisan news consumption with social media habits. Literature predicting belief in misinformation has often focused on questions such as political ideology (Pfattheicher and Schindler 2016), general belief in conspiracy theories (Jolley and Douglas 2014a, 2014b; Lewandowsky, Gignac, and Oberauer 2013), or testing specific media choices like partisan news or internet sources (Garrett 2011; Garrett, Weeks, and Neo 2016; Meirick 2013). In this chapter, we focus explicitly on the role that distinct news media channels play in promoting or limiting beliefs in political misinformation.

Media remain the primary source of political information for the majority of citizens, few of whom have access to personal knowledge about public affairs (McCombs and Shaw 1972). A large body of research shows that news media use is positively related to political knowledge, largely by increasing the availability of political information (Jerit, Barabas, and Bolsen 2006). At the level of the media system, different media outlets and channels should make different kinds of information available for learning.

The media are not a unitary system. The growth and fragmentation of media channels has produced a high-choice media environment, within which people can select a media diet that fulfills their needs and interests—which may mean for some individuals consuming a lot of information about news and politics, while others avoid it completely (Edgerly 2017; Prior 2007). Likewise media choice enables selective exposure, whereby individuals choose to expose themselves to media outlets that tend to support their existing beliefs and worldview (Garrett 2009; Stroud 2010).

Different media repertoires should shape the possibility of learning misperceptions (Garrett, Weeks, and Neo 2016; Kull, Ramsay, and Lewis 2003; Meirick 2013; Nyhan 2010). We expect that partisan news media use should be related to the rate of belief in congruent misperceptions, such that higher levels of partisan media use are positively related to beliefs in electoral misperceptions that favor one's own candidate (H2a) but should be negatively related to beliefs in misperceptions that would be damaging to a preferred candidate (H2b).

We have a similar set of expectations for use of online news media. Online news media facilitate selective exposure to political information because they require a high level of choice on the part of the news user (Prior 2007). Therefore we expect a positive relationship between use of online news media and belief in congruent misinformation (H3a). The selectivity allowed by online media should likewise result in a negative relationship between online media use and belief in incongruent misinformation (H3b).

We expect that use of mainstream news media will be negatively related to electoral misperceptions—both those that are congruent (H4a) and those that are incongruent (H4b) with candidate support. Previous research has shown that use of broadcast television news and newspapers is positively related to (accurate) political knowledge and should be less likely to offer congruent information in general (Wells et al. 2017). Television news remains the most common source of news and information for American adults, with 57% of adults often getting news from television, compared to 38% who often get news online (Mitchell et al. 2016). Moreover, national and local broadcast news has maintained relatively high levels of trust; 77% of those surveyed report having at least "some" trust in national news organizations (Mitchell et al. 2016). During the 2016 election cycle, mainstream news media outlets dedicated substantial resources to fact-checking and combating misinformation in other ways (International Fact Checking Network 2017). Therefore we expect that less overtly partisan news channels may be able to help educate their viewers and reach viewers who otherwise would tune out, potentially reducing misinformation beliefs.

Finally, we expect use of entertainment media to play a role. While entertainment news offers less selectivity than online news use, it offers different affordances than traditional media. Notably, it often features soft news, which may facilitate learning, especially among those otherwise tuned out of the news (Baum 2002, 2003; Becker and Waisanan 2013; Becker and Bode 2017; Xenos and Becker 2008). This is important, given that many people prefer entertainment to news in general, so entertainment media offers some information, whereas they might otherwise opt out of politics entirely (Prior 2007). Entertainment should therefore be a source of information and knowledge, but its relationship to misinformation is less clear. While political comedy and other entertainment programs often take on viral misinformation head-on, it is unclear how effective such correction is. We therefore propose a research question, asking how use of entertainment news is related to belief in misinformation (RQ1).

Most extant research has not adequately considered the role that social media may play in exacerbating or limiting beliefs in misinformation, especially as compared to other components of the media diet. In the aftermath of the 2016 election, many media pundits were quick to point to the role of social media in spreading fake news (Silverman 2016; Mitchell et al. 2016). There is some empirical evidence that social media may disseminate misinformation (Shin et al. 2017) or enhance selective exposure to political information because social networks serve as echo chambers—likeminded enclaves in which only agreeable information circulates widely within a network (Colleoni, Rozza, and Arvidsson 2014, though see Barberá et al. 2015).

On the other hand, social media networks tend to be larger and more diverse than in-person networks. Bakshy, Messing, and Adamic (2015) argue that the diversity of social media networks may enable more exposure to information diversity than other forms of media use. Similarly, when science and health misinformation is immediately corrected on social media by social media platforms or by other users, it may reduce belief in misinformation (Bode and Vraga 2015; Vraga and Bode 2017b). Therefore this heterogeneity of opinion could expose individuals to information they may not otherwise see that leads them to correctly update their beliefs. Thus we believe the role of social media use in predicting political misperceptions remains an open question. We propose RQ2 to examine the relationship between social media use and misperceptions in the aftermath of the 2016 election.

Measuring misinformation

Measuring belief in misinformation is extremely difficult. The majority of falsehoods to which people are exposed are not entirely falsifiable; rather they are subject to at least some degree of interpretation. This complicates whether to classify them as true misinformation—defined as "cases in which people's beliefs about factual matters are not supported by clear evidence and expert opinion" (Nyhan and Reifler 2010, 305)—or something similar but lesser, like misleading information or misguided interpretation. The alternative to this complication is choosing only misinformation that is clearly shown to be untrue by experts, but this significantly narrows the scope of what can be considered, particularly in the political realm, where there is often debate between the parties about the potential outcomes of a particular proposal, founded in differences in worldviews, personalities, and interpretations of the causes for societal ills (Abramowitz 2006; Conover and Feldman 1981; Jost 2017).

In order to focus on misinformation that was important in the 2016 election, we adopt a more inclusive definition of misinformation, including both information that fits the classic definition (i.e., "not supported by clear evidence and expert opinion"), as well as some misinformation that is more subject to interpretation or that was widely believed to be misinformation at the time of our survey. Specifically, we include seven statements and ask respondents, "Please rate whether you think any of the following statements about the 2016 election is: False, mostly false, neither true nor false, mostly true, or true" (where false is 1 and true is 5). The seven statements were chosen to (1) represent important claims made during or directly after the 2016 U.S. presidential election; (2) represent claims that came from both sides of the aisle—that is, any given claim reflected poorly on exactly one of the presidential candidates, but the suite of claims reflected poorly on both major candidates; and (3) represent claims that were a mix of the truly falsifiable and those that were subject to greater interpretation.

The statements were: (1) The FBI has indicted Hillary Clinton for her use of a private email server; (2) Hillary Clinton was the first to say that Barack Obama was not born in America; (3) Hillary Clinton rigged the Democratic primaries; (4) Illegal immigrants are responsible for many of the crimes in this country; (5) ISIS is using Donald Trump videos to recruit new jihadists; (6) Donald Trump's secret ties to Russia affected the outcome of the presidential election; and (7) Hillary Clinton lost because laws prevented many people from voting.

These statements represent a variety of approaches to misinformation. Statements 1 (indictment) and 2 (birther) were both falsifiable and knowable at the time of the election. Fact checks were available on Election Day that indicated that these statements were untrue. Statements 3 (primaries), 4 (crime), 6 (Russia), and 7 (voter ID) are harder to demonstrate as entirely true or false. For instance, the recent book by Donna Brazile (2017) suggests that the Clinton campaign did more than the Sanders campaign in terms of controlling elements of the Democratic National Committee, but stops short of calling it "rigging" the election. Reasonable people could take that information and interpret it in different ways. Similarly, while illegal immigrants commit fewer crimes than do citizens (Nichols 2017), as a population they are still responsible for some amount of crime, and it is up to individual interpretation what constitutes "many" crimes. While there is now consensus that Russia did meddle in the 2016 U.S. presidential election with the intent of helping Trump (Binkowski 2016; Holan 2017), it is not clear whether that activity affected the outcome of the election. And finally, while voter ID laws likely played a role in who voted in 2016 (Cecil 2017), it is not clear that they tipped the election, leaving some amount of interpretation open regarding this statement.

Statements 5 (ISIS) and 6 (Russia) appeared to be untrue at Election Day (Valverde 2017), but information has since come to light that suggests they may in fact be true (Windrem 2017; Holan 2017). This introduces another element of misinformation that is rarely talked about: election narratives may become more or less true over time. The question of how to deal with that in terms of measurement is an interesting one: Should people who thought the statements were true in November 2016 be rewarded for knowing that, or should they still be classified as holding misperceptions, given that evidence did not yet exist to point strongly to their falseness?

Belief in these statements varied substantially, from a low of 2.03 (the FBI has indicted Clinton) to a high of 2.69 (ISIS is using Donald Trump videos to recruit

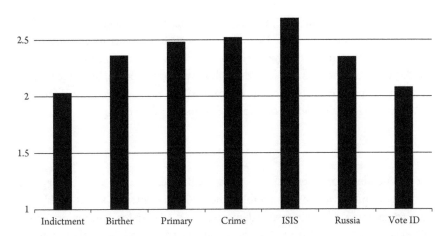

Figure 7.1 Belief in Misinformation Statements.

Note: Statements are: (1) The FBI has indicted Hillary Clinton for her use of a private email server; (2) Hillary Clinton was the first to say that Barack Obama was not born in America; (3) Hillary Clinton rigged the Democratic primaries; (4) Illegal immigrants are responsible for many of the crimes in this country; (5) ISIS is using Donald Trump videos to recruit new jihadists; (6) Donald Trump's secret ties to Russia affected the outcome of the presidential election; and (7) Hillary Clinton lost because laws prevented many people from voting. N = 600. Numbers on the Y axis reflect the mean belief in each statement, on a 5 point scale.

new jihadists) on a 5-point scale (see Figure 7.1). However, it is important to recognize that the public in the aggregate did report that these statements were mostly false. Our analysis follows two lines of inquiry. First, we test our motivating hypotheses and research questions, which examine the factors that predict support of statements that are congruent with one's own beliefs or preferences, as compared to those which go against one's own beliefs or preferences. To do so, we combine statements 1 through 4 into a single measure of statements that favor Trump (largely by discrediting Clinton), and combine statements 5 through 7 into a second measure that favors Clinton (largely by discrediting Trump or undermining his victory). These are then matched to candidate preference (that is, for whom a respondent reported voting), where statements 1–4 would be incongruent and statements 5–7 would be congruent for those who supported Clinton, and the reverse would be true for those who supported Trump (congruent misinformation mean = 2.86, S.D. = 0.87; incongruent misinformation mean = 1.84, S.D. = 0.84). Second, we then examine which of these factors predicts belief in each statement separately, to determine whether there are consistent predictors of belief in misinformation or the extent to which these forces depend on the particular attributes of the misinformation being propagated.

Methods

From November 9 to 14, 2016, we recruited a rolling cross-section of U.S. adults, sampling 100 people per day. This allowed us to test beliefs in election-related narratives directly after the outcome of the election was known. Samples were collected via convenience panels using the online vendor Qualtrics, but were matched via quota sampling on race, income, education, and age to more closely represent the U.S. population. Therefore our starting sample is 600 participants.

Variables

Our independent variables focus on news media use. We draw on a battery of 23 questions about news use and combine them into six different scales (Table 7.5). We also examine whether respondents reported voting for Clinton or Trump. This is coded as "1" if they voted for Trump (44.5%) and "0" if they voted for Clinton (55.5%). All respondents who voted for another candidate, 1.1% of those respondents who reported voting, are dropped from analysis, as are any respondents who reported that they did not vote (20.1%). Finally, we control for standard demographic variables (Table 7.5).

Analysis

Congruent and incongruent misinformation

To test our first hypothesis, we compare the descriptive statistics for congruent and incongruent misinformation. Confirming H1, belief in incongruent misinformation—information that makes one's preferred candidate look bad (mean = 1.84)—is substantially lower than congruent misinformation (mean = 2.86), which conforms to one's worldview ($t = 19.66$, $p < 0.01$).

To test our expectations regarding what predicts belief in congruent and incongruent misinformation, with an emphasis on media use, two ordinary least squares regression models were estimated, with congruent misinformation and incongruent misinformation as the dependent variables. These models are shown in Table 7.1.

There are several overall patterns worth noting before we test our specific hypotheses. First, although belief in congruent misinformation is significantly higher than belief in incongruent misinformation, we have relatively more success in predicting belief in incongruent misinformation ($R^2 = 0.23$) as compared to congruent misinformation ($R^2 = 0.13$), despite being less common.

Several demographic factors predict belief in congruent and incongruent misinformation. Political interest is a significant predictor of both congruent ($\beta = 0.09$) and incongruent ($\beta = -0.12$) misinformation, albeit in competing ways: the more interested you are in politics, the more likely you are to believe congruent

Table 7.1 **Predicting Belief in Congruent and Incongruent Misinformation**

	Congruent Misinformation	Incongruent Misinformation
Political interest	.09†	−.12*
	(.05)	(.04)
Gender (F)	.14	−.23*
	(.09)	(.09)
Age	−.01	−.01*
	(.01)	(.01)
Education	−.06*	−.06†
	(.03)	(.03)
TV news	−.09*	−.10*
	(.05)	(.04)
CNN	−.11*	−.01
	(.04)	(.04)
Fox	.08*	.05
	(.03)	(.03)
MSNBC	.12*	.03
	(.05)	(.04)
Newspaper news	−.01	−.04
	(.05)	(.05)
Entertainment news	.05	.23*
	(.07)	(.06)
Online news	.16†	.24*
	(.09)	(.08)
Social media news	.03	−.09*
	(.04)	(.04)
Voted Trump	.22*	.17†
	(.11)	(.10)
Adjusted R^2	.13	.23

Note: Unstandardized betas reported with standard errors in parentheses.
* p <.05 † p <.10.
N = 600.

misinformation, but the less likely you are to believe incongruent misinformation. This seems consistent with the nature of motivated reasoning: those most interested in politics should be more motivated to protect their identity by believing information consistent with their political preferences (Erisen, Redlawsk, and Erisen 2017; Weeks and Garrett 2014). In contrast, education shows a consistent effect, whereby the more educated are less likely to believe misinformation of either type (congruent β = -0.06, incongruent β = –0.06). While this may suggest a beneficial impact of education on the ability to distinguish credible information from misinformation—a type of literacy that is central to many educational efforts (Kahne, Hodgin, and Eidman-Aadahl 2016; Kahne and Bowyer 2017; Morreale et al. 2016)—it also counters research suggesting that education may enhance motivated reasoning by providing resources to more effectively rebut incongruent information (Meirick 2013; Taber and Lodge 2006). It may be that education on its own offers a benefit, but when combined with specific media habits—especially exposure to partisan news—it creates a polarizing impact on beliefs (Hindman 2012; Meirick 2013).

Two other demographic trends are worth noting, although we have less literature to draw upon to interpret their meaning. Specifically, we find that older adults (β = –0.01) and women (β = –0.23) are both less likely to believe in incongruent campaign narratives. It may be that age has a similar effect as political interest: longer experience with the political process and campaign narratives may enable these older adults to reject incongruent misinformation, without providing the protection or the motivation to reject congruent narratives. The effect of gender is more difficult to explain. In general women tend to attend less to politics than do men, due mainly to differential socialization and structural factors like available leisure time (Bennett and Bennett 1989), but it is unclear how differential interest or attention to politics in general would manifest specifically for rejection of incongruent misinformation.

These analyses also allow us to test whether candidate support uniquely contributed to belief in misinformation. We find that, even when controlling for demographic differences and media use patterns, Trump voters (as compared to Clinton voters) were more likely to report believing in misinformation of both types (congruent β = 0.22; incongruent β = 0.17). There is some research indicating that conservatives may be more susceptible to misinformation than liberals, which could explain this finding (Lewandowsky, Ecker, and Cook 2017; Pfattheicher and Schindler 2016). Alternatively, this could be an artifact of the unique context of the 2016 election or the choices made in terms of misperceptions measured; more research on this topic is needed.

In terms of media variables that are the focus of this chapter, findings are mixed. Several media sources seem to bolster beliefs in misinformation. Specifically, use of partisan cable television channels—Fox News (β = 0.08) and MSNBC (β = 0.12)—predict belief in congruent misinformation, supporting H2a, but not belief in incongruent misinformation, as predicted in H2b. This may reflect the increasingly partisan orientation of these cable channels and underscores their relationship to partisan polarization (Levendusky 2013). Here we demonstrate that use of these channels is related to beliefs in questionable election narratives that support one's own candidate while denigrating the other. Unfortunately, our cross-sectional data do not allow us to show that use of partisan media *cause* beliefs in misinformation. It is likely that partisans who hold misinformed beliefs about election narratives are also more likely to use partisan news media. Existing research suggests that partisan media use and ideological beliefs are related to each other in a reinforcing spiral, such that partisan media use reinforces partisan beliefs and partisan beliefs spur continued use of partisan media (Feldman et al. 2014; Slater 2007). While Feldman et al. showed this process at work in a study of beliefs about climate change, our findings provide hints of similar processes at work for misleading election narratives.

People who use online sources for news are more likely to report believing in both congruent (β = 0.16, supporting H3a) and incongruent (β = 0.24) misinformation, although this relationship is stronger for belief in incongruent misinformation—the opposite of what we expected in H3b. This result offers limited evidence for the proposal that digital media platforms allowed misinformation about the election to spread widely, though again our data do not allow us to tease out causality in this process. Use of online channels for political information tends to be highly selective and driven by existing predispositions (Prior 2007; Borah, Thorson, and Hwang 2015), and media selection and belief outcomes are likely related in a reciprocal process over time.

Finally, we find that use of entertainment media for news is related to belief in incongruent misinformation (β = 0.23, answering RQ1). It may be that seeing entertainment media—especially comedic programs that often mock presidential candidates (Niven, Lichter, and Amundson 2003)—reinforces familiar tropes in an effort to satirize the narratives and thus in a sense create backfire effects. There is some evidence for this in terms of perception of *The Colbert Report* (LaMarre, Landreville, and Beam 2009) and findings that *Saturday Night Live*'s portrayal of Trump actually hurt Clinton's favorability (Becker 2017), but this also counters research suggesting political entertainment has a beneficial effect on learning (Becker and Waisenan 2013; Becker and Bode 2017; Xenos and Becker 2008). Future research should pay special attention to when political comedy can create opportunities for learning or correcting versus reinforcing incorrect beliefs.

The case for media sources and their relationship to misinformation is not entirely bad. In contrast to partisan and online news sources, television news consistently predicts lower misinformation beliefs, both congruent (β = –.09) and incongruent (β = –0.10), while CNN also predicts lower belief in congruent misinformation (β = –0.11). And contrary to what the pundits often suggest, social media news use also predicts lower beliefs in incongruent misinformation (β = –0.09, answering RQ2). Finally, attending to news via newspapers seems to play no role in amplifying or mitigating misperceptions.

Trump and Clinton voters

We further break down the models predicting belief in congruent and incongruent misinformation by Trump and Clinton voters, to see if the influences on them were consistent or different. Several differences stand out. For Trump voters, belief in congruent misinformation (Table 7.2) is predicted by political interest ($\beta = 0.11$). For Clinton voters, on the other hand (Table 7.3), it is predicted by attention to two cable news networks: watching CNN is a negative predictor ($\beta = -0.11$), whereas watching MSNBC is a positive predictor ($\beta = 0.15$). Similar results are seen for incongruent misinformation. For Trump voters, political interest negatively predicts belief in incongruent misinformation ($\beta = -0.10$), as does education ($\beta = -0.12$), television viewing ($\beta = -0.17$), and social media use ($\beta = -0.10$). Use of entertainment ($\beta = 0.35$) and online news ($\beta = 0.28$) is positively associated with belief in incongruent misinformation. For Clinton voters, watching Fox is positively associated with belief in incongruent misinformation ($\beta = 0.23$), as is use of entertainment news ($\beta = 0.13$).

Specific misinformation beliefs

Our final analysis breaks down belief in each individual statement of misinformation (Table 7.4). Seven different models are estimated with each statement as the dependent variable, using the same independent variables from the first set of models. Overall, we are able to explain the greatest variance for the belief in the statement regarding illegal immigrant crime ($R^2 = 0.41$), and we are least successful in predicting belief in the statement about ISIS using Trump for recruitment videos ($R^2 = 0.17$). Beyond that, the models are notable for their different findings. Even variables like political interest and education, which might be expected to consistently reduce misperceptions, are not consistently negative or significant in all models. (Indeed political interest is a significant negative predictor in only a single model.) TV news is frequently a significant predictor of reduced misperceptions (in four out of seven cases), and partisan cable outlets (Fox and MSNBC; at least one is significant in each of the seven models), along with entertainment news (four of the seven models), fairly consistently predict increased misperceptions. Vote choice works in predictable ways: voting for Trump increases misperceptions for statements favorable to Trump and decreases those against him. Notably, social media is significant in only a single model, and in that case—for belief in the statement that Russian interference affected the election outcome—it negatively predicts misperceptions, in line with the analyses reported above.

Table 7.2 **Predicting Belief in Congruent Misinformation for Trump and Clinton Voters**

	Trump Voters	*Clinton Voters*
Political interest	.11†	.08
	(.06)	(.07)
Gender (F)	.12	.22
	(.13)	(.14)
Age	−.01	.01
	(.01)	(.01)
Education	−.05	−0.06
	(.05)	(.05)
TV news	−.08	−.11
	(.06)	(.07)
CNN	−.08	−.11†
	(.07)	(.06)
Fox	.03	.08
	(.05)	(.07)
MSNBC	.09	.15*
	(.07)	(.06)
Newspaper news	.03	.01
	(.08)	(.08)
Entertainment news	.01	.08
	(.11)	(.10)
Online news	.18	.16
	(.12)	(.13)
Social media news	.07	−.01
	(.05)	(.06)
R^2	.12	.09

Note: Unstandardized betas reported with standard errors in parentheses.

* $p < .05$; † $p < .10$.

N = 600.

Table 7.3 **Predicting Belief in Incongruent Misinformation for Trump and Clinton Voters**

	Trump Voters	*Clinton Voters*
Political interest	−.10[†]	−.03
	(.06)	(.06)
Gender (F)	−.31*	−.16
	(.13)	(.12)
Age	−.01	−.01
	(.01)	(.01)
Education	−.12*	−.01
	(.05)	(.04)
TV news	−.17*	−.07
	(.06)	(.06)
CNN	.03	−.05
	(.06)	(.05)
Fox	−.07	.23*
	(.05)	(.06)
MSNBC	.06	−.03
	(.07)	(.05)
Newspaper news	.01	−.08
	(.07)	(.07)
Entertainment news	.35*	.13†
	(.10)	(.08)
Online news	.28*	.16
	(.11)	(.11)
Social media news	−.10*	−.08
	(.05)	(.05)
R^2	.37	.18

Note: Unstandardized betas reported with standard errors in parentheses.
* $p <.05$; † $p <.10$.
N = 600.

Table 7.4 **Predicting Belief in Individual Statements**

	Indictment	Birther	Primary	Crime	ISIS	Russia	Voter ID
Political interest	−.17*	.07	.09	.02	.05	−.11†	−.02
	(.06)	(.07)	(.07)	(.06)	(.07)	(.06)	(.05)
Gender (F)	−.08	.12	−.31*	.05	−.18	.19	−.06
	(.14)	(.14)	(.14)	(.12)	(.14)	(.13)	(.12)
Age	−.02*	.01	−.01*	.01	.01	−.01	−.01
	(.01)	(.01)	(.01)	(.01)	(.01)	(.01)	(.01)
Education	−.10*	−.08	.01	.01	−.03	−.03	−.14*
	(.05)	(.05)	(.05)	(.04)	(.05)	(.04)	(.04)
TV news	−.13†	−.04	−.23*	.06	.01	−.14*	−.20*
	(.07)	(.07)	(.07)	(.06)	(.07)	(.06)	(.06)
CNN	.05	−.1	−.1	−.08	−.08	−.01	−.05
	(.06)	(.06)	(.06)	(.06)	(.06)	(.06)	(.06)
Fox	.01	.16*	.22*	.17*	−.07	−.02	−.09†
	(.06)	(.06)	(.06)	(.05)	(.06)	(.05)	(.05)
MSNBC	.12†	.03	−.05	−.01	.11†	.12†	.19*
	(.07)	(.07)	(.07)	(.06)	(.07)	(.06)	(.06)
Newspaper news	−.05	.01	−.09	−.01	−0.05	.08	−0.01
	(.08)	(.08)	(.08)	(.07)	(.08)	(.07)	(.07)
Entertainment news	.39*	−.02	.06	.02	.17†	.26*	.16†
	(.10)	(.10)	(.10)	(.09)	(.10)	(.09)	(.09)
Online news	.04	.21	.28*	.08	.19	.16	.37*
	(.12)	(.13)	(.13)	(.11)	(.13)	(.12)	(.11)
Social media news	−.03	.02	.04	−.04	−.02	−.11*	−0.06
	(.06)	(.06)	(.06)	(.05)	(.06)	(.06)	(.05)
Voted Trump	.65*	.74*	1.24*	1.36*	−.70*	−.92*	−.53*
	(.15)	(.16)	(.15)	(.13)	(.15)	(.14)	(.13)
R^2	.26	.2	.39	.41	.17	.3	.29

Note: Unstandardized betas reported with standard errors in parentheses.
* $p < .05$; † $p < .10$.
N = 600.

Table 7.5 **Appendix Sources, Scales, and Question Wordings**

Mode of news	Content
Television	*National* nightly news on CBS, ABC, or NBC; *local* television news about your viewing area. Television news use scale (two items, r = 78, mean = 2.87, S.D. = 1.27).
Newspaper	Local newspapers; national newspapers. Newspaper use scale (two items, r = 61, mean = 2.09, S.D. = 1.10).
Entertainment	Entertainment news programs (e.g., *Entertainment Tonight, E! News!*); News satire (e.g., *The Daily Show, Last Week Tonight with Jon Oliver*); Daytime talk shows (e.g., *Ellen, The View*); Late night talk shows (e.g., Jimmy Fallon, Jimmy Kimmel). Entertainment news use scale (four items, α = 82, mean = 1.81, S.D. = 0.93).
Online	Conservative political blogs (e.g., *Instapundit*); liberal political blogs (e.g., *Daily Kos, Talking Points Memo*); international news websites (e.g., *BBC, The Guardian*); emailed newsletters (e.g., *The Skimm, Daily Beast, Washington Post*); internet news aggregators (e.g., Yahoo News, Google News); online only news organizations (Politico, Business Insider, Gawker). Online news use scale (six items, α = 86, mean = 1.73, S.D. = 0.84).
CNN	CNN cable news programs (e.g., Anderson Cooper, Wolf Blitzer). CNN (mean = 2.13, S.D. = 1.33).
Fox	Fox cable news programs (e.g., Bill O'Reilly, Sean Hannity). Fox News (mean = 1.94, S.D. = 1.30).
MSNBC	MSNBC cable news programs (e.g., Rachel Maddow, Chris Matthews). MSNBC (mean = 1.82, S.D. = 1.20).
Social Media	Facebook; Twitter; YouTube; Reddit; Snapchat; Instagram. Social media news use scale (six items, α = 91, mean = 3.15, S.D. = 1.17).
Demographic variables	Age (18 to 89, mean = 44.68, S.D. = 14.47), gender (68% female), education (on a scale from 1 to 5, mean = 2.48 where 2 is "some college" and 3 is "associate's degree," S.D. = 1.48), and political interest (on a scale from 1 to 5, mean = 3.23, S.D. = 1.20).

Note: The prompt for Television, Newspaper, Entertainment, Online, CNN, Fox, and MSNBC is "Please indicate how often in the last week you've consumed content from each source (using any device)"; the prompt for Social Media is "In the past week, how often did you see content about news or current events on each of the following social media sites?"

Discussion and conclusions

The immediate aftermath of the 2016 presidential election saw widespread concerns about misinformation and its causes, especially the role of social media (Bennett and Livingstone 2018). Our results suggest three main findings.

First, in terms of the media's exacerbating public misperceptions, the role of social media may have been overstated. Across seven different incorrect statements about Trump and Clinton, *for each statement more people reported that it was false rather than true.* Social media news use was not related to belief in misinformation that favored one's preferred 2016 presidential candidate, and may even have helped to reduce such beliefs when it came to believing misinformation that was detrimental to a preferred candidate. While this contradicts the popular narrative, it is consistent with previous research that suggests social media does not tend to predict belief in rumors, fake news, or misinformation (Garrett 2016). Given the nature of social media, this makes some amount of sense. Social media is not an echo chamber; rather the diversity of friends on social media tends to consist of weak ties (de Meo et al. 2014) that therefore offer a range of political perspectives (Bode 2016b) and also may lead to incidental exposure to political information (Bode 2016a; Gil de Zúñiga, Weeks, and Ardèvol-Abreu 2017). Online news use, however, is worth investigating further in terms of its ability to bolster belief in misinformation. Likewise, both Fox and MSNBC appear to promote belief in congruent misinformation, whereas CNN works against this pattern. The finding that online and partisan media may spread or reinforce misinformation is consistent with previous research (Garrett, Weeks, and Neo 2016), but the difference between CNN and the two other cable channels validates arguments that the three cable channels cannot be considered equal in terms of their partisan content or informational value (Morris 2005).

Second, what of broadcast news? *In general, television news use consistently predicts lower levels of both types of misinformation.* This suggests an important role of traditional network news in mitigating misinformation in the modern media environment. Indeed television news media around the world are increasingly emphasizing combating misinformation via fact-check segments and other means as part of their broader mission of informing the public (IFCN 2017). Additionally, it may be that partisan selective exposure is less dominant for choices about television news use, reducing the potential for misinformation to spread. But at the same time, when it came to media sources associated with misperceptions, overall, *partisan cable news use is much more consistently related to misperceptions than social media use.*

Third, what drives belief in congruent versus incongruent misinformation? Consistent with motivated reasoning, while people generally disbelieved incongruent misinformation, *they were more willing to believe misinformation that matched their existing worldview.* Misperceptions can arise from a variety of forces, including incomplete knowledge, uncertainty, and simple misunderstandings of scientific or expert consensus (Hinze et al. 2014; Pasek, Sood, and Krosnick 2015; Starbird et al. 2015). But when misperceptions bolster preexisting viewpoints, they are likely to carry additional weight, and thus also be more difficult to correct.

We find that *motivated reasoning drives these processes*. In particular, individuals with higher levels of political interest are more likely to believe congruent misinformation and disbelieve incongruent misinformation. In contrast, education can serve as an important counter to both types of misinformation, which may bolster arguments that increased educational efforts are an important tool to generate skepticism toward misinformation (Kahne and Bowyer 2017; Vraga and Bode 2017a). The beneficial impact of education may be limited to the aggregate, however, as it is possible that educated individuals embedded in specific (and likely partisan) media environments may instead find opportunities to reinforce partisan beliefs (Meirick 2013; Taber and Lodge 2006). Therefore we must be cautious when advocating for education as an unalloyed benefit in combating misinformation (Vraga and Bode 2017a).

Finally, our study uncovered meaningful differences between Trump and Clinton supporters, with Trump supporters particularly likely to believe congruent misinformation (and, to a lesser extent, incongruent misinformation). This matches other extant research about differences in misperceptions among Trump supporters (Pfattheicher and Schindler 2016) and among Republicans in general (Fessler, Pisor, and Holbrook 2017; Lewandowsky, Ecker, and Cook 2017; Sterling, Jost, and Pennycook 2016). Our analysis of Trump versus Clinton voters in terms of belief in congruent misinformation suggests that Trump voters were motivated more by their political interests, whereas watching MSNBC by Clinton voters was related to belief in congruent misinformation. But the small sample size in these analyses limit our confidence in these results.

There are several limitations of our approach and our data. First, we are restricted by the cross-sectional nature of our data collection. As such, we are unable to speak to the causal pathways implied by these associations. It may be, for example, that people who tend to hold misperceptions—either congruent or incongruent—are more likely to seek out information online to validate those viewpoints rather than such information-seeking being the cause for developing these misperceptions in the first place. Perhaps most likely, a growing body of research suggests that partisan beliefs and partisan media use are related to each other in the form of a reinforcing spiral (Feldman et al. 2014; Slater 2007). Our data do not allow us to test this possibility here; we can confirm only that patterns of media use are related to patterns of belief in misinformation, even over and above the role played by variables that are likely to predict media selection (e.g., political interest).

Second, we are limited by the specific misperceptions that we chose to explore—and especially that our measures contained more misperceptions favoring Trump (four) rather than Clinton (three). It is not a simple process to establish "what counts" as a misinformation narrative about the election; verification of election narratives is a dynamic process. Our data collection strove to measure beliefs in statements about the election that were not backed by extensive expert evidence at the time (November 2016) and that were likely to be widely believed across the population of voting citizens. Some of these statements have received evidential support in the months since the election, and others remain difficult to falsify. As we noted, this makes it difficult to engage in normative evaluations of our findings. There is more work to be done to examine the dynamics of misinformation, correction, and media use over time to answer the questions we can only raise here.

Our study complicates traditional media narratives about the aggregate level of belief in various election narratives in the wake of the 2016 U.S. presidential election and the main culprits for its spread. In our data, collected in the days immediately after the election, people often recognized incorrect misinformation—especially, but not only, when such misinformation harmed their preferred candidate. Careful scrutiny of the prevalence and sources of misinformation is necessary before appropriate measures can be taken to counter its potential influence.

Acknowledgments

The authors thank the Carnegie Corporation of New York, the Damm Fund of the Journal Foundation, and the Reynolds Journalism Institute at the University of Missouri for their generous support of the research.

8

Transparency

NANDI VANKA, AVERY DAVIS-ROBERTS, AND DAVID CARROLL

Nonpartisan election observation has become an almost universal global practice (Kelley 2012). By 2006, a total of 1,759 election events in 157 countries, or 80% of elections across the world, were observed by international organizations (Hyde 2011). Citizen observation activities were similarly widespread. Many of these observation missions were funded or supported by the government of the United States or were undertaken by U.S. organizations.

Nonpartisan election observation by international or domestic organizations continues to be seen as a principal tool in the practitioner's toolkit to promote credible elections. Scholars and practitioners note that election observation can contribute to better elections by promoting adherence to international obligations and commitments (Carroll and Davis-Roberts 2013); promoting public trust and confidence in the electoral process and thereby influencing participation (Alvarez, Hall, and Llewellyn 2008a; Birch 2010; Norris 2013); detecting electoral malfeasance (Hyde 2011); influencing perceptions of fairness of the electoral institutions and the electoral environment (Hyde and Marinov 2014; Bush and Prather 2017); and providing analysis and actionable recommendations for election administrators should they seek to improve electoral processes in the future (Martinez i Coma, Nai, and Norris 2016).

Nonpartisan observation can also facilitate citizens' participation in the public affairs of their country, and therefore there are reasons to assume that observation can help improve election processes across regime type.

While the U.S. views itself as a global leader in democracy, with strong institutions and traditions of political participation, it is an outlier in terms of the degree to which election observation is consistently welcomed and conducted at home across the 50 states. This situation is particularly ironic because the United States is a vocal supporter of nonpartisan observation in other countries. There are many instances in the United States when interest in conducting nonpartisan observation of elections has been met with skepticism, or even outright hostility. For example, in 2012 the secretary of state in Iowa and the attorney general in Texas made it clear that international election observation by the Organization for Security and Co-operation in Europe (OSCE) would not be welcome, despite the international commitments of the United States to invite and accept observers (Cervantes 2012; CSCE/OSCE 1990). This skepticism toward observers continues, despite evidence that confidence in the honesty and credibility of electoral processes has declined in the United States over the course of the past decade (see Hasen, this volume).[1]

Although some domestic and international groups conduct observations in the United States, these efforts remain limited, as the practice, experience, and expectations regarding observation vary significantly across the states (Carter Center and National Conference of State Legislatures 2016). For example, since 2004, at the invitation of the U.S. State Department, the OSCE's Office of Democratic Institutions and Human Rights has deployed international election observers. In 2016 the Organization of American States (OAS) also deployed a mission to the United States. At the same time, U.S. civic nonpartisan organizations, often focused on a specific local context, are active in states across the country. In some states, scholars have conducted "educational" or academic observation missions, gaining access to the electoral process with the goal of conducting research and providing insights or recommendations for future processes. And of course, media and partisan observation of elections is a well-known practice.

This chapter presents Carter Center research on questions regarding exactly who can observe what, when, and where, and the variations across the 50 states, particularly regarding nonpartisan observation. Our analysis starts with the premise that the decentralized nature of election administration in the United States is relatively unique and accounts for some of the variation in practices (see Vickery and Szilagyi, this volume).[2] The core of the research outlined below documents the extent of the variation, providing a thorough review of the laws, regulations, and policies across the states regarding who can be considered an observer and what parts of the electoral process observers can access.

While the decentralized structure enables and accounts for much of the variation, our analysis also extends to a preliminary exploration of other possible contributing factors, as well as the potential consequences of the relatively restrictive access for observers in the U.S and the many variations across the states. Are there any discernible patterns to the levels of observer access or restrictions? Why are some states more restrictive than others? What are the implications of this variety on the electoral and administrative processes and on citizen participation? If nonpartisan election observation has the benefits that the United States sees as valuable internationally in other electoral and political contexts, should the United States not consider ways to increase the role and contributions that election observation can make at home?

This chapter considers each of these questions in light of varying restrictions and access for observers across U.S. jurisdictions. The Carter Center's research concludes that levels of access for nonpartisan observers fluctuate across the country; rules for observers are not always standardized across a single state; and a number of states provide little or no access to nonpartisan observers. Inconsistencies in observer access conflict with the United States's international commitments and indicate a general disregard for nonpartisan observation in the United States as a beneficial tool for democratic elections, which we discuss in further detail. First we offer an overview of the Carter Center's review and analysis of the regulatory landscape regarding observation across the 50 states and the District of Columbia, followed by an analysis of trends in policy and practice.

Research design

In order to analyze the rules and regulations regarding election observation and observer access to the electoral process across the United States, as well as to provide better and more information to the public, the Carter Center and the National Conference of State Legislatures examined the laws, regulations, and practices governing election observers in the 50 states and D.C. The research was focused on two overarching questions: (1) Who is allowed to observe what and where? (2) How is observation regulated, or what practices are in place to determine observer access to the various phases of the electoral process?

Working in close collaboration with the National Conference of State Legislatures, the Center undertook statutory research and analysis to assess whether election observation was commonly and/or explicitly regulated in state statutes and what those rules and regulations say about the rights and responsibilities of observers. For the purposes of this work, five main types of observers were identified and are defined as follows:

> *Citizen partisan observers*: "Usually referred to as poll watchers or challengers, these observers represent political parties, candidates, or groups in favor of or against a ballot proposition. Partisan citizen observers generally guard against activity that could undermine their own party or group's interests. Challengers are able to challenge the eligibility of individual voters to cast their ballot" (Carter Center and National Conference of State Legislatures 2016).
>
> *Citizen nonpartisan observers*: "These observers, usually affiliated with a civil society organization, work to protect the integrity of the electoral process and advance electoral quality and accountability regardless of the political outcome" (Carter Center and National Conference of State Legislatures 2016).
>
> *International nonpartisan observers*: "International nonpartisan organizations deploy teams of international observers, who are non-citizens and non-residents of the country where an election is being held. They typically follow a professional methodology based on international and domestic standards for democratic elections. Impartial international observers seek to provide

a credible, data-driven assessment of the conduct of an election and are not interested in the political outcome" (Carter Center and National Conference of State Legislatures 2016).

Academic observers: "Academic observers are associated with higher education institutions, and many study elections with a goal of strengthening democratic practices. Like nonpartisan observers, academics generally do not promote a particular campaign or political outcome" (Carter Center and National Conference of State Legislatures 2016).

Federal observers: "Federal observers represent the Department of Justice and are sent to respond to concerns about compliance with federal laws (notably the Voting Rights Act of 1965). [Complaints] may relate to issues such as potential racial discrimination during the polling process, compliance with bilingual election procedures, or inadequate accessibility for disabled voters" (Carter Center and National Conference of State Legislatures 2016).

Drawing from the Carter Center's experience with international election obser-vation and knowledge of standards for credible election observation, the main re-search questions were formed to assess where, what, and when observers can have access to and assess the electoral process, broken down by observer type. Seven key questions were developed to guide data collection and provide measures for comparing policies across states.

The first key question asked whether rules for observers are specified in statute and, if not, whether they are formalized or standardized in any other resources. The second question asked, "Does an accreditation process for observers exist?" Accreditation for election observers is a common practice in countries that in-vite and allow international observers. Accrediting an observer means that a state or country officially recognizes a person's role as an observer and often entails re-ceiving training and signing a code of conduct.

Questions 3 through 5 were included to understand whether observers have ac-cess to all aspects of the election process, which is common in many other coun-tries and allows observers to view such activities as the preparation of any ballot materials, testing of voting machines, and voter registration, as well as the casting of ballots on election day and postelection activities such as ballot counting and vote tabulation, audits, and any dispute-resolution procedures. Based on international best practices and recognized guidelines, professional observers should be accorded sufficient access to each part of the election process in order to conduct their work and provide a credible assessment, as well as to provide recommendations for improved election administration (OSCE 2005a).

The sixth question posed was "Is access to observe dependent on election officials' discretion (state or local)?" Finally, in order to understand states' interpretations of the law in practice and to gauge if they would be open to allowing observers, ques-tion 7 asked, "Does the state have past experience with observers?"

In addition to legal statutes, the Carter Center and National Conference of State Legislatures referred to state election directors' (SEDs) websites along with state and county poll worker training materials, poll watcher manuals and observer handbooks, political party recruitment guides, county election officials' websites, news articles, journals, and university research studies to answer these questions. The Center also designed customized questionnaires for each of the SEDs and the SED for D.C. The questionnaire template mirrored the research's key questions but also referenced specific laws, any other regulation authorized by state election officials, and the implementation of these rules. As statutory information often contained little reference to observers other than party poll watchers, SED responses formed the basis of much of the data on nonpartisan and academic observers. In total, 43 states and D.C. responded to the Center's inquiry.[3]

The Center also conducted interviews with eight elections experts to supplement the information gathered in person. Interview questions focused on interviewees' experiences seeking access to polling places, working with administrators or observers, and conducting domestic and international observation in the United States, and on lawmakers' and election officials' perspectives on election observation.

Finally, in an effort to provide a more holistic and in-depth view of the diversity of state policies for observers, the Center conducted five case studies on Connecticut, New Mexico, Georgia, California, and North Dakota, which are now available on the National Conference of State Legislatures "Policies for Observers" webpage. A 50-state database of references for observer policies was ultimately compiled and made available online. While the resulting database is relatively comprehensive, it should be noted that clear, standardized, state-level information was not available for every state.

Findings

Here we describe the most significant findings of the regulatory review, including select information that can inform our overall understanding of election observation policies in the United States, how observation is perceived domestically, and how it is practically handled at the state level. Analysis of legislative information is based on standardized policy interpretations where provided by election officials.

Partisan observation of U.S. elections

Almost all states (47 states and D.C.) explicitly allow political parties to appoint partisan election observers, with access to the process generally ranging from watching Election Day procedures (i.e., opening and closing of polling stations, testing of voting machines, casting of ballots, and more) to unhindered access to watch any aspect of the electoral process.[4] Partisan observers, more than any other type of observer, are permitted by law to observe elections across jurisdictions. Party-affiliated observers are often placed in particularly contentious areas to verify that the process or outcome of an election does not disadvantage the interests of their political party. Following an election, information gathered by partisan poll watchers can be used to challenge results.

While most states explicitly grant access to partisan watchers, they are still expected to observe without interference, unless acting as "challengers." The large majority of states also explicitly provide for challengers to be present at polling places during the casting and counting of ballots.

Citizen nonpartisan observation of U.S. elections

Citizen nonpartisan observers *may* be able to gain access in as many as two-thirds of states. Nonpartisan groups' access to the election is largely unaddressed in U.S. state statutes, and as a result, practices vary among states and across counties and are generally at the discretion of election officials. At least 34 states and D.C. appear to allow citizen nonpartisan observers to be present at elections based on statutes or practices authorized at the state level. However, not all counties within the 34 states necessarily grant access to citizen nonpartisan observers consistently, and access for different nonpartisan observer groups is determined on a case-by-case basis.

A closer look at rules for nonpartisan observers reveals that nine states explicitly provide in statute for citizen nonpartisan observers to be present to watch their elections.[5] These states offer varying levels of access to pre-election, Election Day, and postelection procedures. Specifications for how close observers can stand and whether they must watch from behind a guard rail vary from state to state.

An additional nine states provide broad access to the public to be present to watch the elections process, and any type of observer, including citizen nonpartisan, could gain access under these statutes.[6] All nine of these states maintain that the public can watch the entire electoral procedure, but in practice access can vary significantly and may be regulated at the county level, where local election officials are responsible for maintaining order in polling places and may be able to limit the number of people observing at a single time. In addition to these nine states, there are other states that permit members of the public to access certain parts of the electoral process, such as the pre-election testing of voting machines and the counting process or postelection audits, but do not permit the public to access polling sites on Election Day.

Sixteen additional states often grant access to citizen nonpartisan observers in practice.[7] This access is frequently acquired when sought or is provided on a case-by-case basis but is not specified in statute. In these 16 states, citizen nonpartisan observer access is at the complete discretion of state or local officials. As a result, it is difficult to know how frequently citizen nonpartisan observers have gained access in these states, or the exact nature of that access. To learn more about what exactly happens in these states, data was collected to confirm that citizen nonpartisan observers had gained access in at least one case in the past and/or that SEDs would grant access to citizen nonpartisan observers if requested to do so in the future (Figure 8.1).

Among the states that were chosen for case studies, the greatest allowances for citizen nonpartisan observers were provided by North Dakota and California. North Dakota guarantees observers "uniform and non-discriminatory access to all stages of the election process" (North Dakota Century Code §16.1-05-09), while California guarantees public access to observe and permits other "bona-fide associations of citizens" to apply for access to all parts of the process and provides them with formal credentials once accepted (California Elections Code §14221, 15004, 2100(a)(9)).

International nonpartisan observation

Seventeen states do not provide access for international observers, despite the United States's international obligation to invite and allow observers based on its signing of the 1990 Copenhagen Document (CSCE/OSCE 1990). However, at least 33 states and D.C. either explicitly allow international nonpartisan observers to be present at elections or may allow them in practice. A mere five states plus D.C. have explicit guidance in statute or administrative code that permits international nonpartisan observers to be present during elections.[8] In another two states, Hawaii and Virginia, statutory language is inclusive of many types of observers but specifies that access for "additional observers," meaning those who are not party poll watchers, must be authorized by county officials such as the chief election official, county clerk, or the local election board.

In the 28 states where policies for international observers remain ambiguous, access for these types of observers could be possible based either on statutes or on practices that make observation open to the public. Where statutes do not specify, it is impossible to know if international nonpartisan observers would gain access to watch elections. County and state officials' perceptions of the value of international observers, and therefore their openness to their presence during elections, varies widely across states. No standard or guarantee exists to ensure that international nonpartisan observers are allowed to be present where statutes do not specify (Figure 8.2).

Academic observation

While many states have permitted academic observers to be present in at least some counties in previous elections, this category of observers generally is not explicitly permitted or mentioned in statute. In some states, academic observers can gain access to polling places through the same process as citizen nonpartisan observers.

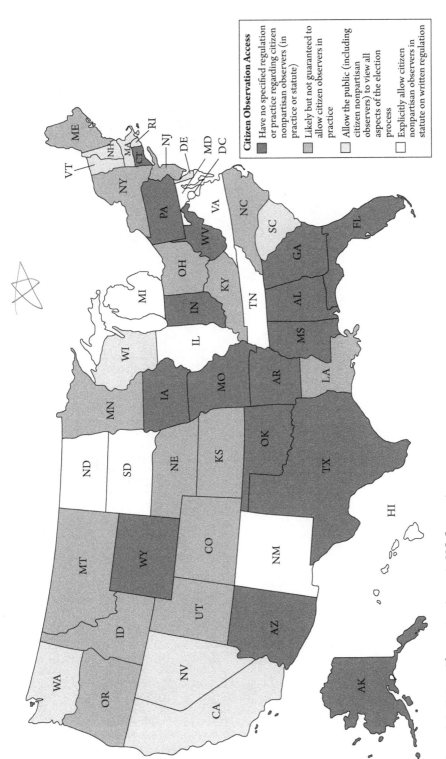

Figure 8.1 Citizen Observation Access in U.S. States n/a
Source: (Carter Center and National Conference of State Legislatures 2016).

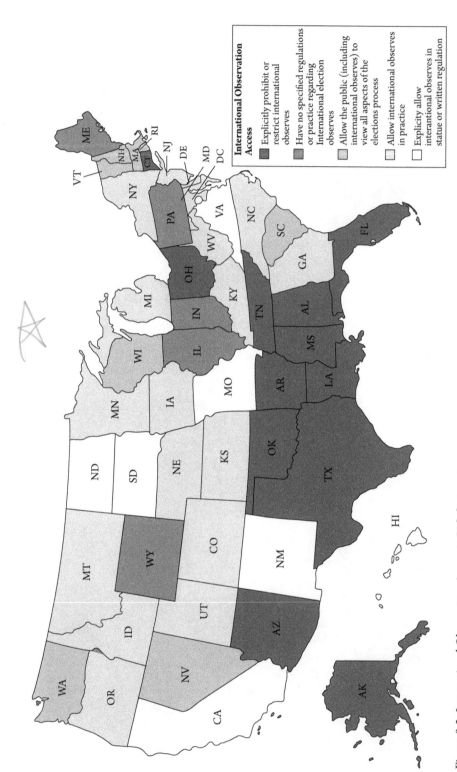

Figure 8.2 International Observation Access in U.S. States n/a

Source: (Carter Center and National Conference of State Legislatures 2016).

Like other nonparty observers, academic observers can gain access when observation is open to the public or when states choose to deal with observers on a case-by-case basis but do not specify in statute.

New Mexico is unique in that it provides explicit access in statute to academic observers, facilitating the work of the Center for the Study of Voting, Elections, and Democracy (C-SVED) at the University of New Mexico. Lonna Rae Atkeson, a political science professor at the university and director of C-SVED, says the academic center has observed New Mexico's elections since 2006, when access was little to none and not easy to acquire. In 2008 a shift in political leadership made those in power more favorable to observation conducted outside of party lines. Since then, C-SVED has forged strong relationships with county election administrators over multiple election cycles. Atkeson stated that the county clerks' offices now expect C-SVED's participation and give serious consideration to their recommendations when reforming election administration practices. Through this cooperation, C-SVED observers have supported election administrators who wish to demonstrate their commitment to improving elections and to working with credible observers.

Federal observation

Information on rules for federal observers was gathered via online research, in news articles and Department of Justice (DOJ) publications. According to these sources and information from SEDs, federal observers have been to specific jurisdictions in at least 40 states.[9] The DOJ's power to deploy observers to U.S. states was significantly curtailed in 2013, when the U.S. Supreme Court struck down sections 5 and 4b of the 1965 Voting Rights Act. These provisions required that states seek federal preclearance before enforcing changes to their voting policies, and they specified increased monitoring of states with histories of discrimination (Tucker 2016). Examples of such issues would be noncompliance with federal bilingual election procedure requirements and voter identification policies that discriminate on the basis of race (Baumgarten and Haltom 2016). States are no longer obligated, however, to accept federal observers and can choose to provide or deny access.

Some state election officials could confirm that federal observers had been present in their states in the past. Most states, however, do not record which observers, federal or other, have participated in past elections. In other countries, this record-keeping often happens in accreditation processes, during which election authorities maintain rosters of officially recognized observers.

Accreditation for observers

In addition to examining policies on observer access, the Carter Center and the National Conference of State Legislatures looked at states' accreditation processes for the different types of observers on the assumption that the existence of accreditation procedures (or lack thereof) would supplement our understanding of the operationalization of observation practices. Accreditation procedures can become, in effect, a contract between the observer and election officials, clearly articulating the rights and responsibilities of observers and usually involving the issuance of identification documents or other credentials required to conduct election observation. Adherence to a code of conduct also may be required. According to international best practices, accreditation should be granted to every person selected to observe, using clearly defined, reasonable, and nondiscriminatory requirements (ACE Electoral Knowledge Network 2017). As we noted, international election observers are commonly accepted and invited by countries around the world, and as a result, clear and centralized accreditation policies for international observers have become a standard practice in countries that allow observation. This is not the case in the United States, where access for observers as well as accreditation are not standardized, or available, in several states.

Based on statutes, county poll worker and poll watcher guides, and responses from SEDs, this study found that 40 states and D.C. have a formal accreditation or appointments process for citizen partisan observers (party poll watchers and challengers).[10] This appointment is managed by local party chairs, candidates, or ballot issue groups and can require approval by election officials or a secretary of state's office. The process usually involves a party or candidate submitting a list of observers' names to county officials by a predetermined date and obtaining a set of signatures authorizing them to send observers to the polls. Unlike accreditation based on international good practice guidelines, this appointment process usually does not require a code of conduct, special training, or identification for observers.

Thirteen states and D.C. have a formal accreditation or appointments process for citizen nonpartisan observers, or those domestic observers not affiliated with a political party.[11] A typical process for accrediting or appointing nonpartisan observers does not exist in the United States. Where it exists, accreditation occurs through collaboration between citizen organizations and state or county election boards, secretary of state offices, and/or county clerks' offices.

Ten states and D.C. have a formal accreditation or appointments process for international nonpartisan observers. Accreditation is first pursued through the U.S. Department of State and then again at the state and/or county levels.[12] A total of seven states do allow citizen partisan, citizen nonpartisan, and/or international nonpartisan observers but have no accreditation or appointment processes to formally recognize any type of observer.[13]

Notable trends

Apart from overall numbers indicating states' openness to different types of observers, some overarching trends and possible correlations were identified.

Access for observers and voting patterns

The first trend is evident by reviewing a map that shows where access for observers is greatest versus most restrictive. While access for partisan observers is broadly available across the large majority of states, access for nonpartisan election observers is greater along the American coasts and is more restricted in southern and midwestern states, with a few exceptions, such as North Dakota, South Dakota, and Wisconsin. In a similar way, "blue," states or states that have voted more liberally and have had a leaning toward the Democratic Party in the past three national elections, generally provide greater access for nonpartisan observers, while conservative or Republican-leaning, "red" states more frequently restrict access for nonpartisan observers. This trend also surfaces when examining SED responses to our interviews, which indicate that even when statutes do not specify policies for nonpartisan observers, SEDs in blue states more frequently interpret the rules to mean that observers could still be allowed because they are not prohibited. In many red states, the lack of clarity in law is often interpreted to mean that observers cannot enter polling places because no statutes specifically allow for it.

Integrity versus access and inclusivity

There are strong political forces at work in the United States that have produced a polarized political system and consistent differences across the partisan divide on a range of issues. One clear example is the ongoing debate on elections, with the Republican Party focusing on the need to ensure "election integrity" and prevent fraud, while Democrats usually stress the importance of inclusivity and expanding access to elections (see Pallister, this volume). These partisan stances may partially explain the differences in statutes and rules along with how they are interpreted.

For states that advocate an emphasis on election integrity, rules and interpretations that restrict access to the electoral process tend to be justified as a means of discouraging fraud, tampering, or outside influence on the conduct of the elections. Alternatively, states that focus on inclusivity and expanding access to elections justify a broader interpretation on the grounds that "sunshine is the best of disinfectants."

Acknowledging that credible observers are present only to observe without interference—including observation of both the problems and the successful aspects of an election—could be beneficial irrespective of a state's stance on election administration. Credible, nonpartisan observation aims to report on the quality of the conduct of elections based on democratic standards and practices. Observers should report and note any instances of voter fraud as well as instances of discrimination or restricted access. Consistent and high-quality independent observers can thus be seen as one means to increase the prospects for positive improvements in the

U.S. electoral process, particularly when implementable, evidence-based recommendations are made (Martinez i Coma, Nai, and Norris 2016).

Law versus practice

In the absence of rules, practice regarding observation, especially nonpartisan observation, varies greatly in the U.S. Lack of specification in statute or written policy does not necessarily mean that observers can or cannot access polling places in a given state. The case-by-case approach adopted by many states permits local jurisdictions to reject not only those observers who they may view as but also those who are credible and non-disruptive. Some states or county officials reserve the right to allow observers who have been deemed credible at the time when they seek access. However, the reality that there is often no policy at the state or county levels—in statute or in practice—is problematic for several reasons.

First, international election obligations protect the right of citizens to participate in the public affairs of their country. By creating uncertainty in the process, and even prohibiting citizen nonpartisan observation in some cases, states effectively undermine this fundamental electoral right.

Next, while the U.S. federal government signed the 1990 Copenhagen Document (CSCE/OSCE 1990) agreeing to provide access for nonpartisan observers in each state, many states have continued to bar access to observers, either as a general practice or as an explicit rule. Hence, while state-level access still needs to be standardized in many cases, no national standard exists, and several states are not in compliance with the U.S. obligation to accept international observers.

Among observer groups, this divide between formal and informal policies can lead to confusion about their ability to gain access to observe, ultimately discouraging their presence in many states. For instance, the OAS decided to deploy observers only to those states that would definitely grant them access. The current system also creates logistical hurdles for organizations interested in observing, which inhibit their activities, even in environments where observation may ultimately be welcome. Not knowing if observers will be able to gain access until they are in-country and/ or in-county (i.e., very close to an election) makes it difficult to plan an observation mission. As a result, some organizations err on the side of caution and will not pursue access to observe in areas where they feel they are not likely to gain it.

The lack of clear rules and procedures also places greater importance on the relationships between observer organizations and election administrators. As the Carter Center's interviews revealed, some citizen nonpartisan and academic observer groups have been able to build strong relationships with administrators in specific counties. These relationships have been integral to those observers gaining access and developing credibility among administrators over time and have served to guarantee their access in states where observation was not granted in statute. However, not all observer groups can afford or are willing to build these relationships over multiple election cycles in order to gain access. For those observers not deemed legitimate when first seeking access, opportunities to build such relationships with election officials and administrators may not be available, and hence access is also unattainable.

Overall, a deeper review and analysis is needed regarding whether observer access should be dependent on election officials' interpretation and discretion. What are the benefits to formalizing access or prohibition of observers in each state? Standardization would not only make it easier for nonpartisan observers and voters to know where they can be present to watch, but it would also be useful for administrators to have clear policies to implement when they are expected to run smooth elections and respond to observers. With standardized frameworks, rules, and expectations, nonpartisan observers could more consistently work to support administrators, serving as their eyes and ears for misconduct or issues, as some observers and administrators reported is already the case. Clarity about observer access could help codify some of the current practices used in states to accommodate observers where statutes do not specify.

Lack of awareness of nonpartisan observation

Interviews with SEDs and legislators revealed that there is a general lack of awareness about the role of credible nonpartisan observers and how they can help to improve elections. Interviews with international nonpartisan, citizen nonpartisan, and academic observers confirmed this finding. Some experts posited that this resistance to observation, especially by non-U.S. groups, is based on an assumption that democracy in the United States is perfectly sound and does not require external scrutiny. Another possible explanation is fear that non-U.S. groups are either foreign government spies looking to rig U.S. elections, which Russian observers have been accused of, or that they are trying to undermine U.S. democracy by exposing cracks in the election administration system (Victor 2016).

Some SEDs expressed disapproval of policies that grant widespread access to observers because this could potentially invite groups looking to cause problems, such as voter intimidation or efforts to weaken trust in the quality of the elections in some way. Some election officials appear not to trust observers because they believe they will have a partisan bias or do not have a nonpartisan interest in improving elections. A few SEDs had poor experiences with disruptive observers in the past who claimed to be nonpartisan but ultimately intimidated voters or acted upon interests in the political outcome. Future research could focus on the paradox of fearing nonpartisan observation while partisan observation remains a widespread practice in the United States.

Overall, the majority of SEDs were not particularly familiar with the roles, responsibilities, or objectives of nonpartisan observers. Only a few SEDs expressed a clear understanding that nonpartisan election observers, especially international observers, follow a professional, impartial methodology that normally requires close coordination with, and respect for the authority of, election administrators.

Outdated laws

After speaking with election officials in many states, it is clear that reforming outdated laws on observer access would require much greater attention at the state level in order to be successful. However, many states have developed practices for observers, such as public access or case-by-case access, to fill in practical gaps not addressed in law. It is possible that administrators in some states are finding ways to include nonpartisan entities in the electoral process because their laws are simply out of date and do not address rules for observers. It is also possible that many states' laws are out of date due to the lack of awareness regarding observation. If the latter is the case, it would not necessarily be indicative, at least on a national level, of resistance to greater observation of U.S. elections, but rather a basic inattention to the subject.

U.S. self-conception as the leader of democracy

Regardless of the possible causes for the current regulatory landscape, it can be argued that the confusing variation and ambiguity of the laws and rules regulating observers has a negative impact on how other nations view the quality and credibility of democracy and elections in the U.S. Restricting the role of observers or making observation more difficult suggests that the United States is not interested in ensuring transparency in our electoral system, even if this is not the reality. As observers at the OSCE mentioned, if the United States does not allow standard access for election observers, it is easy for other member states that signed the 1990 CSCE/OSCE *Copenhagen Document* to do the same. More fundamentally, the United States has obligated itself by the OSCE Copenhagen commitments to ensure effective international observation of its elections. While individual states have the constitutional power to administer elections, that should not allow them to prevent the United States from abiding by its commitments. What does it say about the democratic nature of U.S. elections that impartial observers cannot easily participate?

Conclusions

A broader dialogue is needed in the United States about the role and benefits of election observation, specifically nonpartisan observation. In a sense, elections provide a snapshot and stress test of the health of a society's democracy. Recent elections have seen declines in public confidence in the honesty of elections in the United States and the rise of new and dangerous threats to election integrity in the forms of cyberattacks, hacking, fake news, and other challenges. While the United States has traditionally taken comfort in our self-conception as a global leader on democracy and transparency, it is clear that serious threats to democracy and democratic institutions are growing both domestically and worldwide (Carothers 2016).

In this context, it is important for citizens and political leaders to consider steps that can be taken to help improve election integrity. Expanding the role of nonpartisan election observers could be part of a larger strategy to restore confidence. While election observation alone cannot provide a singular solution for rebuilding trust in the credibility of U.S. elections and democracy, impartial observers could help identify the main challenges and provide recommendations for steps to improve the democratic nature of U.S. election administration. As the Carter Center heard in interviews, some county administrators already use their relationships with nonpartisan observers to demonstrate their efforts to address key issues. These partnerships can lead to meaningful steps to improve election administration and to address criticisms directed at election officials who are committed to transparent elections and electoral reform.

Election observation is a tool for identifying solutions to electoral issues rather than a final solution to all of our electoral problems. Some researchers argue that election observation may not be particularly influential in building confidence in elections, and that it may have a weak effect on citizens' perceptions of election credibility in contexts with high levels of partisanship (Bush and Prather 2017). As the U.S. political and electoral systems are strongly characterized by partisanship, we should continue to consider how nonpartisan observers would affect this dynamic. Research on the impacts of international and domestic election observation should also continue to inform our discussions of the possible role for nonpartisan observers in strengthening elections in the United States. This research is not conclusive on the potential effects of increased election observation across states but aims, rather, to address gaps in awareness and available information on existing regulations in order to support substantive conversation and debate on the subject going forward.

Building on the Carter Center and the National Conference of State Legislatures' review of state policies and practices for observers, a number of areas for further research could be undertaken in order to complement findings about election observation in the U.S. Some larger questions for additional academic research should first consider why partisan observers are viewed as more trustworthy than nonpartisan observers. Given that partisan observers have an allegiance to a specific political party, while nonpartisan observers must work without favoring any political outcome, there is a need for further study of what lies behind this perception and exactly how widely it is held. It is possible that a lack of understanding or awareness of the role of nonpartisan observers has led to this perception, but this explanation would require follow-up research in order to be fully confirmed.

Additional research could also look at the possible correlation between states' and counties' political leanings and their openness to nonpartisan election observers. A related study could consider why international observers generally receive greater support from the U.S. federal government than from state election authorities. Other useful areas for research could include examining the implications that current rules and regulations for observers have on the role of the citizen in the U.S. electoral process. Finally, while some research exists regarding the impact of observation on public perceptions of the electoral process, additional studies should explore whether and how election observation might more specifically help to improve trust in the honesty of U.S. elections.

Notes

1. In 2016, 30% of Americans polled by Gallup expressed confidence in the honesty of elections in general. This was a decline of 10% from the previous year and an almost 30% decline from 2009. According to Gallup, the United States ranked 90th of the 112 countries where Gallup asked that question in 2016 (McCarthy and Clifton 2016).
2. This assessment is based on the Carter Center's experience observing 107 elections in 39 countries over the course of three decades. While most sovereign states have a centralized election commission or authority and a national election law, requirements for elections in the United States vary by individual state, and elections are administered only at the state level.
3. Only Alabama, Arkansas, Maine, Nevada, Pennsylvania, Virginia, and Wyoming did not respond.
4. Nevada, North Dakota, and Wisconsin do not explicitly name partisan observers in statute, but all three states have statutory language providing access to "any person" or "any member of the public." Partisan observers could gain access under these policies.
5. Hawaii, Illinois, Maryland, Michigan, New Mexico, North Dakota, South Dakota, Tennessee, and Virginia as well as D.C.
6. California, Massachusetts, Nevada, New Hampshire, Rhode Island, South Carolina, Vermont, Washington, and Wisconsin.
7. Colorado, Delaware, Idaho, Kansas, Kentucky, Louisiana, Maine, Minnesota, Montana, Nebraska, New Jersey, New York, North Carolina, Ohio, Oregon, and Utah.
8. California, Missouri, New Mexico, North Dakota, and South Dakota.
9. Ten states and D.C. were not confirmed to have had DOJ observers in the past: Arkansas, Colorado, Delaware, Nevada, Oklahoma, Pennsylvania, Rhode Island, Vermont, West Virginia, and Wyoming.
10. Only Maine, Massachusetts, Mississippi, Montana, Nevada, New Hampshire, North Dakota, South Dakota, Vermont, and West Virginia do not have a process for appointing and officially recognizing partisan observers.
11. California, Colorado, Hawaii, Idaho, Illinois, Kansas, Maryland, Michigan, New Mexico, Ohio, Tennessee, Virginia, and Wisconsin, as well as D.C.
12. California, Colorado, Hawaii, Idaho, Kansas, Michigan, New Mexico, Ohio, Virginia, and Wisconsin, as well as D.C.
13. Massachusetts, Mississippi, Montana, New Hampshire, North Dakota, South Dakota, and Vermont.

9

Decentralized Administration

CRAIG ARCENEAUX

U.S. Supreme Court Justice Louis Brandeis famously argued that federalism allows states to act as "laboratories of democracy."[1] According to this idea, federalism allows states to experiment with different policies such that the country as a whole is then able to evaluate which policy choices work better than others. With 50 states as laboratories, not to mention the roughly 13,000 local electoral jurisdictions, the United States would appear primed to advance electoral integrity. But as Norris, Cameron, and Wynter (this volume) and Vickery and Szilagyi (this volume) show, in fact the country lags behind other comparable Western democracies. Could federalism actually be the culprit here? After all, one might just as easily view the mosaic of rules and regulations in these laboratories as a source of confusion, and the flexibility at the local level as worsening parochial interests, consistent standards, and professional electoral administration.

Any move to incriminate federalism must proceed with caution. Federalism is found in almost 30 countries throughout the world, and it is constructed differently from one to another (Anderson 2008). As shown in this chapter, federal states exhibit a wide range of electoral integrity. The chapter compares the United States with Canada, Mexico, and Brazil to show that federalism is compatible with a variety of administrative electoral procedures and decision-making arrangements. Still, it would be wrong to then conclude that federalism has no impact on electoral integrity in the United States, where electoral procedures are so decentralized and instilled in federal relations. Justice Brandeis presents an idealized portrait of the impact of federalism on policy innovation, one that places unwarranted faith in the system to regulate itself and stir improvements. But federalism allows state actors to pursue or to undermine electoral integrity.

I look to Albert Hirschman's model of "exit, voice, and loyalty" to evaluate how federalism, and U.S. federalism in particular, affects the opportunity to improve electoral integrity. This focus on opportunity is significant. Security and inclusiveness are both fundamental to the growth of electoral integrity, but, as Pallister argues in this volume, they can clash. Recognizing how to balance the two values, and that some electoral procedures require trade-offs between the two while others enhance both, is indispensable to any reasoned, evidenced-based set of best practices. But the scholarly identification of good policies addresses only part of the problem for those seeking electoral reform in the United States. The practical pursuit of those reforms must work its way through, and ultimately confront, federal arrangements that have long tailored interests, strategies, and reactions to the established electoral arrangements in the United States. Flawed electoral arrangements often serve powerful interests. Whether these can counter the collective interest in electoral integrity is a matter of inquiry. Hirschman's model of "exit, voice, and loyalty" helps us understand how federal institutions affect the will and motivation of actors to change electoral procedures for good or ill.

Federalism and electoral integrity in comparative perspective

The Perceptions of Electoral Integrity (PEI) survey facilitates analysis of the relationship between federalism and electoral integrity. The study surveys experts on their assessments of the quality of national elections worldwide (Norris, Wynter, and Cameron 2018a). As Latner discusses in this volume, the database collects expert perceptions of the quality of elections on 11 different dimensions and assigns an overall 100-point summary score to a country based upon its national elections.[2] The United States does not fare well on the PEI Index. In 2017, Denmark, Finland, and Norway topped the list, with aggregate scores of 87, 86, and 83, respectively. The United States scored just 61, ranking it 55th of the 164 countries in the index (see Norris, Cameron, and Wynter, this volume). The United States sits at the lowest level of all consolidated democracies, and below several countries, such as Tunisia, Ghana, and Mongolia, where democracy has yet to firmly establish itself (Norris, Garnett, and Grömping 2017). Among the dimensions on which the United States falls short, a few stand out. The country scores 14 on district boundaries, and reaches just 40 on voter registration—two dimensions that fall primarily within the purview of state-level officials. The score of 36 on electoral laws is a drag on the overall score, and it too is influenced considerably by state-level officials. Norris, Cameron, and Wynter (this volume) show that V-Dem's rating of free and fair elections generate similar cross-national rankings, providing independent validity tests.

The low rating of the United States, and its poor scores on dimensions that largely fall under state authorities, beg the question: Does federalism impair electoral integrity? As a first cut, we can take a look at the PEI scores of federal countries. And to better isolate the presumed negative impact of federal institutions, we will look exclusively at federal countries that are fully fledged democracies, as identified by Freedom House (2017). Overall, the 12 federal democratic countries fare quite well on the PEI Index. They score an average of 68, which would collectively rank them at number 33, on par with Japan. Indeed for every problematic federal state, such as the United States (61) or India (59), there is a commendable federal state, such as Germany (81) or Switzerland (79). Importantly, then, federal states exhibit a wide range of electoral integrity. Likewise one cannot pinpoint any specific dimensions of electoral integrity that all federal states uniformly appear to lag on, as one would expect if federalism had a corrosive impact on certain aspects of the democratic machinery. As noted, the United States does very poorly on district boundaries (14), electoral laws (36), and voter registration (40), but the other 11 federal democracies score an average of 58, 64, and 63 on these dimensions, though with significant variation. In all, descriptive statistics provide no evidence to the effect that federal institutions per se generally depress electoral integrity.

Does this mean that federalism has no bearing on electoral integrity? To answer this question, we need to take a closer look at precisely what federalism is, how it is designed, and how this affects electoral administration.

Most countries find it practicable to split the work of politics between the national and subnational governments. Hence, even in unitary states, central governments often delegate some policymaking power to local bodies. But federal systems reinforce this division with a legal guarantee of control at the lower level. While unitary regimes may decentralize some policymaking power, they can conceivably retract it at any given time, while federal states cannot. Sovereignty is therefore shared in a federal system, and this separation between two levels of government can be considered the essence of federalism (Anderson 2008, 4). Nevertheless the degree of political, fiscal, and administrative decentralization varies among federal and unitary states.

In theory, a division of policy responsibilities can be made: the national government often assumes the sole right to engage in international agreements and retains primary responsibility for matters of defense and economic planning, while the lower-level governments focus on social policies such as health, education, welfare, cultural programs, and basic matters of law and order. But in practice, sharing sovereignty is a much messier affair (Elazar 1987). Still, this does not stop countries from attempting to enumerate exclusive policy areas, often with actual lists in sections of their constitution, and often with a nod toward sharing with a third list of concurrent powers. As a safeguard against new policy areas that may arise, and to ensure flexibility, countries may reserve residual powers (powers not expressly mentioned) for the national or subnational level and allow for the growth of implied powers. Clearly, then, while two countries may share the federal label, their precise mix of enumerated, concurrent, residual, and implied powers may differ dramatically. Likewise the placement of electoral policy powers can fluctuate from one country to another.

Relations among the subnational units of a federal system can also vary dramatically from case to case. The drawing of borders and groupings of peoples may create contrasts of scale, economic opportunity, and cultural uniformity. These differences create political asymmetries. Countries can offset this with constitutional asymmetries—that is, legally mandated arrangements that allow some groups to be treated differently or granted distinct self-governing powers (Watts 1999). Commonly, federal countries will attempt to offset political asymmetries with a second legislative chamber, the senate, that grants the constituent units more or less equal representation despite their differences in population. Federal countries may also simply grant constitutional asymmetries to assuage the concerns of politically significant minorities, as Canada does with Quebec and as Spain does with its autonomous communities Catalonia and the Basque Country (McGarry 2005).

Generally speaking, national governments can react to these real power differences among constituent units in one of two ways. The United States embraces competitive federalism, which views differences as sources of innovation and entrepreneurship. Modeled on the free market, federalism allows discrepancies in resources and influence, which are thought to stir creativity, and even out financially in the long run as firms move to lower-cost constituent units. On the other hand, Germany advocates cooperative federalism and uses tools such as equalization transfers to even out economic differences and hopefully reduce disparities and friction in the short run (Watts 2006).

Given the range of choices, it is no surprise that federal systems differ substantially from one country to another. Countries select certain features given their particular needs and as a product of their political values and histories. For example, some federal countries that emerged as formerly independent states grouped themselves together as a larger country. This model of "coming together" federalism is distinguished from "holding together" federalism, whereby a country transforms itself into a federal state to address regional distinctions. Alfred Stepan (1999) notes that this history matters. Predictably, "coming together" federal systems tend to reserve more rights for the states. They are more likely to embrace constitutional symmetry, grant residual powers to the states, and guarantee these features in a more rigid constitution.

But in addition to the distinct characteristics of a given federal system, there is also the question of fit: how the particular design of federalism corresponds to other political institutions found in the political system of the country. Arend Lijphart (1999) provides some ground rules, arguing that federalism works best with bicameralism, a strong judiciary, and rigid constitution. As he puts it, these institutions "are guarantors of federalism rather than components of federalism itself" (188). Bicameralism assures that the subnational governments will have their own representative chamber in a senate. A strong judiciary establishes a referee should disputes emerge between the national and lower-level governments. And a rigid constitution offers the constituent units confidence that their accorded policymaking powers will be respected. As it turns out, these three institutions are commonly found in federal systems, but their appearance—the balance of bicameralism, strength of the judiciary, and rigidity of the constitution—is also a matter of degree. Even more, the institutions are often a matter of compromise with other institutional values held in the political system. For example, the strength and role of the judiciary is significantly affected by whether a country makes use of a code law system, as in Brazil and Mexico, or a common law system, as in Canada and the United States. There is also a host of other institutional choices, such as presidential or parliamentary government, executive power, the party system, relations with international institutions, or majoritarian or proportional electoral systems, that further affect the impact of federalism. In the following section, I provide an overview of four examples of federal systems to illustrate the diversity.

Electoral systems in federal countries: Case studies

Federalism is compatible with a variety of electoral arrangements. Nonetheless federalism plays a critical role in each because of the legal guarantees it may provide to those arrangements as part of the balance of policy authority between national- and state-level governments. A number of components compose electoral arrangements, but some of the most significant are control over the administration of elections and rule making (e.g., district boundaries and electoral formulas), the partisanship of the electoral management board, and the setting for the adjudication of disputes. The United States embraces a system that decentralizes electoral administration and rule making. Brazil takes the opposite tack, with centralization in both areas, while Canada and Mexico rest midway by allowing decentralized rule making but centralizing their electoral administration. In the area of partisanship, the United States and Mexico both staff their electoral boards with partisans, while Brazil and Canada look to nonaligned professionals. Finally, the code law traditions in Brazil and Mexico lead them to establish specialized, central courts to adjudicate electoral disputes, while the United States and Canada remain true to the common law tradition and allow lower-level courts to address disputes in the first instance.

The United States

The 13 original colonies of the United States created a confederacy at independence, and only after tremendous debate accepted federal arrangements under the 1789 Constitution. Theirs was clearly a story of "coming together," with guarantees instilled through constitutional symmetry, residual powers that rest in the states, and a rigid constitution. Within this context, Article I, Section 4 of the Constitution, also known as the Elections Clause, places electoral policy in the hands of state authorities, though with an open condition to significant oversight powers at the national level. The clause reads, "The Times, Places, and Manner of holding Elections for Senators and Representatives, shall be prescribed in each state by the Legislature thereof; but the Congress may at any time make or alter such Regulations." The clause may appear to offer Congress expansive authority, but over time the courts have interpreted its power as limited to a reactive, veto power, exerted only over the core functions of representation and voting when the states take actions that grossly violate constitutional rights (Weinstein-Tull 2016, 776).

The narrow interpretation of the Elections Clause has created an electoral system that has been characterized as hyper-decentralized (Ewald 2009). Many countries may opt for decentralization for whatever reason, whether or not they embrace federal arrangements. The key distinction in the U.S. case is that this decentralization is embedded in and ultimately sheltered by the legal guarantees of federalism and judicial interpretations of the Election Clause. This interlacing of electoral decentralization and federalism in the United States is highlighted by Justin Weinstein-Tull (2016), who discusses the pathology of a system that allows national authorities to legislate on electoral matters but also protects the rights of state-level authorities to delegate responsibilities to local governments. Hence, despite recent national regulations under the National Voter Registration Act of 1993, the Help America Vote Act of 2002, and the Military and Overseas Voter Empowerment Act of 2009, the national government has had difficulty enforcing its mandates in the face of numerous incidents of noncompliance. When brought to court, state agencies have argued that they are not the proper defenders or lack the authority to compel local governments in areas described by the regulations. Though many of the arguments have not succeeded, the litigation has significantly slowed national regulatory powers. In many cases, the courts declare a state noncompliant but sidestep the issue of how to enforce compliance (Weinstein-Tull 2016, 746–75). Perhaps just as significant, the litigious backlash has dulled national attempts to pursue further reforms.

Details on U.S. electoral arrangements are discussed further in this volume by Vickery and Szilagyi. The key here is to recognize how federalism shields this system from significant intrusions by the national government and thereby allows substantial differences to emerge as state and local authorities find tremendous latitude to act on their own. This has allowed partisanship to flourish as parties capture state and local administrative bodies and design procedures to their own liking. A recent application of the PEI Index at the state level illustrated that these differences also exist across electoral integrity, with scores ranging from 73 to 75 in New Mexico, Iowa, New Hampshire, Idaho, and Vermont, but falling to 55 or below in Oklahoma, Tennessee, Wisconsin, and Arizona (Norris, Nai, and Grömping 2016). Reflecting upon his home state of North Carolina, one U.S. scholar lamented, "If it were a nation-state, North Carolina would rank right in the middle of the global league table—a deeply flawed, partly free democracy that is only slightly ahead of the failed democracies that constitute much of the developing world" (Reynolds 2016).[3] These discrepancies place doubt on the "laboratories of democracy" argument. Rather than providing laboratories for experimentation on policies such that states can learn from each other and improve, federalism appears to shelter policies that fail to advance and even subvert electoral integrity. The "exit, voice, and loyalty" model develops this argument below.

Canada

Most scholars understand Canada to have a more decentralized form of federalism than the United States (Simeon 2006).[4] They also understand this to be ironic, because when Canada first forged its federal institutions under the 1867 British North America Act, it did so with the U.S. case in mind and with an eye toward a more centralized version of federalism. From the Canadian perspective, the U.S. Civil War stemmed largely from weak federal authority. And perhaps more important, there was a real fear that the United States might turn its attention north for conquest and an understanding that this threat could best be met with a stronger central government. To underscore its different federal model, Canada placed its residual powers in the national government, in clear contrast to the Tenth Amendment of the U.S. Constitution, which grants residual powers to the state governments. Whatever the intentions, since that time U.S. federalism has increasingly tilted toward the national government, while Canadian federalism has shifted authority toward its provinces. There are many explanations for this: a byproduct of U.S. presidentialism, of U.S. priority to security and defense policies, of Canada's approach to language and cultural divisions by granting greater autonomy to provinces, while the U.S. approach to racial division has been to empower the national government to defend against nefarious state and local authorities. But one common thread in each country ultimately pointed each in a different direction. Both countries make use of a common law system, and thereby afford their courts the power of judicial review to help mold implied powers.

Irrespective of their constitutional founders' intents, the Judicial Committee of the Privy Council (the final court of appeal in Canada up to 1949, when it was replaced by the Supreme Court) has interpreted the division of power to the benefit of the provinces, while the U.S. Supreme Court has tended to side with the national government. The trends may have also been the unintended product of strong bicameralism in the United States and weak bicameralism in Canada.[5] In the United States, the federal lines of debate work their way through Congress and take place at the national level, while in Canada, the provincial governments themselves take primary responsibility for their own interests vis-à-vis the national government.

Scholars can therefore note that Canadian provinces assume a higher proportion of total government revenues and spend with greater autonomy than their U.S. counterparts. But federalism is about control over specific policy areas, and this is often a matter of degree. In fact, in an index of the distribution of powers in federal systems, Ronald L. Watts (2008) finds that the Canadian federal government assumes primary control of 18 policy areas and the provinces take on 23. The numbers for the United States are 11 and 25, respectively. And Canada has 7 shared policy areas to the United States total of 9. One can conclude that Canada is more decentralized, but that may differ in any given policy area, and the administration of elections is one of these exceptions.

Unlike in the United States, in Canada a single institution, Elections Canada, assumes administrative authority over elections (Courtney 2007). The body is hierarchically organized, with a chief electoral officer (CEO) and deputy electoral officer at the top, and a returning officer (RO) in each of the 338 ridings (the term used for districts in Canada), who in turn presides over a deputy returning officer and polling clerk in the approximately 73,000 polling stations in the country. Parliament appoints the CEO for a 10-year term, and the CEO in turn appoints ROs for 10-year terms. The body is an independent agency, with authority to administer elections, oversee the maintenance of the National Register of Electors, engage voter information, oversee campaign finance, and train staff. The Canada Elections Act, along with a series of 2014 amendments known as the Fair Elections Act, provide the primary legal framework for elections. A commissioner of Canada Elections holds responsibility for enforcing the legal framework (including the power to investigate), though all Canadian citizens can either file a complaint through the commissioner's office or make use of the regular courts and ultimately appeal to the Supreme Court. Under the 2014 reforms, the commissioner is appointed to a seven-year term by the director of public prosecutions, where his office is located.

Elections Canada continuously updates the voter lists using various government agency databases (e.g., vehicles, hunting, pensions). Canadian citizens see their information automatically updated, though they are given the right to request that they be removed from the list. Those that may have been overlooked may register on Election Day. All voters are required to confirm their identity and residence at the polls, though Canada has a very inclusive identification process, accepting about 50 different types of ID, from driver's licenses to debit cards, student IDs, library cards, utility bills, and even labels on prescription medicine. Provinces redraw boundaries after each decennial census, but all work according to the same rules. A nonpartisan independent commission is led by a judge appointed by the chief justice of the province. The speaker of the House of Commons appoints two additional members.

Campaign finance is highly regulated. Only citizens and permanent residents can make contributions, and they are limited to 1,500 CAD for each political party, candidate, party district association, or nominee contestant. All contributions over 200 CAD are matters of public record and must be reported to Elections Canada. Candidates can spend 5,000 CAD of their own money and make use of a loan of up to 1,500 CAD. A system of public financing reimburses parties and candidates up to 50% of their spending if they poll over 2% in the national vote. The media is regulated by fair-time rules, and third-party media spending is limited to 150,000 CAD nationally and 3,000 CAD in any given riding. There are spending limits, but the 2014 reforms allowed spending to be proportionate to the length of the campaign. Because the 2015 electoral campaign ran 78 days, nearly double the previous election, overall spending rose from 290 million CAD to 443 million CAD, and public funding rose from about 60 million CAD to 120 million CAD (CBC News 2016).

Mexico

Mexico established a federal system under its first constitution, in 1824, but federalism soon emerged as a cover for regional *caudillo* rule rather than as an ingredient in a democratic, balance-of-power political system. The dictatorship of Porfirio Díaz (1876–1911) ran roughshod over federal lines of authority, so it was little surprise that the Constitution of 1917 attempted to reinstall federal ideas. Nonetheless one-party dominance by the Institutional Revolutionary Party (PRI) created an authoritarian regime up to 2000, when the party finally relinquished control of the presidency after losing elections. Mexico still operates under the Constitution of 1917, and though democratic politics remain fragile in the country, the state governments have emerged as potent players and no longer simply answer to the national government, as under the PRI regime (Beer 2012).

But if politics have grown more decentralized in Mexico, elections have become more centralized (Pérez and González Ulloa 2011). Interestingly, the centralization of elections first served the interests of authoritarianism. Under the Electoral Law of 1946, municipalities lost the power to organize elections, be they municipal, state, or federal, and the national government set more stringent guidelines for the creation of political parties. The law solidified the hegemonic position of the PRI by removing the independent status of the Federal Electoral Commission with flexible appointment powers of its members and placed the power to certify elections in the hands of Congress. The secretary of the interior, a political position, took charge of investigating electoral malpractices. By the 1970s, declining voter turnout, the threat of armed insurrection, and general calls for democratization convinced the PRI of the need for electoral reform to, at a minimum, assuage its critics. Beginning in 1977, a number of reforms looked first to the elements of representation. Parties found it easier to receive recognition, and the allocation of some congressional seats through proportional representation allowed opposition parties to see gains in Congress. Still, the opening of representation was offset by closer oversight of the electoral administration, as in the 1986 electoral reform, which gave the president complete control over appointments to all electoral offices, even at local polling offices.

A resurgence of criticism arose in 1988, after the manifestly fraudulent presidential election. To mitigate the public outcry, a 1989 reform created the Federal Electoral Institute (IFE). Opposition parties gained some power to appoint officials, but the governing PRI retained majority control and the body itself sat under the secretary of the interior. In 1996, a capstone reform made the IFE fully independent and, just as important, created the Electoral Tribunal of the Federal Judiciary (TEPJF) to render final decisions of electoral disputes. (Previously, judicial decisions on electoral matters could be overturned by Congress.) This court would also address municipal and state elections and reach into state politics with the creation of regional courts. Still, alongside this centralization, Mexico retains some decentralization in the rule-making surrounding electoral matters, as with redistricting, which rests within state-level boards and allows for different formulas and approaches across states (López Levi and Reyes Garmendia 2008).

Although analysts rightly portray 2000 as the year of Mexico's democratic transition, the history of reforms shows that the democratization process had an earlier start date, and in fact continues through various political reforms. There is little doubt that Mexico has a much stronger electoral administrative system today. A national code, the General Law on Electoral Institutions and Procedures of Mexico, serves as the basis for all elections, from presidential contests to municipal balloting. The rise of the TEPJF marked the movement of electoral adjudication from the political realm to the judiciary (Berruecos 2003). The National Electoral Institute (INE, which would take over the responsibilities of the IFE; see below) actively updates a general catalog of voters from the census rolls but requires voters to self-register, after which it issues biometric voter ID cards (it includes a photo and fingerprint), and even distributes photos along with lists of voters to polling stations to ensure proper identification. These INE documents compose the federal registry of voters and serve both national and state/municipal elections.

But if under the PRI regime the country saw a gradual growth of representation even while electoral deceit remained and even increased, today the crisis rests within the representative realm. After the jubilation of the 2000 elections, the 2006 and 2012 elections were far more contentious and prompted high-stakes negotiations among the major parties, which actually served to reinstall partisan influence in elections (Serra 2012). After the creation of the IFE, the body saw a general movement of its nine-member General Council from government and party appointees to unaffiliated citizens. But the 2007 reforms allowed Congress to reappoint members of the IFE to satisfy partisan demands for representation. Likewise the reforms created a comptroller to supervise the finances of the IFE, and this comptroller answers directly to Congress. The 2014 reforms replaced the IFE with the INE and ostensibly strengthened it by giving it more complete control over all state electoral boards (previously, it delegated many of the state and local controls it did hold) and expanded powers over regulated campaign finances at lower levels. But the new 11-member General Council retains the partisan quota.

Mexican democracy presents us with a puzzle. Recent reforms have been much more extensive than those described here, including a number of progressive changes. Campaigns face spending caps and work within a media that must offer equal time. The no-reelection provision for congresspersons has been dropped to increase accountability. Citizens now have referendum opportunities. New rules require gender parity in candidate nominations for parties. Independents now have the right to run for office. And previous immunity protections for the presidency have been withdrawn. And yet Mexicans remain distrustful and dissatisfied with their government. Suspicion clouds every reform, often with good reason. The expansion of public financing is viewed not as an equalizing measure but as one that further solidifies the position of the three dominant parties. The abundance of corruption scandals lends little credence to forceful regulations on the use of state resources for political campaigns (Serra 2016). Moves to centralize electoral administration to increase efficiency, professionalization, and transparency are viewed with suspicion as partisan influence grows (*LADB* 2014). One may have expected the 2015 legislative elections to be a celebration of the new reforms, but they were ultimately marred by some of the highest levels of electoral violence in recent decades (*LADB* 2015). On paper and in many ways in practice, Mexico can claim credit for laudable electoral procedures. But that matters little if the public does not have confidence in government to begin with.

Brazil

Brazil democratized in 1985, but its electoral code can be traced to 1932, a product of the Revolution of 1930. Elections in Brazil had been tainted by *coronelismo*— control by local bosses, or patrons (*coronéis*)—since the founding of the Republic in 1889. The code not only improved the integrity of suffrage by adopting the secret ballot and expanding the vote to women and all citizens 18 and over, but it also implemented two procedural changes that continue to characterize the Brazilian voting system. The code moved the management and supervision of elections from the legislature to the courts, and it centralized the administration of voting in the national government. Despite the dramatic political changes in Brazil through the 20th century, the electoral justice system design has remained relatively stable (though it was suspended or restricted on several occasions).

Whereas Mexico assigns responsibility for the management of elections and the adjudication of elections to two separate bodies, Brazil looks to just one institution. The Superior Electoral Tribunal (TSE, Tribunal Superior Eleitoral) takes full responsibility for administering the electoral system, from the registration of voters and printing of ballots to voter information campaigns, the recruitment of poll workers, the enforcement of campaign finance provisions, and the adjudication of disputes (Fleischer and Barreto 2009). The body itself consists of seven members, five of whom are judges and two of whom hail from the legal profession. Those from the legal profession are selected by the president from a list of six provided by the Supreme Federal Tribunal (Brazil's Constitutional Court). Notably, three justices are recruited from the Supreme Federal Tribunal and two from the Superior Tribunal of Justice, and they retain their primary positions even while they serve on the TSE. The crossover appears to facilitate legal understandings, for although the TSE stands as the final court of appeal on electoral matters, if a constitutional question comes into play, the case can be brought to the Supreme Federal Tribunal. Nonetheless there are no cases of the Supreme Federal Tribunal overturning a ruling by the TSE, and in most cases the court refuses to review the decisions (Marchetti 2012, 119). Despite the short two-year tenures of the court officials, the overall insulation of the Brazilian judiciary ensures the autonomy of the electoral court. In fact the court advertises the short terms as a method to insulate it from partisan influence.[6] Directly beneath the TSE rest the regional electoral tribunals in each state and the federal district. These regional courts also consist of five judges and two legal professionals. The regional tribunals then select an electoral judge for each electoral district. This judge receives support from an ad hoc electoral board created just 60 days before the election and consisting of a judge and two to four citizens. Together, the electoral judge and electoral board manage and administrate elections within their district.

Electoral procedures in Brazil receive praise from analysts. Voting is compulsory (but optional for those 16–17 years of age). Voters are expected to self-register and notify the local electoral board should they move, and penalties for not doing so help ensure high registration rates.[7] Brazil embraced e-voting in 1998, and this has significantly enhanced suffrage. Brazil uses an open-list proportional system for its lower house, and before the use of voting machines, voters were faced with ballots that required them to write in the names of their desired candidates. High rates of illiteracy resulted in the spoilage of some 20% of ballots in each election. The voting machines simplify the process by asking voters to touch the portrait of their favored candidate on a screen. F. Daniel Hidalgo (2010) found evidence to argue that e-voting expanded the electorate by 30%. The TSE proudly advertises its use and the advantages of e-voting, even claiming to hold the world record for the quickest vote count.[8] The interest in technology is now moving toward the registration process, with a plan to have all Brazilians enrolled in a biometric registration system that will not only further ensure voter identification but will also allow Brazilians to vote outside their home district. Generally speaking, the relatively high regard Brazilians have for their judiciary (compared to other institutions) has transferred to the TSE, which also gained confidence since democratization.

This is not to say that electoral politics are not problematic in Brazil. While the voting process itself may be praiseworthy, the electoral system has fallen under criticism for stirring corruption scandals. Brazil not only has an open-list proportional representation system, but it also has rather relaxed rules for party recognition, offers significant public financing during the campaign, and gives party leaders few tools for party discipline. Individual competition and intraparty competition is fierce. Faced with strict campaign finance regulations, many candidates look to clandestine sources. And once in office, party leaders feel pressured to make use of bribery to corral their own partisans and cobble together majorities in a system that typically sees some 30-plus parties. The growing corruption is testing the credibility of the electoral justice system, as it ultimately holds responsibility for enforcing the electoral code. In 2015 the Supreme Federal Tribunal took up the case of corporate donations in elections and ruled them illegal. While the decision may have improved the position of the court as a force against corruption, in 2017 the TSE was asked to rule on the use of improper campaign finances by President Michel Temer during the 2014 election, but acquitted him in a 4–3 vote. Chief Judge Gilmar Mendes characterized the issue as one that required a political solution outside the realm of the court.

In all, the Brazilian approach to elections is distinguished by the role of the courts. It is an interesting distinction given the separation of powers principle in the presidential system in place. But in Brazil, the court takes a predominant position in the maintenance, execution, adjudication, and even creation of electoral regulations (through its interpretations and two-year review cycle of recommendations on the electoral code). As a federal system, Brazil's is recognized as one of the most decentralized (e.g., municipalities are not only constitutionally recognized, but even receive enumerated powers). Like Canada, Brazil nests its centralized electoral management in a federal system that is generally more decentralized than in the United States.

The search for electoral integrity: Exit, voice, loyalty, and federalism

Albert O. Hirschman published his seminal work, *Exit, Voice and Loyalty* (1970), in an effort to further develop the field of political economy. In his eyes, while both politics and economics deal with behavior, the former focuses too much on rebellion and the latter on withdrawal as mechanisms to exhibit dissatisfaction. Hirschman wanted to think more holistically and to appreciate how a negative change in any given situation creates two choices for individuals: they can either seek an alternative (exit) or attempt to fix things (voice). He is ultimately concerned with how (or if) a firm, organization, or state receives signals on its decline, and does something about it. After outlining his model, I will apply it to how individuals might react to electoral arrangements.

Individually, exit and voice appear to have rather straightforward consequences and responses. Given a decline in a product, consumers might switch to another item or simply do without it (exit), sending a clear message to the firm to address its problems. On the other hand, if the firm were a monopoly so that the consumers had no exit option, they would voice their grievances until the product was improved. The recognition of exit and voice offers a criticism of the free market model of competition, which depends on consumers to signal their dissatisfaction through exit (withdrawing purchases from one firm and moving to another). But

Hirschman notes that such a model provides little opportunity for recuperation if sales immediately collapse and the firm goes bankrupt. Alternatively, it is better to have a combination of "alert consumers," who exit and thereby signal dissatisfaction, and "inert consumers," who provide a cushion of demand and thereby the time for the firm to adapt (Hirschman 1970, 24). Another criticism of perfect competition, and its reliance on exit, is when all firms experience the same quality decline and consumers simply shift from one to another. This overreliance on exit allows all firms to survive even as quality declines continue, "and that to this extent competition and product diversification is wasteful and diversionary" (28). In such cases, monopoly is preferable to market competition (because it would force consumers to use voice). The insight appears to perfectly describe the plight of consumers who endlessly switch cable and satellite television plans, but it can also be applied to political presumptions. One market-based argument behind federalism is in the presumption that it offers laboratories of democracy. In the United States, there are 50 opportunities to test out public policies or electoral system designs, but this assumes that citizens will make some use of voice and that there will not be 50 different instances of product decline.

According to Hirschman, voice, like exit, can be overdone (or underdone). Again, it is best to have a mixture of alert and inert consumers. Looking specifically at democracy, neither permanent activism nor permanent apathy is desirable. But beyond the recognition of the choice between using exit or not, or between using voice or not, is the fact that in most instances both exit and voice simultaneously exist as strategies. And consumers will not only select between the two, but they may also use them complementarily, as with those who opt for voice but retain the threat of exit as a last resort.

Two broad sets of questions then arise. First, under what conditions will voice be preferred to exit? This opens several inquiries into the costs of voice and the barriers or ease of exit. A second set of questions surrounds the recognition that different groups may react differently—specifically, some consumers may be more quality conscious and others more price conscious, leading them to opt for voice or exit at different moments. Taking a short leap into the realm of politics, consider how this thinking affects our understanding of the dynamics of voting in a two-party system. Hirschman notes that the traditional understanding of the two-party system was largely based on location theories of firms: voters are thought to rest on a linear left-right continuum such that rational parties will move toward the center and collect more voters because those at the ends "have nowhere else to go." Hirschman contends that parties may be more responsive to extreme voters in two-party systems precisely because they have nowhere else to go and thus become more likely to use voice, especially when institutional rules such as malapportionment or gerrymandering (see Magleby et al., this volume) increase sensitivity to voice. In his time, he focused on the Barry Goldwater case, but today Donald Trump comes to mind.

Loyalty comes into play as a lag on exit. Importantly, loyalty is not the same as faith. It is a rational presumption that the organization will right itself in the long run. It does have its limits and can delay exit for only so long. But what loyalty does ensure is that the calculation of exit is more likely to be threatened (rather than used immediately) and thus noticed by the organization. In Hirschman's first writing, he further noted that loyalty (as a calculated decision) might also be the result of severe entry or exit costs. In this case, the loyal will stay the course, hoping for the best, while the firm receives neither the signals of exit nor voice, and the quality of the product will continue to decline.

Many since Hirschman's original publication have criticized his concept of loyalty as an underdeveloped, residual category. Rusbult and Zembrodt (1983; also see Rusbult 1988) argue that while exit and voice are active responses to a deteriorating situation, they are distinct in that voice is constructive and exit destructive. And loyalty is passive and constructive. What is missing is a passive and destructive response, or neglect. The added response is especially helpful to political analyses of governing bodies that do not offer an easy exit option, such as the state itself, because it captures apathy as a response. Other studies have identified distinctive effects of the responses. Hirschman himself noted that the model is geared toward the status quo, presuming that under optimum conditions a firm will receive signals and adjust accordingly to restore the relationship. But some who opt for the voice response may be more motivated by self-interest and attempt to restore the organization in a way that benefits them (Hirschman 1974). Further developing this idea, Dowding et al. (2000) argue that voice could be either collective (in pursuit of the common good) or individual (self-interested).

The addition of political apathy as a form of neglect and the self-interested dimension of individual voice are especially helpful to political studies, electoral design, and the impact of federalism. In this discussion, I apply Hirschman's model in the following way.

A democracy rests on a relationship between active citizens and a responsive government. Elections sit at the crux of this relationship, because they offer opportunities for citizens to communicate their interests and hold standing governments accountable for past preferences. After any given election, there will always be dissatisfied citizens (those whose candidates or parties lost), but in a strong democracy these citizens will remain loyal due to their confidence in the electoral system and the hope that they might win the next time around. In a perfect world, these conditions will bring about stability. Nonetheless, as we well know, electoral procedures need to be regularly adjusted or updated (e.g., as census results call for redistricting and as new technologies offer novel registration or voting practices) and often fall to criticism as societal preferences change (e.g., Should criminals be disenfranchised? Should primaries be open or closed?). Given a rising sense of dissatisfaction with the institutional design of the political system itself rather than the incumbent government, how will a citizen respond?

In the case of the state, exit is a difficult option given the costs of upending one's life and moving to another country. Nonetheless, if a state grows clearly undemocratic and repressive, the calculus may shift toward exit. But within democratic states, federal systems offer more opportunities for exit than do unitary systems. Galston and Mann (2010) recognize the option of exit within the United States, writing, "Because people increasingly prefer to live near others who share their cultural and political preferences, they are voting with their feet and sorting themselves geographically." Even if the costs of moving from one subnational unit to another remain high, federal principles of decentralization may mean that even moving to another county or municipality may offer some satisfaction. This does not mean citizens move in search of improved electoral integrity, but rather that when they move (typically for economic or personal reasons) they consider partisanship. One study found that "as much as 20% of the desirability of a place derives from its partisan location" (Gimpel and Hui 2015). Gerrymandering is a problem (see Magleby et al., this volume), but federalism may compound it as individuals "self-sort." Though exit may bring satisfaction to the citizens that chose it, damage is done to national politics as competition declines and polarization increases. Likewise the preference for exit denies government signals on how it might improve, and as with Hirschman's critique of perfect competition, citizens may simply be moving from one poorly constructed electoral regime to another. These citizens may grow loyal—not to electoral integrity but rather to electoral outcomes that fit their politics. They see no reason to voice concerns over poor electoral integrity.

Neglect is another corrosive response, and it occurs as citizens conclude that the costs of participation outweigh the benefits. Some citizens may be swayed more by high costs, and others by the lack of benefits. Difficult registration procedures, voter ID laws, or outright restrictions, as in the case of convicted felons in certain states, raise costs and keep some citizens from the polls (see Norris, Cameron, and Wynter, and Bergman, Tran, and Yates, this volume); others react to benefits—or the lack thereof—and do not vote because they just feel powerless or look upon all their political choices with dissatisfaction. Neglect can be measured by voter turnout. Federal systems are often criticized for fostering neglect through voter burnout due to the greater number of offices up for election or because the fragmentation resulting from federal institutions makes government less efficient and frustrates voters.

Voice entails an active strategy to change electoral arrangements, but those using voice may take different approaches. Optimally, citizens will face issues of electoral integrity with reasoned debate and evidence-based claims to address administrative or political problems. But though voice may be subdued by loyalty, it can also be distorted by collective action problems as citizens hope to freeride on the efforts of other citizens, or by the complexity of institutional design. (Gerken 2009 refers to this as the "invisibility" of electoral arrangements.) In the end, electoral integrity is a public good, but electoral design is not necessarily. Some political actors, driven by self-interest rather than the public interest, may find an opportunity to manipulate electoral designs to their advantage. This raises an interesting question: Under what conditions are efforts to change electoral design (i.e., voice) swayed by the public interest or by self-interest? Some of the genius of Hirschman's model emerges from his emphasis on how the likelihood of one strategy interacts with other potential strategies. Self-interested voice strategies face competition from other voice strategies (both public interest and self-interest), so it is reasonable to conclude that as more citizens select exit, loyalty, or neglect, and given the collective action problems besetting collective voice, the chances of a self-interested voice strategy increases. And if federal institutions increase exit, loyalty, and/or neglect, self-interested voice strategies grow more common. Under such conditions, we should expect electoral integrity to deteriorate.

Exit, voice, and loyalty in U.S. elections

According to the PEI Index, electoral integrity is troubled in the United States. This section uses Hirschman's model as a platform for evaluating U.S. elections, with an emphasis on the role of federal institutions and with comparisons to Canada, Brazil, and Mexico. As noted, federalism per se can hardly be to blame for the difficulties surrounding U.S. electoral integrity. It is, however, in the particular mix of U.S. federal institutions that we find conditions that maximize individual voice. Table 9.1 summarizes some of the primary distinctions of federal institutions discussed in the case studies.

Hirschman identifies voice and exit as signaling mechanisms that can help an organization recognize its deficiencies. Both occur in the U.S. system, but in ways that fail to help improve the system. In fact they partly contribute to poor electoral integrity. The difficulties of the voting experience from state to state itself are well

Table 9.1 **Federal Institutions in the United States, Canada, Mexico, and Brazil**

	Compulsory Voting	*Registration*	*Electoral Administration*	*Adjudication*	*Electoral Board(s)*	*Rule-making*
United States	No	Passive	Decentralized	Dispersed	Partisan	Decentralized
Canada	No	Active	Centralized	Dispersed	Nonpartisan	Decentralized
Mexico	Yes (not enforced)	Passive	Centralized	Concentrated	Partisan	Decentralized
Brazil	Yes (enforced)	Active	Centralized	Concentrated	Nonpartisan	Centralized

Note: Descriptions based on author's evaluation of national institutions and related legislation.

documented (e.g., Cain, Donovan, and Tolbert 2008; also see Brennan Center for Justice n.d.). The United States also makes use of a majoritarian electoral system, which has been associated with limiting voter choice and increasing dissatisfaction. Gerrymandering only adds to the lack of competition (Magleby et al., this volume). Partly as a result of this, voter turnout is depressed as citizens opt to exit; in an average U.S. presidential election, about 45% of the voting-age population will usually opt out. In off-year congressional elections, over 60% will not participate. And in local elections, often over 80% decide not to vote. Decentralized rule making, and the nonconcurrence of local, state, and national elections, have a cumulative corrosive effect. Off-year congressional elections have an obvious direct impact on national politics as representatives and senators take their seats, and state-level officials elected at this time gain control over many electoral rules and even districting in most states. But again, it is not federalism but U.S. federalism that is the culprit here. The parliamentary system in Canada unifies national elections, and the country's centralized electoral management board removes lower-level officials from most decisions surrounding electoral rules. Brazil has had concurrent national and state elections since 1994. And Mexico changed its rules for election to the senate so that the entire body is reelected every six years, in line with the presidential term. Deputies, who serve three years, are also up for election alongside the president and senate every other term. Like many countries worldwide, Canada, Mexico, and Brazil have national electoral management bodies (Catt et al. 2014).

Exit strategies have a greater impact on the electoral system in the United States than they do in Canada, Brazil, and Mexico. It is not that the incidence of citizens moving to communities with more politically like-minded individuals is greater in the United States than in Canada, Brazil, or Mexico. Rather, given the more decentralized nature of the electoral system, exit in the United States allows citizens to bolster administrative differences across state lines (Oppenheimer 2005). In Hirschman's formula, exit can serve a positive purpose, as an organization sees individuals leave it for another. But he also notes that when all sellers offer an equally deficient good, and thereby both lose and gain buyers, they will not receive the signal and overall quality will continue to decline. Under a similar dynamic, in the United States we see blue states turning bluer and red states turning redder, and while individuals who make the move may feel some initial satisfaction, the impact on electoral integrity is negative. As competition within states declines, victorious parties see their supporters abstain from voice, and instead embrace a pernicious form of loyalty toward the flawed electoral arrangements that guarantee success for their party.

This is not to argue that genuine loyalty does not exist in the United States. Indeed it appears robust, but it is a growing concern. Several polls and studies (e.g., Smith 2016) show declines in tolerance and affinity for basic democratic values in the United States. Still, at this point U.S. attitudes appear far more driven by criticisms of government legitimacy than by democratic legitimacy. Even with growing dissatisfaction over electoral procedures, there is strong aversion to changes in electoral institutions, likely because traditionalism still runs strong, most view the country as successful, and they link regime institutions with these attitudes. It may also be the case that federalism has socialized U.S. citizens toward more conservative attitudes regarding institutional change given the hurdles it faces. Either way, both pernicious loyalty and genuine loyalty temper calls to reform electoral arrangements.

The problems with electoral integrity in the United States would appear to offer a clear motivation for voice. But as Hirschman's framework illustrates, individuals may opt for other strategies. Many opt for neglect or remain loyal, and even when exit is used it largely fails to send recuperative signals and may even reinforce problems. And as Hirschman emphasizes, we also need to consider the set of individuals that opt for a certain strategy. With many looking to exit or neglect, or standing pat with loyalty, those remaining to use voice are more likely to be more extreme, and thus to pursue individual rather than collective goals in their use of voice. In addition, the U.S. electoral system offers tremendous opportunities for individual voice. Lax campaign finance rules allow smaller groups of wealthy individuals to more easily push their positions, and U.S. federalism increases the chances of success because so many important facets of rule-making rest at the state level.

Brazil, Mexico, and Canada all have institutional arrangements that close off other routes and thus direct efforts more toward collective voice to signal changes in electoral procedures. Centralized electoral administrations restrain the pernicious form of loyalty that can emerge in the United States. Brazil shuts out neglect as an option with compulsory voting and concentrates voter attention with the use of simultaneous elections. Opportunities for individual voice are stifled by a relatively insulated and centralized electoral administration and a highly regimented campaign financing scheme. This also undermines exit strategies. Still, as admirable as Brazil's electoral procedures may be, the country's political problems rest in the setting of those procedures. The electoral rules and party system create incentives for corruption, compounded by a weak rule of law. This system appears to be wearing on the loyalty of voters. These institutional differences then partly explain why Brazilian voters are more likely to choose protest (see Justus and Aggio 2018), while U.S. voters settle on neglect, and why any change driven by voice is more likely to be collective in Brazil and individual in the United States.

While Brazil faces growing problems of loyalty, these difficulties have long plagued Mexico, where electoral malfeasance by the authoritarian PRI sullied electoral activities. Electoral authorities faced a difficult task in the effort to build electoral integrity after the 2000 transition and have admirably implemented a number of significant reforms. But the fragile credibility gained by electoral institutions was undermined by the move toward a partisan electoral management board and seemingly intractable problems in the rule of law that direct too many politicians toward corrupt influences rather than the accountability concerns of voters. Canada brandishes praiseworthy electoral institutions, but neglect remains a concern with voter turnout running about 65%. Nonetheless, high levels of loyalty cushion regime legitimacy and deflate significant efforts to pursue electoral reform at the national level, as when Prime Minister Justin Trudeau in 2017 backed down from his campaign promise to implement a proportional representation system. Still, the decentralized nature of rule making in Canada allows provinces to design their own electoral systems, and this may offer a route toward experimentation and gradual acceptance of change. Note, though, the difference with the U.S. system, where decentralization is coupled with partisan influence and easier opportunities for campaign lobbying. In Canada, a nonpartisan and centralized electoral administration steers reform toward a more collective than individual voice.

Conclusions

Federalism cannot be presumed to offer "laboratories of democracy" as a sort of self-regulating mechanism to improve policy, including electoral policy. The institutions within a federal system can be designed in a number of ways, and some constructions may direct actions toward the improvement of electoral integrity, whereas others may fail or even invite individuals to undermine electoral integrity. This chapter has used Albert Hirschman's model of "exit, voice, and loyalty" to illustrate how electoral institutions influence the motivation and capacity of individuals, and thus the opportunity, to effect improvements in electoral integrity. In the case of the United States, it will not be enough to identify and reach agreement on good policy and best practices surrounding electoral integrity. So long as individual voice, exit, and loyalty overshadow collective voice, it will be tremendously difficult to find the support required to implement those good policies and best practices.

Notes

1. *New State Ice Co. v. Liebmann*, 285 U.S. 262, 311 (1932).
2. The dimensions are the following: electoral laws, electoral procedures, district boundaries, voter registration, party registration, media coverage, campaign finance, voting procedures, vote count, results, and electoral authorities.
3. It should be noted that the Electoral Integrity Project does not compare the cross-national and subnational surveys with each other.
4. See "Canadian and U.S. Federalism," special issue of *Publius: The Journal of Federalism* 40 (Summer 2010): 3.
5. In Canada, senators are appointed by the governor general on the advice of the prime minister and hold their positions until age 75. The body holds little legitimacy and influence.

6. See the description of the court on its website: www.tse.jus.br.
7. For example, when applying for public employment or a passport, a voter must supply proof of registration.
8. "Electoral Court Breaks World Speed Record in Vote Counting," *Gaceta Mercantil Online,* October 31, 2006, available at lexisnexis.com.

PART III

CONCLUSIONS

10

America in Comparative Perspective

CHAD VICKERY AND HEATHER SZILAGYI

International technical assistance providers and election observers assess developing democracies across a range of dimensions spanning the electoral cycle, but more established democracies are rarely scrutinized by practitioners in the same manner. This chapter evaluates the fundamental integrity of key elements of the electoral process in the United States by holding them to the same standards routinely applied to developing democracies around the world. Taking this international perspective, we highlight a confluence of factors in the United States that produce many wasted votes (those cast for either a losing candidate or in excess of those required by a winning candidate) and a system of governance that largely fails to reflect the will of a majority of voters.

Exploring this topic is important because the United States has traditionally benefited from a high level of trust in the electoral process, but this trust is eroding (see Norris, Cameron, and Wynter, this volume). This chapter highlights areas where international and American election practitioners differ in their perspective on the integrity of the U.S. electoral process, generating a *blind spot* (Stephanopoulos 2013b, 769). American practitioners do not recognize the myriad ways in which the U.S. electoral process deviates widely from what the international community would be willing to accept in developing democracies. This phenomenon could help to explain, in part, the limited reform initiatives undertaken at the federal level to date and raises doubts about the prospect for such efforts in the future.

Gallup polls discussed in Norris, Cameron, and Wynter (this volume) have shown that the American people have traditionally had considerable trust in outcomes generated by the U.S. electoral process, suggesting that this blind spot may not be limited to election practitioners. For example, in the immediate aftermath of the 2016 presidential race, in which Hillary Clinton won the popular vote but lost the election, Gallup polls report that 84% of voters in the United States considered Donald Trump to be the legitimate president, including 76% of Clinton voters. According to Gallup, these results are similar to those following the hotly contested 2000 election that ended in a protracted Supreme Court battle (Jones 2016). Given the highly controversial circumstances surrounding each of these elections, it is reasonable to conclude that these numbers reflect more diffuse trust in the process that extends beyond any one election or candidate preference.

Increasingly, however, trust in American democracy is being challenged by candidates, parties, and outcomes that do not reflect democratic norms. Gallup has also documented diminishing public confidence in the honesty of elections in the United States in general; while 52% of Americans surveyed expressed confidence in honest elections in 2006, the percentage had declined to 30% when Gallup asked the question in 2016 (Norris, Cameron, and Wynter, this volume; McCarthy and Clifton 2016). Vulnerabilities we will discuss in this chapter are already undermining U.S. democracy, and perceptions of integrity can have real-world implications (Norris 2014). We conclude that if the electoral process in the United States is not reformed in line with international standards, public perceptions of electoral integrity may continue to decline, with serious implications for the sustainability of American democracy.

Methods and evidence

Our research draws on scholarly literature, legal frameworks, U.S. case law, discussions with international election experts, and expert survey findings to identify and analyze the most critical vulnerabilities to the U.S. system through the integrity framework routinely applied to democracies around the world. We employ key features of the International Foundation for Electoral Systems (IFES) Electoral Integrity Assessment (EIA) methodology to evaluate the electoral process in the United States. The EIA methodology is a rigorous tool used to analyze 18 key areas of the electoral process for vulnerabilities to systemic manipulation, malpractice, and fraud. These distinct vulnerability types are defined as follows:

> *Systemic manipulation* is defined as the use of domestic legal provisions and/or electoral rules and procedures that run counter to widely accepted democratic principles and international standards and that purposefully distort the will of voters.
>
> *Malpractice* refers to the breach by a professional of his or her relevant duty of care, resulting from carelessness or neglect.
>
> *Fraud* is defined as the deliberate wrongdoing by election officials or other electoral stakeholders, which distorts the individual or collective will of the voters. (Vickery and Shein 2012)

Vulnerabilities are also considered in light of their substantive impact on the electoral process. Impact is assessed differently depending on the vulnerability type, specifically whether the element of intent is present. Malpractice is assessed in terms of *probable* impact: the likely impact on the next election if the vulnerability is not addressed. Systemic manipulation and fraud, which, unlike malpractice, require intentionality, are assessed in terms of *potential* impact: the possible impact on the next election if the vulnerability (however small) is exploited.

A holistic electoral cycle approach to assessing these vulnerabilities emphasizes that each aspect of the process is intertwined with the others, and vulnerabilities in disparate areas can compound to have a far-reaching impact. IFES has applied the EIA methodology to elections in Afghanistan, the Republic of Georgia, Pakistan, Sri Lanka, Myanmar, and The Gambia. This type of assessment could prove valuable in more established democracies as well, as processes can change over time and no election is without flaws.

We have found—anecdotally—that election practitioners in the United States have come to accept as normal, or even beneficial, what international experts would consider to be glaring deficiencies in the American electoral system. To explore this theory empirically, we conducted an online survey of experts to assess attitudes about different aspects of the electoral process in the United States. Surveys were distributed via email and conducted online from May 9 to June 14, 2017. The questionnaire consisted of a series of factual statements about the U.S. electoral process, and respondents were asked whether the scenario had a positive or negative impact on the credibility of elections in the United States.

There were two target groups of respondents for the survey: international election experts and election practitioners in the United States. We developed the sample of potential respondents by relying on an extensive network of election experts, and their referrals, from IFES's work providing technical assistance and engaging in electoral processes around the world. Drawing on our networks allowed us to leverage IFES's connections with others working in the field of elections and generated a diverse sample. We relied only upon a preexisting network of electoral experts in an effort to ensure that respondents met necessary criteria. U.S. election practitioners included in the sample were individuals who currently or previously played a direct role in administering the electoral process, including secretaries of state, directors of elections, and employees of state or county election boards. International experts were specifically selected on the basis of comparative experience in election administration and limited specific knowledge of the U.S. system. For example, experience observing international elections or providing technical assistance to a variety of electoral processes qualified individuals for inclusion in this group of potential respondents.

The survey was sent to 80 experts (32 international and 48 American), with 32 taking the survey (15 international and 17 American), for a completion rate of 40%.[1] As noted this chapter will seek to evaluate the integrity of the U.S. electoral process in a manner commensurate with the standards used to assess elections around the world. Survey findings supplement technical findings from the application of IFES's EIA methodology though it should be noted that as they draw upon a nonprobability sample with a limited number of responses, these results can be considered indicative and exploratory rather than representative.

We focus on several key areas of the electoral cycle that observers and academics have regularly noted pose acute challenges to the U.S. electoral process: (1) the process of boundary delimitation for congressional districts, (2) the role of the Electoral College in electing the executive, (3) voter registration processes and requirements, and (4) the framework for administering elections. The choice of these topics was reached after a careful review of election observation reports as well as quantitative electoral integrity measures from the Electoral Integrity Project's Perceptions of Electoral Integrity (PEI) data set and in-depth discussions with U.S. election experts. The selected categories were highlighted as overall areas of concern by observer reports and election experts, generally received low scores across the 50 states on the PEI Index, and were determined by our analysis to provide the highest vulnerability to the integrity of the electoral process. The research did not examine positive aspects of election administration in the United States that have been identified by observer reports and other sources.

We evaluate these key stages of the electoral process in the United States by applying comparative international standards and good practice, including vulnerabilities to distinct categories of systemic manipulation, malpractice, and fraud. It should be noted that we do not present complete integrity assessments of each of the 50 U.S. states, which would be required to fully understand the country's electoral integrity profile. The concluding section provides a holistic perspective on the overall impact on the electoral process, emphasizing linkages between categories that compound vulnerabilities and exacerbate impacts.

Boundary delimitation

In a democracy, the electoral system defines the rules of the game for political competition. At its core, the electoral system "translates the votes cast . . . into seats won by parties and candidates," (Reynolds and Reilly 2002, 5). While there is no clear consensus or international standard to direct a country's selection of electoral system, "there is an increasing recognition of the importance of issues that are affected by electoral systems, such as the fair representation of all citizens, the equality of women and men, the rights of minorities, special considerations for the disabled, and so on" (Reynolds and Reilly 2002, 14).

The United States has a bicameral legislature composed of an upper house (Senate) and a lower house (House of Representatives). Each state elects two members to the Senate through a statewide popular vote. Members of the House of Representatives are elected from single-member districts, with 435 seats apportioned among the states on the basis of population. Reapportionment of these seats between states, as well as boundary redistricting within states, occurs every 10 years after a national census. As described below, an upper house whose membership is not contingent on district population is in line with common international practice. This section will therefore focus on integrity issues surrounding the House of Representatives and not discuss possible issues related to the election of senators.

As discussed by Magleby et al. (this volume), the integrity of a majoritarian electoral system is fundamentally tied to the fairness of the boundary delimitation process, known as "redistricting" in the United States. If constituent boundaries are drawn in a way that gives one party or group an unfair advantage over its rivals, the integrity of the process is undermined. Districts that are deliberately drawn to skew demographics to the advantage of one political party or community over others can drastically affect electoral outcomes and the composition of the legislature, disenfranchising individual voters and stymying community representation in government (Handley 2007). However, no single formula exists for demarcating boundaries across all country contexts in a manner commensurate with guaranteeing fair elections and securing optimum representation. For example, in majoritarian electoral systems, any map will leave some votes wasted. According to the definition put forward by the University of Chicago Law School paper articulating the efficiency gap standard, "A vote is wasted if it is cast (1) for a losing candidate, or (2) for a winning candidate but in excess of what she needed to prevail" (Stephanopoulos and McGhee 2015, 831).

Boundary delimitation practices can, either intentionally or unintentionally, significantly increase the number of wasted votes for one party or community to the point where the election may no longer be considered fair or inclusive, or where election outcomes are not considered representative. Two practices commonly used to achieve this effect are "packing" (consolidating supporters or members of one group into a small number of districts) and "cracking" (breaking up supporters or members of one group into many districts so that they do not have a majority in any district) (Levitt 2010).

Given the variety of delimitation practices around the world, few international standards have been proposed for preventing such outcomes and ensuring fair boundaries. However, there is growing evidence that the use of bipartisan or neutral commissions to draw districting maps leads to more competitive elections (Stephanopoulos 2013a). In addition, it is generally accepted that the boundary delimitation process should be transparent and accessible to the public (Handley 2007, 60). However, in our survey, international expert and U.S. election practitioner survey respondents had somewhat divergent views on the credibility of districting bodies.

Beyond the principle of one-person, one-vote,[2] no U.S. federal laws exist to specifically regulate partisan districting, or gerrymandering. This leaves enormous power to the states to determine their own district lines, a job often left to partisan state legislatures, and a wide variety of redistricting practices are used to ultimately determine constituencies for the U.S. House of Representatives. To provide a high-level snapshot, congressional boundaries are drawn by state legislatures in 37 states (six of these have either advisory or backup commissions), by independent commissions in four states (Arizona, California, Idaho, and Washington), and by politician-led commissions in two states (Hawaii and New Jersey). The remaining seven states currently have one congressional district each and therefore do not require districting commissions (Dews 2017).

As evidenced by the U.S. Supreme Court's inability to date to articulate a manageable standard by which to evaluate gerrymandering, untangling the impact of the process on the electoral map can be complicated. Much of this analysis begins with an examination of partisan bias. A recent report from the Brennan Center for Justice uses three popular quantitative methods to test "extreme partisan bias" on the 2012, 2014, and 2016 electoral maps. While coming to a series of ancillary conclusions, the report's macro-level findings have significant implications for the integrity of the electoral process in the United States: "In the 26 states that account for 85% of congressional districts, Republicans derive a net benefit of at least 16–17 congressional seats in the current Congress from partisan bias" (Royden and Li 2017, 1). These results were among the most conservative of the research findings; an efficiency gap analysis found that Republicans gained a net 26–37 extra seats in the 2012 elections, 4–19 seats in 2014, and 17–29 seats in 2016 (Royden and Li 2017; Stephanopoulos and McGhee 2015). The results suggest that seats won due to partisan bias could have been responsible for Republican majorities in 2012 and 2016 (Royden and Li 2017; see Table 10.1).

It is important to note that intentional gerrymandering is reinforced by the tendency of likeminded partisans to live near each other, a phenomenon coined "the big sort" (Bishop 2008). Americans with liberal political leanings tend to live in larger population centers, while conservatives tend to live in less densely

Table 10.1 **Proportionality in North Carolina and Maryland**

	Vote Share		Seat Share		Ratio		Vote-Seat Gap (%)
	% Rep	% Dem	% Rep	% Dem	Rep	Dem	
North Carolina	57	43	77	23	1.35	0.53	20%
Maryland	37	63	11	89	0.29	1.41	26%

Note: This table displays the disparity between seat and vote shares for elections to the U.S. House of Representatives in North Carolina and Maryland in 2016. The gap in North Carolina favored Republicans, while the gap in Maryland benefited Democrats. Votes for a candidate other than a Republican or Democrat were excluded from this analysis.

Source: Data on vote and seat shares from the New York Times 2017a, 2017b.

populated areas. As a result, single-member districts based in part on geography and maintaining communities of interest naturally reflect this partisan divide. Recent reports suggest that this geopolitical polarization at every level, from county to regional, continues to trend upward (Florida 2016). Intentional gerrymandering can exacerbate the effects of this process (Royden and Li 2017), though how much it does so is debated (Dews 2017).

However, Brennan Center research devoted to uncovering the effect of gerrymandering (discussed above) makes the point that the states with the worst partisan bias actually "tend to have fairly even statewide distributions of partisans.... It is, in short, almost certainly no coincidence that the worst degrees of partisan bias are observed (with the exception of Texas) in closely contested and hard fought battleground states" (Royden and Li 2017, 14). This finding calls into question the notion that partisan bias in districting is largely due to "the big sort." Regardless of the precise impact of gerrymandering on the distribution of seats in the House of Representatives, reform is clearly needed from the perspective of international standards.

Contrary to the case of *partisan* distribution, both the United States and the international community have developed clear principles governing considerations of *population* distribution in the delimitation process. The Venice Commission of the Council of Europe's *Code of Good Practice in Electoral Matters* dictates that the distribution of single-member districts in the lower house should ensure "equal voting power," which requires that population be considered in boundary delimitation (2003, 17).[3] The "maximum admissible departure from the distribution . . . should seldom exceed 10% and never 15%" for population-based electoral constituencies (2003, 17).

As described above, the U.S. Congress is a bicameral legislature. The Senate comprises 100 members, two of which are elected from each state. The U.S. Constitution stipulates that each state is represented by two senators regardless of population, resulting in significant population variation in constituency size. However, this approach to allocating seats in the upper house of a bicameral legislature is common in parliamentary systems and in line with accepted international practice.

Members of the House of Representatives are elected in single-member district contests, and the 435 seats are distributed among the states on the basis of population. In *Reynolds v. Sims* (1964), the U.S. Supreme Court held that federal congressional districts *within states* must be of "substantially equal" size to ensure the principle of one-person, one-vote articulated in Article 1, §2 of the Constitution. However, as the Apportionment Act of 1911 establishes 435 as the total number of members in the lower house (with each state granted at least one), the size of the House of Representatives has not expanded in more than a century despite the increasing population of the United States. Accordingly, significant variation in congressional district sizes *between* states persists. For example, based on 2010 census data, the average district size of the House of Representatives in Montana is 88% larger than the average district size in Rhode Island (Burnett 2011). This malapportionment in the lower house is clearly a violation of international good practice, as described by the Venice Commission. As population growth is largest in some of the most populous states (U.S. Census Bureau 2016), the impact of malapportionment on the integrity of the electoral process will continue to grow, absent legislative or judicial intervention.

Considering the various aspects of the delimitation process discussed above, the key electoral integrity vulnerabilities to legislative elections in the United States relate to *systemic manipulation*. Partisan districting, or gerrymandering, of state legislative districts is the most serious vulnerability to systemic manipulation in this category. This finding is supported by the Electoral Integrity Project's PEI expert survey, which found gerrymandering to be consistently the most problematic aspect of U.S. voting since data collection began in 2012 (Norris et al. 2017). Out of 164 countries, only Malaysia and Singapore scored lower than the United States in this category in the most recent release of PEI data (Norris, Wynter, and Cameron 2018a).

The significant malapportionment of single-member district sizes between states is also a clear violation of international standards and, as it is ensured by statute, a significant vulnerability to systemic manipulation. IFES has regularly cited the malapportionment of single-member districts as a vulnerability when conducting integrity assessments around the world. While a substantial majority of international survey respondents viewed the disparity in district sizes between states as contributing to the credibility of the electoral process "somewhat" or "very" negatively, only a small number of U.S. election practitioners agreed with the "somewhat negative" characterization, and none had a "very negative" outlook. Instead, a vast majority of these practitioners viewed the process as having a "neutral" impact on credibility.

While adjusting the size of the House of Representatives to mitigate the effects of malapportionment may seem like an extreme step, developed democracies have regularly engaged in even more significant electoral system reform. For example, New Zealand shifted from a first-past-the-post system to a mixed-member proportional system in 1993 after dissatisfaction with multiple rounds of elections in which the results led to major discrepancies between the ratio of votes to seats for political parties (Harris 2000). After significant public pressure to reform an electoral system seen as contributing to corruption and one-party rule, Japan moved to a parallel electoral system as a way to appease both small and large political parties (Cox 2005). Overall, the combined effects of gerrymandering and the malapportionment of House legislative districts present a high vulnerability to systemic manipulation with a high potential impact on electoral integrity.

The Electoral College

The Electoral College is shorthand for the process by which the executive of the United States is indirectly elected. Popular elections for the presidency are conducted in the states (and the District of Columbia), each of which is assigned a number of "electoral votes" equal to its total number of representatives in Congress. Nationwide, 538 electoral votes are contested, of which 270 are needed to win the presidency. With the exception of Nebraska and Maine, states award their electoral votes to candidates on a winner-take-all basis.

The Electoral College was intentionally designed to be an electoral system as close to direct election as possible without fully handing that power over to the people (Feerick 1968). This process enables a scenario by which a presidential candidate could win a plurality of the popular vote but lose the presidency through the Electoral College, as has happened five times in American history and twice in the five presidential elections since 2000. In fact, according to analysis by National Public Radio, it is theoretically possible to be elected president of the United States with less than 30% of the nationwide vote (Kurtzleben 2016).

As shown in Figure 10.1, international experts with comparative experience in elections had an overwhelmingly negative reaction to the statement "It is possible for a candidate to win the presidency through the Electoral College without

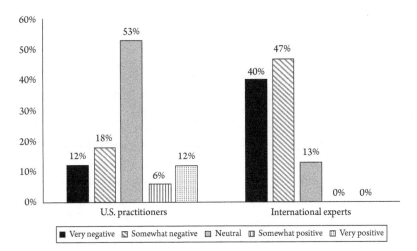

Figure 10.1 Approval of Winning the Presidency without the Popular Vote.
Note: Respondents were presented with background information about the American electoral system and asked to rate how the following statement impacts the credibility of the U.S. electoral process: "It is possible for a candidate to win the presidency through the Electoral College without winning the national popular vote of all American citizens." N = 17 U.S. practitioners; N = 15 international experts. Source: IFES online survey of election experts.

winning the national popular vote of all American citizens." A substantial minority of American election practitioners, however, responded in kind. A majority of that group rated the practice as neutral, and still some respondents found the fact to have a "somewhat" or "very" positive impact on credibility.

Election results are not official until electors cast their ballots at state conventions following Election Day. While some states have instituted rules binding electors to vote for the winner of the popular vote in their respective state, the U.S. Constitution is designed to allow electors to vote for any candidate; they should be influenced by but not bound to the state's popular vote. In practice, so-called faithless electors are rare and have never altered the outcome of a presidential election (Agrawal 2016).

Key integrity vulnerabilities related to elections for the executive pertain to *systemic manipulation*. The ability to lose the popular vote and be elected president is a structural feature of the American electoral system that presents a clear vulnerability with respect to the internationally recognized principle of ensuring representative government. As electoral votes are predicated on the number of members of Congress awarded to each state, this phenomenon is partially a product of malapportionment in the assignment of seats in the House of Representatives that give smaller states an outsized voice in the selection of the president. Additionally, equality of representation among the states in the Senate ensures that small states have added influence in the selection of the president (in addition to enhanced representation in the upper house). Devising a system for choosing the executive was a hotly debated topic of the Constitutional Convention of 1787, and the unique method of an Electoral College was settled upon as a means to "bring the election as close to the people as possible, except for direct election itself" (Feerick 1968, 254). While the Electoral College was created under unique circumstances and influenced by a set of competing interests among the country's founders, it is clear from a comparative perspective that at this point in the evolution of American democracy, a system that enables the candidate with fewer votes to win the presidency undermines the overall integrity of the electoral process.

Regardless of whether victorious presidential candidates lose the popular vote in the future, the presence of this vulnerability has a high *potential* impact on the integrity of the electoral process. Additionally, this phenomenon is likely to continue occurring, or even accelerate in frequency, as demographic changes grant an increasingly outsized voice to less populous states through the Electoral College. Just as the United States has reformed other aspects of its electoral process (through the 14th and 19th Amendments to the Constitution) to increase participation and to ensure that the electoral system is representative of the electorate, it could consider reforming the Electoral College to meet current international standards and reflect the will of a majority of voters.

A constitutional amendment would theoretically be required to abolish the Electoral College, but some groups are actively proposing workarounds that would ensure the president was elected by a nationwide popular vote without eliminating the institution of the Electoral College. Unfortunately, reform efforts, and in particular a push for a constitutional amendment, have historically failed to gain traction due to the lack of political will to reform the process—even following significant flashpoints like the 2000 presidential election. As Princeton University political historian Julian Zelizer (2016) explains, "The power of small states within the Senate combined with the fact that voters don't tend to elevate this issue to the same urgent status of other issues has usually left proposals for an amendment to die on the vine."

Finally, the ability of electors to vote for a candidate who did not receive the popular vote in their state represents a clear vulnerability to systemic manipulation. This power is embedded in the Constitution as a means of guarding against the direct election of the president, and as such an elector casting an electoral vote against the will of the people would be a legitimate application of his or her mandate. The rarity of electors exercising this capacity in practice—even in controversial elections—means that the vulnerability to this particular concern is low, but if it were to be exploited in a meaningful way, the potential impact on electoral integrity would be high.

Voter registration

Article 21 of the *Universal Declaration of Human Rights* states that everyone has the right to take part in government, access public services in his or her country on an equal basis, and vote in elections by way of universal and equal suffrage. As discussed in the chapters in this volume by Pallister and by Bergman, Tran, and Yates, voter registration can serve as either a bridge or a barrier to upholding the principle of universal and equal suffrage. A country's legal and administrative adoption of inclusive voter registration practices can lower rates of political marginalization and enhance electoral integrity. When legal barriers and administrative decisions effectively disenfranchise or further marginalize parts of the population, however, electoral integrity is diminished.

For voter registration to be fair and inclusive, potential voters must be aware of the registration process and have reasonable opportunities and relatively easy access to complete it (ACE Electoral Knowledge Network 2013, 12–15). Maintaining the integrity of an election requires a balance between ensuring that only registered voters may legally vote and preventing ineligible voters from registering. The registration process should also provide mechanisms to transparently remove noneligible persons from the voter registry. To ensure an accurate voter list, a continuous list of voters must be regularly maintained after its initial creation. Since voter registration is not usually compulsory, the election management authority needs to obtain changes in voter information—for example, changes of address or eligibility to vote. If voters are not required by law to notify the election management authority when they move, the voter list may quickly lose currency (ACE Electoral Knowledge Network 2013, 103–106).

As is the case with most aspects of election administration in the United States, the process for registering to vote varies by state. Voter registration is active (the responsibility to register rests with the voter) with minimal federal oversight, though federal law does set basic standards under the National Voter Registration Act and Help America Vote Act. The Help America Vote Act instructs states to maintain updated and accurate voter registration databases, and the National Voter Registration Act establishes some standards to guard against the removal of eligible voters from voter rolls. However, variation in state practices and procedures for record keeping and a lack of centralization of voter information creates opportunities for administrative errors. The absence of a central, independent electoral management body (EMB) with the mandate and resources needed to maintain and protect a centralized registry presents additional challenges for maintaining accurate voter registries for federal elections. Vulnerabilities stemming from the lack of a central EMB will be described in detail in the next section.

The Pew Research Center (2012), a nonpartisan think tank, published a comprehensive report on voter registration in the United States. Concluding that the voter registration process was not up to date with modern technology and a mobile society, the study found that approximately one in eight registrations (about 24 million) were either invalid or "significantly inaccurate." Pew describes the paper-based, manual entry of voter registration data in most states as creating a vulnerability to malpractice. Pew research also revealed more than 1.8 million dead individuals on voter lists and 12.7 million outdated records. In total, Pew found that there were issues, in terms of accuracy or validity, with 13% of voter registration records nationally (approximately 24 million). In reaction to claims of fraud tied to inaccurate voter registration data, the Presidential Advisory Commission on Election Integrity was formed by executive order in 2017. The Commission was seen as partisan by many stakeholders, and its requests to access voter registration from states were denied. The White House (2018) cited issues with obtaining this data when President Trump disbanded the Commission in January 2018, passing the matter over to the Department of Homeland Security.

As voters can legally move and register in a new state without notifying officials in their previous state of residence, the Pew Research Center (2012) found that more than 2.75 million individuals were registered in more than one state. Citing a survey from the Cooperative Congressional Election Study, the report notes that around one in four voters in 2008 believed that voter registration records were updated automatically when they moved, although in reality this is rarely the case (Pew Research Center 2012, 7). Over half of voters did not know that voter registration information could be revised at state departments of motor vehicles. Despite the deceased and outdated registrations clogging the rolls, Pew researchers also estimated that 51 million eligible citizens remained unregistered, accounting for nearly a quarter of the eligible population in 2012.

While the decentralized nature of voter registration in the United States presents a unique set of challenges, there are examples of mature democracies implementing voter registration reform that provide a useful comparison. For example, Canada passed legislation in 1996 that shifted the system of voter registration from one of individual enumerators going door to door to register voters, to an automated national register that would eventually incorporate new information from numerous federal departments. While the previous system was not perceived to be inaccurate, the legislature came to a consensus that a national registry would eliminate duplicate registration efforts between different levels of government and lead to cost savings (Black 2003). The Canadian electoral management body, Elections Canada (2004), claims the National Register of Electors has consistently exceeded the cost-saving expectations originally estimated at 30 million Canadian dollars per election (ACE Electoral Knowledge Network 2012); however, attempts to increase the accuracy of the list are still ongoing.

Vulnerabilities to inaccurate and outdated registries have contributed to the impetus for perhaps the most controversial component of voter registration in the United States: voter identification (see Bergman, Tran, and Yates, this volume). This is an issue that clearly separated international experts and U.S. election practitioners and also generated polarizing responses within the U.S. practitioner group. As shown in Figure 10.2, a vast majority of international respondents indicated that requiring voters to present photo identification positively contributes to the credibility of the electoral process. Possibly reflecting partisan division over the issue, roughly equal numbers of U.S. election practitioners were on each side of the positive/negative divide.

It is crucial to emphasize that while *requiring* some type of identification is in line with international best practices to prevent voter fraud, equal access to qualifying identification must accompany this requirement. As explained in the foreword to a Brennan Center report on the subject, "The problem is not requiring voter ID, per

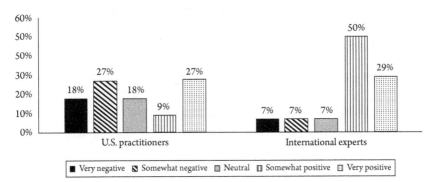

Figure 10.2 State Photo Identification Laws.
Note: Respondents were asked to rate how the following statement impacts the credibility of the U.S. electoral process: "The state legislature passed a law requiring state residents to present a photo identification in order to vote." N = 11 U.S. practitioners; N = 14 international experts.
Source: IFES online survey of election experts.

se—the problem is requiring ID that many voters simply do not have" (Waldman 2012). Both groups of survey respondents were generally agreed that cases in which the nearest office issuing voter identification is inaccessible or maintains limited business hours contributes negatively to the credibility of the electoral process. The Brennan Center report also highlighted financial barriers to obtaining the documents required for identification. For example, birth certificates can cost from $8 to $25, and marriage licenses can cost between $8 and $20 (Gaskins and Iyer 2012). From a comparative perspective, access to identification rather than a legal requirement is the most significant impediment to the integrity of voter registration in the United States.

Much debate in the United States has also focused on whether such discrimination is intentional. Courts have ruled that voter identification laws were implemented with the intent to discriminate in several cases, generally against African American voters. In striking down a North Carolina voter ID law, a federal court found that the provisions "target African Americans with almost surgical precision" (Ingraham 2016). Such obvious evidence of discriminatory intent is uncommon, and many controversial state laws remain on the books. Similar allegations of intentional discrimination have been made in response to a variety of changes to state election law or administration, including restrictions on early voting.

We evaluate voter registration in the United States to be susceptible to all three vulnerability types. First, the decentralized and, in many instances, partisan collection and maintenance of voter registration data for federal elections makes the U.S. voter registration system (or systems) uniquely vulnerable to *systemic manipulation*. Some states are working to improve the quality of voter registration data and their collection practices. A significant number of U.S. states, however, have implemented policies restricting access to the franchise through what many stakeholders believe are overly complex or burdensome registration practices. These policies are generally implemented with the stated goal of preventing fraud, despite an absence of evidence of the widespread nature of this phenomenon (Levitt 2014). Such allegations of voter fraud are also used to cast doubt on and raise questions about the credibility of the overall electoral process (Sweeney, Vickery, and Ellena 2016). Adding to this controversy, courts have found discriminatory intent underlying several policy changes, including in North Carolina, Texas, and Wisconsin. These attempts to disenfranchise voters clearly violate international standards and present a high vulnerability to systemic manipulation.

Further, a reliance on paper-based registration and the manual entry of voter information by election officials creates multiple opportunities for *malpractice*. Most voter registration processes in the United States do not utilize modern technology, predictably contributing to the incorrect entry of voter information and the outdated nature of American voter lists described above. Without a centralized voter register or electoral management body (described in the following section), this problem is compounded by the lack of coordination among states to identify duplicate registrations and between government agencies within states to streamline voter information. The onus is on individuals to accurately maintain their voter registration, though understanding of and access to the process is somewhat limited, as described by the Pew Research Center (2012).

With respect to *fraud* vulnerabilities, the decentralized voter registration process often enables a single voter to register in multiple states without detection. Coupled with the lack of federal voter identification requirements (though some states have implemented strict regulations), this renders the process vulnerable to multiple voting. However, the Pew research suggests that multiple registrations are an accidental byproduct of a mobile population and a lack of coordination between states (which keep independent voter lists), countering the idea that multiple registrations are part of a coordinated attempt to undermine voter registries. If this vulnerability were to be exploited on a massive scale, the impact on electoral integrity would be quite high. Exploiting this system in a meaningful way, however, would require an enormous coordinated effort, and numerous studies that have examined the prevalence of multiple types of voter fraud in the United States, including impersonation and noncitizen/nonresident voting, have concluded that such fraud is incredibly rare (Brennan Center for Justice 2017b). Based on the existing evidence, this type of voter fraud is extremely unlikely to determine electoral outcomes in future.

The administrative framework

"Electoral management body," or EMB, is the commonly accepted term for the institution responsible for the management and administration of elections. International good practice generally prefers a national EMB to ensure that every voter has equal access to the franchise. A national or federal EMB also mitigates vulnerabilities to the politicization of certain areas of the electoral process, including voter registration. While noting that decentralized election administration can have some benefits in terms of transparency and inclusiveness, the ACE Electoral Knowledge Network emphasizes some downsides of this model: "Devolving electoral powers and responsibilities to local authorities without appropriate oversight may make it more difficult to maintain electoral consistency, service, quality and—ultimately—the freedom and fairness of elections. The United States is a good example of this difficulty" (Catt et al. 2014, 17).

As Arceneaux (this volume) explains, the absence of a federal EMB and the administration of elections for the same federal offices entirely by states, with minimal guidance provided by federal regulations, is highly unusual when viewed in cross-national comparison. While a vast majority of international experts found this practice to have "very" or "somewhat" negative impact on electoral credibility, only a fairly small percentage of U.S. practitioners agreed. In fact, a majority of this latter group answered that the practice had a "very" or "somewhat" positive impact.

EMBs around the world take on a variety of institutional structures, but the Venice Commission outlines that the body should always be impartial and enjoy functional independence from the government to ensure the proper conduct of elections, or at a minimum eliminate serious suspicions of irregularity. Public confidence in the fairness of the electoral process and the accuracy of electoral results depends in large measure on both the actual and the perceived impartiality of the EMB.[4]

While some representation of political party members in EMBs is relatively common, they should not form the whole of the institution or entirely control the management of elections. The structure of election administration in the United States varies between states, and it is often highly politicized. For example, secretaries of state, who are elected officials and generally belong to a major political party, serve as the chief election official in 24 states. Chief election officials of states and counties may also stand as candidates in elections that they themselves are administering (OSCE 2016). International experts and American election administrators have strikingly different views on the partisan administration of elections. As highlighted in Figure 10.3, responding to the statement "Secretaries of state, elected statewide officials who generally belong to a major political party, serve as the chief election official in some states," all of the international experts surveyed said it had a "very" or "somewhat" negative impact on the credibility of the electoral process. Fewer than half of American practitioners shared these views, with the majority of respondents giving this factor a "neutral" or "somewhat positive" ranking.

Politicized election management is not a problem unique to the United States, but the disparity in how U.S. practitioners and international experts view the

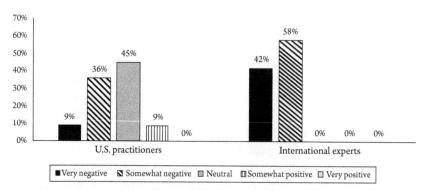

Figure 10.3 Partisan Administration of Elections.

Notes: Respondents were asked to rate how the following statement impacts the credibility of the U.S. electoral process: "Secretaries of state, elected statewide officials who generally belong to a major political party, serve as the chief election official in some states." N = 11 U.S. practitioners; N = 12 international experts.

Source: IFES online survey of election experts.

problem raises doubts about the supply of political will needed for reform. Concern about political party influence over local and state elections led Mexico to pass legislation in 2014 that centralized control over state and local elections in a new national election management body (McNally 2014). Additionally, while the Swedish central EMB was previously incorporated within the national tax agency, it became an independent agency in 2001 after election officials raised concerns that "electoral matters required a separate budget, a specific administrative system as well as an advanced IT/data support system" (Lemon 2005).

In addition to partisan influence, the decentralization of election administration in the United States creates further vulnerabilities to electoral integrity stemming from inconsistent procedures and a lack of oversight. These vulnerabilities include challenges to maintaining up-to-date and accurate voter registration information, as described in the previous section. Additionally, states and local jurisdictions do not use uniform or consistent voting machines or voting technology. A majority of U.S. election practitioners responded that this practice had a "neutral" impact on the credibility of the electoral process, with support for options surrounding this middle-ground split almost evenly. However, a vast majority of international experts felt that this practice had a "very negative" or "somewhat negative" impact on the credibility of the process.

Some have argued that differences in voting machines and procedures between states serve as a safeguard against hacking and external interference (Edwards and Wilson 2016). However, this decentralization makes it much more difficult to ensure that local officials across 3,000 counties in the United States are able to properly secure their election equipment. This view also underestimates vulnerabilities to hacking and interference presented by a decentralized approach to election administration, especially when interference with the vote in a small number of key areas could swing an election. The technical challenges of election equipment technology used in the United States were explained by University of Michigan computer science professor J. Alex Halderman to the Senate Intelligence Committee (Halpern 2017):

> A small number of election technology vendors and support contractors service the systems used by many local governments. Attackers could target one or a few of these companies and spread malicious code to election equipment that serves millions of voters. . . . Before every election, voting machines need to be programmed with the design of the ballot, the races, and candidates. This programming is created on a desktop computer called an election management system, or EMS, and then transferred to voting machines using USB sticks or memory cards. These systems are generally run by county IT personnel or by private contractors. Unfortunately, election management systems are not adequately protected, and they are not always properly isolated from the Internet. Attackers who compromise

an election management system can spread vote-stealing malware to large numbers of machines.

Further, approximately 15 states use Direct Recording Equipment voting machines that do not provide a voter-verified paper trail. A lack of paper records makes it impossible to conduct a meaningful audit of the votes cast in these states, some of which, including Pennsylvania, are hotly contested battleground states (Halpern 2017).

In addition, new voting technologies have not been updated in many states due to a lack of federal, state, and local resources. Both groups of survey respondents had concerns about this phenomenon, but a plurality of U.S. respondents rated it "neutral" compared to a substantial majority of international respondents who rated the statement as having a "very negative" impact on the credibility of the electoral process. The Brennan Center for Justice (2017e) characterizes the problem in this way: "While nearly all of today's voting machines go through a federal certification and testing program, many jurisdictions purchased voting machines before this process was in place. Older machines can have serious security flaws, including hacking vulnerabilities, which would be unacceptable by today's standards." Experts agree that the expected lifespan is 10 to 20 years (and most likely closer to 10) for voting machines purchased since 2000. Forty-three states (and in most, a majority of the districts within them) used some machines that were at least 10 years old in 2016. Machines were at least 15 years old in 14 states. Additionally, "nearly every state is using some machines that are no longer manufactured and many election officials struggle to find replacement parts" (Norden and Famighetti 2015).

The partisan administration of elections in the United States, including the notion that a chief election official may administer an election in which he is also a candidate, runs counter to international good practice and introduces vulnerabilities to *systemic manipulation*. Explicit partisan control over the electoral process, including the fundamental areas of voter registration and voting procedures, at best gives the appearance of impropriety and at worst could enable a manipulation of the rules of the game for either partisan or personal advantage. The potential impact of such manipulation on the integrity of a given electoral process would be high.

There are also significant vulnerabilities to *fraud* in the institutional framework for elections in the United States, most notably with respect to the technological infrastructure for casting and counting ballots. Researchers have found serious security flaws in the obsolescent technologies used in many jurisdictions, and the decentralized nature of the electoral process creates significant apertures for manipulation through hacking or other interference. These security vulnerabilities were on display at a July 2017 computer security conference when hackers broke into U.S. voting machines in less than two hours (Darrow 2017). Recent reporting has also highlighted the extent to which hackers were able to successfully interfere with election technology during the 2016 election, including "at least one successful attempt to alter voter information, and the theft of thousands of voter records that contain private information like partial Social Security numbers" (Calabresi 2017a). As election outcomes can hinge on the results from a handful of counties or states, it is possible for isolated efforts to manipulate voting machines to have an outsized impact on the integrity of the electoral process.

Conclusions and discussion

Our research draws on scholarly literature, legal frameworks, U.S. case law, discussions with international election experts, and survey findings to identify and analyze the most critical vulnerabilities to the U.S. system through the integrity framework IFES routinely applies to democracies around the world. Each discrete issue discussed in this chapter has already been hotly debated and studied in detail by others. After applying IFES's established integrity assessment methodology in six countries, however, we have found that what is most useful from a technical perspective is not only the intricacies of the specific vulnerabilities identified in our reports but how each country's holistic vulnerability profile affects the integrity of the overall electoral process and the credibility of the election results. Identifying linkages among the areas examined here provides insight into a subset of the structural integrity issues plaguing the U.S. electoral system, but a full analysis of each of the 50 states and District of Columbia would be required to obtain a complete picture of the American electoral process.

Our assessment finds that the electoral process for federal offices is beset by entrenched, systemic deficiencies that undermine the credibility of the results and make the system particularly vulnerable to manipulation. These deficiencies include vulnerabilities that would be considered *systemic manipulation*, such as gerrymandering, malapportionment, the institution of the Electoral College, and restrictions on voter eligibility; *fraud*, including the potential for multiple voting due to decentralized voter registration; and *malpractice*, exemplified by different standards for maintaining voter registration data.

The interplay among these vulnerabilities exacerbates the impact of each one on the integrity of the American electoral process and undermines the ideas of majority rule and representative democracy. The forces of gerrymandering, malapportionment in the House of Representatives, and the structure of the Electoral College in particular produce a system that encourages a significant number of wasted votes and representative bodies that do not accurately reflect the demographic makeup of the country. Just one example suggests that by the year 2040, 70 senators will represent only 30% of the American population (Seib 2017).

Vulnerabilities in the voter registration system that, in effect, erode the fundamental right to vote—such as burdensome and potentially discriminatory requirements and mistakes stemming from outdated and poorly understood registration practices—further deepen the impact of these structural forces. In particular, the franchise is threatened among populations already more likely to be underrepresented in the political system due to the impacts of gerrymandering and malapportionment. These problems are made all the more difficult to solve by disparate methods of election administration across state lines and a general lack of resources devoted to the electoral process. Combined with an aging voting system and the other challenges highlighted throughout this chapter, the integrity of the U.S. electoral process is increasingly under threat. Again, this illustrates why a holistic examination of electoral integrity is important, as a vulnerability in one part of the process can prove much more serious when the dots are connected to other identified vulnerabilities. In totality, the threat to the electoral process in the United States is much greater than might otherwise be assumed through an examination of issues in isolation.

As noted previously, vulnerabilities to fraud, malpractice, and systemic manipulation exist in every electoral system. Regardless of whether these vulnerabilities materially alter the results of an election, it is critical to emphasize that the belief or perception that they are widespread can deflate public confidence in the election process and outcomes. The U.S. has traditionally benefited from a great deal of trust in the process and widespread acceptance of election results, despite very real vulnerabilities and, in some instances, a failure to meet the international standards by which developing democracies are judged. Emerging evidence suggests this trust in the integrity of elections has deteriorated (McCarthy and Clifton 2016). Before the 2016 election, the ultimately victorious presidential candidate made public, preemptive allegations of fraud and a "rigged system" (Pramuk 2016), likely to set the groundwork for challenging the results in the event of defeat. Despite this candidate's victory, claims of voter fraud have achieved great prominence in public discourse, distracting from the many other vulnerabilities in the electoral process that receive significantly less attention and represent a much more serious threat when considered holistically.

No democracy is perfect, and we should not be surprised that the United States faces many of the same challenges as a range of democracies around the world. A crucial challenge facing the U.S. system in particular, however, is the lack of awareness and acceptance of the severity of the system's vulnerabilities or a resistance to democratic reform that is an accepted, ongoing process in other democracies. Despite the persistent argument that the United States is too uniquely structured to benefit from comparative examples, this chapter has presented specific cases of developed democracies, including those with a federal structure, introducing reforms in response to identified challenges or vulnerabilities. As emphasized by the survey data, the election practitioners in the United States largely do not acknowledge vulnerabilities within the electoral process. Our survey data supports the conclusion that is evident from looking at both history and the current political environment: the United States is extremely resistant to reforming its electoral process to reflect international standards or to learning from the comparative experience of other countries that have strengthened their electoral systems over time.

Without addressing this blind spot, it will likely be impossible to consider—let alone implement—the serious reform initiatives that are needed to ensure American elections are resilient to new challenges. As they are increasingly shown to have a tangible impact on the electoral process and the quality of representative government, the structural deficiencies we have discussed could also serve to erode the American public's traditional faith in the system. Both actual threats to integrity and perceived threats to credibility of elections have implications for the sustainability and survival of American democracy. The United States has the resources and technical capacity to remedy these ills; what it lacks is the awareness and political will to do so.

Acknowledgments

The authors gratefully acknowledge Magnus Ohman and Madeline Waddell for their research and writing support, as well as Matthew Emery and Rakesh Sharma for their assistance with survey design and implementation. We are also grateful to Erica Shein, Katherine Ellena, and Staffan Darnolf for their thoughtful guidance and review of this chapter.

Notes

1. Full survey data available upon request. Some respondent dropout occurred during the course of the survey, and as a result, the number of respondents is lower for some questions.
2. *Reynolds v. Sims* (1964): "The Equal Protection Clause requires substantially equal legislative representation for all citizens in a State regardless of where they reside."
3. Factors including the number of registered voters and number of resident nationals may also be considered as proxies for establishing equal voting power.
4. This language is drawn from IFES electoral integrity assessment language used to establish and describe international standards and best practices in this area of the electoral process.

11

Lessons for the Reform Agenda

PIPPA NORRIS, THOMAS WYNTER, AND SARAH CAMERON

The book has highlighted a range of contemporary challenges about electoral integrity in America. Some concerns are relatively novel, but others reflect long-standing shortcomings. Successive chapters have analyzed new evidence concerning the importance of implementing both inclusive and secure electoral registers and balloting procedures rather than seeing these as trade-off values (Pallister; Bergman, Tran, and Yates); the need to establish fair and impartial processes to determine district boundaries, thereby strengthening accountability and party competition for the House of Representatives (Magleby et al.); the desirability of a vigorous, pluralistic, and vigilant free press to combat disinformation campaigns and fake news in the post-truth era (Bode, Thorson, and Vraga); the advantages of establishing professional, consistent, and uniform federal standards of electoral administration (Arceneaux); the value of transparent processes for citizens, journalists, party officials, and international monitors observing the ballot process and the vote count (Vanka, Davis-Roberts, and Carroll); and the way that several taken-for-granted features of U.S. elections, like the Electoral College for the presidency, violate basic international standards of electoral integrity (Vickery and Szilagyi).

To draw these ideas together and to provide a broad overview about the severity and distribution of malpractice in America, we offer systematic evidence to evaluate the electoral integrity of 50 U.S. states and D.C., drawing upon data from the Perceptions of Electoral Integrity (PEI) U.S. 2016 survey (Norris, Garnett, and Grömping 2017). The most common problems that are observed concern the effects of gerrymandered district boundaries, the checkerboard of electoral laws generating inconsistent administrative standards from one state to another, the impact of disinformation campaigns in the media, the deregulation of campaign finance, and the need for secure *and* inclusive registration requirements.

We then draw upon the 2017 U.S. World Values Survey and the 2012 American National Election Study to see whether people disaffected with the performance of U.S. elections were usually also more dissatisfied with the state of American democracy and less likely to go to the polls. On the one hand, many of the challenges facing American electoral integrity involve technical and procedural legal matters. These arouse heated debate among election officials, lawyers, politicians, scholars, and policy wonks, but they may not be considered terribly important to the general public, given other vital bread-and-butter issues on the policy agenda. After all, beyond leadership and partisan cues, what does the American public really understand about abstract issues such as the regulation of campaign funding (Milyo and Primo 2017), how the Electoral College works, the pros and cons of single-member pluralist electoral systems, or the legal battles over district maps? On the other hand, public perceptions of electoral malpractice may well erode public confidence in the electoral process, trust in government, and support for democracy by ordinary citizens. The logic is simple: Why bother to participate at the ballot box if you don't believe that the process is honest or the outcome is fair? The evidence scrutinized in this chapter demonstrates that public confidence in elections is closely intertwined with broader feelings of democratic legitimacy and patterns of civic engagement in America.

So what is to be done? We conclude by considering what concrete steps and political reforms could potentially be taken to help rebuild a bipartisan consensus, to strengthen electoral integrity, and to restore public confidence in American democracy. It is argued that four sequential steps should be considered for a comprehensive and strategic package of reforms, including amending electoral laws and regulations for registration and balloting; building the capacity of more impartial, independent, and professional electoral management bodies; monitoring performance and expanding transparency through electoral observers, comparative and state-level performance indicators, and watchdog agencies; and strengthening dispute-resolution mechanisms and oversight agencies.

Lessons learned about major challenges in the 2016 U.S. elections

What are the main lessons from the 2016 U.S. presidential elections about the state of electoral integrity in America? Before considering potential policy reforms, it is important to diagnose the ills of the body politic by disaggregating problems, in terms of identifying the weakest stages of the electoral cycle and also where problems are observed most commonly across America. The expert assessments in the U.S. Perceptions of Electoral Integrity Index (from PEI-US-2016; Norris, Garnett, and Grömping 2017) provide guidance through indicators that can be broken down into its subcomponents, as shown in Table 11.1. Modest differences in the ratings among states should be discounted, given the limited number of expert respondents in each state. More reliable assessments can be constructed by transforming the continuous 100-point scales in the PEI indices into high, medium,

Table 11.1 **Electoral Integrity in U.S. States, 2016**

State	PEI index	Electoral laws index	Electoral procedures	Voting district boundaries	Voter registration	Party and candidate registration	Media coverage	Campaign finance	Voting process	Vote count	Results	Electoral authorities	Rank
Vermont	✓	✓	✓	✗	✓	✓	✓	✓	✓	✓	✓	✓	1
Idaho	✓	!	✓	✗	✓	✓	✓	✓	✓	✓	✓	✓	2
New Hampshire	✓	!	✓	✗	✓	✓	✓	!	✓	✓	✓	✓	3
Iowa	✓	!	✓	✓	!	✓	✓	!	✓	✓	✓	✓	4
New Mexico	✓	!	✓	✓	!	✓	✗	✓	✓	✓	✓	✓	5
Maine	✓	✓	✓	✓	✓	✓	✓	!	✓	✓	!	✓	6
Washington	✓	✓	✓	✗	✓	✓	✗	✗	✓	✓	✓	✓	7
Hawai'i	✓	✓	✓	✓	✓	✓	✓	✓	✓	✓	✓	✓	8
Louisiana	✓	✓	✓	✗	✓	✓	✓	✓	✓	✓	✓	✓	9
Colorado	✓	✓	✓	✗	✓	✓	!	!	✓	✓	✓	✓	10
Maryland	✓	✓	✓	✗	✓	✓			✓	✓	✓	✓	11
Oregon	✓	!	✓	✗	✓	✓	✗	✗	✓	✓	!	✓	12
Minnesota	✓	✓	✓	✗	!	✓	✗	!	✓	✓	✓	✓	13
Delaware	✓	✗	✓	✗	!	✓	!	!	✓	✓	✓	✓	14
Connecticut	✓	!	✓	✗	✓	✓	!	!	✓	✓	✓	✓	15
Montana	✓	✗	✓	✗	!	✓	!	!	✓	✓	✓	✓	16
Massachusetts	✓	!	✓	✗	✓	✓	!	✗	✓	✓	✓	✓	17
Wyoming	✓	✗	✓	✗	✓	✓	✓	!	✓	✓	✓	✓	18
DC	✓	✓	✓	✗	!	✓	✗	!	✓	✓	✓	✓	19
West Virginia	✓	✗	✓	✗	✗	✓	!	!	✓	✓	✓	!	20
Alaska	✓	!	✓	!	!	✓	✗	!	✓	✓	✓	✓	21
Nebraska	✓	✗	✓	✗	!	✓	!	!	✓	✓	✓	✓	22
California	✓	!	✓	✗	!	✓	✗	✗	✓	✓	!	✓	23
Utah	✓	!	✓	✗	!	✓	!	!	✓	✓	✓	✓	24
Illinois	✓	✗	✓	✗	✗	✓	!	✗	✓	✓	✓	✓	25
Missouri	✓	✗	✓	✗	✗	✓	!	!	✓	✓	✓	✓	26

State	PEI index	Electoral laws index	Electoral procedures	Voting district boundaries	Voter registration	Party and candidate registration	Media coverage	Campaign finance	Voting process	Vote count	Results	Electoral authorities	Rank
New Jersey	✓	!	✓	×	✓	✓	×	×	✓	✓	✓	✓	27
Arkansas	✓	×	✓	×	×	✓	×	×	✓	✓	✓	✓	28
Indiana	✓	×	✓	×	×	✓	!	!	✓	✓	✓	!	29
North Dakota	✓	×	✓	×	!	✓	!	×	!	✓	✓	!	30
Kentucky	✓	×	✓	×	×	✓	×	!	✓	✓	✓	✓	31
South Dakota	✓	!	✓	×	!	✓	×	!	✓	✓	✓	✓	32
Kansas	✓	×	✓	×	!	✓	×	!	✓	✓	✓	!	33
Nevada	✓	!	✓	×	!	✓	×	×	✓	✓	✓	✓	34
New York	!	×	✓	×	!	✓	!	×	✓	✓	!	✓	35
Virginia	!	×	✓	×	!	✓	×	×	✓	✓	✓	✓	36
Texas	!	×	✓	×	×	✓	!	×	✓	✓	✓	✓	37
Florida	!	×	✓	×	!	✓	!	×	✓	✓	✓	✓	38
North Carolina	!	×	✓	×	×	✓	×	!	✓	✓	×	✓	39
Alabama	!	×	✓	×	×	✓	×	×	✓	✓	✓	✓	40
Michigan	!	×	✓	×	!	✓	×	×	✓	✓	×	✓	41
Ohio	!	×	✓	×	!	✓	×	×	✓	✓	!	✓	42
Georgia	!	×	✓	×	×	✓	×	×	✓	✓	✓	!	43
Rhode Island	!	×	✓	×	!	!	×	×	✓	✓	!	✓	44
Pennsylvania	!	×	✓	×	×	✓	×	×	✓	✓	✓	✓	45
South Carolina	!	×	✓	×	!	✓	×	×	!	✓	✓	✓	46
Mississippi	!	×	✓	×	×	✓	×	×	!	✓	✓	!	47
Oklahoma	!	×	✓	×	×	!	×	×	!	✓	✓	✓	48
Tennessee	!	✓	✓	×	!	!	×	×	✓	!	!	✓	49
Wisconsin	!	×	✓	×	×	✓	×	×	✓	✓	!	✓	50
Arizona	!	×	!	×	×	✓	×	×	✓	✓	!	!	51

Note: Categories ✓ = High (60+) ! = Moderate (50–59) × = Low (Less than 50).

Source: PEI-US-2016 (Norris, Garnett, and Grömping 2017).

and low categories of electoral integrity, similar to those used to compare countries in Figure 1.4. States can also be ranked from high to low integrity based on the overall summary PEI Index.

Many specific shortcomings and particular flaws help to explain the rank of particular states observed in Table 11.1. On voter registration, for example, Arkansas received one of the lowest evaluations in the expert assessments; it was reported that thousands of eligible voters were removed from voter rolls there prior to the 2016 election, after the secretary of state sent an inaccurate list of felons to county clerks (Hardy 2016). In Wisconsin, new voter ID requirements are estimated to have deterred 1 in 10 eligible registrants from casting a ballot, with the strongest effects on minorities and the poor (Mayer and DeCrescenzo 2017). Among the best-ranked U.S. states in this subcomponent, by contrast, automatic voter registration is a recurring theme; for example, Oregon was the first state to introduce this reform in 2015, and another nine states, including Vermont, West Virginia, and California, have followed. And this change is under consideration in many other places (Brennan Center for Justice 2017a). Therefore many particular factors and contingent events underlie both the framework of electoral laws implemented by the state and also the perceived quality of electoral integrity observed in American states. Chapters in this book, drawing upon multiple methods and approaches, have explored the underlying reasons for these patterns in depth.

What were the most pervasive challenges across America? Overall, as we observed earlier in chapter 1 (Figure 1.5), according to the PEI evidence, the most common flaws in U.S. electoral integrity relate to the following issues:

(i)   Electoral boundaries.
(ii)   Campaign finance.
(iii) Media coverage.
(iv)   Electoral laws and voter registration.

It is therefore worthwhile to focus on these issues, to compare how the scores vary on each of these subcomponents and among U.S. states.

Gerrymandering district boundaries

Issues of partisan gerrymandering have a long legacy in America, but the distorting effects of these practices have worsened in recent years (McGann et al. 2016). The issue of racial gerrymandering and civil rights has been tackled by the courts for many years, but it is only recently that the U.S. Supreme Court has been willing to wade into the issue of standards and measures of partisan gerrymandering (see Hasen, this volume; Magleby et al., this volume; Royden, Li, and Rudensky 2018). Gerrymandering practices ensure that representatives are returned time and again to the House of Representatives based on mobilizing the party faithful, without having to appeal more broadly to constituents across the aisle. Gerrymandering may reduce electoral accountability and thereby potentially exacerbate the bitter partisanship that plagues House politics (McGann et al. 2016). As populations change, periodic redistricting is needed in contests using majoritarian or plurality electoral systems with single-member districts, or proportional representation systems with small multimember districts. In most countries that redraw boundaries, the final decisions rest with either independent nonpartisan boundary commissions, election management bodies, and/or the courts. By contrast, in two-thirds of American states, decisions over redistricting are left in the hands of partisan legislators; France is the only other country following these practices. Recognizing the clear conflict of interest when legislators draw boundaries, important structural reforms to the process have been implemented in states that have adopted bipartisan political commissions or implemented independent commissions composed of nonpartisans.[1]

The expert evidence from PEI suggests that the process of drawing district boundaries, and the way that partisan gerrymandering functions to insulate incumbents from genuine competition, is the single weakest stage of American elections. In the global comparisons of districting practices, the United States scored far worse than other, comparable democracies (Norris, Martinez i Coma, and Grömping 2015; Martinez i Coma and Lago 2017). American experts ranked 46 U.S. states as low in integrity on the process of drawing district boundaries. North Carolina and Wisconsin were the worst performers, and only four U.S. states were ranked high (Iowa, New Mexico, Maine, and Hawai'i). As Magleby et al. (this volume) demonstrated, valid and reliable indicators are now available, allowing the judiciary to determine manipulations of district boundaries that violate electoral integrity. Courts can use these measures to throw out heavily gerrymandered maps. An important step in this direction was taken in February 2018, when the Pennsylvania State Supreme Court decided to throw out the maps enacted by the 2011 Republican state legislature and adopt a substitute plan that was far closer to the political makeup of the electorate (Bycoffe, 2018). At the time of writing, the U.S. Supreme Court is considering two extreme partisan gerrymandering cases, in Maryland (*Benisek v. Lamone*) and in Wisconsin (*Gill v. Whitford*), to judge whether they can come up with a standard to decide whether the cases violate the U.S. Constitution. The outcome is likely to have important consequences for redistricting practices in American elections.

Campaign finance

By all indications, campaign finance is another exceptionally weak link in the U.S. electoral cycle, and a common problem worldwide, as discussed in detail in an earlier volume (Norris and Abel van Es 2016; International IDEA 2018). The hefty $6.4 billion price tag for the 2016 U.S. presidential and congressional elections sets alarm bells ringing, up from $4.3 billion in 2000, after adjusting for inflation. Some minor reforms have been implemented in recent years; for example, almost half of all U.S. states revised their campaign finance regulations during 2017, including strengthening criminal penalties for any violations (NCSL 2018a). But although the public favors stricter control over campaign finance, including on the use of foreign funds in U.S. elections, there has been no effective action by Congress to reform the role of money in politics, the Federal Election Commission has been bitterly divided along partisan lines, and the Supreme Court has moved to deregulate campaign funding. Populist cries of "Drain the Swamp" in Trump rallies reflected genuine concern among Trump's supporters about lobbyists buying access, the influence of wealthy donors over government, and public policies skewed toward corporate interests, not less-well-off Americans. Similar themes also resonated among progressives and played a big part in Bernie Sanders' stump speeches. The Pew Research Center (2018a) polls found that three-quarters of Americans (77%) support limits on the amount individuals and organizations can spend on political campaigns and issues, and two-thirds believe that new laws could be effective in reducing the role of money in politics.

Yet Transparency International's 2017 U.S. Corruption Barometer shows that, despite Trump's campaign reform promises, in fact a majority of Americans believe that things have become worse, that corruption has risen under the Trump administration, and that the White House is the most corrupt of nine key institutions. The need to reform the role of money in politics is a challenge in most countries; many democracies, such as the U.K. and Sweden, have abandoned laissez-faire policies by moving toward growing public funding and greater transparency in the regulation of party political finances (Norris and Abel van Es 2016). By contrast, in recent years America has moved increasingly in the opposite direction, toward deregulation, in particular following *Citizens United v. FEC* (2010) and *McCutcheon v. FEC* (2014). PEI experts judged the issue of campaign finance as of low integrity in half of all American states, although it was regarded as particularly problematic in Wisconsin and South Dakota, compared with six high-rated states, including New Mexico, Vermont, and Idaho (see Table 11.1).

Campaign media

The role of the legacy news media in American democracy has also come under sustained pressure, including from long-term trends in the media environment, the rise of digital technologies, and the economics of the news industry. The decline of public trust in the impartiality and reliability of information provided by major newspapers and network and cable news programs is also a long-term trend, although it has been accelerated among Republicans by Trump's populist mantra "Fake media," used to describe any negative news about his administration. Gallup has monitored American trust in the legacy news media (newspapers, television, radio) since 1972, with a steady decline over the years, from 72% in 1976 to 32% in 2016 (Swift 2017). Democrats have been consistently more trusting of the news media than Republicans; in fact, the partisan gap widened to a chasm after the 2016 elections. In 2017 only 14% of Republicans said they had a "great deal" or "fair amount" of trust in the news media, compared with 72% of Democrats, in part because of the way journalists act as a watchdog over the Trump administration.

This conflux of developments has generated a Petri dish of rich opportunities for Russian and domestic alt-right groups to exploit disinformation campaigns, where intentional falsehoods disguised as news spread virally. The impact of fake news, alternative facts, post-truth, and disinformation campaigns, both online in social media as well as in mainstream media, emerged as one of the major issues of concern after Election Day in the United States and other Western democracies. In a post-truth era, the public appears to have lost faith in the honesty, impartiality, and credibility of the legacy press (Bennett and Livingstone 2018).

Lack of trust in media information was further exacerbated after the 2016 election by publication of the joint intelligence service report on the prevalence of Russian meddling (Office of Director of National Intelligence 2017). The report concludes that Russian state-sponsored outlets such as RT and Sputnik were engaged in propaganda, playing on divisive wedge issues of race and policing through social media. St. Petersburg "troll factories" (the Internet Research Institute) fed polarizing messages through American social media (MacFarquar 2018; Isikoff and Corn 2018). This problem was compounded by cybersecurity breaches of the Democratic National Committee's email server and Hillary Clinton's campaign organization, with information released through WikiLeaks. Sanders supporters, their mistrust deepened, claimed that "rigged" primary debates favored Clinton (Brazile 2017). The climate of suspicion was heighted further by the brouhaha about Cambridge Analytica's breach of confidential records and the misuse of purloined data obtained from 50 to 87 million Facebook users for advertising on behalf of the Trump campaign. Russian interference in the election triggered the Justice Department's appointment of Special Counsel Robert Mueller. Rumors of his investigation, including into potential collusion between the Russians and the Trump campaign, have become increasingly embroiled in intense partisan controversy. This has been exemplified by divergent news framing by Fox News and CNN in February 2018 of the Mueller indictments of Russian operatives (Chang 2018).

The Office of Director of National Intelligence (2017) revealed Russian cybersecurity threats in the 2016 election targeting official voting records in 21 states. Federal officials in the Department of Homeland Security expressed confidence that none of the attacks succeeded in tampering with the registration databases or vote tally, but, despite the implementation of some additional security measures by several states, worries persist about subsequent contests. More than 40 states use balloting systems more than a decade old, built without this sort of threat in mind (Halper 2017a). These events are widely documented, and the basic facts are not in serious dispute. What remains indeterminate is whether officials in the Trump campaign knowingly and intentionally aided Russian efforts, the subject of investigations by Special Counsel Mueller. The Republican report from the House Intelligence Committee disputes the evidence feeding these suspicions, but the bipartisan Senate Intelligence Committee tells a different story. Reactions have been slow; it was only in March 2018, more than a year after coming to office, that the Trump administration expelled Russian diplomats in retaliation for malign cyberattacks targeting the U.S. electoral system and critical infrastructure. The issue is bitterly partisan: Democrats claim that associates of the Trump campaign illegally worked with Russian intelligence officials to interfere with the outcome of the 2016 election, and the cloud of the Mueller investigation continues to dog the White House. Although there have been behind-the-scenes attempts by states to tighten security, it is by no means clear whether these are sufficient to deter potential attacks in future contests.

It is no surprise, then, that media coverage was ranked in PEI-US-2016 as among one of the poorest dimensions of electoral integrity in the 2016 American election. Survey items in this dimension addressed the fair gatekeeping role of the media, including "Newspapers provided balanced election news," "TV news favored the governing party," and "Parties/candidates had fair access to political broadcasts and advertising." Media markets vary in their degree of pluralistic competition and the availability of local newspapers and genuinely local TV stations, a growing problem in many areas. Experts saw the most serious problems with campaign media in 25 low-ranked states, such as Nevada, Arkansas, and Oregon, while a high ranking was observed in nine states, such as Washington, Vermont, and Idaho.

Electoral laws and voter registration

State laws governing the electoral register and balloting process have also become increasingly embroiled in partisan controversy during recent elections. As Pallister (this volume) discusses, registration procedures should ideally meet several principles. On the one hand, the issue of *electoral security* encompasses whether these processes were sufficiently robust so that qualified electors, and only qualified electors, could cast a ballot. Even a few cases of fraud that come to widespread attention can undermine public trust in the process. On the other hand, it is also widely considered to be highly desirable that procedures help to maximize *voter inclusion*, so that laws respect the fundamental rights of all qualified citizens to cast a ballot in a timely and efficient way, without facing undue burdens or administrative hurdles.

America is far from unique in debating the optimal way to strike a balance across these values; other Anglo-American democracies have seen renewed concern about the potential consequences of electoral registration procedures for issues of disenfranchisement and voter rights, fraud and security, and maladministration and accuracy. Thus in Britain, after the return of the Conservative government following the June 2017 general election, the U.K. Electoral Commission (2017b) published a new report investigating the risks of double voting and duplicate registration applications. Stricter voter identification requirements were introduced on a trial basis in several pilot areas during the May 2018 local elections, only to find that almost 4,000 electors without ID were turned away and unable to cast a ballot in these districts (Electoral Reform Society 2018). In Canada in 2014 the Conservative government also implemented stricter registration requirements and eliminated vouching to deter the potential risks of fraud.[2]

The key issue for all countries is how electoral laws and procedures can strike an appropriate balance between the twin values of security and inclusion.

Policies seeking to improve security typically emphasize the importance of photo identification and proof of citizenship requirements, and they may also restrict registration periods, absentee ballot voting, and early voting. Yet it is widely suspected that these moves discourage voter turnout, especially among sectors of the electorate that lack official papers or find it difficult to cast a ballot under the restricted facilities, including the poor, people with disabilities, and minority populations (Wang 2012). The ACLU argues that voting rights are under attack from state laws making it harder for Americans to cast a ballot; such measures cut early voting, implement voter ID laws, or purge electoral rolls.[3] Republican-controlled states that have implemented stricter requirements for voter registration and balloting are alleged to be suppressing voters' rights, a modern form of Jim Crow laws (Bentele and O'Brien 2013). On these grounds, several unduly restrictive voting and registration procedures have been struck down by the courts (see Hasen, this volume). The question of voter inclusion involves respecting the fundamental rights of all qualified and eligible citizens to cast a ballot in a timely and efficient way, without facing undue burdens or administrative hurdles, as discussed by Pallister (this volume). There is also concern about the convenience of the electoral process for the public and any undue hurdles raised by the time and effort required to register and cast a ballot. As Bergman, Tran, and Yates (this volume) demonstrated, the impact of strict photo ID requirements is not neutral; there are partisan effects. In any close elections where the margin of victory is determined by a few votes, reforms like voter ID laws can have a significant impact.

To expand inclusion, many state laws have sought to expand convenience voting, including by Election Day registration, online registration, preregistration (prior to attaining the age of 18), voter identification requirements to cast a ballot, voting rights for felons, absentee ballots, mail ballots, early ballots, provisional ballots, publication of voter leaflets, and publication and distribution of sample ballots. The National Conference of State Legislatures' (NCSL 2017c) Elections Legislation Database documents the election laws and procedures used in all 50 states; these range from voter identification requirements to methods of disseminating voter information. Yet reforms reducing the time and effort to vote can also have a negative impact on security, a major consideration that has prevented the adoption of online voting (Norris 2004).

Both security and inclusion are widely regarded as important principles. Without security, the danger arises that any fraudulent acts that go undetected raise public doubts about the process and outcome. Without respect for basic voting rights, democracy is undermined. While few doubt the importance of both security and inclusion as core components of electoral integrity (Pallister, this volume), in practice the difficulty arises that these values may involve trade-offs in a zero-sum game. It is critical to strike the right trade-off between making registration accessible and making it secure. Easier registration processes, such as by expanding convenience for citizens through online applications and the use of same-day registration, usually strengthen voter turnout. But the introduction of more accessible registration without sufficient verification checks raises security risks of abuse and fraud (U.K. Electoral Commission 2017a). Moreover, these are far from the only criteria that deserve to be considered for elections to meet international standards of electoral integrity; other guiding principles are impartiality, transparency, efficiency, accuracy, honesty, and professionalism (Catt et al. 2014). The PEI expert evaluations of "Election Registration" saw the weakest procedures in Wisconsin and Washington; 14 states rated low and 13 states rated high in this component.

Do these problems matter for trust and legitimacy?

Elites, such as officials, lawyers, politicians, and journalists, express concern about the issues affecting the integrity of American elections. But many involve abstruse technical elements that are not visible to ordinary citizens, including the constitutional and legal procedures regulating the apportionment of electoral districts, the security of voting machines against the risks of cyberattacks, and the constitutional design of the Electoral College. In general, therefore, compared with more bread-and-butter matters like jobs and taxes, do ordinary citizens know and care about these flaws in electoral procedures? In particular, do perceptions of electoral malpractice have the capacity to erode public confidence in American democracy and depress (already low) levels of U.S. voting participation?

To see whether public concerns about malpractice influence political attitudes and behavior, we can analyze data from the 2017 U.S. World Values Survey. This includes a 10-item battery tapping into citizens' evaluations of different qualities of elections. The positive (P) and negative (N) items (see below), with Likert-type responses, fall into the stages of the electoral cycle, including items used to generate two scales. The Survey asks, "In your view, how often do the following things occur in this country's elections?"

Electoral Integrity Scale
- Election officials are fair. (P)
- Women have equal opportunities to run for office. (P)
- Journalists provide fair coverage of elections. (P)
- Voters are offered a genuine choice in the elections. (P)
- Votes are counted fairly. (P)

Electoral Malpractice Scale
- Opposition candidates are prevented from running. (N)
- Rich people buy elections. (N)
- TV news favors the governing party. (N)
- Voters are bribed. (N)
- Voters are threatened with violence at the polls. (N)

Factor analysis suggests that the positive and negative items fall into consistent and robust scales. They can therefore be summed and standardized to 100-point measures for ease of comparison to generate the Electoral Integrity and Electoral Malpractice Scales, respectively.[4]

Table 11.2 shows the two OLS regression models predicting satisfaction with American democracy (measured by a 10-point scale) and the reported frequency of voting in midterm elections from 2008 to 2014. The results confirm that perceptions measured by the Electoral Malpractice Scale were associated with democratic dissatisfaction and lower turnout, while perceptions measured by the Electoral Integrity Scale saw the reverse relationship. These correlations persist after controlling for the standard demographic and attitudinal factors. Thus democratic satisfaction tended to be higher among more educated and affluent Americans and among those with authoritarian values. Democrats proved far more negative, which can be explained as part of the "winners-losers" thesis (Anderson et al. 2005). Indeed, out of all the variables, overall the perceptions of electoral integrity and malpractice proved the strongest factors predicting democratic satisfaction (based on the standardized beta coefficients).

Several factors proved significant predictors for turnout as well; for example, higher participation was observed among whites, the interwar generation, the more educated and affluent, and liberals. The generational cohort and age effects were particularly strong, as widely and consistently observed in numerous previous studies (Wattenberg 2015; Zukin et al. 2016; Garcia-Albacete 2014). Even with these controls, however, public perceptions of electoral malpractice and integrity still proved significant and pointed in the expected direction. To look at the substantive importance of these attitudes, Figure 11.1 shows the reported rates of voting participation in midterm elections in 2010 and 2014. Only a modest (5-point) gap in perceptions of electoral integrity and malpractice was found among the abstainers who said they never voted in these contests. The gap widened among

Table 11.2 **Predicting Democratic Satisfaction and Voting Participation, World Values Survey, 2017**

		Satisfaction with American democracy				Frequency of voting in midterm elections 2008–2014			
		B	SE	Beta	P.	B	SE	Beta	P.
Perceptions	Electoral Malpractice Scale	**-0.02**	**0.00**	**-0.14**	*******	**-0.00**	**0.00**	**-0.06**	*******
	Electoral Integrity Scale	**0.04**	**0.00**	**0.23**	*******	**0.00**	**0.00**	**0.06**	*******
CONTROLS									
Race	White	0.12	0.12	0.03	N/s	0.12	0.04	0.07	***
	Black	0.01	0.21	0.00	N/s	0.13	0.07	0.04	N/s
	Hispanic (Ref)	0.00				0.00			
Gender	Female (Ref)	0.00				0.00			
	Male	0.13	0.11	0.03	N/s	0.07	0.04	0.04	N/s
Generation	Interwar (Ref) 1900–1945	0.00				0.00			
	Baby Boomer 1946–1964	-0.43	0.23	-0.08	N/s	-0.25	0.08	-0.13	***
	Gen X 1965–1979	-0.42	0.23	-0.08	N/s	-0.63	0.08	-0.31	***
	Millennial 1980+	-0.10	0.23	-0.02	N/s	-1.05	0.08	-0.60	***
SES	Education	0.12	0.06	0.05	*	0.13	0.02	0.13	***
	Household Income	0.05	0.01	0.09	***	0.02	0.01	0.07	***
	Financial insecurity (savings)	-0.05	0.06	-0.02	N/s	-0.02	0.02	-0.02	N/s
Partisanship	Democrat	-0.68	0.11	-0.15	***	-0.07	0.04	-0.04	N/s
	Republican	0.16	0.26	0.01	N/s	-0.01	0.09	0.00	N/s
Values	Liberal–Conservative scale	0.00	0.00	-0.03	N/s	0.00	0.00	-0.08	***
	Authoritarian scale Schwartz value of security, conformity, and tradition	0.17	0.07	0.05	**	-0.01	0.03	-0.01	N/s
	(Constant)	4.33	0.52		***	0.89	0.18		***
	Adjusted R2	0.15				0.23			
	N.	1,796				1,814			

Note: OLS regression models with the unstandardized Beta (B), Standard error (SE), standardized betas and significance. * $p < .05$, ** $p < .01$, *** $p < .001$. N/s Not significant.

Source: World Values Survey, U.S. only, 2017.

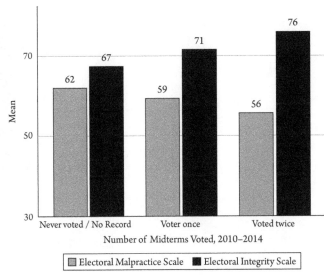

Figure 11.1 Voting Participation by Perceptions of Electoral Integrity, U.S., 2016.
Note: For the construction of the Electoral Malpractice and Electoral Integrity standardized scales, see text. Q: "In your view, how often do the following things occur in this country's elections?" The Electoral Integrity Scale includes responses to the following items: Election officials are fair; Women have equal opportunities to run for office; Journalists provide fair coverage of elections; Voters are offered a genuine choice in the elections; Votes are counted fairly. The Electoral Malpractice Scale includes responses to these statements: Opposition candidates are prevented from running; Rich people buy elections; TV news favors the governing party; Voters are bribed; Voters are threatened with violence at the polls. Source: World Values Survey 2017, U.S. only.

those who reported voting once and expanded to a substantial (20-point) gap among those who reported voting in both congressional elections. That is to say, those who voted more regularly had more favorable perceptions of electoral integrity and lower perceptions of electoral malpractice.

To provide further reliability checks, similar models were run using the 2012 American National Election Study, which carries several identical items on electoral integrity. As shown in Figure 11.2, very similar results can be observed. Those people who expressed considerable confidence that "votes are counted fairly" and "electoral officials are fair" are far more likely to report that they voted compared to those who expressed less confidence.

These findings about the American electorate also confirm previous research (Norris 2014) that has examined similar issues by comparing public opinion in almost two dozen diverse countries around the world (not including the United States), using data from the sixth wave of the World Values Survey (2012–2014). This Survey found that, even after applying a battery of attitudinal, economic, and social controls, public perceptions of electoral integrity

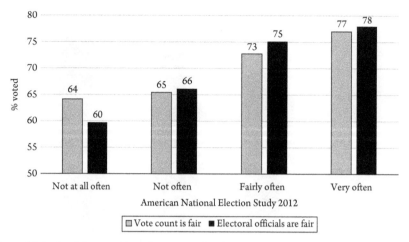

Figure 11.2 Confidence in Fair Elections and Voter Turnout, U.S., 2012.
Source: American National Election Study 2012.

were significantly associated with feelings of legitimacy, including confidence in political parties and legislatures, as well as satisfaction with the performance of democracy and reported voting turnout. The consistent pattern observed across varied nations and types of regimes certainly suggests that positive feelings about the quality of elections are often closely correlated with other indicators of civic engagement. This makes sense logically: the more people feel they can trust elections, that these contests are not rigged, fraudulent, or corrupt, the more likely they are to feel that democracy works and that it is worthwhile to cast a ballot. Conversely, as others have reported, suspicions that elections are deeply flawed have a corrosive effect on democratic satisfaction and voter turnout (Alvarez, Hall, and Llewellyn 2008b; Birch 2008, 2010; Martinez i Coma and Trinh 2017).

At the same time, it is not possible to disentangle the direction of causality in the underlying correlation using a cross-sectional survey taken at a single point in time. The relationship may reflect a rationalization of habitual behavior, whereby those who vote regularly for whatever reason (such as duty or social networks) say that they are more likely to be satisfied with democracy. But it seems more logical to assume that prior attitudes (confidence in the fairness and integrity of American elections) lead to political behavior. Compared with equivalent democracies around the world, U.S. turnout in presidential and congressional general elections is relatively low; just 60% of the eligible electorate voted in the 2016 contest. Rising public concern about the honesty of American elections, whether these perceptions are true or false, is likely to weaken turnout further, although other trends, such as intense partisanship, may serve to counteract these tendencies.

Electoral integrity is therefore important to ordinary Americans, not just an elite concern. Due to the phenomenon of motivated reasoning (Kunda 1990; Edelson et al. 2017), however, there is little consensus among Democrats and Republicans about the precise diagnosis of any problems with U.S. elections. In particular, media bubbles in the contemporary information environment are likely to deepen partisan polarization over what constitutes the most severe risks to electoral integrity, reinforcing preexisting doubts by Republicans about alleged voter fraud and fake news (reinforced by Fox News) and worrying Democrats about alleged Russian meddling and GOP attempts at voter suppression (highlighted by CNN) (Chang 2018). The partisan framing of news coverage seems likely to drive Americans apart rather than broadening a shared compromise about reforming the electoral rules of the game.

This is clearly illustrated in the Pew Research Center (2018a) poll that sought to monitor American attitudes toward democracy and political institutions, including the performance of elections. When asked what was important for elections in the United States, the survey found considerable bipartisan consensus surrounding the several propositions; for example, there was broad agreement that U.S. elections should be free from tampering (90% responded that this was "very important"), congressional districts should be fairly drawn (72%), and there should be high turnout (70%) in presidential elections. As shown in Figure 11.3, however, when asked about the performance of U.S. elections, Republicans and Democrats differed sharply on the underlying debate about voter registration, with Democrats emphasizing the problems of inclusion ("No eligible voters should be denied the vote") while Republicans prioritized problems of security ("No ineligible voters should be permitted to vote").

Reforms strengthening electoral integrity in America

Given all these indicators, the evidence points to a range of enduring problems in American elections, with the capacity to damage civic culture. Most attempts to strengthen U.S. elections involve piecemeal reforms, such as the report by the Bauer-Ginsberg Commission (Bauer et al. 2014). Proposals are often worthwhile but technical in nature and modest in impact. These are equivalent to rearranging the deck chairs on the *Titanic*. Instead, what is needed is a more comprehensive plan addressing systematic and structural weaknesses at the heart of American elections. Several steps can be recommended, illustrated in Figure 11.4, including a sequential process involving improving legal regulations, building the capacity of administrative agencies such that these laws can be implemented efficiently and effectively, monitoring performance, and strengthening accountability and oversight. These are the initiatives used in many countries around the world where electoral assistance seeks to improve electoral integrity (Norris

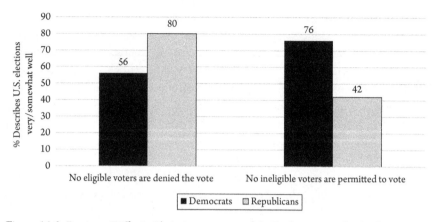

Figure 11.3 Partisans Differ in Their Assessments of the Performance of U.S. Elections.
Note: Percentage who say each statement describes U.S. elections very/somewhat well.
Source: Pew Research Center 2018a.

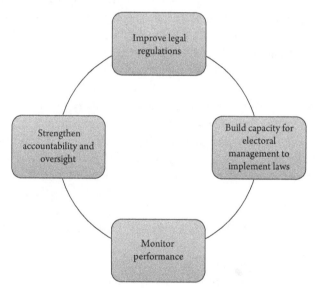

Figure 11.4 Recommended Sequence of Reforms.
Source: Norris 2017a, 55.

2017a). In practice, perhaps the most urgent practical steps in the US involve the following:

(i) Reforming electoral legal regulations for registration and balloting.
(ii) Building more impartial, independent, and professional electoral management bodies.
(iii) Monitoring performance and expanding transparency through electoral observers, comparative and state-level performance indicators, and watchdog agencies.
(iv) Strengthening dispute-resolution mechanisms.

Legal regulations for registration and balloting

The first step would be to overhaul the basic regulation of registration and balloting, the source of so much controversy in U.S. elections. Piecemeal reforms to state laws governing these processes in America have generated a complex hodgepodge of practices. Despite the extensive body of literature evaluating the impact on turnout, it still remains difficult to establish conclusively the effects of any single type of electoral procedure, not least because multiple factors affect voting participation (Smets and van Ham 2013).

Are reforms that implement more convenient forms of registration and voting effective? In one of the seminal early studies on the effects, Rosenstone and Wolfinger (1978) concluded that U.S. states that used the most relaxed registration processes had higher turnout, and their research suggests that similar effects would follow by lowering the costs of registration elsewhere in the country. Similarly, Piven (1988) argued that legal-institutional factors, including registration procedures, are the most important barriers to voting participation for disadvantaged groups in America. Burden et al. (2014) found that Election Day registration had a positive effect on participation, but another convenience measure, early voting, actually tended to depress turnout. So while most empirical studies find that stricter registration and balloting rules do correlate with lower turnout, at the same time, reforms designed to ease the process do not necessarily boost participation substantially (Berinsky 2005; Highton 2004; Hershey 2009). There are several reasons for this.

Turnout is expected to be boosted by reducing the logistical costs of registering and voting. But in practice they do nothing to alter the other informational costs involved in participating, nor do they address the lack of genuine choice among issues, parties, and candidates at the ballot box.

States with a strong participatory culture, such as Minnesota, are the most likely to adopt lenient registration laws, such as Election Day registration. As a result, it may be misleading to extrapolate from these contexts to assume that similar effects would arise from exporting lenient registration facilities to states with a tradition of more restrictive voting rights, such as Alabama (Hanmer 2009; Bowler and Donovan 2011; Norris 2004).

Convenience voting facilities are also most often used by engaged citizens, reinforcing their propensity to vote, but this may thereby exacerbate any social gaps in turnout arising from age, socioeconomic status, education, ethnicity, or sex (Burden et al. 2014; Berinsky 2005).

Additionally, critics claim that well-meaning procedural reforms making legal requirements for the registration and voting process more lenient may also have unintended consequences, such as heightening security risks, undermining the secrecy of the ballot, increasing administrative costs and complexities, producing inconsistent and unequal voting rights across America, and thereby possibly ultimately damaging public confidence in electoral integrity (Burden et al. 2014). Elsewhere, for example in the U.K., the introduction of online registration, while seen as part of the commonsense drive to modernize elections, has made the system more vulnerable to fraud (U.K. Electoral Commission 2017b).

Implementing more convenient voting is therefore often seen as useful as a straightforward fix for low turnout, and the results may well be positive (if modest in size), but in practice, as Pallister (this volume) concludes, the desire for inclusive participation needs to be counterbalanced by the need to protect the security of the ballot.

On the other hand, many state laws have sought to tighten security. As discussed by Bergman, Tran, and Yates and by Vickery and Szilagyi (both this volume), one common way to do this is to implement stricter photo IDs for registration and voting. This process could be less contentious if free and secure photo IDs were provided by state and federal agencies automatically to all eligible citizens, as they are in many countries. In India, for example, all citizens who qualify to vote are provided with free photo IDs by the Indian Electoral Commission.[5] The IDs are matched online to identical photo records listed against all names on the electoral register in local polling places. The card serves as a general identity card for casting votes as well as other official purposes, such as applying for a passport. India is the world's largest democracy, containing over 800 million people, many illiterate. It is also a highly diverse society and federal state. If India can implement a secure system of no-cost voter ID cards, then such a measure should not be beyond the capacity of the United States. This is only one dimension of improving secure voting records, however; the federal government also needs to provide states and localities with the resources to invest in electronic machines that leave a paper trail, for random audits, and digital registration and voting records also need far greater security against the risks of hacking. A combination of these steps could strengthen public confidence in the integrity of the electoral process, reduce the barriers to political participation, and strengthen security.

Building independent, impartial, and professional electoral management

Passing new laws and regulations is only the first step. As the front-line agencies, officials and poll workers need the capacity, skills, and resources to implement them in an impartial and uniform manner. Electoral agencies should ideally meet several general guiding principles designed to ensure legitimate and credible electoral processes and outcomes. These include de facto *independence* from undue interference in their activities from the executive or legislative branch; *integrity* so that the process is free of fraud and corruption; *transparency* to build trust in the accuracy and honesty of the process; *efficiency* so that services are delivered effectively, equitably, and within budget; *impartiality* so that officials are not biased toward any single contestant; and *professionalism* so that staff have the training, expertise, and resources to manage tasks well (Catt et al. 2014).

Countries differ in whether electoral administration is handled by governmental or independent agencies and whether decision-making is largely centralized or localized (Catt et al. 2014). Based on these distinctions, the United States differs from most long-standing democracies in its high degree of partisanship and decentralization. Regulatory policies and administrative procedures are less coherent if decision-making is dispersed across multiple federal, state, and local agencies, weakening coordinated or "joined-up" governance. The decentralization of decision-making to state and local officials means that nuts-and-bolts administrative rules, such as the hours polling places are open, the deadline for registering, and the use of postal voting, vary from one place to another. Thus citizens' fundamental voting rights are not consistently applied across all jurisdictions. Poorly resourced local bodies, needing to ramp up efforts to run contests at periodic intervals, often lack the expertise, professional personnel, and technical capacity to manage these tasks well. Giving considerable discretion to local electoral officials means that when problems arise, it becomes more difficult to establish "where the buck stops" among multiple agencies with overlapping functions, weakening accountability. For all these reasons, structural reforms to the process of electoral management should be considered in the United States, at minimum by strengthening the roles of the Federal Election Commission (regulating campaign finance) and the Electoral Assistance Commission (advising on standards), and promoting more independent administrative agencies to avoid the actual or appearance of partisan conflicts of interest. Whether this is likely to happen without the impetus of a major crisis remains doubtful, however; for example, in July 2017, as part of budget cuts, the House Republicans tried to defund the Electoral Assistance Commission, the primary administrative agency working with the Department of Homeland Security on electoral security.

Monitoring performance

In general, attempts at monitoring electoral integrity are part of a broader set of initiatives concerning governance transparency and accountability. These qualities are generally thought to help plug the leaky pipes of corruption and inefficiency, channel government spending more efficiently, and produce better public services. In the field of electoral governance, greater openness about the rules and procedures, outcomes, and decision-making processes used by electoral authorities is widely assumed to build public trust, improve policymaking, and facilitate accountability.[6] By revealing problems, as Vanka, Davis-Roberts, and Carroll discuss in this volume, it is generally believed that the reports published by election observers, the news media, and citizen watchdog groups will pressure electoral officials and elected representatives to implement reforms and deter malpractice. By contrast, silence and secrecy are powerful tools used by governments to cloak their actions from public scrutiny. Even if unable to generate positive benefits, there is still a presumption in favor of open electoral governance, since "the absence of transparency in electoral processes invariably leads to the suspicion that fraudulent activities are taking place" (Wall 2006, 24). Disclosure alone is unlikely to deliver major benefits, however, unless it is coupled with forms of accountability and penalties or incentives to improve the professional standards of electoral administration and reduce the role of partisan interests (Fung, Graham, and Weil 2008; Norris and Nai 2017). The development of a broader range of performance indicators is another important initiative, allowing triangulation by combining multiple methods, including expert, poll worker, and mass surveys, aggregate indicators from registration and voting records, legal statistics and court cases, forensic autopsies, policy evaluation case studies, and experimental pilot studies (Burden and Stewart 2014).

Improving dispute-resolution mechanisms

The judiciary has traditionally played an active role in determining whether new U.S. state laws governing voting rights and electoral procedures meet constitutional standards, including striking out several attempts to introduce strict photo identification requirements (Hasen 2012). The courts, rather than the legislative branch, have played the most important role in determining contemporary campaign finance regulations. In *Bush v. Gore* in 2000 the rulings by the Supreme Court essentially determined the outcome of the race, allowing George W. Bush's victorious Florida's electoral college votes to stand (Boatright 2015). Similarly, court decisions on gerrymandering are likely to be vital for reforms stamping out excessive partisan bias in mapmaking. But traditional legal appeals usually involve a very lengthy process, and in the interim disputes can fail to be remedied, exacerbating disaffection and protests. To overcome these problems, many countries have established special courts and informal mediation processes to deal with electoral disputes that arise at all stages of the electoral cycle in a timely fashion. Dispute-resolution mechanisms aim to deal with complaints in a prompt, just, and impartial manner, minimizing partisan conflict, upholding rights, and facilitating acceptance of the eventual result by all sides in any dispute. Effective systems of electoral justice safeguard the legality of the process and the rights of citizens, promote consensus, and strengthen the legitimacy of the process. Electoral dispute resolution systems, which are independent of electoral management bodies, take different institutional forms in different countries, as described in a comprehensive global handbook published by International IDEA (2010), but the core idea is now widely accepted. The United States could learn from these practices.

Therefore a comprehensive and strategic package of reforms designed to strengthen electoral integrity in America should ideally consider four sequential steps: amending the legal procedures used for registration and balloting to maximize both security and inclusion; building more impartial, independent, and professional electoral management bodies to replace the highly localized and partisan agencies responsible for electoral administration; monitoring performance and expanding transparency through electoral observers, developing better performance indicators, and strengthening watchdog bodies; and strengthening dispute resolution mechanisms and oversight agencies. These are far from the only reforms to be considered—indeed there is a lengthy list—but they would represent major steps that would facilitate many other improvements. Elections provide essential infrastructure for American democracy, and, like roads, bridges, and tunnels, they need investment to be maintained. It remains to be seen whether there is the will and the capacity to meet the challenges facing electoral integrity in the United States or whether worsening problems of legitimacy and trust will further exacerbate the party polarization, legislative gridlock, social intolerance, and illiberal forces that threaten to tear apart the fabric of American democracy.

Notes

1. Ballotpedia, "State-by-State Redistricting Procedures," https://ballotpedia.org/State-by-state_redistricting_procedures.
2. See "Electoral Reform" at https://www.canada.ca/en/campaign/electoral-reform.html.
3. ACLU, "Fighting Voter Suppression," https://www.aclu.org/issues/voting-rights/fighting-voter-suppression.
4. For more technical details about the factor analysis used for the scale construction and the robustness tests, see Norris 2014, ch. 3.
5. See India's National Voters' Services Portal, http://www.nvsp.in/.
6. See, for example, "Electoral Integrity" at the Open Election Data Initiative, http://www.openelectiondata.net/en/guide/electoral-integrity/public-confidence/.

SELECTED BIBLIOGRAPHY

Abramowitz, Alan I. 2006. "Disconnected, or Joined at the Hip?" In *Red and Blue Nation? Characteristics and Causes of America's Polarized Politics*, edited by Pietro Nivola and David W. Brady, 72–85. Washington, D.C.: Brookings Institution Press.

ACE Electoral Knowledge Network. 2012. "Voter Registration—Cost Implications." *ACE Encyclopedia Version 1.0.* http://aceproject.org/main/english/vr/vrb15.htm.

ACE Electoral Knowledge Network. 2013. "Voter Registration." *The ACE Encyclopedia.* http://aceproject.org/ace-en/pdf/vr/view.

ACE Electoral Knowledge Network. 2016. "Election Integrity: Accrediting Observers." https://aceproject.org/main/english/ei/eie08.htm.

ACE Electoral Knowledge Network. 2017. http://aceproject.org/.

ACE Electoral Knowledge Network. N.d. "Voting Operations: Absentee Voting." Accessed December 11, 2017. http://aceproject.org/ace-en/topics/vo/voa/voa02/voa02b/default.

Agrawal, Nina. 2016. "All the Times in U.S. History That Members of the Electoral College Voted Their Own Way." *Los Angeles Times*, December 20. http://www.latimes.com/nation/la-na-faithless-electors-2016-story.html.

Ahlquist, John S., Kenneth R. Mayer, and Simon Jackman. 2014. "Alien Abduction and Voter Impersonation in the 2012 U.S. General Election: Evidence from a Survey List Experiment." *Election Law Journal* 13 (4): 460–475.

Allcott, Hunt, and Matthew Gentzkow. 2017. "Social Media and Fake News in the 2016 Election." *Journal of Economic Perspectives* 31 (2): 211–236.

Alvarez, R. Michael, Lonna Atkeson, and Thad E. Hall, eds. 2012a. *Confirming Elections: Creating Confidence and Integrity through Election Auditing.* New York: Palgrave Macmillan.

Alvarez, R. Michael, Lonna Rae Atkeson, and Thad E. Hall. 2012b. *Evaluating Elections: A Handbook of Methods and Standards.* New York: Cambridge University Press.

Alvarez, R. Michael, and Bernard Grofman, eds. 2014. *Electoral Administration in the United States.* New York: Cambridge University Press.

Alvarez, R. Michael, and Thad E. Hall. 2008. "Building Secure and Transparent Elections through Standard Operating Procedures." *Public Administration Review* 68 (5): 828–838.

Alvarez, R. Michael, Thad E. Hall, and Susan Hyde, eds. 2008. *Election Fraud.* Washington, D.C.: Brookings Institution Press.

Alvarez, R. Michael, Thad E. Hall, and Morgan Llewellyn. 2008a. "Are Americans Confident Their Ballots Are Counted?" *Journal of Politics* 70 (3): 754–766.

Alvarez, R. Michael, Thad E. Hall, and Morgan Llewellyn. 2008b. "Who Should Run Elections in the United States?" *Policy Studies Journal* 36 (3): 325–346.

Ambinder, Marc. 2014. "Why Internet Voting Is a Very Dangerous Idea." *The Week*, August 28. http://theweek.com/article/index/267191/why-internet-voting-is-a-very-dangerous-idea.

American National Election Studies. (2013). *2012 Time Series Study* [Data file and code book]. Retrieved from https://electionstudies.org/project/2012-time-series-study/.

Amnesty International. 2002. "Amnesty International's 2002 Report on Singapore." May 28. http://www.singapore-window.org/sw02/020528ai.htm.

Anderson, Christopher J., Andre Blais, Shaun Bowler, Todd Donovan, and Ola Listhaug. 2005. *Losers' Consent: Elections and Democratic Legitimacy.* New York: Oxford University Press.

Anderson, George. 2008. *Federalism: An Introduction.* New York: Oxford University Press.

Ansolabehere, Stephen. 2008. "Access versus Integrity in Voter Identification Requirements." *New York University Annual Survey of American Law* 63 (4): 613–630.

Ansolabehere, Stephen, and Eitan Hersh. 2014. "Voter Registration: The Process and Quality of Lists." In *The Measure of American Elections*, edited by Barry C. Burden and Charles StewartIII, 61–90. Cambridge Studies in Election Law and Democracy. Cambridge University Press. https://doi.org/10.1017/CBO9781107589117.003.

Archer, J. Clark, Fiona M. Davidson, Erin H. Fouberg, Kenneth C. Martis, Richard L. Morrill, Fred M. Shelley, Robert H. Watrel, and Gerald R. Webster. 2014. *Atlas of the 2012 Elections.* Lanham, MD: Rowman & Littlefield.

Arthur, Charles. 2014. "Estonian E-voting Shouldn't Be Used in European Elections, Say Security Experts." *The Guardian*, May 12. http://www.theguardian.com/technology/2014/may/12/estonian-e-voting-security-warning-european-elections-research.

Ax, Joseph. 2016. "Jill Stein's Recount Bid Is Over." *Huffington Post*, December 12. http://www.huffingtonpost.com/entry/jill-stein-recount-over_us_584f3b71e4b0bd9c3dfe612e.

Bakshy, Eytan, Solomon Messing, and Lada A. Adamic. 2015. "Exposure to Ideologically Diverse News and Opinion on Facebook." *Science* 348 (6239): 1130–1132.

Barberá, Pablo, John T. Jost, Jonathan Nagler, Joshua A. Tucker, and Richard Bonneau. 2015. "Tweeting from Left to Right: Is Online Political Communication More Than an Echo Chamber?" *Psychological Science* 26 (10): 1531–1542.

Barone, Michael, and Chuck McCutcheon. 2013. *The Almanac of American Politics 2014.* Chicago: University of Chicago Press.

Barreto, Matt A., Stephen A. Nuno, and Gabriel R. Sanchez. 2009. "The Disproportionate Impact of Voter-ID Requirements on the Electorate—New Evidence from Indiana." *PS: Political Science & Politics* 42 (1): 111–116.

Bauer, Robert F., et al. 2014. The American Voting Experience: Report and Recommendations of the Presidential Commission on Election Administration. Washington, D.C. www.supportthevoter.gov.

Bauer, Scott. 2016. "Stein Still Stands to Benefit under Losing Recount Effort." *Associated Press*, December 5. https://apnews.com/000b42099c524f069ecd71d4065e05ca/stein-still-stands-benefit-under-losing-recount-effort.

Baum, Matthew A. 2002. "Sex, Lies, and War: How Soft News Brings Foreign Policy to the Inattentive Public." *American Political Science Review* 96 (1): 91–109.

Baum, Matthew A. 2003. "Soft News and Political Knowledge: Evidence of Absence or Absence of Evidence?" *Political Communication* 20 (2): 173–190.

Baumgarten, Harry, and Sondra Haltom. 2016. "Failure to Observe: The Federal Observer Program after Shelby County." *Campaign Legal Center*, July 21. http://www.campaignlegalcenter.org/news/blog/failure-observe-federal-observer-program-after-shelby-county.

Beauchamp, Zack. 2017. "Democrats Are Falling for Fake News about Russia." *Vox*, May 19. https://www.vox.com/world/2017/5/19/15561842/trump-russia-louise-mensch.

Beaulieu, Emily. 2014. *Electoral Protest and Democracy in the Developing World.* New York: Cambridge University Press.

Becker, Amy B. 2017. "Trump Trumps Baldwin? How Trump's Tweets Transform SNL into Trump's Strategic Advantage." *Journal of Political Marketing*: 1–19.

Becker, Amy B., and Leticia Bode. 2017. "Satire as a Source for Learning? The Differential Impact of News versus Satire Exposure on Net Neutrality Knowledge Gain." *Information, Communication and Society* 21 (4): 1–14.

Becker, Amy B., and Don J. Waisanen. 2013. "From Funny Features to Entertaining Effects: Connecting Approaches to Communication Research on Political Comedy." *Review of Communication* 13 (3): 161–183.

Beer, Caroline C. 2012. "Reinvigorating Federalism: The Emergence of Governors and State Legislatures as Power Brokers and Policy Innovators." In *Oxford Handbook of Mexican Politics*, edited by Roderic Ai Camp, 119–142. New York: Oxford University Press.

Bennett, Corey. 2016. "Guccifer 2.0 Drops More DNC Docs." *Politico*, September 13. https://www.politico.com/story/2016/09/guccifer-2-0-dnc-docs-228091.

Bennett, Lance W., and Steven Livingston. 2018. "The Disinformation Order: Disruptive Communication and the Decline of Democratic Institutions." *European Journal of Communication* 33 (2): 122–139.

Bennett, Linda L. M., and Stephen Earl Bennett. 1989. "Enduring Gender Differences in Political Interest: The Impact of Socialization and Political Dispositions." *American Politics Quarterly* 17 (1): 105–122.

Bentele, Keith G., and Erin E. O'Brien. 2013. "Jim Crow 2.0? Why States Consider and Adopt Restrictive Voter Access Policies." *Perspectives on Politics* 11 (4): 1088–1116.

Berger-Tal, Oded, Jonathan Nathan, Ehud Meron, and David Saltz. 2014. "The Exploration-Exploitation Dilemma: A Multidisciplinary Framework." *PLOS ONE* 10 (3): e0119116. https://doi.org/10.1371/journal.pone.0095693.

Berinsky, Adam J. 2005. "The Perverse Consequences of Electoral Reform in the United States." *American Politics Research* 33 (4): 471–491.

Berman, Ari. 2017. "The Man behind Trump's Voter Fraud Obsession." *New York Times Magazine*, June 13. https://nyti.ms/2siFKzB.

Berruecos, Susana. 2003. "Electoral Justice in Mexico: The Role of the Electoral Tribunal under the New Federalism." *Journal of Latin American Studies* 35: 801–825.

Best, Robin E., Shawn Donahue, Daniel B. Magleby, Jonathan Krasno, and Michael D. McDonald. 2018. "Values and Validations: Proper Standards for Comparing Standards for Packing Gerrymanders." *Election Law Journal* 17: 82–84.

Biggers, Daniel R., and Michael J. Hanmer. 2017. "Understanding the Adoption of Voter Identification Laws in the American States." *American Politics Research* 45 (4): 463–473. https://doi.org/10.1177/1532673X16687266.

Binkowski, Brooke. 2016. "CIA: Russia Interfered with U.S. Elections." *Snopes*, December 10. https://www.snopes.com/2016/12/10/cia-russia-interfered-with-u-s-elections/.

Birch, Sarah. 2008. "Electoral Institutions and Popular Confidence in Electoral Processes: A Cross-National Analysis." *Electoral Studies* 27 (2): 305–320.

Birch, Sarah. 2010. "Perceptions of Electoral Fairness and Voter Turnout." *Comparative Political Studies* 43 (12): 1601–1622.

Bishop, Bill. 2008. *The Big Sort: Why the Clustering of America Is Tearing Us Apart*. New York: First Mariner Books.

Black, Jerome H. 2003. "From Enumeration to the National Register of Electors: An Account and Evaluations." *Institute for Research on Public Policy*, August 21. http://irpp.org/research-studies/choices-vol9-no7/.

Blake, Aaron. 2017. "Donald Trump Claims None of Those 3 to 5 Million Illegal Votes Were Cast for Him. Zero." *Washington Post*, January 26. https://www.washingtonpost.com/news/the-fix/wp/2017/01/25/donald-trump-claims-none-of-those-3-to-5-million-illegal-votes-were-cast-for-him-zero/.

Boatright, Robert G., ed. 2015. *The Deregulatory Moment? A Comparative Perspective on Changing Campaign Finance Laws*. Ann Arbor: University of Michigan Press.

Boczkowski, Pablo J., ed. 2018. *Trump and the Media*. Cambridge, MA: MIT Press.

Bode, Leticia. 2016a. "Political News in the News Feed: Learning Politics from Social Media." *Mass Communication and Society* 19: 24–28. doi:10.1080/15205436.2015.1045149.

Bode, Leticia. 2016b. "Who Sees What? Individual Exposure to Political Information via Social Media." In *Social Media and Politics: A New Way to Participate in the Political Process*, edited by G. W. Richardson, 189–204. Santa Barbara, CA: Praeger.

Bode, Leticia, and Emily K. Vraga. 2015. "In Related News, That Was Wrong: The Correction of Misinformation through Related Stories Functionality in Social Media." *Journal of Communication* 65: 619–638.

Borah, Porismita, Kjerstin Thorson, and Hyunseo Hwang. 2015. "Causes and Consequences of Selective Exposure among Political Blog Readers: The Role of Hostile Media Perception in Motivated Media Use and Expressive Participation." *Journal of Information Technology and Politics* 12 (2): 186–199.

Bowler, Shaun, and Todd Donovan. 2011. "The Limited Effects of Election Reforms on Efficacy and Engagement." *Australian Journal of Political Science* 47 (1): 55–57.

Boye, Joyce Irene. 2012. "Food Allergies in Developing and Emerging Economies: Need for Comprehensive Data on Prevalence Rates." *Clinical and Translational Allergy* 2 (December): 25. https://doi.org/10.1186/2045-7022-2-25.

Brady, Henry E., and John E. McNulty. 2011. "Turning Out to Vote: The Costs of Finding and Getting to the Polling Place." *American Political Science Review* 105 (1): 115–134.

Brazile, Donna. 2017. *Hacks: The Inside Story of the Break-ins and Breakdowns That Put Donald Trump in the White House*. New York: Hachette Books.

Brennan Center for Justice. 2015. "Voting Laws Roundup 2015." Last modified June 3. https://www.brennancenter.org/analysis/voting-laws-roundup-2015.

Brennan Center for Justice. 2016a. *The Case for Automatic Voter Registration*. https://www.brennancenter.org/sites/default/files/publications/Case_for_Automatic_Voter_Registration.pdf.

Brennan Center for Justice. 2016b. "Voting Problems Present in 2016, but Further Study Needed to Determine Impact." November 14. https://www.brennancenter.org/analysis/voting-problems-present-2016-further-study-needed-determine-impact.

Brennan Center for Justice. 2017a. "Automatic Voter Registration." April 17. https://www.brennancenter.org/analysis/automatic-voter-registration.

Brennan Center for Justice. 2017b. "In Their Own Words: Officials Refuting False Claims of Voter Fraud." April 13. https://www.brennancenter.org/quotes-on-voter-fraud.

Brennan Center for Justice. 2017c. "New Voting Restrictions in America." https://www.brennancenter.org/sites/default/files/analysis/New_Voting_Restrictions.pdf.

Brennan Center for Justice. 2017d. "Resources on Voter Fraud Claims." June 26. https://www.brennancenter.org/analysis/resources-voter-fraud-claims.

Brennan Center for Justice. 2017e. "Voting System Security and Reliability Risks." https://www.brennancenter.org/sites/default/files/analysis/Fact_Sheet_Voting_System_Security.pdf.

Brennan Center for Justice. N.d. "New Voting Restrictions in America." https://www.brennancenter.org/new-voting-restrictions-america.

Bump, Phillip. 2016. "Donald Trump Will Be President Thanks to 80,000 People in Three States." *Washington Post*, December 1. https://www.washingtonpost.com/news/the-fix/wp/2016/12/01/donald-trump-will-be-president-thanks-to-80000-people-in-three-states/?utm_term=.f3116f989468.

Burden, Barry C., David T. Canon, Kenneth R. Mayer, and Donald P. Moynihan. 2014. "Election Laws, Mobilization, and Turnout: The Unanticipated Consequences of Election Reform." *American Journal of Political Science* 58 (1): 95–109.

Burden, Barry C., David T. Canon, Kenneth R. Mayer, and Donald P. Moynihan. 2017. "The Complicated Partisan Effects of State Election Laws." *Political Research Quarterly* 70 (3): 564–576.

Burden, Barry C., and Brian J. Gaines. 2013. "Administration of Absentee Ballot Programs." Report prepared for the Presidential Commission on Election Administration, July 15, 2013. http://electionadmin.wisc.edu/bg_absentee_report.pdf.

Burden, Barry C., and Charles StewartIII, eds. 2014. *The Measure of American Elections.* New York: Cambridge University Press.

Burnett, Kristin D. 2011. "Congressional Apportionment: 2010 Census Briefs." U.S. Census Bureau. November. https://www.census.gov/prod/cen2010/briefs/c2010br-08.pdf.

Bush v. Gore, 531 U.S. 98 (2000) (per curiam).

Bush, Sarah, and Lauren Prather. 2017. "The Promise and Limits of Election Observers in Building Election Credibility." *Journal of Politics* 79 (3): 921–935.

Bycoffe, Aaron. 2018. "Pennsylvania's New Map Helps Democrats. But It's Not a Democratic Gerrymander." *FiveThirtyEight,* February 20. https://fivethirtyeight.com/features/pennsylvanias-new-map-helps-democrats-but-its-not-a-democratic-gerrymander/.

Cain, Bruce E., Todd Donovan, and Caroline J. Tolbert. 2008. *Democracy in the States: Experimentation in Election Reform.* Washington, D.C.: Brookings Institution Press.

Calabresi, Massimo. 2017a. "Election Hackers Altered Voter Rolls, Stole Private Data, Officials Say." *Time,* June 22. http://time.com/4828306/russian-hacking-election-widespread-private-data/.

Calabresi, Massimo. 2017b. "Inside Russia's Social Media War on America." *Time,* May 18. http://time.com/4783932/inside-russia-social-media-war-america/.

California Elections Code § 14221, 15004, 2100.

Calingaert, Daniel. 2006. "Election Rigging and How to Fight It." *Journal of Democracy* 17 (3): 138–151.

Callahan, David. 2002. "Expanding the Vote: The Practice and Promise of Election Day Registration." *Demos,* January 1. http://www.demos.org/publication/expanding-vote-practice-and-promise-election-day-registration.

Campbell, Tracy. 2006. *Deliver the Vote: A History of Election Fraud, an American Tradition 1742–2004.* New York: Carroll and Graf.

Carbó, Steven, and Brenda Wright. 2008. "Promise and Practice of Election Day Registration." In *America Votes! A Guide to Modern Election Law and Voting Rights,* edited by Benjamin E. Griffith, 65–90. Chicago, IL: American Bar Association Section of State and Local Government Law.

Carothers, Thomas. 2016. "Look Homeward, Democracy Promoter." *Foreign Policy,* January 27. http://foreignpolicy.com/2016/01/27/look-homeward-democracy-promoter/.

Carroll, David J., and Avery Davis-Roberts. 2013. "The Carter Center and Election Observation: An Obligations-Based Approach for Assessing Elections." *Election Law Journal: Rules, Politics, and Policy* 12 (1): 87–93.

Carroll, Lauren. 2016. "Russia and Its Influence on the Presidential Election." *Politifact,* December 1. http://www.politifact.com/truth-o-meter/article/2016/dec/01/russia-and-its-influence-presidential-election/.

The Carter Center. 2014. *Election Obligations and Standards.* Atlanta, GA: Carter Center.

The Carter Center and National Conference of State Legislatures. 2016. "Policies for Election Observers." October 12. http://www.ncsl.org/research/elections-and-campaigns/policies-for-election-observers.aspx.

Carter, Jimmy, and James A. Baker III. 2005. *Building Confidence in U.S. Elections: Report of the Commission on Federal Election Reform.* September. https://www.eac.gov/assets/1/6/Exhibit%20M.PDF.

Catt, Helena, Andrew Ellis, Michael Maley, Alan Wall, and Peter Wolf. 2014. *Electoral Management Design: Revised Edition.* Stockholm: International Institute for Democracy and Electoral Assistance.

CBC News. 2016. "2015 Federal Election Cost Taxpayers $443M, up 59% from 2011 Election." February 6. http://www.cbc.ca.

Cecil, Guy. 2017. "Priorities USA Voter Suppression Memo." Priorities USA. May 3. https://www.scribd.com/document/347821649/Priorities-USA-Voter-Suppression-Memo.

Century Foundation. 2005. *Balancing Access and Integrity: The Report of the Century Foundation Working Group on State Implementation of Election Reform.* https://tcf.org/content/book/balancing-access-and-integrity/.

Cervantes, Bobby. 2012. "Iowa to Poll-Watchers: Back Off." *Politico,* October 31. http://www.politico.com/story/2012/10/iowa-warns-intl-observers-of-arrest-083108.

Chang, Alvin. 2018. "Fox News's Appalling Past 72 Hours, Analyzed." *Vox,* February 19. https://www.vox.com/2018/2/19/17027456/fox-news-mueller-indictment-trump.

Chen, Jowei, and Jonathan Rodden. 2013. "Unintentional Gerrymandering: Political Geography and Electoral Bias in Legislatures." *Quarterly Journal of Political Science* 8: 239–269.

Chenoweth, Erica, and Jeremy Pressman. 2017. "One Year after the Women's March on Washington, People Are Still Protesting en Masse. A Lot. We've Counted." *Washington Post,* January 21.

Cheung, Gordon W., and Roger B. Rensvold. 2000. "Assessing Extreme and Acquiescence Response Sets in Cross-Cultural Research Using Structural Equations Modeling." *Journal of Cross-Cultural Psychology* 31 (2): 187–212. https://doi.org/10.1177/0022022100031002003.

Cheung, Gordon W., and Roger B. Rensvold. 2002. "Evaluating Goodness-of-Fit Indexes for Testing Measurement Invariance." *Structural Equation Modeling: A Multidisciplinary Journal* 9 (2): 233–255. https://doi.org/10.1207/S15328007SEM0902_5.

Cho, Wendy Tam, and Yan Y. Liu. 2016. "Toward a Talismanic Redistricting Tool: A Fully Balanced Computational Method for Identifying Extreme Redistricting Plans." *Election Law Journal* 15: 351–566.

Cillizza, Chris. 2016. "Hillary Clinton's Campaign Wants to Make One Thing Very Clear: They Don't Want a Recount." *Washington Post,* November 29. https://www.washingtonpost.com/news/the-fix/wp/2016/11/29/hillary-clintons-campaign-didnt-want-this-recount-and-doesnt-think-it-will-change-anything/?utm_term=.5dd4459a604d.

Cillizza, Chris. 2017. "Donald Trump Laughed When Rodrigo Duterte Called the Media 'Spies.' Not Good." *CNN,* November 13. https://www.cnn.com/2017/11/13/politics/trump-duterte-press/index.html.

Citrin, Jack, Donald P. Green, and Morris Levy. 2014. "The Effects of Voter ID Notification on Voter Turnout: Results from a Large-Scale Field Experiment." *Election Law Journal* 13 (2): 228–242.

City of Mobile v. Bolden, 446 U.S. 55 (1980).

CNN. 2016. "Thousands Take to the Streets to Protest Trump Win." November 10. https://edition.cnn.com/2016/11/09/politics/election-results-reaction-streets/index.html.

Cohen, Marshall. 2017. "By the Numbers: The Trump Orbit's Contact with Russians." *CNN,* November 22. http://www.cnn.com/2017/11/21/politics/trump-russia-by-the-numbers/index.html.

Colleoni, Elanor, Alessandro Rozza, and Adam Arvidsson. 2014. "Echo Chamber or Public Sphere? Predicting Political Orientation and Measuring Political Homophily in Twitter Using Big Data." *Journal of Communication* 64 (2): 317–332.

Collier, Paul, and Pedro Vicente. 2011. "Violence, Bribery and Fraud: The Political Economy of Elections in Sub-Saharan Africa." *Public Choice* 153 (1): 1–31.

Conover, Pamela Johnston, and Stanley Feldman. 1981. "The Origins and Meaning of Liberal/Conservative Self-Identifications." *American Journal of Political Science* 25 (4): 617–645.

Cooley, Alexander, and Jack Snyder, eds. 2015. *Ranking the World: Grading States as a Tool of Global Governance.* Cambridge, U.K.: Cambridge University Press.

Coppedge, Michael, John Gerring, Carl Henrik Knutsen, Staffan I. Lindberg, Svend-Erik Skaaning, Jan Teorell, David Altman, Michael Bernhard, Agnes Cornell, M. Steven Fish, Haakon Gjerløw, Adam Glynn, Allen Hicken, Joshua Krusell, Anna Lührmann, Kyle L. Marquardt, Kelly McMann, Valeriya Mechkova, Moa Olin, Pamela Paxton, Daniel Pemstein, Brigitte Seim, Rachel Sigman, Jeffrey Staton, Aksel Sundtröm, Eitan Tzelgov, Luca Uberti, Yi-ting Wang, Tore Wig, and Daniel Ziblatt. 2018. *V-Dem Codebook v8.* Gothenburg: Varieties of Democracy (V-Dem) Project.

Cottrell, David, Michael C. Herron, and Sean J. Westwood. 2018. "An Exploration of Donald Trump's Allegations of Massive Voter Fraud in the 2016 General Election." *Electoral Studies* 51: 123–142.

Courtney, John C. 2007. "Canada's Chief Election Officer: Responsibilities and Independence." *Canadian Parliamentary Review* 30 (1): 32–35.

Cox, Karen. 2005. "Japan: Adapting to a New Electoral System." In *Electoral System Design: The New International IDEA Handbook,* edited by Andrew Reynolds, Ben Reilly, and Andrew Ellis, 114–116. Stockholm: International Institute for Democracy and Electoral Assistance.

Craft, Stephanie, Seth Ashley, and Adam Maksl. 2017. "News Media Literacy and Conspiracy Theory Endorsement." *Communication and the Public* 2 (4): 388–401.

CSCE/OSCE. 1990. *Document of the Copenhagen Meeting of the Conference on the Human Dimension of the CSCE.* June 5–29. http://www.osce.org/odihr/elections/14304?download=true.

Dahl, Robert Alan. 1989. *Democracy and Its Critics.* New Haven, CT: Yale University Press.

Darrow, Barb. 2017. "How Hackers Broke Into U.S. Voting Machines in Less than 2 Hours." *Fortune,* July 31. http://fortune.com/2017/07/31/defcon-hackers-us-voting-machines/.

Daschle, Tom, Dirk Kempthorne, Olympia Snowe, Dan Glickman, and Trent Lott. 2014. "Governing in a Polarized America: A Bipartisan Blueprint to Strengthen Our Democracy." Bipartisan Policy Center Commission on Political Reform report. http://bipartisanpolicy. org/wp-content/uploads/sites/default/files/files/BPC%20CPR%20Governing%20in%20 a%20Polarized%20America.pdf.

Davis v. Bandemer, 478 U.S. 109 (1986).

Davis, Julie Hirschfeld. 2017. "Trump Picks Voter ID Advocate for Election Fraud Panel." *New York Times,* May 11. https://nyti.ms/2pBuE3g.

Davis, Noah. 2013. "The Rise of Food Allergies and First World Problems." *Pacific Standard,* October 1. https://psmag.com/social-justice/rise-food-allergies-first-world-problems-67067.

Daxecker, Ursula E. 2012. "The Cost of Exposing Cheating: International Election Monitoring, Fraud, and Post-Election Violence in Africa." *Journal of Peace Research* 49 (4): 503–516.

de Alth, Shelley. 2009. "ID at the Polls: Assessing the Impact of Recent State Voter ID Laws on Voter Turnout." *Harvard Law & Policy Review* 3 (1):185–202.

De Meo, Pasquale, Emilio Ferrara, Giacomo Fiumara, and Alessandro Provetti. 2014. "On Facebook, Most Ties Are Weak." *Communications of the ACM* 57 (11): 78–84.

Dews, Fred. 2017. "A Primer on Gerrymandering and Political Polarization." *Brookings Now,* July 6. https://www.brookings.edu/blog/brookings-now/2017/07/06/a-primer-on-gerrymandering-and-political-polarization/.

Doherty, Carroll. 2018. *Key Findings on Americans' Views of the U.A. Political System and Democracy.* Washington, D.C.: Pew Research Center.

Douglas, Scott. 2017. "Opinion: The Alabama Senate Race May Have Already Been Decided." *New York Times,* December 11. https://www.nytimes.com/2017/12/11/opinion/roy-moore-alabama-senate-voter-suppression.html.

Dowding, Keith, Peter John, Thanks Mergoupis, and Mark van Vugt. 2000. "Exit, Voice, and Loyalty: Analytical and Empirical Developments." *European Journal of Political Research* 37: 469–495.

Drew, Timeka. 2016. "Voting Rights Organizing Guide." Democracy Square. December 7. https://democracyconvention.org/news/voting-rights-organizing-guide.

Dutton, William H., Bianca Christin Reisdorf, Elizabeth Dubois, and Grant Blank. 2017. "Social Shaping of the Politics of Internet Search and Networking: Moving beyond Filter Bubbles, Echo Chambers, and Fake News." Quello Center Working Paper No. 2944191. https://ssrn.com/abstract=2944191.

The Economist. 2002. "In Praise of Iowa." October 17. https://www.economist.com/node/1394735.

Economist Intelligence Unit. 2018. "Democracy Index 2017: Free Speech under Attack." http://pages.eiu.com/rs/753-RIQ-438/images/Democracy_Index_2017.pdf.

Edelson, Jack, Alexander Alduncin, Christopher Krewson, James A. Sieja, and Joseph E. Uscinski. 2017. "The Effect of Conspiratorial Thinking and Motivated Reasoning on Belief in Election Fraud." *Political Research Quarterly* 70 (4): 933–946.

Edgerly, Stephanie. 2017. "Seeking Out and Avoiding the News Media: Young Adults' Proposed Strategies for Obtaining Current Events Information." *Mass Communication and Society* 20 (3): 358–377.

Edwards, Haley Sweetland, and Chris Wilson. 2016. "It's Almost Impossible for the Russians to Hack the U.S. Election. Here's Why." *Time*, September 21. http://time.com/4500216/election-voting-machines-hackers-security/.

Edwards, Kari, and Edward E. Smith. 1996. "A Disconfirmation Bias in the Evaluation of Arguments." *Journal of Personality and Social Psychology* 71 (1): 5.

Elazar, Daniel. 1987. *Exploring Federalism.* Tuscaloosa: University of Alabama Press.

Elections Canada. 2004. "Completing the Cycle of Electoral Reforms—Recommendations from the Chief Electoral Officer of Canada on the 38th General Election." http://www.elections.ca/content.aspx?section=res&dir=rep/off/r38&document=part21&lang=e.

Electoral Integrity Project. 2017. "Projects." https://www.electoralintegrityproject.com/research-themes/.

Electoral Reform Society. 2018. "Thousands of Voters Turned Away from Polling Stations in Mandatory ID Trials." May 4. https://www.electoral-reform.org.uk/latest-news-and-research/media-centre/press-releases/thousands-of-voters-turned-away-from-polling-stations-in-mandatory-id-trials/.

Elklit, Jorgen, and Palle Svensson. 1997. "What Makes Elections Free and Fair?" *Journal of Democracy* 8 (3): 32–46.

Elmendorf, Christopher S. 2006. "Election Commissions and Electoral Reform: An Overview." *Election Law Journal* 5 (4): 425–446.

Ely, John Hart. 1978. "The Centrality and Limits of Motivation Analysis." *San Diego Law Review* 15: 1155–1161.

Enten, Harry. 2017. "Trump Hasn't Diminished America's Faith in Elections, but He Has Polarized It." *FiveThirtyEight*, May 11. https://fivethirtyeight.com/features/trump-hasnt-diminished-americas-faith-in-elections-but-he-has-polarized-it/.

Erisen, Cengiz, Dave Redlawsk, and Elif Erisen. 2017. "Complex Thinking as a Result of Incongruent Information Exposure." *American Politics Research* 46 (2): 217–245.

European Commission. 2018. "Final Report of the High Level Expert Group on Fake News and Online Disinformation." March 12. https://ec.europa.eu/digital-single-market/en/news/final-report-high-level-expert-group-fake-news-and-online-disinformation.

Ewald, Alec C. 2009. *The Way We Vote: The Local Dimension of American Suffrage.* Nashville, TN: Vanderbilt University Press.

Faris, Robert, Hal Roberts, Bruce Etling, Nikki Bourassa, Ethan Zuckerman, and Yochai Benkler. 2017. *Partisanship, Propaganda, and Disinformation: Online Media and the 2016 US Presidential Election.* Berkman Klein Center Research Publication. https://cyber.harvard.edu/publications/2017/08/mediacloud.

Feerick, John D. 1968. "The Electoral College: Why It Was Created." *American Bar Association Journal* 54 (March): 249–255.

Feldman, Lauren, Teresa A. Myers, Jay D. Hmielowski, and Anthony Leiserowitz. 2014. "The Mutual Reinforcement of Media Selectivity and Effects: Testing the Reinforcing Spirals Framework in the Context of Global Warming." *Journal of Communication* 64 (4): 590–611.

Fessler, Daniel M. T., Anne C. Pisor, and Colin Holbrook. 2017. "Political Orientation Predicts Credulity regarding Putative Hazards." *Psychological Science* 28 (5): 651–660.

Festinger, Leon. 1957. *A Theory of Cognitive Dissonance.* Evanston, IL: Row, Peterson.

Fetzer, Joel S. 2008. "Election Strategy and Ethnic Politics in Singapore." *Taiwan Journal of Democracy* 4 (1): 135–153.

Fidler, David P. 2017. "Transforming Election Cybersecurity." Digital and Cyberspace Policy Program, Council on Foreign Relations. May 17. https://www.cfr.org/report/transforming-election-cybersecurity.

Fife, Brian L. 2010. *Reforming the Electoral Process in America*. Santa Barbara, CA: Praeger.

Fleischer, David, and Leonardo Barreto. 2009. "El impacto de la justicia electoral sobre el sistema politico Brasileño." *América Latina Hoy* 51: 117–138.

Fletcher, Richard, Alessio Cornia, Lucas Graves, and Rasmus Kleis Nielsen. 2018. "Measuring the Reach of 'Fake News' and Online Disinformation in Europe." Reuters Institute, University of Oxford. February. https://reutersinstitute.politics.ox.ac.uk/sites/default/files/2018-02/Measuring%20the%20reach%20of%20fake%20news%20and%20online%20distribution%20in%20Europe%20CORRECT%20FLAG.pdf.

Flores, Thomas Edward, and Irfan Nooruddin. 2016. *Elections in Hard Times*. New York: Cambridge University Press.

Florida, Richard. 2016. "America's 'Big Sort' Is Only Getting Bigger." *CityLab*, October 25. https://www.citylab.com/equity/2016/10/the-big-sort-revisited/504830/.

Foley, Edward. B. 2016. *Ballot Battles: The History of Disputed Elections in the United States*. New York: Oxford University Press.

Fortin-Rittberger, Jessica, Philipp Harfst, and Sarah Dingler. 2017. "The Costs of Electoral Fraud: Establishing the Link between Electoral Integrity, Winning an Election, and Satisfaction with Democracy." *Journal of Elections, Public Opinion and Parties* 27 (3): 350–368.

FoxNewsInsider. 2016. "Oops! Stein Recount Turns Up More Votes than Voters in Detroit." December 14. http://insider.foxnews.com/2016/12/14/steins-recount-turns-more-votes-voters-detroit.

The Franchise Project. 2017. "Voting Access Scorecard." https://thefranchiseproject.com/.

Frank, Richard W., and Ferran Martinez i Coma. 2017. "How Election Dynamics Shape Perceptions of Electoral Integrity." *Electoral Studies* 48: 153–165.

Freedom House. 2017. *Freedom in the World, 2017*. https://freedomhouse.org/report/freedom-world/freedom-world-2017.

Freedom House. 2018. *Freedom in the World, 2018*. https://freedomhouse.org/report/freedom-world/freedom-world-2018.

Friess, Steve. 2009. "Acorn Charged in Voter Registration Fraud Case in Nevada." *New York Times*, May 5. https://www.nytimes.com/2009/05/05/us/05acorn.html.

Frizell, Sam. 2016. "What Leaked Emails Reveal about Hillary Clinton's Campaign." *Time*, October 7. http://time.com/4523749/hillary-clinton-wikileaks-leaked-emails-john-podesta/.

Fukumoto, Kentaro, and Yusaku Horiuchi. 2011. "Making Outsiders' Votes Count: Detecting Electoral Fraud through a Natural Experiment." *American Political Science Review* 105 (3): 586–603.

Fumarola, Andrea. 2016. "Fidesz and Electoral Reform: How to Safeguard Hungarian Democracy." *EUROPP* (blog). http://blogs.lse.ac.uk/europpblog/2016/03/21/fidesz-and-electoral-reform-how-to-safeguard-hungarian-democracy/.

Fung, Archon, Mary Graham, and David Weil, eds. 2008. *Full Disclosure: The Perils and Promise of Transparency*. New York: Cambridge University Press.

Gaffney v. Cummings, 412 U.S. 735 (1973).

Gallup World Poll. 2018. *Country Data Set*. Last modified February 23. http://www.gallup.com/services/177797/country-data-set-details.aspx?utm_source=link_newsv9&utm_campaign=item_230213&utm_medium=copy.

Galston, William A., and Thomas E. Mann. 2010. "The GOP's Grassroots Obstructionists." *Washington Post*, May 16. http://www.washingtonpost.com/wpdyn/content/article/2010/05/14/AR2010051404234.html.

Garcia-Albacete, Gema M. 2014. *Young People's Political Participation in Western Europe*. New York: Palgrave Macmillan.

Garrett, R. Kelly. 2009. "Politically Motivated Reinforcement Seeking: Reframing the Selective Exposure Debate." *Journal of Communication* 59 (4): 676–699.

Garrett, R. Kelly. 2011. "Troubling Consequences of Online Political Rumoring." *Human Communication Research* 37 (2): 255–274.

Garrett, R. Kelly. 2016. "Facebook's Problem Is More Complicated than Fake News." *The Conversation*, 16 November. http://theconversation.com/facebooks-problem-is-more-complicated-than-fake-news-68886.

Garrett, R. Kelly, Brian E. Weeks, and Rachel L. Neo. 2016. "Driving a Wedge between Evidence and Beliefs: How Online Ideological News Exposure Promotes Political Misperceptions." *Journal of Computer-Mediated Communication* 21 (5): 331–348.

Gaskins, Keesha, and Sundeep Iyer. 2012. *The Challenge of Obtaining Voter Identification.* Brennan Center for Justice. http://www.brennancenter.org/publication/challenge-obtaining-voter-identification.

Gaughan, Anthony J. 2017. "Illiberal Democracy: The Toxic Mix of Fake News, Hyperpolarization, and Partisan Election Administration." *Duke Journal of Constitutional Law and Public Policy* 12: 57–139.

Gendreau, Henri. 2017. "The Internet Made 'Fake News' a Thing—Then Made It Nothing." *Wired,* February 27. https://www.wired.com/2017/02/internet-made-fake-news-thing-made-nothing/.

Gerken, Heather K. 2009. *The Democracy Index: Why Our Election System Is Failing and How to Fix It.* Princeton, NJ: Princeton University Press.

Gerken, Heather K. 2013a. "Make It Easy: The Case for Automatic Registration." *Democracy: A Journal of Ideas* 28 (Spring). http://www.democracyjournal.org/28/make-it-easy-the-case-for-automatic-registration.php?page=2.

Gerken, Heather K. 2013b. "The Sweet Spot for Election Reform." Bipartisan Policy Center, October 15. https://bipartisanpolicy.org/blog/sweet-spot-election-reform/.

Gerken, Heather K. 2014. "65 Ways to Improve Our Democracy." *Election Law Blog,* June 24. http://electionlawblog.org/?p=62729.

Gerring, John, and Strom C. Thacker. 2008. *A Centripetal Theory of Democratic Governance.* New York: Cambridge University Press.

Gil de Zúñiga, Homero, Brian Weeks, and Alberto Ardèvol-Abreu. 2017. "Effects of the News-Finds-Me Perception in Communication: Social Media Use Implications for News Seeking and Learning about Politics." *Journal of Computer-Mediated Communication* 22 (3): 105–123.

Gillin, Joshua. 2017. "Fake News Website Starts as Joke, Gains 1 Million Views within 2 Weeks." *Punditfact,* March 9. http://www.politifact.com/punditfact/article/2017/mar/09/fake-news-website-starts-joke-gains-1-million-view/.

Gimpel, James G., and Iris Hui. 2015. "Seeking Politically Compatible Neighbors? The Role of Neighborhood Partisan Composition in Residential Sorting." *Political Geography* 48: 130–142.

Global Commission on Elections, Democracy and Security. 2012. *Deepening Democracy: A Strategy for Improving the Integrity of Elections Worldwide.* Stockholm: IDEA.

Goel, Sharad, Marc Meredith, Michael Morse, David Rothschild, and Houshmand Shirani-Mehr. 2017. "One Person, One Vote: Estimating the Prevalence of Double Voting in U.S. Presidential Elections." *OpenScholar@Harvard.* https://scholar.harvard.edu/files/morse/files/1p1v.pdf.

Gorman, Sean. 2016. "Trump's Pants on Fire for Claiming 'Serious Voter Fraud' Occurred in Virginia." *Politifact,* November 29. http://www.politifact.com/virginia/statements/2016/nov/29/donald-trump/trumps-pants-fire-serious-voter-fraud-claim-virgin/.

Graham, David A. 2016. "What's the Goal of Voter ID Laws?" *The Atlantic,* May 2. https://www.theatlantic.com/politics/archive/2016/05/jim-demint-voter-id-laws/480876/.

Greenbaum, Mark. 2011. "Democrats' Revenge in 2012: A Radical Illinois Gerrymander." *Christian Science Monitor,* June 8. https://www.csmonitor.com/Commentary/Opinion/2011/0608/Democrats-revenge-in-2012-a-radical-Illinois-gerrymander.

Grimmer, Justin, Eitan Hersh, Marc Meredith, Jonathan Mummolo, and Clayton Nall. 2017. "Comment on 'Voter Identification Laws and the Suppression of Minority Votes.'" Stanford University, August 7. https://stanford.edu/~jgrimmer/comment_final.pdf.

Grofman, Bernard. 2003. *Race and Redistricting in the 1990s.* New York: Algora.

Gronke, Paul. 2013. "Early Voting: The Quiet Revolution in American Elections." In *Law and Election Politics: The Rules of the Game,* edited by Matthew J. Streb, 134–148. New York: Routledge.

Gronke, Paul, Michael W. Sances, and Charles Stewart III. 2016. "Americans Have Become Much Less Confident That We Count Votes Fairly." *Washington Post,* August 10. https://www.washingtonpost.com/news/monkey-cage/wp/2016/08/10/are-u-s-voters-confident-in-their-electoral-system-yes-and-no/?utm_term=.583d4a4c6dc2.

Hajnal, Zoltan, Nazita Lajevardi, and Lindsay Nielson. 2017. "Voter Identification Laws and the Suppression of Minority Votes." *Journal of Politics* 79 (2): 363–379.

Hall, Thad E. 2013. "U.S. Voter Registration Reform." *Electoral Studies* 32 (4): 589–596.

Halper, Evan. 2017a. "Cyberthreats to U.S. Elections Are Prominent and Growing." *Government Technology,* August 2. http://www.govtech.com/security/Cyber-Threat-to-US-Elections-Are-Prominent-and-Growing.html.

Halper, Evan. 2017b. "U.S. Elections Are an Easier Target for Russian Hackers Than Once Thought." *Los Angeles Times,* July 28. http://www.latimes.com/politics/la-na-pol-elections-hacking-2017-story.html.

Halpern, Sue. 2017. "Our Hackable Democracy." *New York Review of Books,* August 10. http://www.nybooks.com/daily/2017/08/10/our-hackable-democracy/.

Handley, Lisa. 2007. "Challenging the Norms and Standards of Election Administration." International Foundation for Electoral Systems. January. http://pdf.usaid.gov/pdf_docs/pnadt409.pdf.

Hanmer, Michael J. 2009. *Discount Voting: Voter Registration Reforms and Their Effects.* New York: Cambridge University Press.

Hardy, Benjamin. 2016. "Thousands of Arkansas Voters Flagged for Removal." *Arkansas Times,* August 2. https://www.arktimes.com/arkansas/thousands-of-arkansas-voters-flagged-for-removal/Content?oid=4518444.

Hare, Christopher, and Keith T. Poole. 2014. "The Polarization of Contemporary American Politics." *Polity* 46 (3): 411–429.

Harris v. Arizona Independent Redistricting Commission, 578 U.S. ___ (2016).

Harris, Paul. 2000. "Electoral Integrity: New Zealand's Change to MMP." *ACE Electoral Knowledge Network.* http://aceproject.org/main/english/ei/eiy_nz01.htm.

Hart, P. Sol, and Erik C. Nisbet. 2012. "Boomerang Effects in Science Communication: How Motivated Reasoning and Identity Cues Amplify Opinion Polarization about Climate Mitigation Policies." *Communication Research* 39 (6): 701–723.

Hasen, Richard L. 2012. *The Voting Wars: From Florida 2000 to the Next Election Meltdown.* New Haven. CT: Yale University Press.

Hasen, Richard L. 2016a. "Softening Voter ID Laws through Litigation: Is It Enough?" *Wisconsin Law Review Forward* 1: 100–121.

Hasen, Richard L. 2016b. "Op. Ed.: What an Election Law Expert Worries about on Election Day." *Los Angeles Times,* November 7. http://www.latimes.com/opinion/op-ed/la-oe-hasen-election-day-worries-20161108-story.html.

Hasen, Richard L. 2017a. "New Paper Casts Doubt on Hajnal et al Finding Strict Voter ID Laws Suppress Democratic Votes." https://electionlawblog.org/?p=91581.

Hasen, Richard L. 2017b. "Report of Presidential Commission on Electoral Administration Appears Gone." *Election Law Blog,* January 27. http://electionlawblog.org/?p=90741.

Hasen, Richard L. 2018. "Cheap Speech and What It Has Done (to American Democracy)." *First Amendment Law Review.* 16: 200–231.

Haspel, Moshe, and H. Gibbs Knotts. 2005. "Location, Location, Location: Precinct Placement and the Costs of Voting." *Journal of Politics* 67 (2): 560–573.

Head, Megan L., Luke Holman, Rob Lanfear, Andrew T. Kahn, and Michael D. Jennions. 2015. "The Extent and Consequences of P-Hacking in Science." *PLOS Biology* 13 (3): e1002106. https://doi.org/10.1371/journal.pbio.1002106.

Heer, Jeet. 2017. "No, Liberals Are Not Falling for Conspiracy Theories Just Like Conservatives Do." *New Republic,* May 23. https://newrepublic.com/article/142828/no-liberals-not-falling-conspiracy-theories-just-like-conservatives.

Helle, Svein-Erik. 2016. "Defining the Playing Field: A Framework for Analyzing Fairness in Access to Resources, Media and the Law." *Zeitschrift fur Vergleichende Politikwissenschaft* 10: 47–78.

Hemmer, Nicole. 2017. "From 'Faith in Facts' to 'Fair and Balanced.'" In *Media Nation: The Political History of News in Modern America,* edited by Bruce J. Schulman and Julian E. Zelizer, 126–143. Philadelphia: University of Pennsylvania Press.

Herron, Michael C., and Daniel A. Smith. 2014. "Race, Party, and the Consequences of Restricting Early Voting in Florida in the 2012 General Election." *Political Research Quarterly* 67 (3): 646–665.

Hershey, Marjorie Randon. 2009. "What We Know about Voter-ID Laws, Registration, and Turnout." *PS-Political Science & Politics* 42 (1): 87–91.

Hicks, William D., Seth C. McKee, Mitchell D. Sellers, and Daniel A. Smith. 2015. "A Principle or a Strategy? Voter Identification Laws and Partisan Competition in the American States." *Political Research Quarterly* 68 (1): 18–33.

Hidalgo, F. Daniel. 2010. "Digital Democratization: Suffrage Expansion and the Decline of Political Machines in Brazil." Manuscript, Department of Political Science, University of California, Berkeley.

Highton, Benjamin. 2004. "Voter Registration and Turnout in the United States." *Perspectives on Politics* 2: 507–515.

Hindman, Douglas Blanks. 2009. "Mass Media Flow and Differential Distribution of Politically Disputed Beliefs: The Belief Gap Hypothesis." *Journalism and Mass Communication Quarterly* 86 (4): 790–808.

Hindman, Douglas Blanks. 2012. "Knowledge Gaps, Belief Gaps, and Public Opinion about Health Care Reform." *Journalism and Mass Communication Quarterly* 89 (4): 585–605.

Hinze, Scott R., Daniel G. Slaten, William S. Horton, Ryan Jenkins, and David N. Rapp. 2014. "Pilgrims Sailing the Titanic: Plausibility Effects on Memory for Misinformation." *Memory and Cognition* 42 (2): 305–324.

Hirschfeld, Gerrit, and Ruth von Brachel. 2014. "Multiple-Group Confirmatory Factor Analysis in R—A Tutorial in Measurement Invariance with Continuous and Ordinal Indicators." *Practical Assessment, Research & Evaluation* 19 (7): 1–12.

Hirschman, Albert O. 1970. *Exit, Voice and Loyalty: Responses to Decline in Firms, Organizations, and States*. Cambridge, MA: Harvard University Press.

Hirschman, Albert O. 1974. "Exit, Voice, and Loyalty: Further Reflections and a Survey of Recent Contributions." *Social Science Information* 13 (1): 7–26.

Holan, Angie. 2017. "2017 Lie of the Year: Russian Election Interference Is a 'Made-up Story.'" *Politifact*, December 12. http://www.politifact.com/truth-o-meter/article/2017/dec/12/2017-lie-year-russian-election-interference-made-s/.

Horwitz, Sari. 2016a. "Getting a Photo ID So You Can Vote Is Easy. Unless You're Poor, Black, Latino or Elderly." *Washington Post*, May 23. https://www.washingtonpost.com/politics/courts_law/getting-a-photo-id-so-you-can-vote-is-easy-unless-youre-poor-black-latino-or-elderly/2016/05/23/8d5474ec-20f0-11e6-8690-f14ca9de2972_story.html?utm_term=.44dfce653d57.

Horwitz, Sari. 2016b. "Trial to Start in Lawsuit over North Carolina's Voter-ID Law." *Washington Post*, January 24. https://www.washingtonpost.com/world/national-security/trial-to-start-over-north-carolinas-voter-id-law/2016/01/24/fac97d20-c1d1-11e5-9443-7074c3645405_story.html.

Howard, Philip N., and Robert Gorwa. 2017. "Opinion: Facebook Could Tell Us How Russia Interfered in Our Elections. Why Won't It?" *Washington Post*, May 20. https://www.washingtonpost.com/opinions/facebook-could-tell-us-how-russia-interfered-in-our-elections-why-wont-it/2017/05/19/c061a606-3b21-11e7-8854-21f359183e8c_story.html.

Huddy, Leonie, Lilliana Mason, and Lene Aaroe. 2015. "Expressive Partisanship: Campaign Involvement, Political Emotion, and Partisan Identity." *American Political Science Review* 109 (1): 1–17.

Huefner, Steven F., Nathan Cemenska, Daniel Tokaji, and Edward B. Foley. 2011. *From Registration to Recounts Revisited: Developments in the Election Ecosystems of Five Midwestern States*. A Project of Election Law @ Moritz at the Ohio State University Moritz College of Law. http://moritzlaw.osu.edu/electionlaw/projects/registration-to-recounts/2011edition.pdf.

Hyde, Susan. 2011. *The Pseudo-Democrat's Dilemma: Why Election Observation Became an International Norm.* Ithaca, NY: Cornell University Press.

Hyde, Susan D., and Nikolay Marinov. 2012. "Which Elections Can Be Lost?" *Political Analysis* 20 (2): 191–210.

Hyde, Susan, and Nikolay Marinov. 2014. "Information and Self-Enforcing Democracy: The Role of International Election Observation." *International Organization* 68 (2): 329–359.

ICCPR. 1966. "International Covenant on Civil and Political Rights." *United Nations Human Rights, Office of the High Commissioner.* http://www.ohchr.org/EN/ProfessionalInterest/Pages/CCPR.aspx.

Ingraham, Christopher. 2016. "The 'Smoking Gun' Proving North Carolina Republicans Tried to Disenfranchise Black Voters." *Washington Post,* July 29. https://www.washingtonpost.com/news/wonk/wp/2016/07/29/the-smoking-gun-proving-north-carolina-republicans-tried-to-disenfranchise-black-voters/?utm_term=.5fc7e7235ba9.

International Fact Checking Network. 2017. "Fact-Checking." https://www.poynter.org/channels/fact-checking.

International IDEA. 2010. *The Handbook of Electoral Justice.* Stockholm: International IDEA.

International IDEA. 2014. *International Obligations for Elections: Guidelines for Legal Frameworks.* Stockholm: International IDEA.

International IDEA. 2018. "Political Finance Database." https://www.idea.int/data-tools/data/political-finance-database.

Isikoff, Michael, and David Corn. 2018. *Russian Roulette: The Inside Story of Putin's War on America and the Election of Donald Trump.* New York: Twelve.

Iyengar, Shanto, and Sean J. Westwood. 2015. "Fear and Loathing across Party Lines: New Evidence on Group Polarization." *American Journal of Political Science* 59 (3): 690–707.

Jacobson, Louis. 2018. "Donald Trump Says There's 'Substantial Evidence of Voter Fraud.' There Isn't." Politifact, January 4. http://www.politifact.com/truth-o-meter/statements/2018/jan/04/donald-trump/donald-trump-says-theres-substantial-evidence-vote/.

Jerit, Jennifer, and Jason Barabas. 2012. "Partisan Perceptual Bias and the Information Environment." *Journal of Politics* 74 (3): 672–684.

Jerit, Jennifer, Jason Barabas, and Toby Bolsen. 2006. "Citizens, Knowledge, and the Information Environment." *American Journal of Political Science* 50 (2): 266–282.

Johnson, Timothy, Patrick Kulesa, Young Ik Cho, and Sharon Shavitt. 2005. "The Relation between Culture and Response Styles: Evidence from 19 Countries." *Journal of Cross-Cultural Psychology* 36 (2): 264–277. https://doi.org/10.1177/0022022104272905.

Jolley, Daniel, and Karen M. Douglas. 2014a. "The Effects of Anti-Vaccine Conspiracy Theories on Vaccination Intentions." *PloS One* 9 (2): e89177.

Jolley, Daniel, and Karen M. Douglas. 2014b. "The Social Consequences of Conspiracism: Exposure to Conspiracy Theories Decreases Intentions to Engage in Politics and to Reduce One's Carbon Footprint." *British Journal of Psychology* 105 (1): 35–56.

Jones, Jeffery M. 2016. "In U.S., 84% Accept Trump as Legitimate President." *Gallup,* November 11. http://www.gallup.com/poll/197441/accept-trump-legitimate-president.aspx.

Jost, John T. 2017. "Ideological Asymmetries and the Essence of Political Psychology." *Political Psychology* 38 (2): 167–208.

Justus, Marcelo, and Gustavo Oliveira Aggio. 2018. "Street Protests against Dilma Rousseff's Administration and Corruption in Brazil: The 'Higher Education Effect.'" *Economic Analysis of Law Review* 9 (1): 5–18.

Kahne, Joseph, and Benjamin Bowyer. 2017. "Educating for Democracy in a Partisan Age: Confronting the Challenges of Motivated Reasoning and Misinformation." *American Educational Research Journal* 54 (1): 3–34.

Kahne, Joseph, Erica Hodgin, and Elyse Eidman-Aadahl. 2016. "Redesigning Civic Education for the Digital Age: Participatory Politics and the Pursuit of Democratic Engagement." *Theory and Research in Social Education* 44 (1): 1–35.

Kang, Cecilia, and Adam Goldman. 2016. "In Washington Pizzeria Attack, Fake News Brought Real Guns." *New York Times*, December 6. https://nyti.ms/2h8nPmp.

Katz, Eric. 2017. "House Republicans Want to Eliminate Federal Election Assistance Agency." *Government Executive*, June 30. http://m.govexec.com/management/2017/06/house-republicans-want-eliminate-federal-election-assistance-agency/139123/.

Katz, Jonathan N., and Gary King. 1999. "A Statistical Model for Multiparty Electoral Data." *American Political Science Review* 93 (1): 15–32.

Kelley, Judith G. 2012. *Monitoring Democracy: When International Election Observation Works, and Why It Often Fails.* Princeton, NJ: Princeton University Press.

Kendall, Maurice G., and Alan Stuart. 1950. "The Law of the Cubic Proportion in Election Results." *British Journal of Sociology* 3: 183–196.

Kessler, Glenn. 2016. "Donald Trump's Bogus Claim That Millions of People Voted Illegally for Hillary Clinton." *Washington Post*, November 27. https://www.washingtonpost.com/news/fact-checker/wp/2016/11/27/trumps-bogus-claim-that-millions-of-people-voted-illegally-for-hillary-clinton/?utm_term=.325988fc19e9.

Keyssar, Alexander. 2009. *The Right to Vote: The Contested History of Democracy in the United States.* New York: Basic Books.

Kimball, David C., Martha Kropf, Donald Moynihan, Carol L. Silva, and Brady Baybeck. 2013. "The Policy Views of Partisan Election Officials." *UC Irvine Law Review* 3: 551–574.

King, Gary, Christopher J. L. Murray, Joshua A. Salomon, and Ajay Tandon. 2004. "Enhancing the Validity and Cross-Cultural Comparability of Measurement in Survey Research." *American Political Science Review* 98: 191–207.

Klass, Brian. 2017. *The Despot's Apprentice.* New York: Hot Books.

Knack, Stephen. 2001. "Election-Day Registration: The Second Wave." *American Politics Quarterly* 29 (1): 65–78.

Knight Foundation. 2018. "American Views: Trust, Media and Democracy." Knight-Gallup. January 16. https://knightfoundation.org/reports/american-views-trust-media-and-democracy.

Kousser, J. Morgan. 1974. *The Shaping of Southern Politics: Suffrage Restriction and the Establishment of the One-Party South, 1880–1910.* New Haven, CT: Yale University Press.

Kraft, Patrick W., Milton Lodge, and Charles S. Taber. 2015. "Why People 'Don't Trust the Evidence': Motivated Reasoning and Scientific Beliefs." *Annals of the American Academy of Political and Social Science* 658 (1): 121–133.

Kropf, Martha, and David C. Kimball. 2011. *Helping America Vote: The Limits of Election Reform.* New York: Routledge.

Kull, Steven, Clay Ramsay, and Evan Lewis. 2003. "Misperceptions, the Media, and the Iraq War." *Political Science Quarterly* 118 (4): 569–598.

Kunda, Ziva. 1990. "The Case for Motivated Reasoning." *Psychological Bulletin* 108 (3): 480–498.

Kurtzleben, Danielle. 2016. "How to Win the Presidency with 23% of the Popular Vote." *National Public Radio*, November 2. http://www.npr.org/2016/11/02/500112248/how-to-win-the-presidency-with-27-percent-of-the-popular-vote.

LADB—Latin American Digital Beat. 2014. "New Electoral Watchdog Agency Starts Work under Cloud of Suspicion." April 9. http://lab.unm.edu.

LADB—Latin American Digital Beat. 2015. "Murders, Intimidation Widespread in Mexico ahead of June 7 Elections." June 3. http://lab.unm.edu.

Lakeman, Enid. 1982. *Power to Elect: The Case for Proportional Representation.* London: Heinemann.

LaMarre, Heather L., Kristen D. Landreville, and Michael A. Beam. 2009. "The Irony of Satire: Political Ideology and the Motivation to See What You Want to See in *The Colbert Report*." *International Journal of Press/Politics* 14 (2): 212–231.

Lawyers' Committee for Civil Rights under Law. 2016. "Striving to Protect Our Vote in 2016." *Election Protection,* December 1. https://lawyerscommittee.org/wp-content/uploads/2017/02/Election-Protection-2016-PostElection-Report-Final.pdf.

Lehoucq, Fabrice Edouard. 2003. "Electoral Fraud: Causes, Types, and Consequences." *Annual Review of Political Science* 6: 233–256.

Lehoucq, Fabrice Edouard, and Iván Molina Jiménez. 2002. *Stuffing the Ballot Box: Fraud, Electoral Reform, and Democratization in Costa Rica.* New York: Cambridge University Press.

Lemon, Kristina. 2005. "The Swedish Election Authority—Independence vs. Government Control." Report presented at Venice Commission Unidem Seminar Organisation of Elections by an Impartial Body meeting in Belgrade, Serbia, June 24–25. http://www.venice.coe.int/webforms/documents/?pdf=CDL-UD(2005)007-e.

Lessig, Lawrence. 2015. *Republic, Lost: Version 2.0.* Revised edition. New York: Twelve.

Levendusky, Matthew S. 2013. "Why Do Partisan Media Polarize Viewers?" *American Journal of Political Science* 57 (3): 611–623.

Levine, Sam. 2017. "Some of Trump's New Election Investigators Don't Seem to Have Much Election Experience." *Huffington Post,* June 22. http://www.huffingtonpost.com/entry/trump-voter-fraud-commission_us_594c1068e4b01cdedf01e75e?3pa.

Levitsky, Steven, and Lucan Way. 2010. *Competitive Authoritarianism: Hybrid Regimes after the Cold War.* New York: Cambridge University Press.

Levitsky, Steven, and Daniel Ziblatt. 2018. *How Democracies Die.* New York: Crown.

Levitt, Justin. 2007. *The Truth about Voter Fraud.* New York: Brennan Center for Justice.

Levitt, Justin. 2010. "A Citizen's Guide to Redistricting." Brennan Center for Justice. https://www.brennancenter.org/sites/default/files/legacy/Democracy/CitizensGuidetoRedistricting_2010.pdf.

Levitt, Justin. 2012. "Election Deform: The Pursuit of Unwarranted Electoral Regulation." *Election Law Journal* 11 (1): 97–117.

Levitt, Justin. 2014. "A Comprehensive Investigation of Voter Impersonation Finds 31 Credible Incidents out of One Billion Ballots Cast." *Washington Post,* August 6. https://www.washingtonpost.com/news/wonk/wp/2014/08/06/a-comprehensive-investigation-of-voter-impersonation-finds-31-credible-incidents-out-of-one-billion-ballots-cast/?utm_term=.506c95b2e2eb.

Lewandowsky, Stephan, Ullrich K. H. Ecker, and John Cook. 2017. "Beyond Misinformation: Understanding and Coping with the 'Post-Truth' Era." *Journal of Applied Research in Memory and Cognition* 6 (4): 353–369.

Lewandowsky, Stephan, Ullrich K. H. Ecker, Colleen M. Seifert, Norbert Schwarz, and John Cook. 2012. "Misinformation and Its Correction: Continued Influence and Successful Debiasing." *Psychological Science in the Public Interest* 13 (3): 106–131.

Lewandowsky, Stephan, Gilles E. Gignac, and Klaus Oberauer. 2013. "The Role of Conspiracist Ideation and Worldviews in Predicting Rejection of Science." *PloS One* 8 (10): e75637.

Lewandowsky, Stephan, and Klaus Oberauer. 2016. "Motivated Rejection of Science." *Current Directions in Psychological Science* 25 (4): 217–222.

Lijphart, Arend. 1999. *Patterns of Democracy: Government Forms and Performance in Thirty-Six Countries.* New Haven, CT: Yale University Press.

Lindberg, Staffan I., Michael Coppedge, John Gerring, and Jan Teorell. 2014. "V-Dem: A New Way to Measure Democracy." *Journal of Democracy* 25 (3): 159–169. https://doi.org/10.1353/jod.2014.0040.

Lopez, German. 2017. "Voter Suppression in Alabama: What's True and What's Not." *Vox,* December 12. https://www.vox.com/policy-and-politics/2017/12/12/16767426/alabama-voter-suppression-senate-moore-jones.

López Levi, Liliana, and Ernesto Soto Reyes Garmendia. 2008. "Federalismo y redistritación electoral en México." *Política y Cultura* 29: 125–147.

Lynch, Michael S., and Chelsie L. M. Bright. 2017. "How Advertising Campaigns Can Help to Mitigate the Negative Effects of Voter ID Laws on Turnout." *USApp-American Politics and Policy Blog*, April 7. http://eprints.lse.ac.uk/75999/.

MacFarquar, Neil. 2018. "Inside the Russian Troll Factory: Zombies and a Breakneck Pace." *New York Times*. February 18. https://www.nytimes.com/2018/02/18/world/europe/russia-troll-factory.html

Madison, James. 1792. "Equality: James Madison, Parties." Founders' Constitution. http://press-pubs.uchicago.edu/founders/documents/v1ch15s50.html.

Magleby, Daniel B., and Daniel B. Mosesson. 2018. "A New Approach for Developing Neutral Redistricting Plans." *Political Analysis* 26: 147–167.

Marchetti, Vitor. 2012. "Electoral Governance in Brazil." *Brazil Political Science Review* 6 (1): 113–131.

Martin, David O. 2016. "Iowa's Redistricting Model Deserves Bipartisan Support." *Wisconsin State Journal*, May 7. https://host.madison.com/wsj/opinion/column/david-o-martin-iowa-s-redistricting-model-deserves-bipartisan-support/article_f68b31de-d792-5c1c-ac15-10741e9bab03.html.

Martin, Jonathan, and Alan Rappeport. 2016. "Debbie Wasserman Schultz to Resign D.N.C. Post." *New York Times*, July 24. https://www.nytimes.com/2016/07/25/us/politics/debbie-wasserman-schultz-dnc-wikileaks-emails.html.

Martinez i Coma, Ferran, and Ignacio Lago. 2017. "Gerrymandering in Comparative Perspective." *Party Politics* 24 (2): 99–104.

Martinez i Coma, Ferran, and Minh Trinh. 2017. "How Electoral Integrity Affects Voter Turnout in Democracies." *Australian Journal of Political Science* 52 (1): 53–74.

Martinez i Coma, Ferran, Alessandro Nai, and Pippa Norris. 2016. "Democratic Diffusion: How Regional Organizations Strengthen Electoral Integrity." Executive Report. University of Sydney, Harvard Kennedy School, and Electoral Integrity Project. http://www.oas.org/fpdb/press/FINAL-Democratic-Difusion-English-Exec.pdf.

Massicotte, Louis, André Blais, and Antoine Yoshinaka. 2004. *Establishing the Rules of the Game: Election Laws in Democracies.* Toronto: University of Toronto Press.

May, Kenneth O. 1952. "A Set of Independent Necessary and Sufficient Conditions for Simple Majority Decision." *Econometrica* 20 (4): 680–84. https://doi.org/10.2307/1907651.

Mayer, Kenneth R., and Michael G. DeCrescenzo. 2017. "Estimating the Effect of Voter ID on Nonvoters in Wisconsin in the 2016 Presidential Election." Elections Research Center. https://elections.wiscweb.wisc.edu/wp-content/uploads/sites/483/2018/02/Voter-ID-Study-FAQ.pdf.

McCarthy, Justin, and Jon Clifton. 2016. "Update: Americans' Confidence in Voting, Election." *Gallup*, November 1. http://www.gallup.com/poll/196976/update-americans-confidence-voting-election.aspx.

McCombs, Maxwell E., and Donald L. Shaw. 1972. "The Agenda-Setting Function of Mass Media." *Public Opinion Quarterly* 36 (2): 176–187.

McDonald, Michael D., and Robin E. Best. 2015. "Unfair Partisan Gerrymandering in Politics and Law: A Diagnostic Applied to Six Cases." *Election Law Journal* 14: 312–330.

McFadden, Cynthia. 2018. "Russians Penetrated U.S. Voter Systems, Top U.S. Official Says." *NBC News*, February 8. https://www.nbcnews.com/politics/elections/russians-penetrated-u-s-voter-systems-says-top-u-s-n845721.

McFaul, Michael. 2016. "Let's Get the Facts Right on Foreign Involvement in Our Elections." *Washington Post*, December 16. https://www.washingtonpost.com/news/global-opinions/wp/2016/12/10/lets-get-the-facts-right-on-foreign-involvement-in-our-elections/?utm_term=.a1ad3083409c.

McGann, Anthony. 2006. *The Logic of Democracy: Reconciling Equality, Deliberation, and Minority Protection.* Ann Arbor: University of Michigan Press.

McGann, Anthony J., Charles Anthony Smith, Michael Latner, and J. Alex Keena. 2015. "A Discernable and Manageable Standard for Partisan Gerrymandering." *Election Law Journal: Rules, Politics, and Policy* 14 (4): 295–311. https://doi.org/10.1089/elj.2015.0312.

McGann, Anthony J., Charles Anthony Smith, Michael Latner, and Alex Keena. 2016. *Gerrymandering in America*. New York: Cambridge University Press.

McGarry, John. 2005. "Asymmetrical Federalism and the Plurinational State." In *Third International Conference on Federalism*, edited by F. Geerkings, 302–324. Tielt, Belgium: Lannoo.

McGinnis, Briana L. 2018. "Beyond Disenfranchisement: Collateral Consequences and Equal Citizenship." *Politics: Groups and Identities* 6 (1): 59–76.

McGovern, Tony. 2016. "County Level Election Results." GitHub. https://github.com/tonmcg/County_Level_Election_Results_12-16.

McIntyre, Lee. 2018. *Post-Truth*. Cambridge, MA: MIT Press.

McKee, Seth C. 2015. "Politics Is Local: State Legislator Voting on Restrictive Voter Identification Legislation." *Research & Politics* 2 (3): 1–7. https://doi.org/10.1177/2053168015589804.

McNally, Dylan. 2014. "Mexico's National Electoral Institute: Ensuring Fair Elections at the Local Level." Rice University's Baker Institute for Public Policy. http://www.bakerinstitute.org/research/mexico-ensuring-fair-elections-local-level/.

Mebane, Walter R. 2017. *Election Forensics Toolkit and Guide*. IIE. https://www.iie.org:443/en/Research-and-Insights/Publications/DFG-UM-Publication.

Meirick, Patrick C. 2013. "Motivated Misperception? Party, Education, Partisan News, and Belief in 'Death Panels.'" *Journalism and Mass Communication Quarterly* 90 (1): 39–57.

Merry, Sally Engle, Kevin E. Davis, and Benedict Kingsbury, eds. 2015. *The Quiet Power of Indicators: Measuring Governance, Corruption, and Rule of Law*. New York: Cambridge University Press.

Michigan Department of State. 2017. "Executive summary of Audits Conducted in Detroit and Statewide in Relation to the November 8, 2016 General Election." February 9. http://www.michigan.gov/documents/sos/Combined_Detroit_Audit_Exec_summary_551188_7.pdf.

Milyo, Jeffrey D. and David M. Primo. 2017. "Public Attitudes and Campaign Finance." Report prepared for the Campaign Finance Task Force. https://bipartisanpolicy.org/wp-content/uploads/2018/01/Public-Attitudes-and-Campaign-Finance.-Jeffrey-D.-Milyo-David-M.-Primo.pdf.

Minnite, Lorraine C. 2007. "Election Day Registration: A Study of Voter Fraud Allegations and Findings on Voter Roll Security." Demos. http://www.demos.org/sites/default/files/publications/edr_fraud.pdf.

Minnite, Lorraine Carol. 2010. *The Myth of Voter Fraud*. Ithaca, NY: Cornell University Press.

Minnite, Lori, and David Callahan. 2003. "Securing the Vote: An Analysis of Election Fraud." Demos. http://www.demos.org/publication/securing-vote-analysis-election-fraud.

Mitchell, Amy, Jeffrey Gottfried, Michael Barthel, and Elisa Shearer. 2016. "The Modern News Consumer: News Attitudes and Practices in the Digital Era." *Pew Research*, July 7. http://www.journalism.org/2016/07/07/the-modern-news-consumer/.

Møller, Jørgen, and Svend-Erik Skaaning. 2010. "Beyond the Radial Delusion: Conceptualizing and Measuring Democracy and Non-democracy." *International Political Science Review* 31 (3): 261–283. https://doi.org/10.1177/0192512110369522.

Morreale, Sherwyn P., Scott A. Myers, Philip M. Backlund, and Cheri J. Simonds. 2016. "Study IX of the Basic Communication Course at Two- and Four-Year US Colleges and Universities: A Re-examination of Our Discipline's 'Front Porch.'" *Communication Education* 65 (3): 338–355.

Morris, Jonathan S. 2005. "The Fox News Factor." *Harvard International Journal of Press/Politics* 10 (3): 56–79.

Mounk, Yascha. 2018. *The People vs. Democracy: Why Our Freedom Is in Danger and How to Save It*. Cambridge, MA: Harvard University Press.

Munck, Gerardo L., and Jay Verkuilen. 2002. "Conceptualizing and Measuring Democracy: Evaluating Alternative Indices." *Comparative Political Studies* 35 (1): 5–34. https://doi.org/10.1177/001041400203500101.

National Democratic Redistricting Committee. 2017. Homepage. https://democraticredistricting.com/.

National Public Radio. 2018. "Kris Kobach on What Led to the Disbandment of Controversial Election Commission." *All Things Considered*, January 4. https://www.npr.org/2018/01/04/575774092/kris-kobach-on-what-led-to-the-disbandment-of-controversial-election-commission.

NCSL (National Conference of State Legislatures). 2012. "Voter List Maintenance: Why, How and When." *The Canvass*, 32 (July/August). http://www.ncsl.org/documents/legismgt/elect/Canvass_Jul-Aug_2012_No_32.pdf.

NCSL (National Conference of State Legislatures). 2013. "Election Day Registration: FAQs." *The Canvass*, 40 (May). http://www.ncsl.org/documents/legismgt/elect/Canvass_May_2013_No_40.pdf.

NCSL (National Conference of State Legislatures). 2017a. "2017 State and Legislative Partisan Composition." http://www.ncsl.org/portals/1/documents/elections/Legis_Control_2017_March_27_11am.pdf.

NCSL (National Conference of State Legislatures). 2017b. "Absentee and Early Voting." August 17. http://www.ncsl.org/research/elections-and-campaigns/absentee-and-early-voting.aspx.

NCSL (National Conference of State Legislatures). 2017c. "State Elections Legislation Database." http://www.ncsl.org/research/elections-and-campaigns/elections-legislation-database.aspx.

NCSL (National Conference of State Legislatures). 2017d. "Elections and Campaigns." http://www.ncsl.org/research/elections-and-campaigns.aspx.

NCSL (National Conference of State Legislatures). 2017e. "Online Voter Registration." http://www.ncsl.org/research/elections-and-campaigns/electronic-or-online-voter-registration.aspx.

NCSL (National Conference of State Legislatures). 2018a. "2017 Campaign Finance Enactments." January 3. http://www.ncsl.org/research/elections-and-campaigns/2017-campaign-finance-enactments.aspx.

NCSL (National Conference of State Legislatures). 2018b. "Voter Identification Requirements: Voter ID Laws." May 15. http://www.ncsl.org/research/elections-and-campaigns/voter-id.aspx.

New York Times. 2016. "Election 2016: Exit Polls." November 8. https://www.nytimes.com/interactive/2016/11/08/us/politics/election-exit-polls.html?mcubz=0.

New York Times. 2017a. "Maryland Results." Accessed May 8. https://www.nytimes.com/elections/results/maryland.

New York Times. 2017b. "North Carolina Results." Accessed May 8. https://www.nytimes.com/elections/results/north-carolina.

Newkirk, Vann R. 2017. "How Voter ID Laws Discriminate." *Atlantic*, February 18. https://www.theatlantic.com/politics/archive/2017/02/how-voter-id-laws-discriminate-study/517218/.

Nichols, Chris. 2017. "Mostly True: Undocumented Immigrants Less Likely to Commit Crimes than U.S. Citizens." *Politifact*, August 3. http://www.politifact.com/california/statements/2017/aug/03/antonio-villaraigosa/mostly-true-undocumented-immigrants-less-likely-co/.

Nisbet, Erik C., Kathryn E. Cooper, and R. Kelly Garrett. 2015. "The Partisan Brain: How Dissonant Science Messages Lead Conservatives and Liberals to (Dis)Trust Science." *Annals of the American Academy of Political and Social Science* 658 (1): 36–66.

Niven, David, S. Robert Lichter, and Daniel Amundson. 2003. "The Political Content of Late Night Comedy." *Harvard International Journal of Press/Politics* 8 (3): 118–133.

Norden, Lawrence, and Christopher Famighetti. 2015. "America's Voting Machines at Risk." Brennan Center for Justice, September 15. https://www.brennancenter.org/publication/americas-voting-machines-risk.

Norden, Lawrence, and Ian Vandewalker. 2017. "Securing Elections from Foreign Interference." Brennan Center for Justice. https://www.brennancenter.org/sites/default/files/publications/Foreign%20Interference_0629_1030_AM.pdf.

Norris, Pippa. 2004. "Will New Technology Boost Turnout?" In *Electronic Voting and Democracy: A Comparative Analysis*, edited by Norbert Kersting and Harald Baldersheim, 193–225. London: Palgrave.

Norris, Pippa. 2012. *Making Democratic Governance Work: How Regimes Shape Prosperity, Welfare, and Peace.* Cambridge, UK: Cambridge University Press.

Norris, Pippa. 2014. *Why Electoral Integrity Matters.* New York: Cambridge University Press.

Norris, Pippa. 2015. *Why Elections Fail.* New York: Cambridge University Press.

Norris, Pippa. 2017a. *Strengthening Electoral Integrity.* New York: Cambridge University Press.

Norris, Pippa. 2017b. *Why American Elections Are Flawed (and How to Fix Them).* Ithaca, NY: Cornell University Press.

Norris, Pippa, and Andrea Abel van Es, eds. 2016. *Checkbook Elections? Political Finance in Comparative Perspective.* New York: Oxford University Press.

Norris, Pippa, Richard Frank, and Ferran Martinez i Coma. 2014. *Advancing Electoral Integrity.* New York: Oxford University Press.

Norris, Pippa, Richard Frank, and Ferran Martinez i Coma. 2015. "Contentious Elections: From Votes to Violence." In *Contentious Elections: From Ballots to Barricades,* by Pippa Norris, Richard Frank, and Ferran Martinez i Coma. New York: Routledge.

Norris, Pippa, Holly Ann Garnett, and Max Grömping. 2017. "Perceptions of Electoral Integrity: The 2016 American Presidential Election." Electoral Integrity Project, the University of Sydney. https://www.electoralintegrityproject.com/pei-us-2016/.

Norris, Pippa, and Ronald Inglehart. 2018. *Cultural Backlash: Trump, Brexit and Authoritarian-Populism.* New York: Cambridge University Press.

Norris, Pippa, and Alessandro Nai. 2017. *Election Watchdogs.* New York: Oxford University Press.

Norris, Pippa, Alessandro Nai, and Max Grömping. 2016. "Perceptions of Electoral Integrity—US 2016." (PEI_US_1.0) Harvard Dataverse, V1, UNF:6:1cMrtJfvUs9uBoNewfUKqA==. https://doi.org/10.7910/DVN/YXUV3W.

Norris, Pippa, Ferran Martinez i Coma, and Max Grömping. 2015. "The Year in Elections, 2014." Electoral Integrity Project. https://www.electoralintegrityproject.com/policy-reports/.

Norris, Pippa, Thomas Wynter, and Sarah Cameron. 2018a. *Corruption and Coercion: The Year in Elections, 2017.* Sydney: Electoral Integrity Project, University of Sydney.

Norris, Pippa, Thomas Wynter, and Sarah Cameron. 2018b. "Perceptions of Electoral Integrity (PEI-6.0)." https://doi.org/10.7910/DVN/Q6UBTH.

Norris, Pippa, Thomas Wynter, and Max Grömping. 2017. "Perceptions of Electoral Integrity (PEI-5.5)." Harvard Dataverse, V2, UNF:6:orsycndtUZPrE58BWhCdtg==. https://doi.org/10.7910/DVN/EWYTZ7.

Norris, Pippa, Thomas Wynter, Max Grömping, and Sarah Cameron. 2017. "The Year in Elections, 2017 Mid-Year Update." Electoral Integrity Project. https://www.electoralintegrityproject.com/policy-reports/.

North Carolina State Conference of the NAACP v. McCrory, North Dakota Century Code §16.1-05-09.

Nyhan, Brendan. 2010. "Why the 'Death Panel' Myth Wouldn't Die: Misinformation in the Health Care Reform Debate." *The Forum* 8 (1): https://doi.org/10.2202/1540-8884.1354.

Nyhan, Brendan. 2017. "Why More Democrats Are Now Embracing Conspiracy Theories." *New York Times,* February 15. https://nyti.ms/2likcup.

Nyhan, Brendan, and Jason Reifler. 2010. "When Corrections Fail: The Persistence of Political Misperceptions." *Political Behavior* 32 (2): 303–330.

O'Connor, Gabe, and Avie Schneider. 2017. "How Russian Twitter Bots Pumped Out Fake News during the 2016 Election." *NPR,* April 3. http://www.npr.org/sections/alltechconsidered/2017/04/03/522503844/how-russian-twitter-bots-pumped-out-fake-news-during-the-2016-election.

Office of Director of National Intelligence. 2017. National Intelligence Council, ICA 2017-01D. "Background to 'Assessing Russian Activities and Intentions in Recent US Elections': The Analytic Process and Cyber Incident Attribution." January 6. https://www.dni.gov/files/documents/ICA_2017_01.pdf.

Olson, Randal S. 2014. "U.S. Racial Diversity by County." Randal S. Olson blog, April 29. http://www.randalolson.com/2014/04/29/u-s-racial-diversity-by-county/.

Oppenheimer, Bruce I. 2005. "Deep Red and Blue Congressional Districts." In *Congress Reconsidered*, 8th edition, edited by Lawrence C. Dodd and Bruce I. Oppenheimer, 135–157. Washington, D.C.: Congressional Quarterly Press.

OSCE (Organization for Security and Cooperation in Europe). 2005a. "Declaration of Principles for International Election Observation and Code of Conduct for International Election Observers." October 27. https://www.osce.org/odihr/16935.

OSCE (Organization for Security and Cooperation in Europe). 2005b. "Ukraine Presidential Election, 31 October, 21 November and 26 December 2004: Final Report." May 11. http://www.osce.org/odihr/elections/ukraine/14674.

OSCE (Organization for Security and Cooperation in Europe). 2014. "Hungary, Parliamentary Elections, 6 April 2014: Statement of Preliminary Findings and Conclusions." April 7. http://www.osce.org/odihr/elections/117205.

OSCE (Organization for Security and Cooperation in Europe). 2016. "General Elections, 8 November 2016." Election Observation Mission press conference, November 9. https://www.osce.org/odihr/elections/usa/246356.

Page, Scott E. 2008. *The Difference: How the Power of Diversity Creates Better Groups, Firms, Schools, and Societies.* Princeton, NJ: Princeton University Press.

Pallister, Kevin. 2017. *Election Administration and the Politics of Voter Access.* London: Routledge.

Parker, Ashley. 2016. "Donald Trump, Slipping in Polls, Warns of 'Stolen Election.'" *New York Times*, October 13. https://www.nytimes.com/2016/10/14/us/politics/trump-election-rigging.html.

Pasek, Josh, Gaurav Sood, and Jon A. Krosnick. 2015. "Misinformed about the Affordable Care Act? Leveraging Certainty to Assess the Prevalence of Misperceptions." *Journal of Communication* 65 (4): 660–673.

Patterson, Thomas. 2016. "News Coverage of the 2016 General Election: How the Press Failed the Voters." Shorenstein Center. December 7. https://shorensteincenter.org/news-coverage-2016-general-election/.

Pearson, Rick. 2011. "Federal Court Upholds Democrat's Map of Illinois Congressional Districts." *Chicago Tribune*, December 15. http://www.chicagotribune.com/news/local/politics/chi-federal-court-upholds-democrats-map-of-illinois-congressional-districts-20111215-story.html.

Penzenstadler, Nick, Brad Heath, and Jessica Guynn. 2018. "We Read Every One of the 3,517 Facebook Ads Bought by Russians. Here's What We Found." *USA Today*, May 11. https://www.usatoday.com/story/news/2018/05/11/what-we-found-facebook-ads-russians-accused-election-meddling/602319002/?utm_source=newsletter&utm_medium=email&utm_campaign=sendto_newslettertest&stream=top-stories.

Pérez, Germán, and Pablo González Ulloa. 2011. "De la descentralización al centralismo en los procesos electorales en México." *Asian Journal of Latin American Studies* 24 (2): 45–68.

Pérez, Myrna. 2017. "Election Integrity: A Pro-Voter Agenda." Brennan Center for Justice. https://www.brennancenter.org/sites/default/files/publications/Election_Integrity.pdf.

Perlroth, Nicole. 2017. "Hackers Are Targeting Nuclear Facilities, Homeland Security Dept. and F.B.I. Say." *New York Times*, July 6. https://nyti.ms/2tRVPN7.

Perlroth, Nicole, Michael Wines, and Matthew Rosenberg. 2017. "Russian Election Hacking Efforts, Wider Than Previously Known, Draw Little Scrutiny." *New York Times*, September 1. https://www.nytimes.com/2017/09/01/us/politics/russia-election-hacking.html.

Persily, Nathaniel. 2017. "Can Democracy Survive the Internet?" *Journal of Democracy* 28: 63–76.

Pew Center on the States. 2010. "Upgrading Democracy: Improving America's Elections by Modernizing States' Voter Registration Systems." November. http://www.pewtrusts.org/~/media/legacy/uploadedfiles/pcs_assets/2010/upgradingdemocracyreportpdf.pdf.

Pew Charitable Trusts. 2014. "Understanding Online Voter Registration." http://www.pewtrusts.org/~/media/legacy/uploadedfiles/pcs_assets/2013/UnderstandingOnlineVoterRegistrationpdf.pdf.

Pew Charitable Trusts. 2016. "Elections Performance Index." http://www.pewtrusts.org/en/multimedia/data-visualizations/2014/elections-performance-index.

Pew Charitable Trusts. 2017. "Request for Applications Signals Next Step in Voting Information Project Transition." Voting Information Project. June 14. http://www.votinginfoproject.org/news/request-applications-signals-next-step-voting-information-project-transition/.

Pew Research Center. 2012. *Inaccurate, Costly, and Inefficient: Evidence That America's Voter Registration System Needs an Upgrade*. Washington, D.C.: Pew Charitable Trusts.

Pew Research Center. 2016a. "Elections Performance Index." August 9. http://www.pewtrusts.org/en/multimedia/data-visualizations/2014/elections-performance-index#indicator; https://thefranchiseproject.com/voter-scorecards/.

Pew Research Center. 2016b. "Hispanic Population Growth and Dispersion across U.S. Counties, 1980–2014." http://www.pewhispanic.org/interactives/hispanic-population-by-county/.

Pew Research Center. 2018a. "The Public, the Political System and American Democracy." April 26. http://www.people-press.org/2018/04/26/the-public-the-political-system-and-american-democracy/.

Pew Research Center. 2018b. "Publics Globally Want Unbiased News Coverage, but Are Divided on Whether Their News Media Deliver." January 11. http://www.pewglobal.org/2018/01/11/publics-globally-want-unbiased-news-coverage-but-are-divided-on-whether-their-news-media-deliver/.

Pfattheicher, Stefan, and Simon Schindler. 2016. "Misperceiving Bullshit as Profound Is Associated with Favorable Views of Cruz, Rubio, Trump and Conservatism." *PloS One* 11 (4): e0153419.

Piven, Francis Fox. 1988. *Why Americans Don't Vote*. New York: Pantheon.

Power, Samantha. 2018. "Beyond Elections: Foreign Interference with American Democracy." In *Can It Happen Here? Authoritarianism in America*, edited by Cass R. Sunstein. New York: HarperCollins, 81–104.

Pramuk, Jacob. 2016. "On Election Day, Trump Still Says It's 'Largely a Rigged System.'" *CNBC*, November 8. https://www.cnbc.com/2016/11/08/on-election-day-trump-still-says-its-largely-a-rigged-system.html.

Prather, Lauren, and Erik S. Herron. 2007. "Enfranchising Displaced Voters: Lessons from Bosnia-Herzegovina." *Election Law Journal* 6 (4): 354–371.

Preliminary EOM Report. 2016. "OAS Observation Mission Highlights Institutional Strength of the U.S. System." OAS. http://www.oas.org/fpdb/press/eom-preliminary-report-usa-2016-final.pdf.

Prior, Markus. 2007. *Post-Broadcast Democracy: How Media Choice Increases Inequality in Political Involvement and Polarizes Elections*. New York: Cambridge University Press.

Project Vote. 2010. "Maintaining Current and Accurate Voter Lists." http://www.projectvote.org/wp-content/uploads/2010/02/List-Maintenance-Policy-Paper-March-2010.pdf.

Qvortrup, Matt. 2005. "Absentee Voting in a Comparative Perspective: A Preliminary Assessment of the Experiences with Postal Voting." Submission for the Joint Standing Committee on Electoral Matters, Australian Federal Parliament. http://www.academia.edu/2881324/Absentee_Voting_in_a_Comparative_Perspective_A_Preliminary_Assessment_of_the_Experiences_with_Postal_Voting.

Rankin, Jennifer. 2017. "EU Anti-Propaganda Unit Gets €1m a Year to Counter Russian Fake News." *The Guardian*, Nov 25. https://www.theguardian.com/world/2017/nov/25/eu-anti-propaganda-unit-gets-1m-a-year-to-counter-russian-fake-news.

Reporters without Borders. 2017. "2017 World Press Freedom Index: Tipping Point?" April 26. https://rsf.org/en/news/2017-world-press-freedom-index-tipping-point.

Reynolds v. Sims, 377 U.S. 533 (1964).

Reynolds, Andrew. 2016. "North Carolina Is No Longer Classified as a Democracy." News and Observer, December 22. http:/www.newsobserver.com.

Reynolds, Andrew, and Ben Reilly. 2002. Electoral System Design: The New International IDEA Handbook. Stockholm: International Institute for Democracy and Electoral Assistance.

Reynolds, Andrew, and Marco Steenbergen. 2006. "How the World Votes: The Political Consequences of Ballot Design, Innovation and Manipulation." Electoral Studies 25 (3): 570–598.

Richey, Mason. 2018. "Contemporary Russian Revisionism: Understanding the Kremlin's Hybrid Warfare and the Strategic and Tactical Deployment of Disinformation." Asia Europe Journal 16 (1): 101–113.

Richie, Robert, and Steven Hill. 1999. Reflecting All of Us: The Case for Proportional Representation. Boston: Beacon Press.

Riley, Michael, and Jordan Robertson. 2017. "Russian Cyber Hacks on U.S. Electoral System Far Wider than Previously Known." Bloomberg, June 13. https://www.bloomberg.com/news/articles/2017-06-13/russian-breach-of-39-states-threatens-future-u-s-elections.

Rocheleau, Matt. 2016. "Stein Raises $2.3 Million for Recount Requests in Three Key States." Boston Globe, November 23. https://www.bostonglobe.com/metro/2016/11/23/jill-stein-seeks-recount-wisconsin-michigan-and-pennsylvania/gmziuhamGOjDgYitbQpWSJ/story.html.

Romo v. Detzner, Final Judgement, CA-412 (2nd Jud. Cir. Fla.) (2014).

Roper. 2015. "How Groups Voted in 1988." Roper Center for Public Opinion Research, November 8. https://ropercenter.cornell.edu/polls/us-elections/how-groups-voted/how-groups-voted-1988/.

Rosenberg, Jennifer S., with Margaret Chen. 2009. "Expanding Democracy: Voter Registration around the World." Brennan Center for Justice. http://www.brennancenter.org/content/resource/expanding_democracy_voter_regi stration_around_the_world.

Rosenberg, Matthew, and Maggie Haberman. 2017. "Trump Advisor Had Twitter Contact with Figure Tied to Russians." New York Times, March 11. https://nyti.ms/2mdQtFx.

Rosenblatt, Joel. 2016. "Michigan Presidential Ballot Recount Ended by Court Ruling." Bloomberg, December 7. https://www.bloomberg.com/news/articles/2016-12-08/michigan-allowed-by-judge-to-end-recount-sought-by-greens-stein.

Rosenstone, Steven J., and Raymond E. Wolfinger. 1978. "The Effect of Registration Laws on Voter Turnout." American Political Science Review, 72: 27–45.

Rosenthal, Robert, and Ralph L. Rosnow. 1991. Essentials of Behavioral Research: Methods and Data Analysis. Boston: McGraw-Hill Humanities Social.

Roth, Kenneth. 2017. "The Dangerous Rise of Populism: Global Attacks on Human Rights Values." Human Rights Watch, November 6. https://www.hrw.org/world-report/2017/country-chapters/dangerous-rise-of-populism#537fde.

Royden, Laura, and Michael Li. 2017. "Extreme Maps." Brennan Center for Justice. May 9. https://www.brennancenter.org/publication/extreme-maps.

Royden, Laura, Michael Li, and Yurij Rudensky. 2018. "Extreme Gerrymandering and the 2018 Midterm." Brennan Center. March 23. https://www.brennancenter.org/publication/extreme-gerrymandering-2018-midterm.

Rusbult, C. E. 1988. "Impact of Exchange Variables on Exit, Voice, Loyalty, and Neglect: An Integrative Model of Responses to Declining Job Satisfaction." Academy of Management Journal 31 (3): 599–627.

Rusbult, C. E., and I. M. Zembrodt. 1983. "Responses to Dissatisfaction in Romantic Involvements: A Multidimensional Scaling Analyses." Journal of Experimental Social Psychology 19: 274–293.

Sainato, Michael. 2016. "DC Leaks Exposes Clinton Insider's Elitist and Embarrassing Emails." Observer, October 7. https://www.observer.com/2016/10/dc-leaks-exposes-clinton-insiders-elitist-and-embarrassing-emails.

Schaffer, Frederic Charles. 2002. "Might Cleaning Up Elections Keep People Away from the Polls? Historical and Comparative Perspectives." *International Political Science Review* 23 (1): 69–84.

Schaffer, Frederic Charles. 2008. *The Hidden Costs of Clean Election Reform.* Ithaca, NY: Cornell University Press.

Schaffer, Frederic Charles, and Tova Andrea Wang. 2009. "Is Everyone Else Doing It? Indiana's Voter Identification Law in International Perspective." *Harvard Law & Policy Review* 3 (2): 397–412.

Schedler, Andreas. 2002. "The Menu of Manipulation." *Journal of Democracy* 13 (2): 36–50.

Seib, Gerald F. 2017. "The Varied—and Global—Threats Confronting Democracy." *Wall Street Journal,* November 21. https://www.wsj.com/amp/articles/the-variedand-globalthreats-confronting-democracy-1511193763.

Senate Intelligence Committee. 2018. "Russian Targeting of Election Infrastructure during the 2016 Election: Summary of Initial Findings and Recommendations." May 8. https://www.burr.senate.gov/imo/media/doc/RussRptInstlmt1-%20ElecSec%20Findings,Recs2.pdf.

Serra, Gilles. 2012. "The Risk of Partyarchy and Democratic Backsliding: Mexico's 2007 Electoral Reform." *Taiwan Journal of Democracy* 8 (1): 93–118.

Serra, Gilles. 2016. "Vote Buying with Illegal Resources: Manifestations of a Weak Rule of Law in Mexico." *Journal of Politics in Latin America* 8 (1): 129–150.

Shane, Scott. 2017. "The Fake Americans Russia Created to Influence the Election." *New York Times,* September 7. https://nyti.ms/2xdVuXM.

Shane, Scott, and Vindu Goel. 2017. "Fake Russian Facebook Accounts Bought $100,000 in Political Ads." *New York Times,* September 6. https://nyti.ms/2xPJ0m9.

Shin, Jieun, Lian Jian, Kevin Driscoll, and François Bar. 2017. "Political Rumoring on Twitter during the 2012 US Presidential Election: Rumor Diffusion and Correction." *New Media and Society* 19 (8): 1214–1235.

Shin, Jieun, and Kjerstin Thorson. 2017. "Partisan Selective Sharing: The Biased Diffusion of Fact-Checking Messages on Social Media." *Journal of Communication* 67 (2): 233–255.

Shugart, Matthew S., and Rein Taagepera. 2017. *Votes from Seats: Logical Models of Electoral Systems.* Cambridge, U.K.: Cambridge University Press.

Silverman, Craig. 2016. "This Analysis Shows How Viral Fake Election News Stories Outperformed Real News on Facebook." *Buzzfeed,* November 17. https://www.buzzfeed.com/craigsilverman/viral-fake-election-news-outperformed-real-newsonfacebook?utm_term=.tyObMY7dkX#.xxXN5lO3rD.

Silverman, Craig, and Lawrence Alexander. 2016. "How Teens in the Balkans Are Duping Trump Supporters with Fake News." *Buzzfeed,* November 3. https://www.buzzfeed.com/craigsilverman/how-macedonia-became-a-global-hub-for-pro-trump-misinfo?utm_term=.vrAjGwJRZB#.raLAaGKvpP.

Simeon, Richard. 2006. "Making Federalism Work." In *Open Federalism: Interpretations, Significance,* edited by Keith Banting, 1–5. Kingston, Ontario: Institute of Intergovernmental Relations, Kingston University.

Slater, Michael D. 2007. "Reinforcing Spirals: The Mutual Influence of Media Selectivity and Media Effects and Their Impact on Individual Behavior and Social Identity." *Communication Theory* 17 (3): 281–303.

Smets, Kaat, and Carolien van Ham. 2013. "The Embarrassment of Riches? A Meta-analysis of Individual-Level Research on Voter Turnout." *Electoral Studies* 32 (2): 344–359.

Smidt, Corwin D. 2017. "Polarization and the Decline of the American Floating Voter." *American Journal of Political Science* 61 (2): 365–381.

Smith, Amy Erica. 2016. "Do Americans Still Believe in Democracy?" *Washington Post,* April 20. https://www.washingtonpost.com/news/monkey-cage/wp/2016/04/09/do-americans-still-believe-in-democracy/?utm_term=.d4fe338b59de.

Solon, Olivia. 2016. "Facebook's Failure: Did Fake News and Polarized Politics Get Trump Elected?" *The Guardian,* November 10. https://www.theguardian.com/technology/2016/nov/10/facebook-fake-news-election-conspiracy-theories.

SPLC. 2017. "Southern Poverty Law Center: Post-Election Bias Incidents Up to 1,372: New Collaboration with ProPublica." *Southern Poverty Law Center.* https://www.splcenter.org/hatewatch/2017/02/10/post-election-bias-incidents-1372-new-collaboration-propublica.

Starbird, Kate, Emma Spiro, Ahmer Arif, Fang-Ju Chou, Sindhuja Narisimhan, Jim Maddock, Kelley Shanahan, and John Robinson. 2015. "Expressed Uncertainty and Denials as Signals of Online Rumoring." Presented at *Collective Intelligence 2015,* San Francisco, CA. http://faculty.washington.edu/kstarbi/ExpressedUncertainty-Final.pdf.

Stark, Stephen, Oleksandr S. Chernyshenko, and Fritz Drasgow. 2006. "Detecting Differential Item Functioning with Confirmatory Factor Analysis and Item Response Theory: Toward a Unified Strategy." *Journal of Applied Psychology* 91 (6): 1292–1306. https://doi.org/10.1037/0021-9010.91.6.1292.

Stedman, Stephen John. 2015. "Electoral Integrity." *The American Interest* (blog). October 10. https://www.the-american-interest.com/2015/10/10/electoral-integrity/.

Stepan, Alfred. 1999. "Federalism and Democracy: Beyond the U.S. Model." *Journal of Democracy* 10 (4): 19–34.

Stephanopoulos, Nicholas. 2013a. "The Consequences of Consequentialist Criteria." *UC Irvine Law Review* 3: 669.

Stephanopoulos, Nicholas. 2013b. "Our Electoral Exceptionalism." *University of Chicago Law Review* 80: 769.

Stephanopoulos, Nicholas, and Eric McGhee. 2015. "Partisan Gerrymandering and the Efficiency Gap." *University of Chicago Law Review* 82: 831–900.

Sterling, Joanna, John T. Jost, and Gordon Pennycook. 2016. "Are Neoliberals More Susceptible to Bullshit?" *Judgment and Decision Making* 11 (4): 352.

Stevens, John Paul. 2014. *Six Amendments: How and Why We Should Change the Constitution.* New York: Little, Brown.

Stewart, Charles, III. 2011. "Adding Up the Costs and Benefits of Voting by Mail." *Election Law Journal* 10 (3): 297–301.

Stewart, Charles. 2017a. "2016 Survey of the Performance of American Elections: Final Report." *Harvard Dataverse,* June 16. https://dataverse.harvard.edu/dataverse/SPAE.

Stewart, Charles, III. 2017b. "Graphic of the Week #1: Polarization in State Voter Confidence." *Election Updates,* June 5. http://electionupdates.caltech.edu/2017/06/05/graphic-of-the-week-1-polarization-in-state-voter-confidence/.

Stewart, Charles, III. 2017c. "A Mirror Site of the PCEA Is Now Up." *Election Updates,* January 31. http://electionupdates.caltech.edu/2017/01/31/a-mirror-site-of-the-pcea-is-now-up/.

Stewart, Charles, III. 2018a. "Partisans Divide over Election Hacking." *Election Updates,* March 7. https://electionupdates.caltech.edu/2018/03/07/partisans-divide-over-election-hacking/.

Stewart, Charles, III. 2018b. "Trump's Controversial Election Integrity Commission Is Gone. Here's What Comes Next." *Washington Post,* January 4. https://www.washingtonpost.com/news/monkey-cage/wp/2018/01/04/trumps-controversial-election-integrity-commission-is-gone-heres-what-comes-next/?utm_term=.ebdcb8e85435.

Stewart, Charles, III, Stephen Ansolabehere, and Nathaniel Persily. 2016. "Revisiting Public Opinion on Voter Identification and Voter Fraud in an Era of Increasing Partisan Polarization." *Stanford Law Review* 68 (6): 1455–1489.

Stroud, Natalie Jomini. 2010. "Polarization and Partisan Selective Exposure." *Journal of Communication* 60 (3): 556–576.

Sunstein, Cass R., ed. 2018. *Can It Happen Here? Authoritarianism in America.* New York: HarperCollins.

Sweeney, Latanya, Ji Su Yoo, and Jinyang Zang. 2017. "Voter Identity Theft: Submitting Changes to Voter Registrations Online to Disrupt Elections." *Journal of Technology Science,* September 6. https://techscience.org/a/2017090601/.

Sweeney, William R., Chad Vickery, and Katherine Ellena. 2016. "Yes, the U.S. Presidential Election Could Be Manipulated." *Washington Post*, September 2. https://www.washingtonpost.com/opinions/global-opinions/yes-the-us-presidential-election-could-be-manipulated/2016/09/02/b125885e-6afe-11e6-ba32-5a4bf5aad4fa_story.html?utm_term=.78238ba183cc.

Swift, Art. 2017. "Democrats' Confidence in Mass Media Rises Sharply from 2016." Gallup, September 21. http://news.gallup.com/poll/219824/democrats-confidence-mass-media-rises-sharply-2016.aspx?g_source=link_newsv9&g_campaign=item_225755&g_medium=copy.

Taagepera, Rein. 2008. *Making Social Sciences More Scientific: The Need for Predictive Models*. Oxford: Oxford University Press.

Taber, Charles S., and Milton Lodge. 2006. "Motivated Skepticism in the Evaluation of Political Beliefs." *American Journal of Political Science* 50 (3): 755–769.

Teorell, Jan, Nicholas Charron, Stefan Dahlberg, Sören Holmberg, Bo Rothstein, Petrus Sundin, and Richard Svensson. 2014. "The Quality of Government Dataset, Version 20Dec13." University of Gothenburg, The Quality of Government Institute. http://www.qog.pol.gu.se.

Thorson, Emily. 2016. "Belief Echoes: The Persistent Effects of Corrected Misinformation." *Political Communication* 33 (3): 460–480.

Tocqueville, Alexis de. 2003. *Democracy in America*. New York: Barnes & Noble Books.

Tomz, Michael, Joshua A. Tucker, and Jason Wittenberg. 2002. "An Easy and Accurate Regression Model for Multiparty Electoral Data." *Political Analysis* 10 (1): 66–83.

Transparency International. 2017. "Corruption in the USA." December 2. https://www.transparency.org/news/feature/corruption_in_the_usa_the_difference_a_year_makes

Tucker, Eric. 2016. "Fewer Election Observers from the Justice Dept. at Polls." Associated Press, October 19. https://www.usnews.com/news/politics/Articles/2016-10-19/us-justice-department-to-dispatch-fewer-election-observers.

U.S. Election Assistance Commission. 2017. "Election Security Preparedness." https://www.eac.gov/election-officials/election-security-preparedness/.

Udani, Adriano, and David C. Kimball. 2018. "Immigrant Resentment and Voter Fraud Beliefs in the US Electorate." *American Politics Research* 46 (3): 402–433.

U.K. Electoral Commission. 2014. "Electoral Fraud in the UK: Final Report and Recommendations." http://www.electoralcommission.org.uk/find-information-by-subject/electoral-fraud/electoral-fraud-vulnerabilities-review?a=164609.

U.K. Electoral Commission. 2017a. Electoral Fraud Vulnerabilities Review. http://www.electoralcommission.org.uk/find-information-by-subject/electoral-fraud/electoral-fraud-vulnerabilities-review.

U.K. Electoral Commission. 2017b. "Electoral Registration at the June 2017 UK General Election: Report on the UK Parliamentary General Election Held on 8 June 2017." https://www.electoralcommission.org.uk/__data/assets/pdf_file/0003/232761/Electoral-registration-report-July-2017.pdf.

Underhill, Wendy. 2013. "No Lines Online." *NCSL State Legislatures Magazine* (May). http://www.ncsl.org/research/elections-and-campaigns/no-lines-online.aspx.

UNDP. 2017. "United Nations Development Programme: Our Projects." http://open.undp.org/#2017/filter/focus_area-2.

USAID. 2013. "Best Practices in Electoral Security: A Guide for Democracy, Human Rights and Governance Programming." https://www.usaid.gov/documents/2496/best-practices-electoral-security-guide-democracy-human-rights-and-governance.

USAID. 2016. "USAID Dollars to Results." https://explorer.usaid.gov//results.

U.S. Census Bureau. 2015. "SAIPE State and County Estimates for 2015." https://www.census.gov/data/datasets/2015/demo/saipe/2015-state-and-county.html.

U.S. Census Bureau. 2016. "Utah Is Nation's Fastest-Growing State, Census Bureau Reports." United States Census Bureau Press Releases: Release Number: CB16-214, December 20. https://www.census.gov/newsroom/press-releases/2016/cb16-214.html.

U.S. Department of Agriculture, Economic Research Service. 2016. "Data for Rural Analysis." Last modified November 17. https://www.ers.usda.gov/topics/rural-economy-population/rural-classifications/data-for-rural-analysis/.

U.S. Department of Justice. 2017. "About Federal Observers and Election Monitoring." March 15. https://www.justice.gov/crt/about-federal-observers-and-election-monitoring.

Valverde, Miriam. 2017. "No Proof ISIS Leaders Using Donald Trump's Travel Ban for Recruitment." *Politifact*, February 7. http://www.politifact.com/truth-o-meter/statements/2017/feb/07/seth-moulton/mostly-false-claim-isis-already-using-trumps-execu/.

Van Deth, Jan W., ed. 2013. *Comparative Politics: The Problem of Equivalence*. Revised edition. Colchester, U.K.: ECPR Press.

Vanhanen, Tatu. 2000. "A New Dataset for Measuring Democracy, 1810–1998." *Journal of Peace Research* 37 (2): 251–265. https://doi.org/10.1177/0022343300037002008.

Venice Commission. 2003. *Code of Good Practice in Electoral Matters*. Opinion no. 190/2002. May 23. http://www.venice.coe.int/webforms/documents/default.aspx?pdffile=CDL-AD(2002)023rev-e.

Vercellotti, Timothy, and David Andersen. 2009. "Voter-Identification Requirements and the Learning Curve." *PS: Political Science & Politics* 42 (1): 117–120.

Verified Voting. 2017. "Internet Voting." https://www.verifiedvoting.org/resources/internet-voting/.

Vickery, Chad, and Erica Shein. 2012. "Assessing Electoral Fraud in New Democracies: Refining the Vocabulary." *International Foundation for Electoral Systems*. May. http://www.ifes.org/sites/default/files/assessing_electoral_fraud_series_vickery_shein.pdf.

Victor, Daniel. 2016. "Three U.S. States Turn Down Russian Requests to Monitor Elections." *New York Times*, October 21. https://www.nytimes.com/2016/10/22/us/politics/united-states-elections-russian-requests-monitor.html?mcubz=0.

Vieth v. Jubelirer, 541 U.S. 267 (2004). quoting *Black's Law Dictionary* 1999, 696.

Vijver, Fons van de, and Norbert K. Tanzer. 2004. "Bias and Equivalence in Cross-Cultural Assessment: An Overview." *European Review of Applied Psychology* 54 (2): 119–135. https://doi.org/10.1016/j.erap.2003.12.004.

Von Spakovsky, Hans A. 2013. "Mandatory Voter Registration: How Universal Registration Threatens Electoral Integrity." Heritage Foundation. http://s3.amazonaws.com/thf_media/2013/pdf/bg2780.pdf.

Voting Integrity Institute. 2017. "Automatic Voter Registration." http://www.votingintegrityinstitute.org/issues/automatic-voter-registration/.

Vozzella, Laura, and Ted Melinik. 2018. "Va. Election Officials Assigned 26 Voters to the Wrong District. It Might've Cost Democrats a Pivotal Race." *Washington Post*, May 13. https://www.washingtonpost.com/local/virginia-politics/voters-assigned-to-wrong-districts-may-have-cost-democrats-in-pivotal-virginia-race/2018/05/13/09a9dd8a-5465-11e8-a551-5b648abe29ef_story.html?utm_term=.093fdd5949e6.

Vraga, Emily K., and Leticia Bode. 2017a. "Leveraging Institutions, Educators, and Networks to Correct Misinformation: A Commentary on Lewandowsky, Ecker, and Cook." *Journal of Applied Research in Memory and Cognition* 6 (4): 382–388.

Vraga, Emily K., and Leticia Bode. 2017b. "Using Expert Sources to Correct Health Misinformation in Social Media." *Science Communication* 39 (5): 621–645.

Waldman, Michael. 2012. "Foreword." In *The Challenge of Obtaining Voter Identification*, edited by Keesha Gaskins and Sundeep Iyer. New York: Brennan Center for Justice. http://www.brennancenter.org/publication/challenge-obtaining-voter-identification.

Wall, Alan, Andrew Ellis, Ayman Ayoub, Carl W. Dundas, Joram Rukambe and Sara Staino. 2006. *Electoral Management Design: The International IDEA Handbook*. Sweden: International IDEA.

Wand, Jonathan N., Kenneth W. Shotts, Jasjeet S. Sekhon, Walter R. Mebane Jr., Michael C. Herron, and Henry E. Brady. 2001. "The Butterfly Did It: The Aberrant Vote for Buchanan in Palm Beach County, Florida." *American Political Science Review* 95 (4): 793–810.

Wang, Tova Andrea. 2012. *The Politics of Voter Suppression: Defending and Expanding Americans' Right to Vote.* Ithaca, NY: Cornell University Press.

Wattenberg, Martin P. 2015. *Is Voting for Young People?* 4th edition. New York: Routledge.

Watts, Ronald L. 1999. "The Theoretical and Practical Implications of Asymmetrical Federalism." In *Accommodating Diversity: Asymmetry in Federal States,* edited by R. Agranoff, 22–42. Baden Baden, Germany: Nomos.

Watts, Ronald L. 2006. "Origins of Cooperative and Competitive Federalism." In *Territory, Democracy, and Justice,* edited by S. L. Greer, 201–223. London: Palgrave.

Watts, Ronald L. 2008. *Comparing Federal Systems.* Ottawa: Institute of Intergovernmental Relations.

Wayne, Stephen J. 2018. *Is This Any Way to Run a Democratic Election?* 6th edition. New York: Routledge.

Weeks, Brian E. 2015. "Emotions, Partisanship, and Misperceptions: How Anger and Anxiety Moderate the Effect of Partisan Bias on Susceptibility to Political Misinformation." *Journal of Communication* 65 (4): 699–719.

Weeks, Brian E., and R. Kelly Garrett. 2014. "Electoral Consequences of Political Rumors: Motivated Reasoning, Candidate Rumors, and Vote Choice during the 2008 US Presidential Election." *International Journal of Public Opinion Research* 26 (4): 401–422.

Weinstein-Tull, Justin. 2016. "Election Law Federalism." *Michigan Law Review* 114: 747–802.

Wells, Chris, Katherine J. Cramer, Michael W. Wagner, German Alvarez, Lewis A. Friedland, Dhavan V. Shah, Leticia Bode, Stephanie Edgerly, Itay Gabay, and Charles Franklin. 2017. "When We Stop Talking Politics: The Maintenance and Closing of Conversation in Contentious Times." *Journal of Communication* 67 (1): 131–157.

The White House. 2018. "Statements and Releases: Statement by the Press Secretary on the Presidential Advisory Commission on Election Integrity." January 3. https://www.whitehouse.gov/briefings-statements/statement-press-secretary-presidential-advisory-commission-election-integrity/.

Whitford v. Gill, 218 F. Supp. 3d 387 (W.D. Wis.) 3:15-cv-421 (2016).

Windrem, Robert. 2017. "ISIS, Al Qaeda Use Trump to Rally Jihadis." *NBC News,* May 20. https://www.nbcnews.com/storyline/isis-uncovered/isis-al-qaeda-use-trump-rally-jihadis-n762201.

Wines, Michael. 2016. "Some Republicans Acknowledge Leveraging Voter ID Laws for Political Gain." *New York Times,* September 16. https://www.nytimes.com/2016/09/17/us/some-republicans-acknowledge-leveraging-voter-id-laws-for-political-gain.html.

Wines, Michael. 2017. "Culling Voter Rolls: Battling Over Who Even Gets to Go to the Polls." *New York Times,* November 25. https://www.nytimes.com/2017/11/25/us/voter-rolls-registration-culling-election.html.

Wisely, John, and J. C. Reindl. 2016. "Detroit's Election Woes: 782 More Votes than Voters." *Detroit Free Press,* December 18. http://www.freep.com/story/news/local/michigan/detroit/2016/12/18/detroit-ballots-vote-recount-election-stein/95570866/.

Wolf, Stephen. 2014. "DRA Update: 2012 President & Downballot Election Results Estimates + Display Table Template." *Daily Kos,* August 5. http://www.dailykos.com/stories/2014/8/4/1318876/-DRA-Update-2012-President-Downballot-Election-Results-Estimates-Display-Table-Template.

Woodall, Hunter. 2016. "Kris Kobach Agrees with Donald Trump That 'Millions' Voted Illegally but Offers No Evidence." *Kansas City Star,* November 30. http://www.kansascity.com/news/politics-government/article117957143.html.

World Net Daily. 2016. "Stealing the Vote: Recount Uncovers Serious Voter Fraud in Detroit." December 8. https://www.wnd.com/2016/12/recount-uncovers-serious-fraud-in-detroit/.

World Values Survey. 2017. 2017 Data U.S. Only. www.worldvaluessurvey.org.

Xenos, M. A., and A. B. Becker. 2008. "Moments of Zen: The Daily Show, Information Seeking, and Partisan Heuristics." Paper presented at annual meeting of the International Communication Association, Montreal, Quebec, Canada. http://citation.allacademic.com/meta/p233925_index.html.

Zaller, John. 1992. *The Nature and Origins of Mass Opinion*. New York: Cambridge University Press.

Zelizer, Julian. 2016. "Sorry, Lady Gaga. We're Not Reforming the Electoral College Any Time Soon." *Washington Post*, November 12. https://www.washingtonpost.com/posteverything/wp/2016/11/12/sorry-lady-gaga-were-not-reforming-the-electoral-college-any-time-soon/?utm_term=.24f47667aaca.

Zukin, Cliff, Scott Keeter, Molly Andolina, Krista Jenkins, and Michael X. Delli Carpini. 2006. *A New Engagement? Political Participation, Civic Life and the Changing American Citizen*. New York: Oxford University Press.

INDEX

Figures and tables are indicated by an italic *f* and *t* following the page number.

absentee voting, 50–52
academic observers
    definition and role, 137
    U.S. findings, 140–143
access, election observers, 145
access, voter
    vs. election integrity, 145–146
    vs. election security, complementarities,
        48*t*, 54–58
    vs. election security, trade-offs, 47–54, 48*t*
    Voting Access Scorecard, 22, 72–75, 73*t*
access-*vs.*-security framing, 44, 45–46
accreditation, election observers, 137, 143–144
ACE Electoral Network, 62
Adamic, Lada, 119
Adams, J. Christian, 36
additive aggregation rule, 64
administration, election
    decentralized, 135, 150n2, 151–171 (*see also*
        decentralized administration)
    framework, U.S. *vs.* other countries, 189–193, 190*f*
    improvement and de-escalation, 41–42
    partisan, systemic manipulation, 192
    recounts, 2016 election, 30–31, 39–41
    snafus, 39–41
alert consumers, 164
Alliance for Securing Democracy, 8
American National Elections Survey, 209–210, 210*f*
anchoring vignettes, 65–66
anxiety, new risks on, 4
apathy, political, 164, 165
Arizona
    gerrymandering, 84
    redistricting and gerrymandering, 84
Assange, Julian, 37
authoritarian-populist rhetoric, 3
authorities, electoral, 62, 63*t*

Bakshy, Eytan, 119
ballot
    legal regulations, 213–214
    secret, 47–48
Barreto, Matt, 104
Bauer-Ginsberg commission
    on cooperation, federal, state, and local, 42
    final report, 39
Bayesian modeling, voter identification, 106, 113n3
Benisek v. Lamone, 201
bicameralism, 154–155, 178–179, 181
Biggers, Daniel, 104
"the big sort," 180–181
Bipartisan Policy Center, on federal, state, and
    local cooperation, 42
Blackwell, Ken, 35–36
Blais, André, 54, 57
blind spot, 175
blue state election law, 31
boundaries, electoral. *See also* gerrymandering
    (partisan)
    alternative measures, 76*t*
    delimitation, U.S., 178–182, 180*t*
    gerrymandering, U.S. 2016 election, 198*f*–199*f*,
        200–201
    PEI survey, 62, 63*t*, 65, 68–71, 68*t*, 70*f*, 73*t*, 74,
        76, 76*t*, 79n12
    redistricting, 179
Brandeis, Justice Louis, 151
Brazil
    code law system, 155
    electoral systems, 161–163, 171n7
    exit, voice, and loyalty, 169
    exit strategies, 168
    federal institutions, 167–168, 167*t*
Brazile, Donna, 120
Brennan Center for Justice, 105

British North America Act, 157
Burden, Barry, 51, 104–105, 213
Bush, George W., 31
Bush v. Gore, 3, 31, 216

Cambodia, multimember districts, 71
Cambridge Analytica, 203
campaign finance, 62, 63t
    2016 U.S. elections, 198f–199f, 201–202
    Canada, 158–159
    PEI index, 65
campaign media, 62, 63t
    2016 U.S. elections, 198f–199f, 202–204
Canada
    campaign finance, 158–159
    common law system, 155
    electoral systems, 157–159, 170n5
    exit, voice, and loyalty, 169–170
    exit strategies, 168
    federal institutions, 167–168, 167t
    parliamentary system, 168
    voter registration reform, 187
Carter Center, 134–150. *See also* transparency
    Election Obligations and Standards database, 14
Center for the Study of Voting, Elections, and
    Democracy (C-SVED), 143
challenges, American elections, 3–28. *See also*
    specific topics
    comparisons, across similar countries, 17–20,
        18f–19f
    comparisons, across U.S. states, 22, 22f
    confidence, 3–6, 9, 10f
    electoral cycle, weaknesses and strengths,
        20–22, 21f
    electoral integrity, concept, 13–15, 15f
    electoral integrity, measurement, 16–17
    fakery, 6–7
    fraud, 5–6
    meddling and information warfare, 8–11, 10f, 11f
    new risks, 4
    partisan polarization, 3, 4
    precedents, 3
    red flags, contemporary era, 3
    Russian meddling, 3–4, 25, 36–38, 203–204
    time, changes over, 23–24, 23f
    trust and legitimacy, 3–5, 9–10, 10f, 11f, 175–176
citizen nonpartisan observers
    definition and role, 136
    findings, U.S. elections, 139–140, 141f
citizen observers, 134
citizen partisan observers, 136
Citizens United v. FEC, 202
Clinton, Hillary
    media coverage skewed against, 4
    misinformation on, motivated reasoning and
        beliefs in, 116, 120 (*see also* fake news;
        misinformation)

popular vote win, 24, 34–35, 175
Russian meddling, 8, 36–38, 203
Wisconsin loss and voter ID laws, 110–111
code law system, 155
Code of Good Practice in Electoral Matters, 181
cognitive dissonance theory, 115
"coming together" federalism, 154, 155
common law system, 155
comparisons, electoral integrity
    across similar countries, 17–20, 18f–19f
    across U.S. states, 22, 22f
    Electoral Integrity Project, 170n3
    federalism and, by country, 152–155
    U.S. *vs.* other countries, 175–195 (*See also*
        United States, comparative perspective)
competitive federalism, 154
confidence
    Constitution on, rigid, 154–155
    in legitimacy of American elections and
        democracy, 4–5, 6, 9, 10f, 30–31
    in media, 3, 4
    in representative institutions, 3
confidence, in electoral integrity
    cyberattacks and hacks on, 41
    electoral cycle stages, 15–16, 15f
    electoral management body on, 190
    in fair elections, on voter turnout, 210, 210f
    fairness, 41
    integrity on, 61
    legal reforms on, well-meaning, 213–214
    malpractice beliefs/ perceptions on, 194,
        197, 206
    Mexico, Ukraine, and Zimbabwe, 12
    strong democracy, 165
    transparency for, 134 (*see also* transparency)
    U.S., 4–5, 6, 9, 10f, 30–31
    U.S., Gallup Poll (2006), 176
    in voters *vs.* non-voters, 209
confirmatory factor analysis, 66, 68t, 75, 79n1
congruent misinformation, 122–125. *See also*
    fake news
    factors driving belief, 131–132
    measurement and analysis, 122–125, 123t
    predicting belief, 122, 123t
    Trump *vs.* Clinton voters, 126, 127t, 132
congruent misperceptions, 114, 116–117
Connecticut, gerrymandering, 94–95, 94f
conspiracy theories, 2016 election
    recounts, 39–41
constitution, rigid, 154–155
constitutional asymmetries, 154
consumers, alerts *vs.* inert, 164
conventions, 14
cooperative federalism, 154
Copenhagen Document (1990), 146, 148
coronelismo, 161
cracking gerrymanders, 86, 99, 179
cyberattacks

potential future, 41
Russian, 7, 36–38
state election systems, 8–9, 37, 203
cyberhacking, Russian, 8, 36–38
cybersecurity, election, 3
Democratic National Committee and Clinton
campaign, 8, 36–38, 203
fraud deterrence, 47
needs, 41–42
Russia 2016 U.S. presidential election,
8, 36–38
Secure Elections Act for, 9
U.S., Department of Homeland Security, 8–9
voter registries and machines, 41, 47, 206
voting technology upgrades, 39

Dahl, Robert, 13
Daily Kos, 88, 100n4
Davis v. Bandemer, 83
deadwood, voter roll purging, 50
decentralized administration, 151–171
electoral integrity, exit, voice, and loyalty,
federalism and, 163–167
electoral integrity, exit, voice, and loyalty,
U.S. elections, 167–170, 167t
electoral integrity, loyalty, 165
electoral systems in federal countries, case
studies, 155–163 (*see also* electoral systems
in federal countries, case studies)
federalism, 151
federalism and electoral integrity, countries
compared, 152–155
policy responsibilities, national and subnational
governments, 153–154
uniqueness, 135, 150n2
decentralized polling places, 58
declarations, 14
de-escalation, 41–42
delegitimization of electoral process, Trump
and, 34–36
democracy
American, satisfaction with, 207, 208t
election administration improvement and
de-escalation, 41–42
electoral integrity and, 61–62
malpractice on, 61–62
partisan manipulation and erosion of, 10
U.S., flawed *vs.* full, 10
Democratic National Committee
Clinton campaign control of, 120
Russian hacking and WikiLeaks, 8, 36–38, 203
Department of Homeland Security
election cybersecurity, state, 8–9, 37, 203
Electoral Assistance Commission, 215
diagnosing electoral integrity, 60–79. *See also*
metrics, electoral integrity
Díaz, Porfirio, 159

Direct Recording Equipment voting
machines, 192
disinformation. *See also* fake news; meddling
alt-right groups, domestic, 203
combating, 196
definition, 7
Russian campaign, 7, 21, 23, 24, 203
Russian Internet Research Agency, 8
dispute resolution mechanisms, 216–217
Dowding, Keith, 165

early (in-person) voting, 58
efficiency gap standard, 179, 180–181, 180t
election, U.S. 2016. *See also specific topics*
campaign finance, 198f–199f, 201–202
campaign media, 198f–199f, 202–204
Electoral College, 24
electoral laws, 198f–199f, 204–206
gerrymandering, 198f–199f, 200–201
PEI index, by state, 197–200, 198f–199f
recounts, conspiracy theories, 39–41
voter registration, 198f–199f, 204–206
voting wars, "normal," 31–33, 31f–32f
election, U.S. 2016, challenges, 197–206,
198f–199f
campaign finance, 198f–199f, 201–202
campaign media, 198f–199f, 202–204
electoral laws and voter registration, 198f–199f,
204–206
gerrymandering district boundaries,
200–201
PEI index by state, 197–200, 198f–199f
election (selection), 62, 63t
Election Day registration (voter), 56–57
Election Integrity Commission, 35–36
Election Obligations and Standards (EOS)
database, 14
election observers (observation)
academic, 137
academic, U.S. findings, 140–143
access, 145
accreditation, 137, 143–144
citizen, 134
citizen nonpartisan, 136, 139–140, 141f
citizen partisan, 136
federal, 137
federal, U.S. findings, 143
international nonpartisan, 136–137,
140, 142f
nonpartisan, 134, 147–148
Organization for Security and Co-operation in
Europe, 135
Organization of American States, 135
partisan, 138–139
skepticism toward, U.S. elections,
134–135, 150n1
Election Protection, 103

elections, free and fair, 102, 112
Anglo-American, expert assessments, 10, 11*f*
legal procedures undermining, 13
rhetoric, 12
U.S., V-Dem ratings, 17, 20, 152
Elections Canada, 158, 187
Elections Clause, 155–156
electoral authorities, 62, 63*t. See also*
administration, election
electoral boundaries. *See* boundaries, electoral;
gerrymandering (partisan)
Electoral College, 183–185, 184*f*
2016 election, 24
vs. popular win, Trump, 24
electoral cycle
3 phases, 62
11 steps, 14–15, 15*f*, 62, 63*t*
phases, 62, 63*t*
stages, 178
weaknesses and strengths, 20–22, 21*f*
electoral democracy benchmark, 13
electoral integrity. *See also specific topics*
vs. access and inclusivity, 145–146
across states, U.S., 22, 22*f*
assessment methodology, 176–178
changes over time, 23–24, 23*f*
concept, 13–15, 15*f*
definition, 61
democracy and, 61–62
diagnosing, 60–79 (*see also* metrics, electoral
integrity)
federalism and, comparative, 152–155
fundamentals, 11–13
importance, 102, 211
malpractice on, 61–62
manipulation, systematic and
intentional, 12–13
measurement, 16–17
postindustrial democracies (2017), 17–20,
18*f*–19*f*
public on, 102
reforms strengthening, 211–212, 212*f*
electoral integrity assessment (EIA), 176–178, 195n4
Electoral Integrity Project (EIP), 60. *See also*
metrics, electoral integrity; Perceptions of
Electoral Integrity (PEI) index
on American elections performance, 2016
cycle, 21, 21*f*
on American elections performance, 2016 *vs.*
2012 and 2014, 22, 22*f*
comparisons, 17, 170n3
diagnosing electoral integrity, 60 (*see also*
metrics, electoral integrity)
on perceptions of electoral integrity, by
U.S. state, 23, 23*f*
on U.S. election problems, 10
Electoral Integrity Scale, 207

electoral integrity standards
11-step electoral cycle, 14–15, 15*f*, 62, 63*t*
Election Obligations and Standards, 14
violating, 15–16
Electoral Law of 1946, 159
electoral laws. *See* laws, electoral
Electoral Malpractice Scale, 207
electoral management, independent, impartial,
and professional, 214–215
electoral management body (EMB), 189–191
Brazil, Canada, and Mexico, 155, 163, 168–170
U.S. lack, 186, 188, 217
Electoral Performance Index (EPI), 22,
72–75, 73*t*
electoral systems
in democracies, 178
U.S., 178–179
electoral systems in federal countries, case studies,
155–163
Brazil, 161–163, 171n7
Canada, 157–159, 170n5
majoritarian, 168
Mexico, 159–161
United States, 155–157
Electoral Tribunal of the Federal Judiciary
(TEPJF), 160
Ely, John Hart, 100n2
equalization transfers, 154
equal voting power, 181, 195n3
equivalence, diagnosing via global and U.S. PEI
indices, 66–72
exit, 163
exit, voice, and loyalty, 151–152
federalism and, 163–167
U.S. elections, 167–170, 167*t*
Exit, Voice and Loyalty (Hirschman), 163–166

fair elections. *See also* elections, free and fair
confidence in, 209–210, 210*f*
fake news, 6–7, 38, 114–133
discussion and conclusions, 131–133
foreign meddling and, 36–38, 203–204 (*see also*
meddling)
literature review, 115–119
misinformation, measuring, 119–121, 121*f*
misinformation, motivated reasoning and,
115–119, 131–132
partisan media, 114, 131
pro-Trump and Russian propaganda, 38
social media, 114, 131
fake news, study methods, 122–130
analysis, 122–130
analysis, congruent and incongruent
misinformation, 122–125, 123*t*
analysis, specific misinformation beliefs,
126–129, 129*t*

analysis, Trump and Clinton voters, 126, 127t–128t
  participants, 122
  variables, 122, 130t
fakery, 6–7
federal countries, electoral systems in, case studies, 155–163
  Brazil, 161–163, 171n7
  Canada, 157–159, 170n5
  Mexico, 159–161
  United States, 155–157
Federal Electoral Commission, 159
Federal Electoral Institution (IFE), 159–160
federalism, 151
  "coming together" *vs.* "holding together," 154, 155
  competitive, 154
  cooperative, 154
  decentralized administration, 151
  electoral integrity, countries compared, 152–155
  exit, voice, and loyalty, 163–167
  exit, voice, and loyalty, U.S. elections, 167–170, 167t
  gerrymandering and, 166
  "laboratories of democracy," 151, 157
  market-based argument, 164
  PEI index and, 152–153
  shared sovereignty, 153
federal observers
  definition and role, 137
  U.S. findings, 143
finance, campaign. *See* campaign finance
Florida, gerrymandering, 84–85
fraud, electoral (voter), 5–6
  American elections, modern, 12
  assessment methods, 177
  cybersecurity, deterrence, 47
  definition, 12, 176
  electoral malpractice and, 46–47
  immigrant voting, 45
  residency, 49
  rhetoric, irresponsible, 42
  security vulnerabilities, 192–193
  Trump on, 5–6, 30, 35, 36, 102
  voter identification, 46
  vs. voter participation maximization, 45–46
  voter registration, 189
free and fair elections. *See* elections, free and fair
Freedom House, 16
  on American elections, 3
  on democratic institutions, erosion, 10
  measures of liberal democracy, 16
Fukumoto, Kentaro, 49

Gaffney v. Cummings, 85
Gaines, Brian, 51

Galston, William, 166
Gaughan, Anthony J., 34
Georgia, gerrymandering and bias, 96, 97–98, 99f
Gerken, Heather, 54, 58
Germany, cooperative federalism, 154
Gerry, Elbridge, 84
gerrymandering (partisan), 9, 83–101, 168
  Arizona, 84
  "the big sort," 180–181
  cautions, 96–98, 98f, 99f
  Connecticut, 94–95, 94f
  courts on, 83–85, 97, 99, 100n2, 180
  cracking gerrymanders, 86, 99, 179
  definition, 71, 84, 85
  determinations, 93–96, 94f, 96f
  entrenching one part, 83
  federalism and, 166
  findings, 90–93, 91f–92f
  Florida, 84–85
  Gaffney v. Cummings, 85
  Georgia, 96, 97–98, 99f
  Illinois, 96, 97, 98f
  intentional, 100n1, 180–181, 180t
  Iowa, 84
  Justice Stevens on, 83
  laws regulating, 179–180
  Maryland, 93–94, 94f, 95, 100–101n5, 201
  Massachusetts, 84
  North Carolina, 70, 201
  Obama on, 83
  Ohio, 95–96, 96f
  packing gerrymanders, 86–87, 89, 179
  Pennsylvania, 201
  prevalence, U.S., 83
  purpose, 85
  recognizing, 86–89
  recognizing, analytical sequence, 88–89
  recognizing, setting baseline, 87–88
  seat-based claims, 85
  silencing minority voices, 83
  standard, 84, 180
  state legislative districts, 182
  threats, 83
  U.S. 2016 election, 198f–199f, 200–201
  on U.S. elections, 20
  vote dilution, 84–86
  Wisconsin, 70, 201
Gill v. Whitford, 201
Global Commission on Elections, Democracy, and Security, 61
Gore, Al, 31
graph-partitioning algorithms, 87
Grimmer, Justin, 104
Grömping, Max, 67f–70f, 76t
Guccifer 2.0, 37

Haberman, Maggie, 37
Hajnal, Zoltan, 104
Halderman, J. Alex, 191–192
Hanmer, Michael, 104
Harris v. Arizona Redistricting Commission, 84
HB 589 (North Carolina), 33
Help America Vote Act (2002), 39, 186
Hicks, William, 104
Hidalgo, F. Daniel, 162
Hirschman, Albert, 151, 163–169
"holding together" federalism, 154
Horiuchi, Yusaku, 49
hot cognition, 116
Hungary, malapportionment and single-seat
    plurality rules, 71

identification, voter. *See* voter identification
Illinois, gerrymandering and bias, 96, 97, 98*f*
immigrant voting, historical impediments, 45
impact, 176. *See also specific topics*
inclusion-versus-security framing, 44, 45–46,
    204–206
    secret ballot, 47–48
    voter access *vs.* election security,
        complementarities, 48*t*, 54–58 (*see also*
        voter access *vs.* election security,
        complementarities)
    voter access *vs.* election security, trade-offs,
        47–54, 48*t* (*see also* voter access *vs.* election
        security, trade-offs)
inclusivity *vs.* election integrity, 145–146
incongruent misinformation, 122–125. *See also*
    fake news
    factors driving belief, 131–132
    measurement and analysis, 122–125, 123*t*
    predicting belief, 122, 123*t*
    Trump *vs.* Clinton voters, 126, 128*t*, 132
incongruent misperceptions, 114, 116–117
indelible ink, on voters' fingers, 47, 56, 58, 59n2
Indian Electoral Commission, free photo IDs, 214
inert consumers, 164
information warfare, 8–11, 10*f*, 11*f. See also* meddling
Institutional Revolutionary Party (PRI), 159
integrity, electoral. *See* electoral integrity
International Foundation for Electoral Systems
    (IFES), 176
international nonpartisan observers
    definition and role, 136–137
    U.S. findings, 140, 142*f*
Iowa, gerrymandering, 84

Japan, 182
Johnson, Jeh, 37–38
Judicial Committee of the Privy Council, 157
judiciary, strong, 154–155

Katz, Jonathan, 106
King, Gary, 106
Kobach, Kris, 35, 102

Lajevardi, Nazita, 104
laws, electoral, 30–43, 62, 63*t*
    2016 U.S. elections, 198*f*–199*f*, 204–206
    de-escalation and election administration
        improvement, 41
    foreign meddling and "fake news," 36–38
    party and candidate, expert ratings, 21, 21*f*
    restrictive voting, 30
    Trump and delegitimization of electoral
        process, 34–36
    voting machine concerns, election administration
        snafus, and conspiracy theories, 39–41
    voting wars, 30
    voting wars, "normal" (2016), 31–33, 31*f*–32*f*
    weaponry escalation, 30
Lawyers' Committee for Civil Rights under
    Law, 103
legitimacy
    of American elections and democracy,
        confidence in, 3–6, 9–10, 10*f*, 11*f*, 30–31,
        175–176
    public malpractice concerns on, 206–211, 208*t*,
        209*f*, 210*f*
level playing field, 12
liberal democracy benchmark, 13
Lijphart, Arend, 154
loyalty, 165. *See also* exit, voice, and loyalty

Magleby, Danie, 87
mail voting, 50–52
majoritarian electoral system, 168
    integrity, 179
majority rule, political equality and, 61
malapportionment, 71, 182
    Cambodia, Zimbabwe, and Uganda, 71
    Hungary, 71
    single-member district sizes, 65, 182
    U.S., 181–182, 184, 193–194
    voice and, 164
malpractice, electoral
    definition, 14, 176
    on electoral integrity and democracy, 61–62
    forms, 46
    paper-based voter registration, 186, 188–189
    U.S. *vs.* other countries, 176–177
    vs. voter fraud, 46–47
manipulation, systematic and intentional, 12–13
manipulation, systemic, 182
    assessment methods, 177
    definition, 176
    Electoral College, 182, 184

partisan administration of elections, 192
voter identification, 188
voter registration, 188
Mann, Thomas, 166
Marshall, Justice, 100n2
Maryland
  gerrymandering, 93–94, 94*f*, 95,
    100–101n5, 201
  proportionality, 180, 180*t*
Massachusetts, gerrymandering, 84
Massicotte, Louis, 54, 57
McCutcheon v. FEC, 202
McGhee, Eric, 85
McGovern, Tony, 105
McKee, Seth, 104
meddling, 8–11, 10*f*, 11*f*
  foreign, fake news, 36–38, 203–204
  Russian (*see* Russian meddling, 2016
    U.S. presidential election)
media
  confidence and trust in, 3–5, 7
  growth and fragmentation, 117
  liberal media bias, 6
  party and candidate, expert ratings, 21, 21*f*
  political information from, 117
media, campaign, 62, 63*t*
  2016 U.S. elections, 198*f*–199*f*, 202–204
media, news
  entertainment (soft news), 118
  "fake news," 6–7
  "fake news," foreign meddling and, 36–38,
    203–204
  mainstream, 118
  online, 118
  online, misinformation belief and, 131
  partisan, 117
  partisan, fake news, 114, 131
  television (broadcast), 118, 131
media use
  misperceptions and, 117
  social identities and, 115
Mendes, Chief Judge Gilmar, 163
Messing, Solomon, 119
metrics, electoral integrity, 60–79
  alternative measures, 72–77, 73*t*, 76*t*
  alternative measures *vs.* PEI, 75–76, 76*t*
  availability and quality, 60
  consensus, 60
  cross-sectional validity problems, 77
  data intensity, 78
  electoral cycle, 3 phases, 62, 63*t*
  electoral cycle, 11-step, 14–15, 15*f*, 62, 63*t*
  Electoral Performance Index, 22, 72–75, 73*t*
  equivalence, global and U.S. PEI indices, 66–72,
    67*f*, 68*t*–69*t*, 70*f*
  integrity and democracy, 61–62
  majority rule and political equality, 61

National Council of State Legislatures, 73*t*, 74
Perceptions of Electoral Integrity, 62–66
  (*see also* Perceptions of Electoral Integrity
    (PEI) index)
Southern Poverty Law Center, 73*t*, 74
U.S. elections issues, 78–79
Voting Access Scorecard, 22, 72–75, 73*t*
Mexico
  code law system, 155
  electoral systems, 159–161
  exit, voice, and loyalty, 169–170
  exit strategies, 168
  federal institutions, 167–168, 167*t*
Michigan recount, 2016 presidential election,
  30–31, 39–41
midterm elections, voting participation by
  electoral integrity, 207–209, 209*f*
misinformation. *See also* fake news
  definition, 119
  measuring, 119–121, 121*f*
  motivated reasoning, 115–119, 131–132
  online media use, 131
  social media use, 118–119, 131
  specific beliefs, 126, 129*t*
misinformation, congruent, 122–125
  factors driving belief, 131–132
  measurement and analysis, 122–125, 123*t*
  predicting belief, 122, 123*t*
  Trump *vs.* Clinton voters, 126, 127*t*, 132
misinformation, incongruent, 122–125
  factors driving belief, 131–132
  measurement and analysis, 122–125, 123*t*
  predicting belief, 122, 123*t*
  Trump *vs.* Clinton voters, 126, 128*t*, 132
misperceptions
  candidate supported on, 126, 127*t*–128*t*, 132
  congruent, 114, 116–117
  entertainment news on, 126, 127*t*–128*t*
  incongruent, 114, 116–117
  media and social media use on, 115, 117, 118,
    119, 125
  motivated reasoning and, 115–116, 132
  partisan cable news on, 126, 127*t*–130*t*, 131
  political interest and education on, 126,
    127*t*–128*t*
  social media on, 126, 127*t*–128*t*, 131
  sources of, 131–132
  TV news on, 126, 127*t*–128*t*
mobile polling stations, 52
Mosesson, Daniel, 87
motivated reasoning, 211
  misinformation and, 115–119, 131–132
  misperceptions and, 115–116
  partisan, 115–116
  tendencies and cognitive dissonance theory, 115
  theories, 4
Mueller, Robert, 8, 203–204

Nai, Alessandro, 67f–70f, 76t
National Conference of State Legislatures
    (NCSL), 73t, 74, 105, 134–150. *See also*
    transparency
National Electoral Institute (INE), 160
National Register of Electors, 158
National Voter Registration Act, 50, 186
neglect, 166
Newport News, VA 2017 state elections, 5
New Zealand, 182
Nielson, Lindsay, 104
nongovernmental organizations (NGOs), assuring
    voting system integrity, 41–42
nonpartisan observers, 134
    lack of awareness of, 147–148
Norris, Pippa, 67f–70f, 76t
North Carolina
    gerrymandering, 70, 201
    PEI index, 156
    proportionality, 180, 180t
    voter identification law, 103, 188
*North Carolina State Conference of the NAACP
    v. McCrory*, 33
Nuno, Stephen, 104

observers (observation), election. *See* election
    observers (observation)
Office of Director of National Intelligence, 203
Ohio, gerrymandering, 95–96, 96f
Olson, Randal, 105
one-person, one-vote, 179, 181
online voter registration, 42, 55–56
online voting, 53–54
opinions, new information enforcing, 4
Organization for Security and Co-operation
    in Europe (OSCE), U.S. election
    observation, 135
Organization of American States (OAS), 135, 146
outdated election laws, 148

packing gerrymanders, 86–87, 89, 179
paper-based voter registration, 55, 59n5, 186,
    188–189
paperless voter registration, 55–56
participation, voter
    absentee and mail voting, 50
    factors predicting, 207, 213
    maximizing, *vs.* electoral fraud, 45–47
    midterm elections, by electoral integrity,
        207–209, 209f
    reducing barriers to, 214
    residence, changing, 49
    voter identification on (*see* voter identification)
partisan media, fake news, 114, 131
partisan-motivated reasoning, 115–116

partisan observation, U.S. elections, 138–139
partisan polarization, 3, 4. *See also specific topics*
    on electoral security, 9
    inclusion-versus-security framing, 45–46
    interpreting new information via, 3
    on reforms, 3
    voting wars, 30
party registration, 62, 63t
    U.S., expert ratings, 21, 21f
Pence-Kobach Presidential Advisory Committee
    on Electoral Integrity, 6
Pennsylvania, gerrymandering, 201
Perceptions of Electoral Integrity (PEI) index,
    16–17, 60, 62–66, 152
    11 subdimensions, 14–15, 15f, 62, 63t, 67, 68t
    49 variables, 62–64
    additive aggregation rule, 64
    advantages *vs.* other indices, 64–65
    vs. alternative measures, 72–77, 73t, 76t
    anchoring vignettes, 65–66
    context, 65
    electoral cycle, weaknesses and strengths,
        20–22, 21f
    equivalence, global and U.S. perceptions, 66–72,
        67f, 68t–69t, 70f
    federal institutions on, 152–153
    instrument use, 65
    postindustrial democracies (2017), 17–20, 18f–19f
    purpose, 60
    strengths, 77
    traits, configuration, 65
    U.S., states, 156–157
    U.S. 2016 elections, by state, 197–200,
        198f–199f
    U.S. *vs.* other countries, 152, 167
    voter eligibility requirements, 77
    weaknesses, 78
performance monitoring, 215–216
performance of U.S. elections, partisan differences,
    211, 212f
Pew Charitable Trusts
    Electoral Performance Index, 22, 72–75, 73t
    on federal, state, and local cooperation, 42
photo IDs, 102, 105, 107t–108t, 113n1, 187, 187f.
    See also voter identification
    free, India, 214
Piven, Frances, 213
Pizzagate scandal, 38
Podesta, John D., 37
polarization, partisan. *See* partisan polarization
political equality, majority rule and, 61
Polity IV, violating, 16
polling places
    decentralized, 58
    mobile stations, 52
polyarch, 13
postelection (processing), 62, 63t

precedents, 3
pre-election (exploring), 62, 63t
principal component analysis, 75, 79n1
procedures
  electoral, 62, 63t
  voting (*see* voting procedures)
propaganda, Russian and social media, 7, 8, 30, 33, 38, 42, 203. *See also* fake news; meddling; Russian meddling

reapportionment, 178–179
reasoning, motivated, 4, 115–119, 131–132, 211. *See also* motivated reasoning
recount, Michigan, 2016 presidential election, 30–31, 39–41
red flags, contemporary era, 3
redistricting, 165. *See also* gerrymandering (partisan)
  2010-2012, 83, 93
  controversies, 33
  Mexico, 160
  U.S., 178–180, 201
  U.S., Illinois, 97
red state election law, 31
reform agenda, lessons for, 196–217
  2016 U.S. elections challenges, 197–206, 198f–199f (*see also* 2016 U.S. elections, challenges)
  dispute resolution mechanisms, 216–217
  electoral management, independent, impartial, and professional, 214–215
  performance monitoring, 215–216
  reforms strengthening electoral integrity, 211–212, 212f
  registration and balloting, legal regulations, 213–214
  technical and procedural legal matters, 197
  trust and legitimacy, public malpractice concerns on, 206–211, 208t, 209f, 210f
reforms, partisan polarization on, 3
regimes, classifying, 13
registration. *See* party registration; voter registration
reprecincting, 100n3
residence change rules, voter, 49–50
residency fraud, 49
residual powers, 153
Reynolds v. Sims, 100n2, 181, 195n2
rhetoric, authoritarian-populist, 3
risks, new, 4
Romo v. Detzner, 85
Rosenberg, Jennifer, 37
Rosenstone, Steven, 213
Rusbult, C. E., 165
Russian collusion, Trump campaign, 9, 203
Russian cyberhacking, 8, 36–38

Russian Internet Research Agency, 8
  state election hacking (2016), 23–24
Russian meddling, 2016 U.S. presidential election, 25, 203–204, 211
  disinformation campaigns, 7
  election, 3, 4
  intelligence and news reports, 4
  propaganda, social media, and fake news, 7, 8, 30, 33, 36–38, 42, 203–204

Sanchez, Gabriel, 104
Sanders, Bernie, 202
satisfaction, with American democracy, 207, 208t
Schaffer, Frederic, 48
Schumpeter, Joseph, 13
secret ballot, 47–48
Secure Elections Act, 9
security, electoral. *See also* cybersecurity, election
  access-*vs.*-security framing, 44, 45–46
  Congressional funding, 9
  inclusion-versus-security framing, 44, 45–46, 204–206 (*see also* inclusion-versus-security framing)
  partisan polarization on, 9
  vs. voter access, complementarities, 48t, 54–58
  vs. voter access, trade-offs, 47–54, 48t
  vulnerabilities, 192–193
Singapore, multimember plurality districts, 71
single-seat districts (SSD), 65, 71
single-seat plurality rules, 71
skew, vote percentage distribution, 86–87
Smidt, Corwin, 116
social identities
  media use, 115
  partisan, 115–116
social media
  fake news, 114, 131
  misinformation from, 118–119, 131
  on misperceptions, 115, 117–119, 125, 126, 127t–128t, 131
  Russian meddling, 2016 U.S. presidential election, 7, 8, 30, 33, 36–38, 42, 203–204
Southern Poverty Law Center (SPLC), 73t, 74
standards, electoral integrity
  11-step electoral cycle, 14–15, 15f, 62, 63t
  Election Obligations and Standards, Carter Center, 14
  violating, 15–16
states, U.S. *See also specific states*
  blue state election law, 31
  cybersecurity and election system cyberattacks, 8–9, 37, 203
  electoral integrity across, 22, 22f
  electoral integrity over time, 23–24, 23f
  PEI index, 156–157, 197–200, 198f–199f
  perceptions of electoral integrity by, 23, 23f

states, U.S. (*Cont.*)
  red state election law, 31
  Russian election hacking (2016), 23–24
Stein, Jill, 30–31, 39
Stepan, Alfred, 154
Stephanopoulos, Nick, 85
Stevens, Justice John Paul, 83, 85
Stone, Roger, Jr., 35, 37
Superior Electoral Tribunal (TSE), 161–162
Supreme Federal Tribunal, 161, 163
survey data, limitations, 105, 113n2
systemic manipulation. *See* manipulation, systemic

Temer, Michel, 163
Texas, voter identification law, 103
The Franchise Project (TFP)
  purpose and work, 72
  Voting Access Scorecard, 22, 72–75, 73*t*
time, changes over, 23–24, 23*f*
Tocqueville, Alexis de, 77
Tomz, Michael, 106
transparency, 134–150
  academic observers, 137
  access for observers and voting patterns, 145
  accreditation, election observers, 137, 143–144
  citizen nonpartisan observers, 136
  citizen observation, 134
  citizen partisan observers, 136
  election observation, 135
  federal observers, 137
  findings, 138–144
  findings, academic observation, 140–143
  findings, citizen nonpartisan observation,
    139–140, 141*f*
  findings, federal observation, 143
  findings, international nonpartisan observation,
    140, 142*f*
  findings, observer accreditation, 143–144
  findings, partisan observation, 138–139
  integrity *vs.* access and inclusivity, 145–146
  international nonpartisan observers, 136–137
  law *vs.* practice, 146–147
  nonpartisan observation, 134, 147–148
  outdated laws, 148
  research design, 136–138
  trends, notable, 144–148
  U.S. election observation, skepticism,
    134–135, 150n1
  U.S. self-conception as leader of
    democracy, 148
  vote count, 41
Transparency International, 202
Tribe, Laurence, 38
Tribunal Superior Electoral (TSE), 161–162
Trudeau, Justin, 170
Trump, Donald

  delegitimization of electoral process, 34–36
  Election Integrity Commission, 35–36
  Electoral College win *vs.* popular vote loss, 24,
    34–35, 175
  extreme voters, 164
  fake news and media mistrust, 6–7, 36, 38
  media coverage, disproportionate, 23
  rigged system and voter fraud claims, 5–6, 30,
    35, 36, 102
  Russian collusion, 9, 203
  Russian meddling favoring, 36–38 (*see also*
    Russian meddling, 2016 U.S. presidential
    election)
trust
  in American democracy, 176
  in American elections, declining, 3–5, 9–10,
    10*f*, 11*f*, 175–176
  public malpractice concerns on, 206–211, 208*t*,
    209*f*, 210*f*
Tucker, Joshua, 106
turnout, voter identification laws on, 59n4, 63,
  104–105

United Nations International Covenant on Civil
  and Political Rights (ICCPR), 61
United States. *See also specific topics*
  bicameral legislature, 178–179, 181
  common law system, 155
  competitive federalism, 154
  electoral systems, 155–157
  exit strategies, 168
  federal institutions, 167–168, 167*t*
  majoritarian electoral system, 168
  malapportionment, 181–182, 184, 193–194
  redistricting, 179
United States, comparative perspective, 175–195.
    See also specific topics
  administrative framework, 189–193, 190*f*
  blind spot, 175
  boundary delimitation, 178–182, 180*t*
  conclusions and discussion, 193–195
  Electoral College, 183–185, 184*f*
  electoral cycle stages, 178
  electoral integrity assessment methodology,
    176–178
  fraud, 176–177
  impact, 176
  malpractice, 176–177
  methods and evidence, 176–178
  respondents, target groups, 177
  systemic manipulation, 176–177
  trust in electoral process, 175–176
  voter registration, 185–189, 187*f*
  vulnerabilities, 176–177
Universal Declaration of Human Rights, 13–14,
  48, 185

U.S. Election Assistance Commission, 42
U.S. presidential election 2016, 4
  cybersecurity and Russian meddling, 8
  Michigan recount, 30–31, 39–41
  recounts, 30–31, 39–41

Vanhanen Index, 64
Varieties of Democracy (V-Dem) project, on
    U.S. free and fair elections, 9–10, 11*f*, 17
  electoral integrity measurement, 16
  electoral/ liberal democracy benchmark
    method, 13
  U.S. ratings, 17, 20, 152
voice, 163, 166. *See also* exit, voice, and loyalty
vote count, 62, 63*t*
  U.S. rating, 21, 21*f*
vote dilution, via gerrymandering, 84–86
vote percentage distribution, skew, 86–87
voter access *vs.* election security,
    complementarities, 48*t*, 54–58
  polling places, decentralized, 58
  voter registration, automatic, 54–55
  voter registration, Election Day, 56–57
  voter registration, online and paperless, 55–56
  voter rolls, posting provisional, 57–58
  voting, early (in-person), 58
voter access *vs.* election security, trade-offs,
    47–54, 48*t*
  absentee and mail voting, 50–52
  mobile polling stations, 52
  online voting, 53–54
  secret ballot, 47–48
  voter identification, 33, 53, 59n4
  voter registration requirement, 48–49
  voter residence change rules, 49–50
  voter rolls, purging deadwood, 50
voter eligibility requirements, PEI index, 77
voter fraud. *See* fraud, electoral (voter)
voter identification, 53, 59n4, 102–113,
    187–188, 187*f*
  Bayesian modeling approach, 106, 113n3
  causes and consequences, 104–105
  counties requiring, 105, 106*t*
  courts on, 103
  critics on, 102–103
  data and findings, 105–110, 106–108*t*,
    109*f*–110*f*
  discussion, 112
  electoral fraud and, 46
  misapplication, deleterious impact, 103
  North Carolina, 103, 188
  North Carolina law, 103, 188
  North Carolina State Conference of the NAACP
    v. McCrory, 33
  other states, 111–112, 111*t*
  on party voter share, 105–110, 109*f*–110*f*, 113n5

photo ID, 102, 105, 107*t*–108*t*, 113n1,
    187, 187*f*
photo IDs, free (India), 214
proponents on, 102
Republican support, 102–103
strict *vs.* not strict, 102
survey data limitations, 105, 113n2
as systemic manipulation, 188
Texas, 103
on turnout, 59n4, 63, 104–105
Wisconsin, 103, 110–111, 111*t*
voter inclusion. *See* inclusion-versus-security framing
voter participation. *See* participation, voter
voter registration, 62, 63*t*
  Britain, 45
  Canadian reforms, 187
voter registration, U.S.
  2016 elections, 198*f*–199*f*, 204–206
  automatic, 54–55
  cybersecurity, 41, 47, 206
  decentralized, 186
  Election Day, 56–57
  expert ratings, 21, 21*f*
  laws impeding, 32–33
  legal regulations, 213–214
  motives, 45
  onerous requirements, 9
  online, 42, 55–56
  vs. other countries, 185–189, 187*f*
  paper-based, 55, 59n5, 186, 188–189
  paperless, 55–56
  requirement, 48–49
voter residence change rules, 49–50
voter rolls
  posting provisional, 57–58
  purging deadwood, 50
voter tabulation districts (VTDs), 87,
    100n3, 100n4
voting
  absentee and mail, 50–52
  convenience, 213–214
  early (in-person), 58
  laws impeding, 32–33
  online, 53–54
Voting Access Scorecard, 22, 72–75, 73*t*
voting machines, 191–192
  cybersecurity, 41, 47, 206
  Direct Recording Equipment, 192
  technology concerns, 39–41
voting procedures, 44–59
  electoral malpractice and voter fraud, 46–47
  inclusion (access)-*vs.*-security framing, 44, 45–46
  U.S. rating, 21, 21*f*
  voter access *vs.* election security trade-offs, 47–54
voting process, 62, 63*t*
voting wars, 30
  "normal" (2016), 31–33, 31*f*–32*f*

vulnerabilities. *See also specific types*
  assessment methods, 176
  holistic electoral cycle approach, 177

Wasserman-Schultz, Debbie, 37
Watts, Ronald L., 157–158
Weinstein-Tull, Justin, 156
White, Byron, 86
Whitford v. Gill, 83
WikiLeaks, Russian cyberhacking, 8, 37
Wisconsin
  gerrymandering, 70, 201

voter identification law, 103, 110–111, 111*t*
Wittenberg, Jason, 106
Wolf, Stephen, 88, 100n4
Wolfinger, Raymond, 213
Women's March, 24
Wynter, Thomas, 67*f*–70*f*

Yoshinaka, Antoine, 54, 57

Zelizer, Julian, 185
Zembrodt, I. M., 165

CPSIA information can be obtained
at www.ICGtesting.com
Printed in the USA
BVHW031330271019
562157BV00003B/7/P

9 780190 934170